KETTRIDGE'S FRENCH IDIOMS

FRENCH IDIOMS

AND FIGURATIVE PHRASES

WITH MANY QUOTATIONS

By

J. O. KETTRIDGE

Officier d'Académie, F.S.A.A., etc.

LONDON

ROUTLEDGE & KEGAN PAUL LTD.

BROADWAY HOUSE: 68–74 CARTER LANE, E.C.4.

First published 1939
by Routledge and Kegan Paul Ltd
Broadway House, 68-74 Carter Lane
London, E.C.4

Second edition (revised) 1949
Reprinted 1956, 1961, 1964, 1970

Printed in Great Britain by
Redwood Press Limited
Trowbridge & London

ISBN 0 7100 1668 9

PREFACE

So full of shapes is fancy,
That it alone is high fantastical.
Twelfth Night I, 1.

The French language abounds in idioms, figures of speech, and proverbs. It has been said that the French are never happy unless they can reduce the gist of everything to a cut and dried phrase. The meanings of some of these phrases can be gathered from the wording ; others are unintelligible, necessitating resort to a book of reference.

There are many quotations in this book, principally from Shakespeare, " the myriad-minded." These quotations, by parallels and contrasts, throw into relief the likenesses and differences between French and English thought and those between archaic and modern English. They also show that many similes, lost in current English, are still preserved in French. Also, it is hoped, they will serve to establish the true sense of the French phrase and help to fix it in the memory. And, finally, the beauty of these quotations can hardly fail to make a joy of the study.

It may be of service to point out the difference between an idiom and a figurative phrase, as contrasted. An idiom is an expression the meaning of which as a whole cannot be deduced from its component parts ; as, Être sur les dents (To be done up [with fatigue]), L'échapper belle (To have a narrow escape). In a figurative phrase, the words have their ordinary connections and relations, but are used metaphorically ; as, Porter de l'eau à la mer (To carry coals to Newcastle), La boîte de Pandore (Pandora's box).

Following is a quotation from Voltaire's *La Princesse de Babylone* VIII : " Après un quart d'heure de silence, il regarda un moment Amazan, et lui dit, *How d'ye do*, à la lettre, *comment faites-vous faire ?* et dans la langue du traducteur, *comment vous portez-vous ?* ce qui ne veut rien dire du tout en aucune langue." *How do you do ?* and *Comment vous portez-vous ?* are therefore idioms.

ABBREVIATIONS, CONVENTIONAL SIGNS, AND REFERENCES

Cf. Compare.

fig. figuratively.

lit. literally.

[Brackets] enclose words, or parts of words, which can be used or omitted at will.

, Virtually synonymous meanings are separated by commas.

; Essentially different meanings are separated by semicolons.

The following references are to Shakespeare's plays of those names : *All's Well That Ends Well* (*Tout est bien qui finit bien*), *Antony and Cleopatra* (*Antoine et Cléopâtre*), *As You Like It* (*Comme il vous plaira*), *The Comedy of Errors* (*La Comédie des Erreurs*), *Coriolanus* (*Coriolan*), *Cymbeline* (*Cymbeline*), *Hamlet* (*Hamlet*), *Julius Caesar* (*Jules César*), *King Henry IV, V, VI, VIII* (*Henri IV, V, VI, VIII*), *King John* (*Le roi Jean*), *King Lear* (*Le roi Lear*), *King Richard II, III* (*Richard II, III*), *Love's Labour's Lost* (*Peines d'amour perdues*), *Macbeth* (*Macbeth*), *Measure for Measure* (*Mesure pour mesure*), *The Merchant of Venice* (*Le Marchand de Venise*), *Merry Wives of Windsor* (*Les Joyeuses Commères de Windsor*), *A Midsummer Night's Dream* (*Le Songe d'une nuit d'été*), *Much Ado About Nothing* (*Beaucoup de bruit pour rien*), *Othello* (*Othello*), *Pericles, Prince of Tyre* (*Périclès, Prince de Tyr*), *Romeo and Juliet* (*Roméo et Juliette*), *The Taming of the Shrew* (*La Mégère apprivoisée*), *The Tempest* (*La Tempête*), *Timon of Athens* (*Timon d'Athènes*), *Titus Andronicus* (*Titus Andronicus*), *Troilus and Cressida* (*Troïlus et Cressida*), *Twelfth Night* (*La Nuit des Rois*), *Two Gentlemen of Verona* (*Les Deux Gentilshommes de Vérone*), *The Winter's Tale* (*Le Conte d'hiver*). *Note.*—Some of the Acts and Scenes of Shakespeare's plays are numbered differently in various editions.

FRENCH - ENGLISH

A

a. N'avoir pas fait une panse d'a, Not to have written a stroke.

abandonner. *See* CHAMP, PARTIE.

abattre. Abattre de la besogne, To get through a lot of work.

La sursomme abat l'âne, It is the last straw that breaks the camel's back.

Petite pluie abat grand vent, Small rain lays great dust (*sometimes very little will end a great quarrel*).

See also BRIDE, CORNEILLE.

abbaye. Pour un moine l'abbaye ne faut pas *ou* ne chôme pas, No one is indispensable.

abbé. Le moine répond comme l'abbé chante, Like master like man.

Nous l'attendrons comme les moines font l'abbé, If he does not arrive punctually for dinner, we will start without him.

abîme. C'est un abîme de science, He is a fount of learning.

Creuser un abîme sous les pas de quelqu'un (*fig.*), To dig a pit for someone (*Psalms* cxix, 85).

L'abîme appelle l'abime (*fig.*), Deep calls (*or* calleth) to deep (*one excess, one exaggeration, one sin, leads to another*). *Quotation under* PAS.

aboi. Être aux abois, To be at bay; To be in desperate straits, To be hard (*or* sore) pressed, To be on one's beam ends; To be about to succumb.

Réduire (*ou* Mettre) aux abois, To bring to bay; To reduce to the last extremity. "Here wast thou bay'd, brave hart; Here didst thou fall; and here thy hunters stand, Sign'd in thy spoil, and crimson'd in thy Lethe."—*Julius Caesar* III, 1. (*Note.*—Lethe = death.)

abondance. Parler avec abondance, To speak fluently, To have an easy flow of speech.

Parler d'abondance, To speak off-hand *or* extempore. "*Quince.* Snug, the joiner, you, the lion's part . . . *Snug.* Have you the lion's part written? pray you, if it be, give it me, for I am slow of study. *Quince.* You may do it extempore, for it is nothing but roaring."—*A Midsummer Night's Dream* I, 2.

Parler d'abondance de cœur, To speak one's mind freely.

See also NUIRE.

abonder. Abonder dans le sens de quelqu'un, To entirely agree with someone.

Abonder dans son sens, To be wedded to one's own opinion.

aborder. Aborder la question, To tackle the question, To broach the subject.

aboutissant. *See* TENANT.

aboyer. Aboyer à la lune (*fig.*), To appeal to deaf ears.

Chien qui aboie ne mord pas *ou* Tous les chiens qui aboient ne mordent pas, His bark is worse than his bite.

absence. *See* BRILLER.

absent. *See* CHAT.

accepter. *See* AUGURE, REFUS.

accommoder. Accommoder quelqu'un d'importance *ou* de toutes pièces, To give someone a good dressing down (*thrashing or scolding*).

accorder. *See* CHIEN, FLÛTE.

accoutrer. Accoutrer quelqu'un de toutes pièces, To give someone a good dressing down (*thrashing or scolding*).

accrocher. *See* BRANCHE.

accroire. En faire accroire à quelqu'un, To impose [up]on someone.

Faire accroire à quelqu'un que . . ., To make someone believe that . . .

S'en faire accroire, To over-estimate one's own importance, To think too much of oneself, To have [got] a swelled head.

acculer. *See* RETRANCHEMENT.

accuser. *See* CHIEN, EXCUSER.

acérer. Avoir une langue acérée, To have a sharp (*or* a caustic) (*or* a stinging) tongue. " For she had a tongue with a tang, Would cry to a sailor, ' Go, hang.' "—*The Tempest* II, 2.

acheter. *See* CHAT, OR, PAIN.

achever. *See* PEINDRE.

achoppement. *See* PIERRE.

acier. *See* CŒUR.

acquérir. Je vous suis acquis, I am at your service.

See also BIEN, CONSISTANCE.

acquit. Faire quelque chose par acquit de conscience *ou* pour l'acquit de sa conscience, To do something for conscience (*or* conscience') sake *or* as a matter of duty.

Faire quelque chose par manière d'acquit, To do something for form's sake *or* as a matter of form *or* perfunctorily.

acquitter. Acquitter sa conscience, To satisfy one's conscience.

acte. Faire acte de bonne volonté, To give (*or* To show) proof of good will. " Upon thy cheek lay I this zealous kiss, As seal to this indenture of my love."—*King John* II, 1.

Faire acte de diligence, To give proof that one has set about doing it (*something*).

Faire acte de présence, To put in an appearance (*legally or socially*).

action. Ses actions haussent *ou* remontent, Ses actions baissent, His stock is going up, His stock is going down (*his credit is rising, falling*).

See also HOMME.

actualité. *See* PREMIER.

actuel. *See* HAUTEUR.

Adam. *See* ÈVE.

adieu. Adieu paniers, vendanges sont faites, It 's all over and beyond recall.

See also FÊTE.

adorer. Adorer le soleil levant, To curry favour with the rising power. " Vouchsafe to show the sunshine of your face, That we, like savages, may worship it."—*Love's Labour's Lost* V, 2.

Adorer le veau d'or, To worship the golden calf. " What a god's gold, That he is worshipp'd in a baser temple Than where swine feed ! " —*Timon of Athens* V, 1. " All gold and silver rather turn to dirt ! And 'tis no better reckon'd, but of those Who worship dirty gods."—*Cymbeline* III, 6. " The learned pate Ducks to the golden fool."—*Timon of Athens* IV, 3.

adoucir. *See* ANGLE.

ad patres. Aller *ad patres*, To join (*or* To go over to) the [great] majority.

Envoyer quelqu'un *ad patres*, To send someone to kingdom come (*slang*). *Quotations under* MONDE.

adresse. C'est à l'adresse d'un tel, That's a hit at so-and-so.

Le trait est arrivé (*ou* est allé) à son adresse, The shaft (*of ridicule, of satire*) struck (*or* went) home.

adresser. *See* SAINT.

advenir. *See* FAIRE.

affaire. C'est une affaire faite, Done, That's settled.

C'est une affaire faite, ou autant vaut, It is as good as done *or* settled.

En voici une affaire, Here's a pretty go *or* a pretty kettle of fish *or* a fine how-d'ye-do. " Here's goodly gear ! "—*Romeo and Juliet* II, 4.

Faire son affaire (*à soi-même*), To make one's pile (*fortune*).

Faire son affaire à quelqu'un, To do for someone (*ruin, or even kill, him*),

To cook someone's goose, To settle someone's hash.

Son affaire est bonne, He's for it (*destined for punishment, misfortune*) (*slang*).

Son affaire est faite, He's done for, It's all up with him, His number's up.

See also AUTRE, BALLOTTER, BRANLE, BRASSEUR, CLAIR, CŒUR, CORSER, COURANT, DEMAIN, DESSUS, ÉCUMEUR, ENGRENER, ÉTAT, ÉTRANGLER, FONDS, HORS, INCOMMODER, MARCHER, MENER, MOMENT, MOT, NEZ, OR, PARTIE, PLI, PLONGER, POCHE, PRENDRE, REPOS, RIEN, SAC, SOMMEIL, TIRER, TRAÎNER, TROUSSER, VOIR.

affamer. *See* VENTRE.

affiche. *See* VEDETTE.

affiler. *See* BEC, LANGUE.

affreux. C'est un homme affreux, He is a hideous[ly ugly] man ; He is a perfect beast (*vile*).

affront. Empocher (*ou* Boire) (*ou* Dévorer) un affront, To pocket (*or* To swallow) an insult.

See also DOUBLER.

âge. *See* APPRENDRE, BAS, BEAU 17, 32, CONNAISSANCE, DEMEURANT, DONNER, ENTRE, FORCE, HOMME, INGRAT, MOURIR, PLAISIR, PRENDRE, RAISON, TIRER.

agglomération. L'agglomération londonienne, parisienne, bruxelloise, etc., Greater London, Paris, Brussels (*the city and its suburbs*).

agir. Voici ce dont il s'agit, The thing is this.

See also AUTRE, CONNAISSANCE, DÉCOUVERT, DESSOUS.

agneau. *See* DOUX.

agonie. L'agonie du jour, The dying day.

agréable. Avoir pour agréable, To [kindly] allow *or* permit : Ayez pour agréable que je vous amène cette personne, que j'attende encore un peu, [Kindly] allow me to bring this person along, to wait a little longer.

C'est un(e) agréable, He (She) is a pleasant person *or* is an agreeable.

Faire l'agréable auprès de quelqu'un, To make oneself pleasant to someone.

See also COMMERCE.

ahan. *See* SUER.

ahurir. C'est un ahuri, une ahurie, He (She) is all in a fluster *or* a flurry. Quelle ahurie ! How flustered she becomes !

aide. Dieu lui, vous, soit en aide, God help him, her, you.

Un peu d'aide fait grand bien, Every little helps.

See also BON 17.

aider. Aide-toi, le ciel t'aidera, God helps those who help themselves. " Our remedies oft in ourselves do lie, Which we ascribe to heaven : the fated sky Gives us free scope ; only doth backward pull Our slow designs when we ourselves are dull." —*All's Well That Ends Well* I, 1.

Dieu aidant, With God's help. " The means that heaven yields must be embrac'd And not neglected ; else, if heaven would, And we will not, heaven's offer we refuse, The proffer'd means of succour and redress."—*King Richard II* III, 2.

See also MATIN.

aigle. C'est un aigle, He is a mastermind *or* a genius *or* (*relatively*) a king *or* a lion : Cet homme-là est un aigle au prix de ceux dont vous parlez, That man is a king compared with those you mention. C'est l'aigle de leur société, He is the lion of their company *or* the king of their castle.

See also CRIER.

aigre. Avoir un caractère aigre comme verjus, To be as sour as vinegar, To be of a vinegary (*or* crabbed) disposition. " Some that will evermore peep through their eyes, And laugh, like parrots, at a bag-piper : And other of such vinegar aspéct, That they'll not show their teeth in way of smile, Though Nestor swear the jest be laughable."—*The Merchant of Venice* I, 1.

aiguille. C'est chercher une aiguille dans une botte de foin, It is like looking for a needle in a bottle (*or* a bundle) of hay *or* in a haystack.

De fil en aiguille, Little by little, Bit by bit, Gradually (*one thing leading to another*) : Il nous a raconté toute l'histoire de fil en aiguille, He told us the whole story little by little.

Disputer, Raisonner, sur une pointe d'aiguille, sur des pointes d'aiguille, To dispute, To argue, over a mere trifle, over mere trifles, To split hairs, To quibble, To cavil.

Faire passer quelqu'un par le trou d'une aiguille, To make it very awkward for someone.

aiguiller. Aiguiller une discussion, To switch on to another subject, To side-track a subject.

S'aiguiller dans une voie nouvelle, To change one's tack, To try another tack.

aiguillon. *See* REGIMBER.

aiguiser. Aiguiser ses (*ou* les) couteaux, To prepare for the fight.

aile. Avoir du plomb dans l'aile, To be hard hit.

Ne battre [plus] que d'une aile, To be in a bad way, To be a lame duck, To be on one's last legs.

See also AVOIR, NOUVELLE, PEUR, PIED, PLUME, PRENDRE, ROGNER, TALON, VOLER.

ailleurs. Allez conter cela ailleurs, Go and tell that to the marines.

See also ESPRIT.

aimable. Il est aimable comme une porte de prison, He is a most unpleasant person.

See also POUVOIR.

aimer. Aimer la bonne chère *ou* Aimer la table, To like good things to eat, To be fond of good living.

Qui aime bien, châtie bien, Spare the rod and spoil the child. "And chastise with the valour of my tongue All that impedes thee from the golden round."—*Macbeth* I, 5.

Qui m'aime, aime mon chien, Love me, love my dog.

See also AISE, BESOGNE, BOUTEILLE, MÉTIER, MORCEAU, SUCRERIE.

ainsi. Ainsi dit, ainsi fait, No sooner said than done.

Pour ainsi dire, So to speak, As it were.

See also PASSER, TEMPS.

air. Avoir grand air, To look distinguished (*of persons*) ; To look well (*of things*).

Avoir toujours le (*ou* un) pied en l'air, To be always on the go ; To be always on the move.

Avoir un air de famille, To have a family likeness.

Avoir un faux air de quelqu'un, To bear a slight (*or* a remote) resemblance to someone.

Être en l'air, To be in a state of confusion *or* of pie (*as a room*) ; To be in a flutter, To be agog [with excitement] (*as a populace, a town*) ; To be ill-secured (*of one's fortune*).

Je connais des paroles sur cet air-là, I have heard that tale before.

L'air du monde est contagieux, Bad habits are catching.

N'être pas dans l'air, To be out of tune (*in singing*).

Ne faire que battre l'air (*fig.*), To be only beating the air. "For it is, as the air, invulnerable, And our vain blows malicious mockery."—*Hamlet* I, 1.

Prendre (*ou* Se donner) des airs *ou* de grands airs, To give oneself airs, To put it on.

Prendre (*ou* Avoir) des airs penchés, To strike affecting attitudes.

Prendre l'air du bureau, To see how

the land lies, To see which way the wind is blowing.

Prendre l'air (*ou* un air) du feu, To have a warm at the fire.

Se donner de l'air, To show a clean pair of heels.

Vivre de l'air du temps, To live on air *or* on next to nothing. " Eating the air on promise of supply."—2 *King Henry IV* I, 3.

See also BEAU 4, BIENHEUREUX, BON 9, CAPABLE, CONQUÉRANT, CRACHER, DÉPLUMER, DÉTERRER, LEVER, MÉCHANT, PARLER, QUATRE, TOUCHER, VAINQUEUR.

airain. Avoir un front d'airain, To have a brazen (*or* a brassy) impudence. " Can any face of brass hold longer out ? "—*Love's Labour's Lost* V, 2. " What a brazen-faced varlet art thou, to deny thou knowest me ! "—*King Lear* II, 2.

Les injures s'écrivent sur l'airain et les bienfaits sur le sable, " Men's evil manners live in brass ; their virtues We write in water."—*King Henry VIII* IV, 2. " The evil that men do lives after them ; The good is oft interred with their bones." —*Julius Caesar* III, 2.

Un ciel d'airain, A sky of brass, A brassy sky (*drought*).

Un siècle d'airain (*fig.*), An age of stress, A stressful age.

See also CŒUR.

aise. Aimer ses aises, To like creature comforts.

Être mal à son aise, To feel ill.

Vous en parlez bien à votre aise, It is easy enough for you to talk.

aisé. Cela est plus aisé à dire qu'à faire, That is easier (*or* more easily) said than done.

Cela vous est bien aisé à dire, It is easy enough for you to talk.

Être aisé à vivre, To be easy to get on with, To be pleasant to deal with.

ajuster. Vous voilà bien ajusté, You do look a sight, What a sight you look !

See also FLÛTE.

alambic. Cette affaire a passé par l'alambic, This matter has been well thrashed out.

alarme. L'alarme est au camp, A scare has been raised, There is a fluttering in the dovecotes.

Mettre l'alarme au quartier *ou* au camp, To raise a scare, To flutter the dovecotes.

alléger. *See* AVRIL.

alléguer. *See* IGNORANCE.

allemand. *See* HAUT, QUERELLE.

aller. Aller aux renseignements (*ou* aux informations) sur quelqu'un, sur quelque chose, To make enquiries about (*or* To inquire about *or* as to) someone, something.

Aller son chemin *ou* Aller toujours son chemin *ou* Aller son petit bonhomme de chemin *ou* Aller son petit train, To go one's way, To jog along, To go plodding on. " Jog on, jog on, the footpath way, And merrily hent the stile-a: A merry heart goes all the day, Your sad tires in a mile-a."—*The Winter's Tale* IV, 2. (*Note.*—hent = take.)

Aller sur les erres de quelqu'un, To follow (*or* To tread) in someone's footsteps.

Aller vite en besogne, To be quick about it, Not to be long about it. " Come, answer not, but to it presently ; I am impatient of my tarriance."—*Two Gentlemen of Verona* II, 7.

Allez vous promener *ou* Allez vous coucher, Be off [with you], Get along with you, Off you go, Pack off, Hook it (*slang*), Beat it (*slang*), Hop it (*slang*). " Get you hence, sirrah ; saucy fellow, hence ! "—*Julius Caesar* IV, 3. " Avoid ! hence from my sight ! "—*Cymbeline* I, 1. " Rogues, hence, avaunt ! vanish like hailstones, go ; Trudge, plod, away, o' the hoof; seek shelter, pack!"—*Merry Wives of Windsor* I, 3. "Go, hop me over every kennel home."—*Taming of the Shrew* IV, 3.

Au long aller, In the long run, In time.

Au long aller, petit fardeau pèse, The lightest weight tires in time.

C'est un homme fait pour aller à tout, There is no height (*or* eminence) to which this man cannot attain (*fig.*).

Cela (*ou* Il) va de soi *ou* va de suite *ou* va sans dire, That (*or* It) is a matter of course, It stands to reason, It goes without saying.

Cela va tout seul, It is all plain sailing.

Faire aller quelqu'un, To order someone about.

Il s'en est allé comme il était venu, He went away empty-handed.

Il va sur [ses] dix ans, He is getting (*or* going) on for ten, He is nearly (*or* will soon be) ten [years old].

La vente va, ne va pas, Business (*i.e., sales*) is good, is not good.

N'y pas aller de main morte, To put one's back (*or* some vim) into it, To set about it in dead earnest, To go it hammer and tongs, To lay it on.

N'y pas aller par quatre chemins, To go (*or* To come) straight to the point, Not to beat about the bush, Not to mince matters. "Hoyday, a riddle! neither good nor bad! What need'st thou run so many miles about, When thou mayst tell thy tale the nearest way? Once more, what news?"—*King Richard III* IV, 4.

Tout y va, la paille et le blé, Everything has gone, lock, stock, and barrel, Nothing has been spared.

Y aller carrément *ou* rondement *ou* Y aller de franc jeu, To go (*or* To come) straight to the point, To be quite straightforward about it; To go about it openly. "Well, how then? come, roundly, roundly."—1 *King Henry IV* I, 2.

See also ADRESSE, AILLEURS, ANGLAIS, AVANT, AVIS, BAISSER, BÂTIMENT, BLANC, BON 7, 75, BOUDIN, BRIDE, BRISÉES, CEINTURE, CHASSE, CHASSE-MARÉE, CHEMIN, CHEVILLE, CHOU, CLAQUET, COMPÈRE, CORNEILLE, CROÎTRE, CROIX, CRUCHE, DÉBANDADE, DÉRIVE, DEVANT, DIABLE, DIRECTEMENT, DROIT, ÉCREVISSE, FESSE, FIL, FORCE, FUMÉE, GALOP, GANT, JAMBE, LAISSER, LANGUE, MARMITE, MÉNAGER, MERVEILLE, MONDE, MOUVEMENT, NEZ, NUE, PAIR, PENDRE, PISTOLET, PLAIN-PIED, PLAIRE, POSTE, POUSSER, PRESSER, PROVIDENCE, PROVISION, QUEUE, ROME, ROULETTE, SOULIER, TÊTE, TRAIN, TROUPE, VAU-L'EAU, VENIR, VENT, VOIR.

allonger. Allonger la courroie, To make the most of it, To make a little go a long way, To eke it out. "I speak too long; but 'tis to peise the time, To eke it, and to draw it out at length, To stay you from election."—*The Merchant of Venice* III, 2.

Allonger le pas, To step out, To put one's best foot (*or* leg) foremost. "Make haste; the better foot before."—*King John* IV, 2.

Avoir le visage allongé *ou* la mine allongée, To pull a long face, To have a face as long as a fiddle.

allumer. Un visage allumé, A ruddy face; A flushed face.

allumette. Ce bois brûle comme des allumettes, This wood burns like matchwood.

See also SEC.

allure. *See* PRENDRE.

almanach. C'est un almanach de l'an passé, It has gone out of date.

Faire (*ou* Composer) des almanachs, To make airy predictions; To spin theories.

Un faiseur d'almanachs, An airy

prognosticator; A spinner of theories.

Une autre fois, je prendrai, je ne prendrai plus, de ses almanachs, Another time, I shall take notice, I shall take no notice, of what he says (*predicts*).

alors. Alors comme alors, We shall see [then], We must wait and see, Time enough when that comes.

alouette. Il attend que les alouettes lui tombent toutes rôties [dans le bec], He expects a fortune to drop from heaven.

S'éveiller, Se lever, au chant de l'alouette, To wake, To rise, with the lark. " Stir with the lark tomorrow, gentle Norfolk."—*King Richard III* V, 3. " It was the lark, the herald of the morn, . . . look, love, what envious streaks Do lace the severing clouds in yonder east."—*Romeo and Juliet* III, 5. " Hark, hark ! the lark at heaven's gate sings, And Phoebus 'gins arise."—*Cymbeline* II, 3. " Lo ! here the gentle lark, weary of rest, From his moist cabinet mounts up on high, And wakes the morning." —SHAKESPEARE, *Venus and Adonis*.

Si le ciel tombait, il y aurait bien des alouettes prises, Pigs might fly.

altesse. Donner de l'altesse à quelqu'un, To call someone Your Highness *or* my lord (*to flatter him*).

amasser. *See* PIERRE.

ambassade. Il a fait une belle ambassade, A nice mess he has made of it *or* of the affair.

ambre. *See* FIN.

ambulant. *See* BIBLIOTHÈQUE, CADAVRE, DICTIONNAIRE, ENCYCLOPÉDIE.

âme. Être l'âme damnée de quelqu'un, To be someone's cat's-paw, To be a mere tool in someone's hands, To do someone's dirty work for him.

See also ARRACHER, BOUE, CHEVILLER, ŒIL, PÉTRIR.

amende. [C'est la coutume de Lorris,] les battus paient l'amende, [It is the way of the world,] the weakest goes to the wall.

amender. Cela n'amendera pas votre marché, That won't help you.

S'amender, To mend one's ways, To turn over a new leaf.

amener. *See* AURORE, MALHEUR, VENT.

amer. Ce qui est amer à la bouche est doux au cœur, Unpleasant things are often salutary. " Thy wit is a very bitter sweeting ; it is a most sharp sauce."—*Romeo and Juliet* II, 4.

See also BÊTISE, DRAGÉE.

américain. *See* ŒIL.

amertume. *See* CALICE.

ami. *See* AUTEL, BESOIN, BON 53, BOURSE, CŒUR, DÉPENDRE, HEURE, HONTEUX, PAIRE.

amitié. Nouer (*ou* Lier) amitié avec quelqu'un, To strike up a friendship (*or*, *slang*, To pal up) with someone.

amorce. See BRÛLER.

amour. C'est un amour, He (She) is a love of a child.

Cet ouvrage est fait avec amour, This work is a labour of love *or* has been done con amore.

Il n'y a point de laides amours, Beauty is in the eyes of the beholder, Beauty lies in lovers' eyes. " Beauty is bought by judgment of the eye, Not utter'd by base sale of chapmen's tongues."—*Love's Labour's Lost* II, 1. " The lover, . . . Sees Helen's beauty in a brow of Egypt."—*A Midsummer Night's Dream* V, 1. " Thy love is black as ebony.—Is ebony like her ? O wood divine ! "—*Love's Labour's Lost* IV, 3.

L'amour et la pauvreté font ensemble mauvais ménage, When poverty comes in by the door, love flies out of the window. " Besides, you know Prosperity's the very bond of love, Whose fresh complexion and whose heart together Affliction alters."—*The Winter's Tale* IV, 3.

L'Amour Médecin, Doctor Cupid. " Flower of this purple dye, Hit with Cupid's archery, Sink in apple of his eye ! When his love he doth espy, Let her shine as gloriously As the Venus of the sky.—When thou wak'st, if she be by, Beg of her for remedy."—*A Midsummer Night's Dream* III, 2. " I'll apply To your eye, Gentle lover, remedy." *A Midsummer Night's Dream* III, 2.

Ne demander qu'amour et simplesse, To ask only for peace and quiet.

On revient toujours à ses premières amours, First love, last love, best love.

Pour l'amour de Dieu, For the love of God ; For goodness' sake ; (*ironically*) Reluctantly.

See also BATTRE, FÉRIR, FILER, RUSE, SERRURE.

amphibie. C'est un amphibie, He is amphibious (*connected with two unrelated professions*) ; He is a time-server.

amuser. S'amuser à la moutarde, To do nothing useful, To twiddle one's fingers.

See also TAPIS.

an. *See* ALMANACH, BON 15, 19, CHAGRIN, MOIS, MOQUER, OUTRAGE, QUINZE, SOUCIER.

ancre. *See* SALUT.

âne. C'est un vrai âne bâté, He is a perfect ass.

Il cherche son âne et il est dessus, He is looking for something that is in his hands. "Look, Lucius, here's the book I sought for so ; I put it in the pocket of my gown."—*Julius Caesar* IV, 3.

Il fait l'âne pour avoir du son, He pretends to be silly in order to dupe others, He is not such a fool as he makes himself out to be, There's method in his madness. " Though this be madness, yet there is method in't."—*Hamlet* II, 2.

Il ressemble à l'âne de Buridan, He can't make up his mind (*as between two alternatives*).

L'âne du commun est toujours le plus mal bâté *ou* Il n'y a point d'âne plus mal bâté que celui du commun, Everybody's business is nobody's business.

On ne saurait faire boire un âne s'il n'a soif *ou* un âne qui n'a pas soif, You may take a horse to the water, but you can't make him drink.

Pour un point (*ou* Faute d'un point), Martin perdit son âne, For want of a nail, the shoe was lost ; For want of one point, the game was lost.

See also ABATTRE, COQ, COUP 19, GRATTER, LAVER, MÉCHANT, PEAU, PONT, SÉRIEUX, TÊTU.

ange. Être aux anges, To be in the seventh heaven [of delight], To be in raptures. " She speaks :—O, speak again, bright angel ! for thou art As glorious to this night, being o'er my head, As is a winged messenger of heaven Unto the white-upturned wondering eyes Of mortals that fall back to gaze on him When he bestrides the lazy-pacing clouds And sails upon the bosom of the air."—*Romeo and Juliet* II, 2. *See also quotation under* RAVIR.

See also DÉCHOIR, RIRE.

anglais. S'en aller (*ou* Partir) (*ou* Filer) à l'anglaise, To go off without saying good-bye, To take French leave. *Quotation under* BRÛLER.

angle. Adoucir les angles, To rub off the rough corners (*fig.*).

angoisse. *See* AVALER.

anguille. Il y a quelque anguille sous roche, There is something afoot *or* something brewing *or* something in the wind, There is more here than meets the eye, I smell a rat.

See also ÉCORCHER.

animal. *See* HABITUDE.

année. Année commune[, année moyenne], [Taking] one year with another (*on an average between the years*).

anse. Faire danser l'anse du panier, To make a bit out of it (*in marketing for someone*), To receive a secret commission.

Faire le pot à deux anses, To set (*or* To stand with) one's arms akimbo.

antichambre. Faire antichambre, To wait in the waiting room ; To hang around soliciting favours ; To lobby. *See also* PROPOS.

antienne. *See* MÊME.

antipode. Ce sont les antipodes, They (*these two men, these two things*) are as opposite as the poles *or* are poles apart, They are exact opposites, They are diametrically opposed, They are as like (*or* as different) as chalk and cheese. " Thou art as opposite to every good As the antipodes are to us, Or as the south to the septentrion." 3 *King Henry VI* I, 4.

Cet homme est l'antipode du bon sens, This man is utterly devoid of common sense.

Être aux antipodes de quelqu'un, To be the exact opposite of someone.

Je voudrais que cet homme fût aux antipodes, I wish this man in Jericho.

antique. C'est un homme de mœurs antiques *ou* C'est un homme antique, He is a gentleman of the old school.

apache. Une ruse d'apache, A devilish trick.

Apocalypse. C'est un vrai cheval de l'Apocalypse, It is a veritable jade *or* a sorry nag (*Revelation* vi, 4–8).

Un style d'Apocalypse *ou* Un style apocalyptique, An obscure (*or* involved) style.

apothicaire. Un mémoire (*ou* Un compte) d'apothicaire, An exorbitant bill.

apôtre. C'est un bon apôtre, He is a sanctimonious rascal.

Faire le bon apôtre, To play the saint.

apparence. Garder les apparences, To keep up the illusion (*false impression*).

Sauver (*ou* Ménager) les apparences, To keep up appearances.

appartenir. *See* CÉSAR.

appel. Faire appel à la force, To resort to force.

Faire appel à ses souvenirs, To try to remember, To tax one's memory.

appeler. Appeler un chat un chat *ou* Appeler les choses par leur nom, To call a spade a spade. " We call a nettle but a nettle ; and The faults of fools but folly."—*Coriolanus* II, 1. *Another quotation under* NOMMER.

Il en a appelé, He has got over it, He has recovered (*from a severe illness*).

J'appelle de votre décision *ou* J'en appelle [de votre sentence], I beg to differ.

See also ABÎME, CHIEN, LÉGION, PARLER.

appétit. Avoir un appétit de loup *ou* de cheval, To be ravenous, To be as hungry as a hunter *or* as a wolf. " And appetite, an universal wolf."—*Troilus and Cressida* I, 3.

C'est un homme qui a bon appétit (*fig.*), He is a man who is never satisfied [with what he has got].

Demeurer (*ou* Rester) sur son appétit (*fig.*), To curb one's desires.

Il n'est sauce (*ou* Il n'est chère) que d'appétit, Hunger is the best sauce.

L'appétit vient en mangeant (*fig.*), The more a man gets the more he wants, Much would have more.

Manger de bon appétit, To eat heartily, To play a good knife and fork.

See also ASSAISONNER, OUVRIR, PAIN.

applaudir. Applaudir à tout rompre *ou* à tout casser, To applaud to the echo, To bring the house down. "I would applaud thee to the very echo, That should applaud again." —*Macbeth* V, 3.

appliquer. Appliquer un soufflet (*ou* une gifle) à quelqu'un, To slap (*or* To smack) someone's face, To give someone a clout.

apprendre. Cela vous apprendra, That will teach you, Serve you right, That'll larn ye (*jocular or vulgar*). " And learn me how to lose a winning match."—*Romeo and Juliet* III, 2.

Il fait bon vivre, on apprend toujours, Live and learn, Those that live longest will see the most.

Je lui apprendrai [bien] à vivre, I'll teach him how to behave.

On apprend à tout âge, It is never too late to learn.

See also DÉPENS, NAGER, RENOMMÉE, SINGE.

appuyer. *See* CHANTERELLE, ROSEAU.

âpre. Être âpre à la besogne, To be a keen worker.

Être âpre à la curée, To be greedy of gain, of honours.

après. *See* COUP 77, DÉLUGE, ÉCHELLE, MORT, MOUTARDE, OS, PLUIE.

à quia. Être à quia, To be in a quandary, To be up a gum tree.

araignée. Avoir une araignée dans le plafond, To have a bee in one's bonnet *or* a screw (*or* a tile) loose, To have something wrong in the upper storey, To have bats in the belfry.

arbalète. *See* TRAIT.

arbre. Se tenir au gros de l'arbre, To be on the safe side.

Tel arbre, tel fruit, " By their fruits ye shall know them."—*Matthew* vii, 20.

See also COGNÉE, ÉCORCE, EMPÊCHER, FOURCHU, PREMIER.

arc. *See* CORDE, DÉBANDER, DÉTENDRE.

arche. C'est l'arche du Seigneur *ou* l'arche sainte, It is forbidden ground (*fig.*).

archives. Mettez cela dans vos archives (*fig.*), Keep that with care.

arçon. Perdre ses arçons, To be out of countenance, To be disconcerted.

See also FERME.

ardent. *See* CHARBON, MARCHER.

argent. En avoir pour son argent, To have (*or* To get) one's money's worth, To have a run for one's money.

Faire valser son argent, To make the money fly.

Point d'argent, point de suisse, Nothing for nothing, No pay, no piper, Show me first your penny. " Said the pieman to Simple Simon, 'Show me first your penny;' Said Simple Simon to the pieman, 'Sir, I have not any.' "—*Nursery rhyme of early and unknown authorship.*

Un homme d'argent, A money-grubber.

See also AUTRUI, BARRE, BESOGNE, BON 18, 51, 75, BOURREAU, BRÛLER, COMPTANT, CONNAÎTRE, COULER, COURIR, COURT, COÛTER, DRAP, EMBARRAS, FENÊTRE, FONDRE, FOU, HUILE, MAIN, NERF, ODEUR, OR, PAROLE, PLAIE, PLEUVOIR, REMUER, ROULER, SEMER, TEMPS, TRAVAILLER.

argile. Une statue d'or aux pieds d'argile (*fig.*), A golden image with feet of clay (*Daniel* ii, 33, 34, 42).

argument. Un argument à deux tranchants, A two-edged argument, An argument that cuts both ways.

arlequin. C'est un arlequin, He is a weathercock. *Quotations under* TOURNER.

Un habit d'arlequin (*fig.*), A medley, A miscellany, An omnium gatherum.

arme. C'est une arme à deux

tranchants, It is a two-edged sword (*fig.*), It cuts both ways.

Elle est sous les armes, She is got up to kill.

Faire arme de tout, To leave no stone unturned.

Faire tomber à quelqu'un les armes des mains (*fig.*), To disarm someone.

Les armes sont journalières, The fortunes of war are uncertain (*lit.* & *fig.*).

See also COURTOIS, RÂTELIER, RESTER, SORT.

armée. *See* ORDRE.

armer. Être armé jusqu'aux dents *ou* Être armé de toutes pièces *ou* de pied en cap, To be armed to the teeth (*lit.* & *fig.*). " Arm'd at all points exactly, cap-à-pé."—*Hamlet* I, 2.

See also PATIENCE.

arracher. Il vaut mieux laisser son enfant morveux que de lui arracher le nez, One may go farther and fare worse.

Je lui ai arraché une dent, I wrung some money out of him.

On se l'arrache, He, She, It, is in great request *or* is all the rage.

Vous lui arracheriez plutôt la vie *ou* le cœur *ou* l'âme, He would sooner lose his right arm, It would break his heart to do it.

See also PLUME.

arracheur. *See* MENTIR.

arranger. Elle est bien arrangée, She is well dressed.

Je l'ai bien arrangé *ou* Je l'ai arrangé de la belle manière, I gave him a good dressing down.

Vous voilà bien arrangé, You do look a sight, What a sight you look !

arrêt. Être en arrêt, To have one's curiosity (*desire to know*) aroused, To be appealed to: Il est en arrêt devant toutes les nouveautés, Any new invention arouses his curiosity *or* appeals to him.

arrêter. *See* CHEMIN.

arrière. *See* DEMEURER, RETOURNER.

arrière-ban. *See* BAN.

arriver. Arriver [à ses fins], To gain one's end[s], To achieve one's purpose, To get what one wants, To succeed, To get on.

Il en arrivera ce qu'il pourra, Let what may happen *or* come. " Come what may come, Time and the hour runs through the roughest day."—*Macbeth* I, 3. " Befall what may befall."—2 *King Henry VI* III, 2.

Un homme arrivé, A successful (*or* A made) man.

See also ADRESSE, BON 8, FAIRE, MALHEUR, MARÉE, MARS, NU, PREMIER, PROPOS.

arroi. Être en mauvais arroi, To be in a sorry plight *or* in a sad pickle.

arroser. Arroser la terre de ses sueurs (*fig.*), To till (*or* To labour) the earth in the sweat of one's brow (*Genesis* iii, 17–19).

Arroser ses créanciers, To put off one's creditors with something on account.

Arroser son pain de larmes, To water one's bread with tears.

Du courage arrosé, Dutch courage. " They were red-hot with drinking: So full of valour that they smote the air For breathing in their faces ; beat the ground For kissing of their feet."—*The Tempest* IV, 1.

J'ai été bien arrosé, I got a thorough wetting, I got wet through.

S'arroser la gorge, To wet one's whistle.

Artaban. *See* FIER.

article. C'est un autre article, That's quite another matter.

Ce n'est pas article de foi, It (*this thing*) is hard to believe. *Cf.* Croire tout comme article de foi *under* CROIRE.

Être à l'article de la mort, To be at the point of death *or* in the article of death *or* in articulo mortis.

artifice. C'est un vrai feu d'artifice (*fig.*), It is a fine display of fireworks (*wit*).

artisan. À l'œuvre on connaît l'artisan, The workman is known by his work, The proof of the pudding is in the eating.

aspect. Présenter une affaire sous un autre aspect, To put a different complexion on a matter.

assaillant. *See* TOURNER.

assaisonner. La faim (*ou* L'appétit) assaisonne tout, Hunger is the best sauce.

assassin. Des yeux assassins, Bewitching (*or* Killing) eyes. " *Juliet.* If they do see thee they will murder thee. *Romeo.* Alack, there lies more peril in thine eye Than twenty of their swords."—*Romeo and Juliet* II, 2.

assaut. Faire assaut d'esprit avec quelqu'un, To vie in wit (*or* To engage in a skirmish *or* a battle *or* an encounter of wit) with someone. " There is a kind of merry war betwixt Signior Benedick and her: they never meet but there is a skirmish of wit between them."—*Much Ado About Nothing* I, 1.

assembler. *See* RESSEMBLER.

assiette. *See* CASSEUR, PIQUER, PIQUEUR.

assigner. *See* BROUILLARD.

assise. Tenir ses assises dans une maison, dans une compagnie, To be the oracle in a house, in a company. " As who should say, ' I am Sir Oracle, And, when I ope my lips, let no man bark ! ' "—*The Merchant of Venice* I, 1.

assommoir. *See* COUP 11.

athlète. Les athlètes de la foi *ou* Les athlètes de Jésus-Christ, The champions of the faith (*The martyrs*).

atout. Avoir tous les atouts dans son jeu (*fig.*), To hold all the winning cards. " Have I not here the best cards for the game, To win this easy match play'd for a crown ? "—*King John* V, 2.

atrocité. Débiter des atrocités sur quelqu'un, To say dreadful things about someone, To cast aspersions on someone.

attache. Il est là comme un chien à l'attache *ou* comme un chien d'attache *ou* Il est toujours à l'attache, He has to stick there the whole day long, He is always tied to his duties *or* chained to his office.

attacher. Ce spectacle attache les yeux *ou* l'attention, This spectacle rivets (*or* compels) the attention.

Je meurs où je m'attache, Faithful unto death.

See also BROUTER, GRELOT, INTÉRÊT, SAUCISSE, SOLIDE.

attaquer. *See* BEC, CORNE, DÉCOUVERT.

atteindre. *See* CRÉTINISME, MANQUER.

atteler. C'est une charrette (*ou* une charrue) mal attelée, They are an ill-matched pair *or* an ill-assorted couple (*husband and wife or partners*); They are an ill-assorted set (*partners*).

attendre. Attendez-moi sous l'orme, You may wait for me till doomsday *or* till the cows come home.

Attendez-vous-y, May you get it, You may whistle for it.

C'est où (*ou* C'est là que) je l'attends, There (*or* That's where) he will go down (*fail*) ; That's where I shall have him (*gain advantage over him*).

Ne t'attends qu'à toi seul, Rely on yourself [alone].

Tout vient à point (*ou* à temps) à qui sait (*ou* à qui peut) attendre, Everything comes to him who waits.

Un coup n'attendait pas l'autre, Blow followed blow.

See also ABBÉ, ALOUETTE, GRUE, MARÉE, PELOTER, VENIR.

attente. *See* BON 73, PIERRE, TABLE.

attention. *See* ATTACHER.

attique. C'est un attique, He is a man of Attic wit *or* of refined amenity of language.

attiser. Attiser le feu (*fig.*), To stir up strife.

attraper. Attrape ! (*fig.*), Sold again ! (*You are caught*) ; Take that (*blow*) !

Attrape qui peut, Scramble for it.

See also FIN, VOL.

auberge. *See* TENIR.

audace. *See* COUP 62, PAYER.

au-delà. *See* SOUCI.

au-dessous. *See* DESSOUS.

au-dessus. *See* DESSUS.

au-devant. *See* DEVANT.

auge. *See* MÉTIER, PORC.

Augias. *See* NETTOYER.

augure. C'est un oiseau de bon augure, de mauvais augure, He is a bird of good omen, of ill (*or* of evil) omen. " Thou ominous and fearful owl of death."—1 *King Henry VI* IV, 2.

J'en accepte l'augure, I take that as a good sign. " If I may trust the flattering eye of sleep, My dreams presage some joyful news at hand." —*Romeo and Juliet* V, 1.

aumône. *See* COIN.

aune. Au bout de l'aune faut le drap, All things have an end ; Waste not, want not.

Savoir ce que vaut l'aune, To know what it costs (*in trouble, expense—from bitter experience*).

Tout du long de l'aune, With a vengeance, And no mistake.

See also MESURER.

aurore. C'est l'aurore d'un beau jour (*fig.*), It is the dawn[ing] of a better day.

L'Aurore aux doigts de rose (*poetic*), Rosy-fingered Aurora (*dawn*). " But, look, the morn, in russet mantle clad, Walks o'er the dew of yon high eastern hill."—*Hamlet* I, 1.

Les pleurs de l'aurore (*poetic*), The dew. " Many a morning hath he there been seen, With tears augmenting the fresh morning's dew, Adding to clouds more clouds with his deep sighs."—*Romeo and Juliet* I, 1. " So sweet a kiss the golden sun gives not To those fresh morning drops upon the rose, As thy eyebeams, when their fresh rays have smote The night of dew that on my cheeks down flows : Nor shines the silver moon one half so bright Through the transparent bosom of the deep, As doth thy face through tears of mine give light."—*Love's Labour's Lost* IV, 3.

Travail d'aurore amène l'or, Early to bed and early to rise, Makes a man healthy, wealthy, and wise.

Une beauté dans son aurore, A budding beauty (*girl*).

aussi. *See* DIABLE.

aussitôt. Aussitôt dit, aussitôt fait *ou* Aussitôt pris, aussitôt pendu, No sooner said than done.

autant. Autant de têtes, autant d'avis *ou* d'opinions, So many men, so many minds.

C'est autant de pris sur l'ennemi *ou* C'est toujours autant de pris, That is so much to the good.

C'est fini, ou autant vaut, It is as good as finished.

See also AFFAIRE, CHARGE, CHIEN, PARLER, PENDRE, REGRETTABLE, SOUVENIR (SE), VENT.

autel. Dresser des autels à quelqu'un (*fig.*), To raise altars to someone.

Élever autel contre autel, To cause, To promote, a schism ; To pit one's credit, one's power, against that of another ; To start a rival concern.

Il prendrait sur l'autel *ou* sur le maître-autel, He is a grab-all. " He will steal, sir, an egg out of a cloister."—*All's Well That Ends Well* IV, 3.

Qui sert à l'autel doit vivre de l'autel *ou* Le prêtre vit de l'autel *ou* Il faut que le prêtre vive de l'autel, The labourer is worthy of his hire (*Luke* x, 7).

Un ami jusqu'aux autels, A friend who will do anything for one, except what goes against conscience or religion.

autorité. Faire autorité, To be regarded as an authority (*on some subject*).

autour. *See* TOURNER.

autre. À d'autres ! Nonsense !, Don't tell me [that], I know better, Tell that to the marines.

Ah ! cet autre ! *ou* Écoutez ce que nous dit cet autre ! Just listen to him, I don't believe a word he says.

Autre chose est de parler, autre chose d'agir, Talking is one thing, doing another.

Autres temps, autres mœurs, Other days, other ways, Manners change with the times. " So our virtues Lie in the interpretation of the time."—*Coriolanus* IV, 7.

C'est une autre affaire *ou* une autre histoire *ou* une autre musique *ou* une autre paire de manches, That's [quite] another matter, That is another story, That's another pair of shoes. *Cf.* Voilà bien une autre histoire *below*.

Comme dit l'autre *ou* cet autre, As the saying goes, As people say.

En voici [bien] d'un (*ou* d'une) autre, How strange, Well, I'm blowed (*slang*), That puts the lid on [it] (*slang*).

Il n'en fait pas (*ou* jamais) d'autres, That's just like him, He's always doing that (*stupid*) kind of thing, He's at it again.

J'en ai vu bien d'autres, That's nothing, *i.e.*, I have seen stranger things than that ; I have seen (*or* known) worse things in my time.

J'en sais [bien] d'autres, I know a trick worth two of that.

Voilà bien une autre histoire, [Here is] more trouble.

See also ARTICLE, ASPECT, ATTENDRE, AVEUGLE, BARBIER, BATTRE, BIEN, BOUCHER, CHANSON, CHANTER, CHASSER, DEMEURANT, FAIT, FOIS, FOUETTER, HABITUDE, LOUP, MALHEUR, MESURER, MONDE, NU, NUIRE, ŒIL, OREILLE, PAQUET, PASSER, PLEURER, PORTER, PROCÈS, RAISON, SOUFFLET, TENDRE, TIRER, TOURNURE, UN, VIOLON, VOYAGE.

autrefois. *See* HOMME.

autruche. Pratiquer la politique de l'autruche, To pursue an ostrich policy, To bury one's head in the sand.

See also ESTOMAC.

autrui. Argent d'autrui nul n'enrichit, Ill got, ill gone. " Didst thou never hear That things ill got had ever bad success ? "—3 *King Henry VI* II, 2.

Mal d'autrui n'est que songe, Others' griefs are but a dream. " Every one can master a grief but he that has it."—*Much Ado About Nothing* III, 2.

See also CHASSER, FAIRE.

avaler. Avaler des couleuvres, To pocket many affronts, To suffer many humiliations, To eat humble pie. " Well, ruffian, I must pocket up these wrongs." — *King John* III, 1.

Avaler la pilule *ou* la dragée *ou* le calice *ou* le morceau *ou* des poires d'angoisse, To swallow the pill, To swallow a bitter pill.

Il avale cela doux comme lait, He takes it all in.

Il avalerait la mer et les poissons, He is insatiable.

See also CHAMEAU, ENNUYER.

avancer. *See* HÂTER.

avant. Aller de l'avant, To go (*or* To forge) ahead.

See also CHANTER, ÉCORCHER, TEMPS.

avantage. Avoir l'avantage, To have the advantage *or* the pull *or* the upper hand *or* (*slang*) the grab.

Tirer avantage d'une circonstance,

To take advantage of (*or* To profit by) a circumstance.

avare. À père avare fils prodigue, A miserly father will have a spendthrift son.

avènement. Le don de joyeux avènement, The fee exacted from a newcomer for his footing (*on accession to office*): Accordez-moi cette faveur, ce sera notre don de joyeux avènement, Grant me this favour, I shall look upon it as my fee for your footing.

avenir. Qui peut pénétrer l'avenir? Who can see into the future? " If you can look into the seeds of time, And say which grain will grow, and which will not, Speak then to me."—*Macbeth* I, 3. " O that a man might know The end of this day's business ere it come! But it sufficeth that the day will end, And then the end is known."—*Julius Caesar* V, 1. " O God! that one might read the book of fate, . . . Oh, if this were seen, The happiest youth,—viewing his progress through, What perils past, what crosses to ensue,—Would shut the book, and sit him down and die."—2 *King Henry IV*, III, 1.

See also VUE.

aventure. Dire la bonne aventure, To tell fortunes.

Dire la bonne aventure à quelqu'un, To tell someone's fortune.

Se faire dire sa bonne aventure, To have one's fortune told.

See also BRUSQUER, CHERCHER, TENTER.

avenue. Les avenues de la fortune, de la renommée, The roads to fortune, to fame.

aversion. *See* BÊTE.

avertir. Se tenir pour averti, To be on one's guard, To take it as a warning: Tenez-vous pour averti, Take this as a warning, You have been warned.

Un homme (*ou* Un bon) averti en vaut deux *ou* Qui dit averti dit muni, Forewarned is forearmed.

avertissement. C'est un avertissement du ciel, This gives one furiously to think.

See also LECTEUR.

aveu. Un homme sans aveu, A vagrant, An outcast.

aveugle. Au royaume des aveugles les borgnes sont rois, Among the blind the one-eyed is king, Among the dunces the mediocre shine.

C'est un aveugle qui en conduit un autre *ou* qui mène l'autre, It is [a case of] the blind leading the blind. " And if the blind lead the blind, both shall fall into the ditch."—*Matthew* xv, 14.

Changer (*ou* Troquer) son cheval borgne contre un aveugle, To make a bad exchange.

Il en parle (*ou* Il juge de la chose) comme un aveugle des couleurs, He doesn't know what he's talking about. " If thou hadst been born blind, thou mightst as well have known all our names as thus to name the several colours we do wear."—2 *King Henry VI* II, 1.

Le sort est aveugle, Fortune is blind. " That goddess blind, That stands upon the rolling restless stone."—*King Henry V* III, 5.

See also CRIER, TAUPE.

avis. Aller aux avis, To put the question to the vote.

Deux avis valent mieux qu'un, Two heads are better than one.

Dire son avis, To speak one's mind.

Sauf meilleur avis, Unless we think better of it.

See also AUTANT, CHANGER, LECTEUR.

aviser. Un fou avise bien un sage, A wise man may learn of a fool. " When I did hear The motley fool thus moral on the time, My lungs began to crow like chanticleer, That fools should be so deep contemplative; And I did laugh, sans intermission, An hour by his dial.—O noble fool ! A worthy fool !—Motley's the only wear."—*As You Like It* II, 7. " He that a fool doth very wisely hit Doth very foolishly, although he smart, Not to seem senseless of the bob ; if not, The wise man's folly is anatomiz'd Even by the squandering glances of the fool."—*As You Like It* II, 7.

avocat. *See* BON 16.

avoir. En avoir à (*ou* contre) quelqu'un, To be angry (*or* cross) with someone, To have a grudge against someone.

En avoir [dans l'aile], To be hard hit.

En avoir pour son compte, To suffer a severe blow (*misfortune or accident*), To get it in the neck (*slang*).

Tant [il] y a, [But] the fact remains (que = that).

Vous en aurez, You'll catch it.

See also ARGENT, DOIGT, DONNER, DOS, ÉBRÉCHER, MONDE, NOUVELLE, ŒIL, PAROLE, PLEURER, POULE, RIEN, TAPER, VALOIR.

avouer. S'avouer coupable, To admit one's guilt, To plead guilty. " To my sick soul, as sin's true nature is, Each toy seems prologue to some great amiss: So full of artless jealousy is guilt, It spills itself in fearing to be spilt."—*Hamlet* IV, 5. " If his occulted guilt Do not itself unkennel."—*Hamlet* III, 2. " And then it started like a guilty thing Upon a fearful summons."—*Hamlet* I, 1.

S'avouer vaincu, To admit oneself beaten, To throw up the sponge, To throw in one's hand *or* one's cards.

See also PARDONNER.

avril. Donner un poisson d'avril à quelqu'un, To make an April fool of someone.

En avril ne quitte pas un fil *ou* ne t'allège pas (*ou* ne te découvre pas) d'un fil, Ne'er cast a clout till May be out.

B

B. Être marqué au B (=*borgne, bigle, bossu, ou boiteux*), To have a (*certain*) bodily defect, viz., To be one-eyed, squint-eyed, hunch-backed, or lame. " If thou . . . wert grim, Ugly, . . . Full of unpleasing blots and sightless stains, Lame, foolish, crooked, swart, prodigious, Patch'd with foul moles and eye-offending marks."—*King John* III, 1. " I, that am rudely stamp'd . . . Deform'd, unfinish'd." —*King Richard III* I, 1. " But after silence spake Some Vessel of a more ungainly Make ; ' They sneer at me for leaning all awry ; What ! did the Hand then of the Potter shake ? ' "—EDWARD FITZGERALD, *Rubaiyat of Omar Khayyam* XCIII.

Ne parler que par B et par F, To be always cursing and swearing.

Babel. C'est la tour de Babel, It is a perfect babel *or* a pandemonium.

bâbord. *See* FEU.

bagage. Plier bagage (*fig.*), To decamp ; To make off, To pack [off] ; To make one's exit (*die*).

Trousser bagage (*fig.*), To decamp; To make off, To pack [off].

bagou. Avoir du bagou, To have the gift of the gab *or* a glib tongue. *Quotations under* LANGUE.

bague. C'est une bague au doigt, It is as good as ready money ; It is a soft (*or* a cushy) job.

baguette. Mener (*ou* Commander) quelqu'un à la baguette, To rule someone with a rod of iron.

See also PASSER.

bail. Il a fait un bail avec la vie, He doesn't look like dying yet, His health gives no cause for anxiety (*of an old man*).

bailler. La bailler bonne à quelqu'un To humbug (*or* To impose on) someone.

Vous m'en baillez d'une belle *ou* Vous

me la baillez belle *ou* la baillez bonne, [A pretty tale] you're telling me, Tell that to the marines.

bâiller. Bâiller à se décrocher (*ou* à se démonter) la mâchoire, To yawn one's head off.

bain. C'est un bain qui chauffe, There will be another downpour before long [although the sun is shining at the moment]. *Quotation under* COUVRIR.

baiser. Ils se sont donné le baiser de paix, They have made it up.

Je vous baise les mains (*ironically*), I am sorry I can't agree with you ; Not likely, No fear, So there, Nothing doing, I'll see myself further (*or* damned) first. *Quotation under* SERVITEUR.

Le baiser de Judas, The Judas kiss. " So Judas kiss'd his master, And cried, all hail ! when as he meant all harm."—3 *King Henry VI* V, 7.

Vous devriez baiser la trace (*ou* baiser chacun) de ses pas, You should be very grateful to him.

See also CUEILLIR.

baisser. Baisser l'oreille *ou* le nez, To be crestfallen. " As crest-fallen as a dried pear."—*Merry Wives of Windsor* IV, 5.

Faire baisser le ton (*ou* le nez) à quelqu'un, To make someone sing small, To take someone down a peg or two, To crop someone's feathers.

Il semble qu'il n'y ait qu'à se baisser et à prendre, It seems as easy as kissing one's hand, It looks so easy (*but it isn't*).

Y aller tête baissée, To go at (*or* for) it for all one is worth *or* (*slang*) bald-headed.

Y donner tête baissée, To go at (*or* for) it for all one is worth *or* (*slang*) bald-headed ; To fall headlong into the trap.

See also ACTION, CRAN, ÉPAULE, HAUSSER, PAVILLON, TÊTE.

bal. Donner le bal à quelqu'un, To give someone a good dressing down (*thrashing*).

Mettre le bal en train (*fig.*), To open the ball, To set the ball [a-]rolling.

See also COUREUR, GRAND.

balai. C'est le balai neuf *ou* Il n'est rien tel que balai neuf, A new broom sweeps clean.

Faire balai neuf, To work well at first.

Rôtir le balai, To lead a fast (*or* disorderly) life, To go the pace.

See also COUP 23.

balance. Faire pencher (*ou* Emporter) la balance (*fig.*), To turn the scale. " By heaven, thy madness shall be paid by weight, Till our scale turn the beam."—*Hamlet* IV, 5.

ballade. *See* REFRAIN.

balle. À vous la balle (*fig.*), The ball is with you, It's your turn (*or* innings) now.

Au bon joueur la balle *ou* La balle [va] au joueur, He is the right man in the right place, He is just the man for the job.

C'est enfant de la balle, He follows his father's trade.

Ce sont balles perdues, It is all wasted effort.

Juger la balle (*fig.*), To take in the situation.

La balle cherche le bon joueur, The job is calling (*or* crying out) for the right man.

La balle n'a été prise que du second bond, The affair only succeeded on the second attempt *or* after a struggle.

Prendre la balle au bond, To seize the opportunity. " Who seeks, and will not take when once 'tis offer'd, Shall never find it more."— *Antony and Cleopatra* II, 7.

Quand la balle me viendra, When a favourable opportunity occurs.

Renvoyer la balle à quelqu'un, To

pass it on to someone, To pass the buck to someone.

Se renvoyer la balle, To engage in a battle of wits with each other.

See also COUP 75.

ballon. Lancer un ballon d'essai, To put out a feeler, To see how the land lies.

See also ENFLER.

ballotter. Ballotter quelqu'un, To play battledore and shuttlecock with someone, To drive someone from pillar to post, To keep some-one dangling [on a string].

Ballotter une affaire, To thrash a matter out.

bamboche. Faire [une] bamboche *ou* des bamboches, To go on the spree, To go gay.

ban. Convoquer le ban et l'arrière-ban, To appeal to all and sundry (*or* to each and all) for help.

Mettre quelqu'un au ban de l'opinion publique, To put someone under the ban of society, To banish someone from society, To ostra-cize someone.

banc. Être sur les bancs, To be at school. " These strange flies, these fashion-mongers, these *pardonnez-mois*, who stand so much on the new form that they cannot sit at ease on the old bench."—*Romeo and Juliet* II, 4.

Se mettre sur les bancs, To go to school.

bande. Faire bande à part, To keep oneself to oneself, To hold aloof.

bander. Avoir l'esprit bandé, To be deep in thought.

Bander son esprit, To concentrate (*or* To focus) one's mind.

bandit. C'est un vrai bandit, He is a social outlaw.

See also FAIRE.

bannière. *See* CROIX, RANGER.

banqueroute. Faire banqueroute à l'honneur, To commit a breach of honour.

Faire banqueroute à quelqu'un, To fail someone (*in a promise, an appointment*).

banquette. Jouer devant (*ou* pour) les banquettes, To play to empty benches *or* to an empty house (*Theatre*).

baptême. Le baptême du tropique *ou* de la ligne, Crossing the line ducking.

barbe. Faire quelque chose à la barbe de quelqu'un, To do something to someone's face.

Il a la barbe trop jeune *ou* Il n'a pas de barbe au menton, He is too young (*inexperienced*) to do it. " The juvenal, the prince your master, whose chin is not yet fledged."—2 *King Henry IV* I, 2. " *Pandarus*. And, you know, he has not past three or four hairs on his chin.— *Cressida*. Indeed, a tapster's arithmetic may soon bring his particulars therein to a total. *Pan*. Why, he is very young."—*Troilus and Cressida* I, 2.

Une barbe grise *ou* Une vieille barbe, A greybeard. " Have I in conquest stretch'd mine arm so far, To be afeard to tell greybeards the truth ?" —*Julius Caesar* II, 2.

Une jeune barbe, A beardless youth. " Shall a beardless boy, A cocker'd silken wanton, brave our fields ? " —*King John* V, 1. (*Note*.—cocker'd wanton = pampered pet.)

See also FLEUVE, RIRE.

barbet. Suivre quelqu'un comme fait un barbet, To follow someone about like a little dog. " The hearts That spaniel'd me at heels." —*Antony and Cleopatra* IV, 12.

See also CROTTER.

barbier. Un barbier rase l'autre, People in the same profession (*or* Those with common interests) should support each other.

barbon. Il fait déjà le barbon, He already has an old head on young shoulders. " I never knew so young a body with so old a head." —*The Merchant of Venice* IV, 1. " His years but young, but his experience old ; His head unmellow'd, but his judgment ripe."—*Two Gentlemen of Verona* II, 4.

barbouiller. Barbouiller du papier (*fig.*), To spill ink (*write uselessly or write trash*).

Le temps se barbouille, We are going to have dirty weather.

barbouilleur. Un barbouilleur [de papier], An ink-spiller, A scribbler.

barder. Être bardé de cordons, To be plastered with decorations (*orders, medals*), To be dripping with stars and crosses.

Être bardé de ridicules, To be covered with ridicule.

barème. C'est un barème, He is wonderful at mental arithmetic.

barque. La barque à (*ou* de) Caron *ou* La barque fatale, Charon's boat *or* ferry. " I pass'd, methought, the melancholy flood With that grim ferryman which poets write of, Unto the kingdom of perpetual night."—*King Richard III* I, 4. " I stalk about her door, Like a strange soul upon the Stygian banks Staying for waftage. O, be thou my Charon, And give me swift transportance to those fields Where I may wallow in the lily beds Propos'd for the deserver ! "—*Troilus and Cressida* III, 2.

Mener (*ou* Conduire) (*ou* Gouverner) bien sa barque, To manage one's affairs well, To play one's cards well.

Mener (*ou* Conduire) (*ou* Gouverner) la barque, To manage the business, To run the show (*slang*). " And you yourself shall steer the happy helm." —2 *King Henry VI* I, 3.

Mener (*ou* Conduire) seul sa barque, To paddle one's own canoe (*fig.*).

barre. Avoir barres sur quelqu'un, To have an advantage over (*or* the pull of) someone.

C'est de l'argent (*ou* de l'or) en barre, It is as good as ready money.

Cet homme est raide comme une barre de fer *ou* est une barre [de fer], This man never gives way an inch (*is inexorable*).

Ne faire que toucher barres, To be only stopping a moment (*at a place*).

Vous lui donnez barres sur vous, You are giving him the advantage over you *or* the pull of you.

barrer. Barrer [le chemin à] quelqu'un (*fig.*), To put obstacles in someone's way, To thwart someone.

barrique. *See* GROS.

bas. Avoir l'oreille basse, To be run down ; To be crestfallen. *Quotation under* BAISSER.

Avoir la vue basse, To be short-sighted *or* near-sighted.

Dans (*ou* En) ce bas monde, Here below.

Faire main basse sur, To lay hands on (*seize, appropriate*) ; To give no quarter to (*enemy*) ; To be down on (*regard with disfavour*).

Le bas âge, Infancy.

Le jour est bas, The day is declining, It is getting dark.

Le temps (*ou* Le ciel) est bas, The clouds are low (*rain threatens*).

Les eaux sont basses chez lui, He is in low water, His fortunes are at a low ebb.

Partir l'oreille basse, To go off with one's tail between one's legs.

Un bas bleu, A bluestocking.

See also CHAPEAU, HAUT, PAVILLON, SAUTER.

bas-fond. Les bas-fonds de la société, The underworld.

basilic. Faire à quelqu'un des yeux de basilic, To cast a withering glance on someone, To kill someone with looks. " Come, basilisk, And kill the innocent gazer with thy sight." —2 *King Henry VI* III, 2. " This will so fright them both that they will kill one another by the look, like cockatrices."—*Twelfth Night* III, 4. (*Note.*—cockatrice = basilisk.)

Basque. *See* MARCHER.

basque. *See* PENDRE.

bât. *See* BLESSER, CHEVAL.

bataille. *See* CHAMP, CHEVAL, LIVRER.

bateau. Monter un bateau à quelqu'un, To take (*or* To get) a rise out of someone, To pull someone's leg, To take someone in, To lead someone up (*or* down) the garden path (*slang*).

bâter. *See* ÂNE.

bâtiment. Être du bâtiment, To belong to that (*i.e., some particular*) trade *or* (*professional*) fraternity.

Quand le bâtiment va, tout va, Slackness in the building trade is a sign of bad trade generally.

bâtir. Une maison bâtie de plâtras *ou* bâtie de boue et de crachat[s], A jerry-built house.

Voilà comme je suis bâti, I'm made that way (*such is my nature, my character*).

See also CHÂTEAU, CHAUX.

bâton. À bâtons rompus, By fits and starts, Desultorily, Off and on.

Ce sera son bâton de maréchal, That will be the highest degree to which he can attain *or* the highest position to which he can get.

Cet enfant sera un jour votre bâton de vieillesse, This child will be one day a support for you in your old age. " The boy was the very staff of my age, my very prop."—*The Merchant of Venice* II, 2.

Faire faire quelque chose à quelqu'un le bâton haut, To force someone to do something.

Le tour (*ou* Le retour) de bâton, A secret commission, Questionable perquisites, Some pickings.

Mener quelqu'un le bâton haut, To force someone to obey.

Mener une vie de bâton de chaise, To lead a fast life.

Mettre (*ou* Jeter) des bâtons dans la roue à quelqu'un, To put a spoke in someone's wheel.

Tout soldat porte son bâton de maréchal dans sa giberne, Every soldier carries a field-marshal's baton in his knapsack (*may one day attain highest military rank*).

See also CRIER, EAU.

batterie. Changer de batterie *ou* Changer ses batteries, To change one's tactics.

Démasquer ses batteries, To show one's hand.

Démonter la batterie (*ou* les batteries) de quelqu'un (*fig.*), To silence someone's batteries *or* guns, To frustrate someone's plans.

Dresser ses batteries, To lay one's plans.

batteur. Un batteur d'estrade, A prowler (*man on the prowl, prowling the streets*).

Un batteur de fer, A fencing master ; A fencing fan ; A swashbuckler.

Un batteur de pavé, A loafer about the streets, A man on the loaf.

battre. À battre, faut l'amour, Come blows, love goes.

Avoir les yeux battus, To have rings under the eyes.

Battre à plate couture, To rout utterly, To beat hollow.

Battre du pays, To roam about *or* around; To treat of many subjects, To cover much ground.

Battre en brèche un argument, To demolish an argument.

Battre en brèche une théorie, une entreprise, To batter [down] a theory, a scheme, To knock a theory, a scheme, on the head. *Cf.* Battre quelqu'un en brèche *below.*

Battre en retraite, To beat a retreat.

Battre froid à quelqu'un, To give someone the cold shoulder, To cold-shoulder someone.

Battre l'estrade, To be on the prowl, To prowl the streets.

Battre la breloque (*fig.*), To be all at sea; To wander *or* To ramble [in one's mind].

Battre la campagne (*fig.*), To wander from one's subject, To digress; To return only a vague answer; To wander [in one's mind], To be delirious.

Battre la grosse caisse (*fig.*), To beat the big drum.

Battre le fer, To have long practice: Il y a longtemps qu'il bat le fer, He has had long practice.

Battre le fer pendant qu'il est chaud, To strike the iron while it is hot, To make hay while the sun shines. " Strike now, or else the iron cools."—3 *King Henry VI* V, 1. " And now, While it is hot, I'll put it to the issue."—*King Henry VIII* V, 1. " We must do something, and i' the heat."—*King Lear* I, 1. " The sun shines hot; and, if we use delay, Cold biting winter mars our hop'd-for hay."—3 *King Henry VI* IV, 8.

Battre le pavé, To tramp the streets.

Battre le pays (*fig.*), To cover the ground: Dans cette conversation, nous avons battu bien du pays en peu de temps, During this conversation, we covered a lot of ground in a short time.

Battre le rappel des recrues, de ses amis, To beat up recruits, one's friends.

Battre monnaie, To raise money *or* (*slang*) the wind *or* the dust.

Battre quelqu'un en brèche, To give someone a clincher *or* (*slang*) one on the knob, To bowl someone over *or* down (*fig.*).

Battre quelqu'un sur le dos d'un autre, To cast innuendoes at someone.

Battre son plein, To be at its height, To be in full swing.

Battre un homme à terre (*fig.*), To strike (*or* To hit) a man when he is down.

Je m'en bats l'œil, I don't care in the least, I don't care a brass farthing *or* a rap *or* a button *or* a fig *or* a pin *or* a straw *or* a tinker's dam[n] *or* a damn *or* two hoots.

Ne pas se tenir pour battu (*fig.*), Not to know when one is beaten.

Se battre contre des moulins à vent, To fight windmills.

Se battre les flancs pour quelque chose, To goad oneself into doing something.

Se laisser battre à terre, To take it lying down.

See also AILE, AIR, AMENDE, DIABLE, EAU, FOIN, HERBE, MENER, MONTAGNE, MUR, NEUF, OISEAU, PLÂTRE, POITRINE, REBATTRE, TAMBOUR.

Baucis. *See* PHILÉMON.

baudruche. Un grand homme en baudruche, A tin god.

baume. Cela fleure comme baume, (*Lit.*) That smells delicious; (*Fig.*) That is in good odour.

Je n'ai pas de foi dans son baume, I have no faith in what he says, in what he promises.

bavard. *See* PIE.

bavette. Être à (*ou* N'être encore qu'à) la bavette, To be still too young (*to take part*).

See also TAILLER.

bayer. Bayer aux corneilles, To gape at the moon, To star-gaze, To catch flies.

beau. 1. À beau jeu, beau retour, One good turn deserves another.

2. Avoir la partie belle, To have the ball at one's feet.

3. Belle question! *ou* [Voilà une] belle demande! What a question! Of course! That goes without saying.

4. C'est un homme du bel air, He is a distinguished-looking man.

5. Comme vous voilà beau (belle)

aujourd'hui, How nice you look to-day, You do look smart to-day.

6. De plus belle, More than ever; Worse than ever; [Once] again. *See also phrases under* RECOMMENCER, REDONNER.

7. Donner (*ou* Faire) beau jeu à quelqu'un, To play into someone's hands.

8. Faire la belle, To show one's graces, To show off, To strut about (*of a woman*).

9. Faire le beau, To show one's graces, To show off, To strut about (*of a man*); To beg (*of an animal*).

10. Il a fait un beau rêve, It was very nice while it lasted; It has turned out far better than he expected.

11. Il en a fait de belles, Pretty (*or* Fine) things he's been up to. " A trim exploit."—*A Midsummer Night's Dream* III, 2.

12. Il fait beau voir . . . (*ironiquement*), [It is] a fine, a strange, thing to see . . . , *e.g.*, Il fait beau vous voir, à votre âge, vous amuser à ces bagatelles, A fine thing to see you, at your age, amuse yourself with such trifles. Il ferait beau que . . . , It would be strange if. . .

13. Il fera beau [temps] quand je retournerai chez lui, It will be a long time before I go and see him again *or* before he catches me at his house again (= *never*).

14. Il y a beau temps que . . . *ou* Il y a beau[x] jour[s] que . . . , It is many a long day since . . .

15. L'avoir beau *ou* L'avoir belle, To have a good opportunity.

16. Le beau idéal, The ideally beautiful, The highest type of beauty, of excellence, The acme of perfection.

17. Le bel âge, [The days of] youth. " Youth's sweet-scented manuscript."—EDWARD FITZGERALD, *Rubaiyat of Omar Khayyam* CIV. " Youth's proud livery."—SHAKESPEARE, *Sonnets* II.

18. Les beaux esprits se rencontrent, Great minds think alike.

19. Les beaux jours, The fine weather; The palmy days. " In the most high and palmy state of Rome."—*Hamlet* I, 1. Mes beaux jours sont passés, I have had my day. " Alack, our terrene moon Is now eclips'd."—*Antony and Cleopatra* III, 13. " What! we have many goodly days to see: The liquid drops of tears that you have shed Shall come again, transform'd to orient pearl, Advantaging their loan with interest Of ten times double gain of happiness."—*King Richard III* IV, 4.

20. Mettre quelque chose dans un beau jour, To explain something clearly.

21. Nous en verrons de belles, si tel événement se réalise, There will be a fine how-d'ye-do, if such a thing happens.

22. Peindre quelqu'un en beau, To make the most of someone.

23. Peindre quelque chose en beau (*fig.*), To paint something in rosy colours.

24. Perdre à beau jeu (*fig.*), To fail when success seemed assured.

25. Pour les, Pour ses, Pour vos, beaux yeux, For love, For the love (de = of); Just to gratify him, her, you, For her pretty face; For nothing (*without payment*).

26. Sa belle-famille, One's in-laws.

27. Se faire beau, belle, To make oneself look nice *or* smart.

28. Tout cela est bel et bon, mais . . . , That is all well and good (*or* all very fine), but . . .

29. Trancher du bel esprit, To set oneself up for a wit.

30. Un beau geste (*fig.*), A noble gesture, A display of magnanimity.

31. Un beau mâle, A real he-man. " A combination and a form, indeed, Where every god did seem to set his seal, To give the world

assurance of a man."—*Hamlet* III, 4. " They say he is a very man *per se*, And stands alone."—*Troilus and Cressida* I, 2. " His life was gentle ; and the elements So mix'd in him that Nature might stand up And say to all the world, ' This was a man.' "—*Julius Caesar* V, 5.

32. Un bel âge, A good old age. *Cf.* Le bel âge, *above*.

33. Vous avez beau faire et beau dire, . . . , It is useless to do or say anything, . . . , [You may] do or say what you like, . . . (*it won't alter matters*).

34. Vous avez beau jeu, You have a good chance, Now's your chance.

35. Vous me la donnez belle, [A pretty tale] you're telling me, Tell that to the marines.

See also AMBASSADE, AURORE, BAILLER, BESOGNE, BRIN, CAMPAGNE, CHEMIN, CONTER, COUP 43, 44, CREUX, CRIER, DÉCHIRER, DEVOIR, DRAP, ÉCHAPPER, ÉCORCHER, EMPLETTE, ÉTOILE, FAUTE, FILS, FLEURON, FOURCHETTE, FOURNIR, HISTOIRE, HONTEUX, HORREUR, INSTRUMENT, JAMBE, JOUER, LOIN, MALHEUR, MALICE, MANIÈRE, MERLE, MOURIR, NATURE, NID, NOUVEAU, PAGE, PARURE, PLUIE, PLUME, PORTER, RACONTER, REVÊTIR, STATUE, TAIRE, VENANT, VOIR.

beaucoup. *See* FALLOIR, MANQUER, PRÈS, RABATTRE.

beauté. *See* AURORE, CRÉPUSCULAIRE, ÉBLOUIR, PARURE.

bec. Attaquer quelqu'un du bec et des ongles, To go for someone tooth and nail.

Avoir bec et ongles *ou* Avoir bon bec, To be well able to defend oneself.

Avoir le bec bien affilé, To have a sharp tongue.

C'est un bec fin, He is an epicure.

Causer bec à bec, To have a private talk.

Se prendre de bec avec quelqu'un, To have a set-to with someone.

Tenir quelqu'un le bec dans l'eau, To keep someone in suspense *or* on a string.

Une prise de bec, An altercation, A squabble, A set-to.

See also ALOUETTE, CAQUET, CLORE, CLOUER, COUP 24, ENFARINER.

bécasse. C'est une bécasse, She's a goose.

bêcher. *See* MÉTIER.

béguin. Avoir un béguin pour quelqu'un, To take a fancy to someone, To have a pash for someone (*slang*).

bêler. Brebis qui bêle perd sa goulée, Those that talk overmuch at table go short of food.

bénédictin. Un travail de bénédictin, A laborious work of erudition.

bénédiction. Que c'est une bénédiction, With a vengeance, And no mistake.

Une maison de bénédiction, A thrice-blessed house ; A house of plenty. " Although The air of paradise did fan the house And angels offic'd all."—*All's Well That Ends Well* III, 2. " Hand in hand, with fairy grace, Will we sing, and bless this place."—*A Midsummer Night's Dream* V, 2. " Every fairy take his gait ; And each several chamber bless, Through this palace, with sweet peace ; E'er shall it in safety rest, And the owner of it blest."—*A Midsummer Night's Dream* V, 2.

See also PAYS.

bénéfice. Il faut prendre le bénéfice avec les charges, One must take the rough with the smooth.

bénir. C'est pain bénit, It serves him right.

De l'eau bénite de cour, Empty (*or* Insincere) fair words (*as of flattery*), Court holy water (*archaic*). " Court holy water in a dry house is better than this rain-water out o' door."—*King Lear* III, 2.

bénitier. Se démener comme le diable au fond d'un bénitier *ou* comme un diable dans un bénitier, To be like a cat on hot bricks (*very agitated*).

berceau. *See* ÉTOUFFER.

berger. L'heure du berger, Trysting-time, The hour of trysting (*of lovers*). " Trip no further, pretty sweeting ; Journeys end in lovers' meeting."—*Twelfth Night* II, 3.

La réponse du berger à la bergère, A clincher.

bergerie. *See* LOUP.

Berthe. *See* FILER.

besace. Être jaloux de quelque chose comme un gueux de sa besace, To cherish something (*or* To hold something as dear) as the apple of one's eye.

besogne. Aimer besogne faite, To dislike work, To be work-shy.

Donner (*ou* Tailler) bien de la besogne à quelqu'un (*fig.*), To cut out his work for someone, To give someone a lot of bother.

Être mou à la besogne, To be a slacker.

Faire de [la] bonne besogne, To work to some purpose.

Faire de [la] mauvaise besogne, To work to no purpose.

Il a fait là une (*ou* de) belle besogne (*ironiquement*), He has made a nice mess of it, A nice mess he has made of it.

Ne songer qu'à [faire] sa besogne *ou* Être tout à sa besogne, To stick to one's last ; To be absorbed in one's work.

Selon l'argent, la besogne, No pay, no work.

See also ABATTRE, ALLER, ÂPRE, BOUDER, BRUIT, CHEVAL, ENDORMIR, MÂCHER, MOURIR.

besoin. C'est dans le besoin qu'on connaît ses vrais amis *ou* On connaît le véritable ami dans le besoin, A friend in need is a friend indeed. " For who not needs shall never lack a friend ; And who in want a hollow friend doth try, Directly seasons him his enemy."—*Hamlet* III, 2.

bête. C'est la bête du bon Dieu, He is absurdly credulous ; He is generous to the point of foolishness.

C'est la bête noire du pays, He is the best hated man in the country.

C'est ma bête noire *ou* ma bête d'aversion, He (She) (It) is my pet aversion.

C'est une bonne bête, He is a good-natured fool.

C'est une fine (*ou* une maligne) bête, He's a wily one.

Être bête comme un pot *ou* Être bête à manger du foin, To be as stupid as an owl. " Thou art the cap of all the fools alive."—*Timon of Athens* IV, 3. " *Titania.* Or say, sweet love, what thou desir'st to eat. *Bottom.* Truly, a peck of provender ; I could munch your good dry oats. Methinks I have a great desire to a bottle of hay: good hay, sweet hay, hath no fellow."—*A Midsummer Night's Dream* IV, 1.

Être condamné (*ou* livré) aux bêtes (*fig.*), To be thrown to the lions.

Faire la bête, To pretend ignorance (*of a happening*) ; To behave foolishly (*against one's own interests*).

La bête est dans nos filets, He is taken in the (*or* in our) toils.

Pas si bête, I am not so foolish as all that, Not if I know it.

Remonter sur sa bête, To get on one's legs again (*fig.*), To regain one's position.

See also CORNE, DINDON, MORT, POIL.

bêtise. Faire des bêtises, To play the fool, To wear motley, To act the goat. " *Jacques.* O that I were a fool ! I am ambitious for a motley coat. *Duke Senior.* Thou shalt have one. *Jacques.* It is my only suit."—*As You Like It* II, 7. " This fellow's wise enough to play the fool ; And, to do that well, craves a kind of wit."—*Twelfth Night* III, 1.

Il est d'une bêtise amère, He is a perfect fool.

beurre. On ne saurait (*ou* On ne peut) manier du beurre qu'on ne s'en graisse les doigts, " Rich preys make true men thieves."—SHAKESPEARE, *Venus and Adonis.*

See also POCHER, PROMETTRE.

biais. Prendre une affaire de tous les biais, To approach a thing from every angle, To study all sides of a question.

Prendre une affaire du bon biais, du mauvais biais, To go the right way, the wrong way, to work on a thing.

Prendre une chose de biais, To go about a thing in an indirect way.

Prendre une personne de biais, To outwit a person.

bibliothèque. C'est une bibliothèque vivante *ou* ambulante, He is a walking encyclopaedia.

See also RAT.

bien. À bien prendre les choses, Rightly speaking.

Avoir du bien au soleil, To be a property owner *or* a person of property.

Bien lui a pris de sortir, It was lucky (*or* a good thing) for him that he went out.

Bien lui en prit, It was lucky for him that he did.

En tout bien et [en] tout honneur, With the best and most honourable intentions, On the square.

Être bien, To be going on well *or* progressing favourably (*of a patient*).

Être bien dans les papiers (*ou* dans l'esprit) de quelqu'un *ou* Être bien vu de quelqu'un *ou* Être bien avec quelqu'un *ou* Se faire bien venir de quelqu'un, To be in someone's good books *or* good graces. " I see, lady, the gentleman is not in your books."—*Much Ado About Nothing* I, 1.

Être bien ensemble, To be good friends.

La connaissance (*ou* La science) du bien et du mal (*Genèse* ii, 9), The knowledge of good and evil (*Genesis* ii, 9).

Le bien cherche le bien *ou* Un bien en acquiert un autre, Money begets money. " Foul cankering rust the hidden treasure frets, But gold that's put to use more gold begets."—SHAKESPEARE, *Venus and Adonis.*

Le, Nous, Vous, voilà bien, Now he is, we are, you are, in a fine fix *or* in a pretty pickle.

Nul bien sans peine, No gains without pains.

Prendre (*ou* Interpréter) quelque chose en bien, To put a favourable construction on something.

Qui bien engrène, bien finit, A good start is half the battle.

Rendre le bien pour le mal, To return good for evil.

S'y prendre bien, To go the right way to work.

Tant bien que mal, Somehow or other, After a fashion.

Tenir bien à ce qu'on tient, To keep tight hold of (*or, slang,* To freeze on to) what one has.

Tomber bien, To come just at the right moment *or* in the nick [of time].

Tout est bien qui finit bien, All's well that ends well.

Vouloir du bien à quelqu'un, To wish someone well ; To be favourably disposed towards someone.

See also AIDE, AIMER, AUTRE, BON 45, CHAIR, CHOSE, COMMENCER, COUR, CROIRE, DIRE, DORMIR, ENTENDRE, ENVIE, FAIRE, FIN, HISTOIRE, MALADE, MENER, MIEUX, MONDE, MONTER, MONTRER, MOURIR, NUIRE, PARTIE, PERDRE, PLACE, PLACER, PORTER, POUVOIR, RÉFLÉCHIR, RENVOYER, RIRE, SELLE, TENIR, TERRAIN,

TOURNER, TRAITER, TROUVER, VILLAGE, VIVRE.

bienfait. Un bienfait insoupçonné, A blessing in disguise.

Un bienfait n'est jamais perdu, Kind deeds they never die.

See also AIRAIN.

bienheureux. Avoir l'air d'un bienheureux, To have a venerable and serene appearance ; To look supremely (*or* blissfully) happy.

Se réjouir comme un bienheureux, To be supremely (*or* blissfully) happy.

bienséance. Par droit de bienséance, (*in order*) To meet one's private ends, Merely to suit one's own purpose.

bientôt. Cela est (*ou* C'est) bientôt dit, That is easier said than done.

See also SAC.

bienvenu. Vous ne seriez pas bienvenu (*ou* bien venu) à lui aller dire cela, If you go and tell him that, you will be sent away with a flea in your ear.

bière. Ce n'est pas de la petite bière, It's no small matter *or* no small beer, It's not to be sneezed at. " To suckle fools and chronicle small beer."—*Othello* II, 1.

Ne pas se prendre pour de la petite bière, To think no small beer of oneself.

bile. Décharger (*ou* Épancher) sa bile, To vent one's spleen.

Émouvoir (*ou* Échauffer) la bile à (*ou* de) quelqu'un, To stir up someone's bile, To rub someone up the wrong way, To rouse someone to anger, To rile someone.

Se faire de la bile, To distress oneself.

bilieux. C'est un homme bilieux, He is a man of a bilious (*or* peevish) nature.

bille. Ils sont à billes pareilles *ou* à billes égales, They are level *or* even [with each other] (*in a competition*).

billet. *See* PARTERRE.

billot. *See* MAIN, TÊTE.

bissac. *See* TOUR.

blâme. *See* DÉVERSER.

blanc. Aller (*ou* Passer) (*ou* Changer) du blanc au noir, To swing round to the opposite opinion ; To go from one extreme to the other.

Faire blanc de son épée, To be over-confident, To make rash promises, To promise more than one is sure of being able to perform.

Mettre du noir sur du blanc, To write, To sling ink (*slang*).

Saigner quelqu'un à blanc, To bleed someone white, To suck someone dry.

Se faire [tout] blanc de son épée, To play the bully, To use vain and boastful menaces, To bluster.

See also BONNET, BUT, CARTE, CHARBON, COUDRE, LOUP, MANGER, MERLE, NUIT, OIE, PAIN, PLUME, REGARDER, ROUGE.

blanchir. Des sépulcres blanchis, Whited sepulchres (*Matthew* xxiii, 27).

Tête de fou ne blanchit jamais, A fool's head is never grey. " How ill white hairs become a fool."—2 *King Henry IV* V, 5. " The silver livery of advised age."—2 *King Henry VI* V, 2.

See also HARNOIS.

blason. *See* REDORER.

blé. C'est du blé en grenier, It is a safe [and sound] investment.

See also ALLER, CRIER, MANGER, PRENDRE.

blesser. Blesser l'oreille (*fig.*), To grate upon the ear.

Blesser les yeux (*fig.*), To offend the eye.

Blesser quelqu'un au cœur, To wound someone's feelings deeply, To sting someone to the quick.

[L'endroit] où le bât (*ou* le soulier) le blesse, [The place] where the shoe pinches. " Alas, poor shepherd !

searching of thy wound, I have by hard adventure found mine own."—*As You Like It* II, 4.

bleu. Être (*ou* Nager) dans le bleu, To live in a dream-world, To be oblivious of the world about one.

N'y voir que du bleu, To be unable to see through it (*be deceived*).

Passer au bleu une chose, To pass something into the limbo of forgetfulness, To take no further interest in a thing.

Un conte bleu, A fairy tale (*tale about fairies*), A bedtime story ; A fairy tale (*absurd or incredible statement*), A bedtime story, A cock-and-bull story, A tar[r]adiddle.

See also BAS, COLÈRE, CORDON, PEUR.

blinder. *See* GOSIER.

bloc. Mettre quelqu'un au bloc, To put someone in quod *or* in clink, To run someone in.

bœuf. C'est un bœuf [pour le travail], He is a glutton for work.

C'est un [gros] bœuf, He is a huge man *or* is a hulk. " O, my sweet beef." — (*to Falstaff*) — 1 *King Henry IV* III, 3. " This huge hill of flesh."(*Falstaff*)—1 *King Henry IV* II, 4. " The hulk Sir John." (*Falstaff*)—2 *King Henry IV* I, 1.

See also CHARRUE, CORNE, FORT, LOURD, ŒUF, SOUFFLER, VENT.

boire. Avoir toute honte bue, To be lost (*or* dead) to all sense of shame.

Boire à la grande tasse, To drown oneself in the sea, To find a watery grave, To be gone (*or* To be sent) to Davy Jones' locker. " Full fathom five thy father lies."—*The Tempest* I, 2.

Boire à sa soif, To drink only when one is thirsty.

Boire à tire-larigot *ou* comme un trou *ou* comme un templier *ou* comme un sonneur *ou* comme une éponge *ou* Boire la mer et ses poissons, To drink like a fish. " My sick fool Roderigo . . . hath to-night carous'd Potations pottle deep."—*Othello* II, 3. " I will do nothing, Nerissa, ere I will be married to a sponge." — *The Merchant of Venice* I, 2.

Boire le calice (*fig.*), To drink the cup (*submit to as inevitable*). " For some we loved, the loveliest and the best That from his Vintage rolling Time has pressed, Have drunk their Cup a Round or two before, And one by one crept silently to rest."—EDWARD FITZGERALD, *Rubaiyat of Omar Khayyam* XXII.

Boire le calice (*ou* la coupe) jusqu'à la lie (*fig.*), To drain the cup to the dregs.

Boire sec, To drink hard ; To drink one's wine (*or* spirits) neat.

Boire un bouillon, To suffer a heavy loss, To make a bad spec. (*speculation*).

C'est la mer à boire, It can't be done. " Alas, poor duke ! the task he undertakes Is numbering sands, and drinking oceans dry."—*King Richard II* II, 2.

Ce n'est pas la mer à boire, That is not such a difficult matter.

Il en perd (*ou* en oublie) le boire et le manger, He is so wrapped up in his work, in the object of his affection, that he neglects his meals.

Il y a à boire et à manger, It is a muddy drink ; It is a many-sided affair ; It is good in parts, like the curate's egg.

[Quand] le vin est tiré, il faut le boire, In for a penny, in for a pound.

Qui a bu boira, He'll do it again, He'll never alter, He will never mend his ways.

Qui fait la faute, la boit, The offender should be the sufferer.

See also AFFRONT, ÂNE, FONTAINE, TUER.

bois. C'est un bois que cette maison de jeu, This gaming house is a den of thieves.

Il est du bois dont on fait les héros, He is the stuff heroes are made of.

Nous ne nous chauffons pas du même bois, We have nothing in common.

On saura (*ou* On verra) de quel bois je me chauffe, I'll show them the stuff I'm made of. " You must not think That we are made of stuff so flat and dull."—*Hamlet* IV, 7.

See also CAUTÈRE, COIN, DÉMÉNAGER, ÉCORCE, FAIM, FEU, FLÈCHE, GUEULE, HÔTE, MOURIR, VISAGE.

boîte. Il faudrait que cette personne fût toujours dans une boîte, This person should be kept in a glass case (*he, she, is so delicate*).

Il semble qu'il sorte d'une boîte, He looks as if he had [just] come (*or* stepped) out of a bandbox.

La boîte à Perrette, The secret chest *or* funds (*of an association*).

La boîte de Pandore, Pandora's box.

See also PETIT.

boiteux. Il ne faut pas clocher devant les boiteux, One must not remind people of their infirmities.

bombarder. Bombarder quelqu'un à une place, à un poste, To pitchfork someone into an office, into a position.

Bombarder quelqu'un de questions, de compliments, de sarcasmes, To bombard someone with questions, with compliments, with taunts. " Zounds ! I was never so bethump'd with words."—*King John* II, 1.

bombe. Ça y est, la bombe va éclater, Now the fat is in the fire.

Il est tombé dans notre société comme une bombe, He burst in among us like a bombshell.

bon. 1. À bon chat, bon rat, Tit for tat, A Roland for an Oliver.

2. À bon droit, With good reason, Rightly.

3. À bon entendeur demi-mot suffit *ou* À bon entendeur, salut *ou* À bon entendeur peu de paroles, A word [is enough] to the wise, Let this be a warning to you, Verb. sap., Verbum [sat] sapienti.

4. [À] bon jour, bonne œuvre, The better the day the better the deed

5. À bon port, Safely ; To a happy issue.

6. À la bonne heure, Well and good, All right, Capital, Splendid ; I don't mind. *Cf.* Arriver à la bonne heure *below*.

7. Aller de bon pied dans une affaire, To be getting on fine (*or* going on swimmingly) in a business.

8. Arriver à la bonne heure *ou* au bon moment, To arrive in the nick of time.

9. Avoir bon air, To look well, To be becoming.

10. Avoir bon dos (*fig.*), To have a broad back.

11. Avoir bon marché de quelqu'un, de quelque chose, To make short work of someone, of something.

12. Avoir bon pied, bon œil, To be hale and hearty ; To be on one's guard. *Cf.* Bon pied, bon œil *below*.

13. Avoir le bon bout par devant soi *ou* Tenir le bon bout [par devers soi], To be on the right tack *or* track, To have hold of the right end of the stick.

14. Avoir une bonne tête, To have a funny [-looking] face ; To have a nice kind face.

15. Bon an, mal an, [Taking] one year with another (*on an average between the years*).

16. Bon avocat, mauvais voisin, A good lawyer makes a bad neighbour. " *Dick the Butcher*. The first thing we do, let's kill all the lawyers. *Jack Cade*. Nay, that I mean to do. Is this not a lamentable thing, that of the skin of an innocent lamb should be made parchment ? that parchment, being scribbled o'er, should undo a man ? "—2 *King Henry VI* IV, 2.

17. Bon droit a besoin d'aide, The best cause is none the worse for support.
18. Bon jeu, bon argent, Seriously speaking, Honour bright.
19. Bon jour et bon an, Good morning and a happy new year to you.
20. Bon pied, bon œil, Be on your guard, Look out.
21. Bonne renommée vaut mieux que ceinture dorée, A good name is better than riches. " Good name in man and woman, dear my lord, Is the immediate jewel of their souls: Who steals my purse steals trash; 'tis something, nothing; 'Twas mine, 'tis his, and has been slave to thousands; But he that filches from me my good name Robs me of that which not enriches him, And makes me poor indeed."—*Othello* III, 3. *See also quotation under* ÉCHAFAUD.
22. C'est un bon cœur [d'homme] *ou* C'est une bonne pâte [d'homme], He is a good-hearted (*or* kind-hearted) (*or* good-natured) man *or* a good sort [of a fellow].
23. C'est un bon diable *ou* un bon enfant, He is a jolly good fellow *or* a jolly good sort. *Cf.* Il est [bien] bon enfant de croire cela *under* ENFANT.
24. C'est une bonne cervelle, He is a level-headed man.
25. C'est une bonne tête [d'homme], He is a clever man.
26. Ce qui est bon à prendre est bon à garder *ou* est bon à rendre, Findings are keepings. *Quotation under* FOSSÉ.
27. Cet homme est bon à l'user, This man improves on acquaintance.
28. Donner (*ou* Souhaiter) le bonjour, le bonsoir, à quelqu'un. To bid (*or* To wish) someone good day, good evening. " Give you good night."—*Hamlet* I, 1. " *Valentine.* Madam and mistress, a thousand good morrows. *Speed.* O, give you good even !—Here's a million of manners."—*Two Gentlemen of Verona* II, 1. " God give you good den, fair gentlewoman."—*Romeo and Juliet* II, 4. (*Note.*—den = evening.)
29. En être quitte (*ou* S'en tirer) à bon compte, To get off cheaply (*without much damage*).
30. En voilà une bonne, I like that, That's a good one *or* a good joke.
31. Être bonne personne, To be a good sort.
32. Être dans la bonne voie, To be on the right track.
33. Être dans les bonnes grâces de quelqu'un, To be in someone's good graces *or* books.
34. Être de bon compte, To be honest about it (*to admit it, not to quibble about it*).
35. Être en [bonne] voie *ou* en [bonne] passe de réussir, To be in a fair way (*or* To bid fair) to succeed, To stand a good chance of succeeding, To be on the high road to success.
36. Être en mouvement de bonne heure, To be early astir.
37. Être sur un bon pied, To be flourishing (*of a business*).
38. Faire bon marché d'une chose, To hold a thing cheap.
39. Faire bon marché de sa peau, To hold one's life cheap.
40. Faire bon visage à quelqu'un, To smile on someone, To make someone welcome.
41. Faire bonne bouche, To leave a pleasant taste in the mouth.
42. Faire bonne contenance, To show a bold front, To put a good face on it, To carry it off.
43. Faire bonne mine à mauvais jeu *ou* à mauvaise fortune *ou* Faire à mauvaise fortune bon visage *ou* Faire contre [mauvaise] fortune bon cœur *ou* Faire bonne contenance devant l'ennemi, To smile in

the face of adversity. To keep smiling, To grin and bear it, To make the best of a bad job, To put a brave face on things, To keep a stiff upper lip. " Happy is your grace, That can translate the stubbornness of fortune Into so quiet and so sweet a style."—*As You Like It* II, 1. " Though fortune's malice overthrow my state, My mind exceeds the compass of her wheel."—3 *King Henry VI* IV, 3. " Yield not thy neck to fortune's yoke, but let thy dauntless mind Still ride in triumph over all mischance."—3 *King Henry VI* III, 3.

44. Garder quelque chose pour la bonne bouche, To keep the best (*or* the titbit) till last (" Lo, as at English feasts, so I regreet The daintiest last, To make the end more sweet."—*King Richard II* I, 3.); To give someone the most unkindest cut of all (*Julius Caesar* III, 2).
45. Il est bien bon de croire cela, He must be very simple to believe that.
46. Il est bon comme le (*ou* comme du) bon pain, He is a good, kind-hearted man, He is a good man and true.
47. Il m'en a dit de bonnes, Some fine (*incredible*) tales he told me.
48. Il n'y a (*ou* Il n'est) si bon cheval qui ne bronche *ou* Il n'y a si bon charretier qui ne verse, It is a good horse that never stumbles, The best horse will stumble sometimes. " A good leg will fall." —*King Henry V* V, 2.
49. Il ne serait pas bon à jeter aux chiens, Not the slightest notice would have been taken of it (*if someone else had done it, had said it*).
50. Je suis, Vous êtes, etc., dans une bonne passe, It is all plain sailing.
51. Jouer bon jeu, bon argent, To play a straight game, To play on the square ; To mean business.
52. Laisser quelqu'un sur la bonne bouche, To finish off the meal (*given to someone*) with a choice morsel ; To come away (*from someone*) at the psychological moment (*after having made a good impression*).
53. Les bons comptes font les bons amis, Short reckonings make long friends.
54. Les bons marchés ruinent, Don't be tempted by cheapness to buy more than you want.
55. Mettre quelqu'un sur la [bonne] voie, To put someone on the right track.
56. N'avoir une chose que par le bon bout, To have to pay dearly for a thing ; To have to take a thing forcibly : S'il en a envie, il ne l'aura que par le bon bout, If he wants it, he will have to pay dearly for it ; If he wants it, he will have to take it by force.
57. N'être bon ni à rôtir, ni à bouillir, To be good for nothing.
58. On n'a jamais bon marché de mauvaise marchandise, A bad article is dear at any price, The best is cheapest in the end.
59. Pour de bon, In earnest.
60. Prendre les choses par le bon côté, To look on the bright side of things. " You do look, my son, in a moved sort, As if you were dismay'd : be cheerful, sir."—*The Tempest* IV, 1.
61. Prendre pour bon, To take for gospel [truth].
62. Prendre une chose par le bon bout, To tackle a thing the right way.
63. Regarder (*ou* Voir) une chose d'un bon œil, To look favourably on a thing.
64. Regarder (*ou* Voir) une personne d'un bon œil, To view a person with a friendly eye.

65. Rester (*ou* Demeurer) sur la bonne bouche, To stop eating, drinking, at the right moment (*before the food or drink cloys*); To leave well alone.
66. Se retirer sur la bonne bouche, To leave it at that.
67. Son compte est bon, He'll catch it.
68. Tout de bon, In earnest.
69. Trouver bon de faire quelque chose, To think fit (*or* To find it advisable) to do something.
70. Trouver bon que quelqu'un fasse une chose, To approve of someone doing something; To allow someone to do something: Je reviendrai, si vous le trouvez bon, I shall come back, if you will allow me.
71. Un bon moment, A pleasant moment; A fairly long time.
72. Une bonne bouche, A titbit, A choice morsel.
73. Une bonne fuite vaut mieux qu'une mauvaise attente, Discretion is the better part of valour. *Quotation under* PEAU.
74. Une bonne pièce, A decent fellow; A vicious (*or* spiteful) person.
75. Y aller bon jeu, bon argent, To go straight to the point, To be quite straightforward about it; To go about it openly; To set about it in good earnest.

See also ACTE, AFFAIRE, AIMER, APÔTRE, APPÉTIT, APPRENDRE, AUGURE, AVENTURE, AVERTIR, BAILLER, BALLE, BEAU 28, BEC, BESOGNE, BÊTE, BIAIS, BREBIS, CABOCHE, CAQUET, CHASSER, CHATOUILLER, CHEMIN, CHIEN, COFFRE, COMMERCE, COMPAGNIE, COMPAGNON, COMPÈRE, COMPOSITION, COURIR, COURT, CREUX, DÉFRAYER, DERNIER, DIABLE, DONNER, DORMIR, ÉCOLE, ÉCRIRE, ENSEIGNE, FIN, FLÈCHE, FOIS, FORTUNE, FRAPPER, GARDER, GRÉ, GROS, INTENTION, IVRAIE, MAIN, MAISON, MALHEUR, MANIÈRE, MARMITE, MAUVAIS, MENER, MORCEAU, MOTIF, MOUVEMENT, MOYEN, NAÎTRE, NEZ, NOUVELLE, OREILLER, OUTIL, OUVRIR, PAPILLOTE, PETIT, PINTE, PLI, PREMIER, PRENDRE, PRINCE, QUART, QUITTER, QUOI, RAPPORT, RENTRER, RIRE, RUSE, SANG, SAUCE, SENS, SENTIR, SOUTENIR, TEMPS, TENIR, TRAIN, TROMPETTE, VENT, VÉRITÉ. (" O, their *bons*, their *bons !* "—*Romeo and Juliet* II, 4.)

bond. Ne faire qu'un bond, To make one rush (*towards someone, something*).

[Tant] de bond que de volée, Somehow or other, By hook or by crook.

See also BALLE, SAUT.

bonde. *See* LÂCHER.

bondir. Cela fait bondir le cœur, That turns me sick, It makes me heave.

Bondy. *See* FORÊT.

bonheur. Au petit bonheur, At a venture, Hit or miss, Sink or swim.

Jouer de bonheur, To be in luck, To have a run of good luck, To be lucky. " The very dice obey him." —*Antony and Cleopatra* II, 3.

Le bonheur du célibat, Single blessedness. " Thrice blessed they that master so their blood To undergo such maiden pilgrimage: But earthlier happy is the rose distill'd, Than that which, withering on the virgin thorn, Grows, lives, and dies in single blessedness."—*A Midsummer Night's Dream* I, 1.

See also INSOLENT, VEINE.

bonhomme. *See* ALLER, CHIC.

bonjour. *See* BON 28, SIMPLE.

bonnet. Avoir la tête près du bonnet, To be hot-tempered.

Avoir mis son bonnet de travers, To have got out of bed on the wrong side *or* with the wrong leg.

C'est bonnet blanc et blanc bonnet, It is six of one and half a dozen of the other, It's as broad as it's long.

Ce sont deux, trois, etc., têtes dans [un] même bonnet *ou* sous le même bonnet, They are hand in (*or* hand and) glove together, They are as thick as thieves.

Jeter son bonnet par-dessus les moulins, To fling aside all restraint.

Parler à son bonnet, To talk to oneself. " Dost dialogue with thy shadow ? "—*Timon of Athens* II, 2.

Prendre quelque chose sous son bonnet, To take something into one's head (*imagine it*) ; To take something upon oneself, To do something on one's own responsibility *or* off one's own bat.

See also GROS, OPINER, TRISTE.

bonsoir. *See* BON 28.

bord. Avoir un mot, un nom, sur le bord des lèvres, To have a word, a name, on the tip of one's tongue.

Être du bord de quelqu'un, To be of someone's mind, To side with someone.

See also EMMIELLER, FOSSE.

bordée. Une bordée [d'injures], A volley (*or* A shower) of abuse. *Quotation under* INJURE.

See also COURIR.

border. Border la haie, To line the route (*of troops*).

borgne. *See* AVEUGLE, PIE.

borne. Cela passe les bornes, That is going too far *or* beyond a joke.

Passer (*ou* Dépasser) toutes les bornes, To go beyond (*or* To pass) all bounds, To know no bounds. " Let's teach ourselves that honourable stop, Not to out-sport discretion. "—*Othello* II, 3.

See also PLANTER.

bosse. *See* PLAIE, ROULER.

botte. Porter (*ou* Pousser) une botte à quelqu'un (*fig.*), To have a thrust (*or* a tilt) at someone ; To deal someone a blow.

Porter une vilaine (*ou* une rude) botte à quelqu'un (*fig.*), To deal someone a nasty blow, To give someone a rude shock.

Prendre ses bottes de sept lieues, To take one's seven-league boots (*prepare to travel rapidly*).

See also AIGUILLE, FOIN, GRAISSER, PROPOS.

bouc. Ils l'ont pris pour leur bouc émissaire, They made him their scapegoat.

bouche. À bouche que veux-tu, Any amount, Enough and to spare, To one's heart's content, Unstintingly.

Avoir toujours quelque chose à la bouche, To have something always on one's lips *or* on one's tongue (*keep repeating it*). " Familiar in their mouths as household words."—*King Henry V* IV, 3.

Bouche close *ou* Bouche cousue, Mum's the word, Not a word, mind. " Seal up your lips, and give no words but mum : The business asketh silent secrecy."—2 *King Henry VI* I, 2. " Stall this in your bosom."—*All's Well That Ends Well* I, 3.

C'est [un] saint Jean bouche d'or, He is a most outspoken man ; He is a most eloquent man.

Être [porté] sur la bouche, To be fond of good living, To be an epicure.

Faire la bouche en cœur, To screw up one's mouth (*in an affected manner*), To be over-nice.

La dépense de bouche, The cost of one's food.

N'avoir ni bouche ni éperon, To be dull and insensible (*of person*).

Prendre sur sa bouche les charités qu'on fait, To encroach on one's [own] livelihood (*or* on one's [own] bread and butter) [to pay] for the assistance one gives to others.

See also AMER, BON, 41, 44, 52, 72, BOURSE, CLORE, CLOUER, DÉESSE, EAU, ENFARINER, FERMER, LANGUE, MEUBLER, ÔTER, OUVRIR, PETIT.

bouchée. *See* DOUBLE.

boucher. Avoir l'esprit bouché *ou* Être bouché, To be dull-witted, To be dense.

Avoir les yeux bouchés, To turn a blind eye.
Boucher un trou (*fig.*), To pay off a debt ; To make good a loss.
Faire un trou pour en boucher un autre, To rob Peter to pay Paul.
Se boucher les oreilles, To stop one's ears, To refuse to listen. " Put armour on thine ears."—*Timon of Athens* IV, 3.
Se boucher les yeux, To turn one's eyes away (*not to wish to see*).
boucler. Boucler quelqu'un, To run someone in, To put someone in quod *or* in clink.
bouder. Bouder à la besogne, To shirk one's share of work, To be work-shy.
Bouder contre son ventre (*fig.*), To cut off one's nose to spite one's face.
Ne pas bouder à la besogne *ou* à l'ouvrage, To be no shirker, To set to work in [good] earnest.
boudin. S'en aller en eau de boudin, To come to nothing, To fizzle out, To dissolve (*or* To melt) into thin air (*fig.*) (*of an enterprise*).
boue. C'est une âme de boue, He has a gross mind.
Ne pas faire plus de cas d'une chose que de la boue de ses souliers, To look upon a thing as dirt.
Tirer quelqu'un de la boue (*fig.*), To drag someone from the mire, Tc raise someone from the gutter.
Traîner quelqu'un dans la boue (*fig.*), To drag someone through the mire (*vilify him*).
See also BÂTIR, PÉTRIR.
bouffée. Il ne s'adonne au travail que par bouffées, He only works by fits and starts.
bouger. Il ne bouge pas plus qu'un terme, He doesn't budge an inch, He is standing there stock-still. *Quotation under* PLANTER.
bouillant. *See* CHAUD.
bouillie. C'est de la bouillie pour les chats, It is slipshod work.
Faire de la bouillie pour les chats, To labour over making some useless thing, To plough the sand[s].
bouillir. La tête (*ou* La cervelle) me bout (*fig.*), My head is burning hot.
See also BON 57, MARMITE, POT.
bouillon. Dans les premiers bouillons de sa colère, In the first paroxysms of his rage.
Un bouillon d'onze heures, A poisoned draught.
See also BOIRE.
boule. Faire la boule de neige, To grow like a rolling snowball, To become larger and larger. " As a little snow, tumbled about, Anon becomes a mountain."—*King John* III, 4.
boulet. Tirer sur quelqu'un à boulets rouges, To attack someone mercilessly (*with reproaches, abuse, or epigrams*), To go for someone baldheaded (*slang*) (" Shall quips and sentences, and these paper bullets of the brain awe a man from the career of his humour ?"—*Much Ado About Nothing* II, 3.) ; To make exorbitant demands on someone's purse.
Traîner le boulet (*fig.*), To slave in drudgery, To drudge.
boulette. Faire une boulette, To make a blunder *or* (*slang*) a bloomer, To drop a brick (*slang*).
bouquet. Réserver une chose pour le bouquet, To reserve a thing for the climax *or* for the grand finale.
bourbier. Se mettre dans un bourbier (*fig.*), To get into a scrape *or* a mess.
bourreau. C'est un bourreau d'argent, He is a spendthrift, He plays ducks and drakes with his money. *Quotation under* FENÊTRE.
Être le bourreau de soi-même, To be one's own enemy (*to neglect one's health—Also, in this sense* Être le bourreau de son corps—*or to torment oneself needlessly*).

bourrique. *See* TOURNER.

bourse. Délier les cordons de la bourse, To loosen the purse-strings.

Donner la bourse à garder au larron, To set the fox to mind the geese. *Quotations under* LOUP.

Loger le diable dans sa bourse, To have an empty purse.

N'avoir (*ou* Ne faire) qu'une bourse, To share expenses, To pool resources.

Ne pas laisser voir le fond de sa bourse, To hide one's true financial position.

Sa bourse est bien plate, His purse is very light (*he is hard up*). " The clergy's bags Are lank and lean."—2 *King Henry VI* I, 3. " I can get no remedy against this consumption of the purse : borrowing only lingers and lingers it out, but the disease is incurable."—2 *King Henry IV* I, 2. *See also quotation under* COURT.

Sa bourse est ouverte à ses amis, He has an open hand.

Sans bourse délier, Without putting one's hand in one's pocket, Without spending a penny.

Selon ta bourse gouverne ta bouche, Cut your coat according to your cloth.

Serrer les cordons de la bourse, To tighten the purse-strings.

Tenir les cordons de la bourse, To hold the purse-strings, To keep the cash. " Thou, Iago, who hast had my purse, As if the strings were thine."—*Othello* I, 1.

Toutes les bourses sont fermées, It is impossible to borrow [money].

Un ami jusqu'à la bourse, A fair-weather friend, A friend until it comes to lending one money. " All gone ! and not One friend to take his fortune by the arm And go along with him."—*Timon of Athens* IV, 11.

See also COMMUN, SAIGNÉE.

boussole. *See* PERDRE.

bout. À tout bout de champ, At every turn.

Au bout du compte, When all is said and done.

Au bout du fossé la culbute, He is (You are) riding for a fall.

Aux deux bouts de la terre, To the ends of the earth, Throughout the world.

Avoir de l'esprit (*ou* des yeux) au bout des doigts, To have sensitive (*or* deft) (*or* clever) fingers.

Avoir de l'esprit jusqu'au bout des doigts *ou* jusqu'au bout des ongles, To be extremely witty.

Avoir de la peine à joindre les deux bouts [de l'année], To have difficulty in making both ends meet.

Avoir un mot, un nom, sur le bout de la langue, To have a word, a name, on the tip of one's tongue.

Brûler la chandelle par les deux bouts, To burn the candle at both ends.

C'est [tout] le bout du monde, At the [very] outside, That is the [very] utmost (*in price, in value*).

C'est une économie de bouts de chandelle, It is a cheese-paring policy, That is penny-wise, pound-foolish, That is spoiling the ship for a ha'p'orth of tar. " Doth like a miser spoil his coat with scanting A little cloth."—*King Henry V* II, 4.

Cette lettre est restée au bout de ma plume, This letter slipped my attention, my memory (*I omitted, I forgot, to write it*).

Dire quelque chose à bout portant, To say something point-blank.

Être à bout [de champ] *ou* à bout de voie, To be brought to a standstill, To be at the end of one's resources, Not to know which way to turn *or* what is to become of one.

Être au bout de son latin, To be at one's wit's end.

Être au bout de son rouleau, To be at the end of one's tether *or* on one's beam ends ; To be on one's last legs (*near death or end*).

Être ménager de bouts de chandelle, To be stingy in little things [only], To take care of the pence.

Il n'est pas au bout [de ses peines], He is not at the end of his troubles, He is not yet out of the wood.

Le bout du monde, The end of the world, The back of beyond.

Montrer (*ou* Laisser passer) (*ou* Laisser percer) le bout de l'oreille *ou* un bout d'oreille, To show the cloven hoof.

On ne sait pas par quel bout le prendre, One does not know how to tackle him.

On y touche du bout du doigt (*fig.*), It (*the event*) is at hand.

Pousser quelqu'un à bout, To drive someone into a corner (*in a discussion*).

Pousser quelqu'un à bout *ou* Pousser (*ou* Mettre) à bout la patience de quelqu'un, To drive someone to extremities, To exhaust someone's patience. " Thou driv'st me past the bounds Of maiden's patience." —*A Midsummer Night's Dream*, III, 2. " The devil take Henry of Lancaster and thee ! Patience is stale, and I am weary of it."—*King Richard II* V, 5.

Tirer sur quelqu'un à bout portant, To abuse someone to his face.

Un [petit] bout d'homme, A [tiny] little man, A midget, A chit, A manikin, A shrimp. " This weak and writhled shrimp."—1 *King Henry VI* II, 3. (*Note.*—writhled = distorted.)

Venir à bout de [la résistance de] quelqu'un, To break down someone's resistance.

Venir à bout de quelque chose, Venir à bout de faire quelque chose, To succeed in doing (*or* To manage to do) (*or* To contrive to do) something.

See also AUNE, BON 13, 56, 62, HAUT, MANGER, PENDRE, RIRE, SAVOIR.

bouteille. Aimer la bouteille, To be fond of the bottle, To be addicted to drinking.

C'est la bouteille à l'encre, It is as clear as mud, It is a hopeless muddle, There is no making head or tail of it. " This is as strange a maze as e'er men trod."—*The Tempest* V, 1. " Confusion now hath made his masterpiece!"—*Macbeth* II, 3.

Laisser sa raison au fond de la bouteille, To get fuddled. " O God, that men should put an enemy in their mouths to steal away their brains ! that we should, with joy, pleasance, revel, and applause, transform ourselves into beasts ! " —*Othello* II, 3.

N'avoir rien vu que par le trou d'une bouteille, To know nothing of the world.

See also SI.

boutique. C'est une boutique, It is a horrid (*or* a beastly) (*or* a most undesirable) place (*the people in it are such*).

Fermer boutique, To shut up shop (*lit. & fig.*).

Se mettre en boutique, To set up shop.

boutoir. *See* COUP 16.

bouton. *See* SERRER.

boutonner. C'est un homme toujours boutonné [jusqu'à la gorge *ou* jusqu'au menton], He is a most uncommunicative (*or* reticent) man.

boutonnière. Faire une boutonnière à quelqu'un, To pink someone, To stab (*or* To pierce) someone with a pointed weapon.

boyau. Cette salle est un boyau *ou* n'est qu'un boyau, This hall is like a corridor (*so narrow*).

braie. S'en tirer (*ou* En sortir) les braies nettes, To come off in (*or* with) a whole skin, To get off scot-free. " Show me one scar charácter'd on thy skin: Men's flesh preserv'd so whole do seldom win."—2 *King Henry VI* III, 1.

braise. Passer sur quelque chose comme chat sur braise *ou* comme un chat sur la braise, Not to dwell (*or* linger) on something (*some matter one does not want to go too deeply into*), To skate over thin ice.

See also CHAUD, TOMBER.

branche. Être comme l'oiseau sur la branche, To be very unsettled, Not to know what is going to happen to one *or* what is going to become of one.

S'accrocher à toutes les branches, To clutch at (*or* To catch at) every and any means of escape (*from a danger, a predicament*).

See also RACCROCHER.

brandon. Les brandons (*ou* Le brandon) de la discorde, The seed[s] of discord.

Un brandon de discorde, A fire-brand, A mischief-maker. " Our firebrand brother, Paris, burns us all."—*Troilus and Cressida* II, 2.

branle. Être (*ou* Se mettre) en branle, To be (*or* To get) going (*in action, working*): Quand il est (*ou* Quand il se met) une fois en branle, When once he is (*or* gets) going.

Mettre en branle une affaire *ou* Donner le branle à une affaire, To set a thing going, To give an impetus to an affair.

See also COMMENCER, MENER, OUVRIR.

branler. Tout ce qui branle ne tombe pas, A creaking gate hangs long.

braque. C'est un braque, He is a madcap.

bras. Avoir les bras rompus (*fig.*), To have worked (*or* worn) one's fingers to the bone.

Avoir quelqu'un sur les bras (*fig.*), To have someone on one's hands.

Casser (*ou* Couper) bras et jambes à quelqu'un (*fig.*), To render someone helpless *or* powerless, To paralyse someone, To bowl someone over ; To stun someone (*with astonishment*), To strike someone all of a heap.

Frapper à tour de bras *ou* Frapper à bras raccourcis, To strike with all one's might.

Ils marchaient en se donnant le bras *ou* Ils marchaient bras dessus, bras dessous, They walked arm in arm.

Je lui romprai bras et jambes, I'll beat him black and blue. *Quotation under* OS.

Les bras m'en tombent *ou* m'en sont tombés, I am dumbfounded *or* flabbergasted.

Saisir (*ou* Prendre) quelqu'un à bras-le-corps, To seize someone round the waist.

Tirer quelqu'un d'entre les bras (*ou* quelqu'un des bras) de la mort, To snatch someone from the jaws of death.

Tomber sur les bras de quelqu'un, To come on someone's hands, To have to be supported (*or* provided for) by someone.

Tomber sur quelqu'un à bras raccourcis, To go for someone tooth and nail, To pitch into someone.

Traiter quelqu'un de monsieur, de monseigneur, gros comme le bras, To call someone sir, my lord, at every turn. " Anon, Francis ? No, Francis; but to-morrow, Francis ; or, Francis, on Thursday ; or, indeed, Francis, when thou wilt. But, Francis,— "—1 *King Henry IV* II, 4.

See also CROISER, DONNER, DROIT, LONG.

brasier. C'est un brasier que son corps, He is in a burning fever.

Sa tête est un brasier, His head is afire (*fig.*).

brasseur. Un brasseur d'affaires, A

man with many irons in the fire; A shady financier.

brassière. Tenir quelqu'un en brassières, To keep someone in leading strings.

brave. Un brave à trois poils, A man who is afraid of nothing *or* who does not know what fear is. " Cowards die many times before their deaths; The valiant never taste of death but once."—*Julius Caesar* II, 2.

braver. *See* QU'EN-DIRA-T-ON.

brebis. C'est bien la brebis du bon Dieu, He can't say bo[h] to a goose (*is so meek*).

Faire un repas de brebis, To eat without drinking.

See also BÊLER, ÉGARER, GALEUX, LOUP, TONDRE.

brèche. Être toujours sur la brèche (*fig.*), To be always [standing] in the breach.

See also BATTRE.

bref. Avoir le parler bref *ou* la parole brève, To be a man of few words; To be curt of speech. " I thank you: I am not of many words, but I thank you."—*Much Ado About Nothing* I, 1. " Speak, breathe, discuss; brief, short, quick, snap." —*Merry Wives of Windsor* IV, 5.

See also FOU.

breloque. *See* BATTRE.

brevet. Donner à quelqu'un [son] brevet d'étourdi, de charlatan, etc., To dub someone a scatter-brain, a quack, etc.

bric. De bric et de broc, By hook or by crook.

bride. À cheval donné on ne regarde pas à la bride, One should not look a gift horse in the mouth.

Aller à toute bride, To go as fast as one's legs can carry one, To go at top speed, To go hell for leather.

Aller bride en main dans une affaire, To proceed cautiously (*or* warily) in a matter.

Courir à bride abattue à sa ruine, à sa perte, To rush headlong to one's ruin, to perdition.

Il a plus besoin de bride que d'éperon, He needs a curb rather than a spur. " Her fume needs no spurs."—2 *King Henry VI* I, 3.

Il fait toujours bon tenir son cheval par la bride, It is always advisable to have control of one's property, of the business in which one is interested.

Lâcher la bride à quelqu'un *ou* Mettre à quelqu'un la bride sur le cou, To give someone his head. " I must have liberty Withal, as large a charter as the wind, To blow on whom I please."—*As You Like It* II, 7.

Lâcher la bride à ses passions, To throw (*or* To give) the reins to (*or* To give rein, *or* vent, to) one's passions.

Tenir quelqu'un en bride, To hold someone in check, To keep someone within bounds.

Tenir quelqu'un la bride haute *ou* la bride courte, To keep a tight rein on someone.

brider. Brider son cheval par la queue, To go the wrong way to work.

Un oison bridé (*fig.*), A goose, A simpleton.

briller. Briller par son absence, To be conspicuous by one's absence.

Faire briller la vérité aux yeux de quelqu'un, To bring the truth home to someone.

See also OR.

brin. C'est un beau brin d'homme, He is a well set-up (*or* a fine upstanding) young man.

brisées. Aller sur les brisées de quelqu'un, To try to supplant someone.

See also SUIVRE.

briser. *See* CRUCHE, OS, PLUME, TYMPAN.

broc. *See* BRIC.

brocher. Brochant sur le tout, To crown (*or* To cap) all.

broncher. *See* BON 48.

bronzer. Le malheur a bronzé son cœur, Misfortune has hardened his heart.

brosser. Brosser quelqu'un (*fig.*), To dust someone's jacket, To give someone a good thrashing.

Se brosser [le ventre], To go hungry (*there being nothing to eat*) ; To have to do without, To have to want.

Tu peux te brosser, Don't you wish you may get it !

brouillard. Je n'y vois que du brouillard, I am very hazy about it, I can't make head or tail of it. *Quotation under* TÉNÈBRES.

Un esprit plein de brouillards, A hazy intellect.

Une créance assignée (*ou* établie) (*ou* hypothéquée) sur les brouillards de la Seine, A debt having no valid security.

brouiller. Brouiller les cartes (*fig.*), To embroil matters.

Cet homme est brouillé avec le bon sens, This man won't listen to reason.

Être brouillé avec la grammaire, To use bad grammar, To break Priscian's head.

Se brouiller avec la justice, To fall foul of the law.

broussailles. Se sauver (*ou* S'échapper) par les broussailles, To get out of it (*a scrape*) as best one can.

brouter. Où la chèvre est attachée, il faut qu'elle broute, One must make the best of things.

See also HERBE.

broyer. *See* NOIR.

bruit. C'est un bruit si grand qu'on n'entendrait pas Dieu tonner, The noise is so great that one cannot hear oneself think.

Faire beaucoup de bruit pour rien, To make much ado about nothing.

Faire plus de bruit que de besogne, To make more noise than anything else.

Il fait plus de bruit que de mal, His bark is worse than his bite.

Il n'est bruit que de cela, People talk of nothing but that.

Un bruit à fendre la tête *ou* Un bruit à tête fendre, A deafening (*or* An ear-splitting) noise.

Un bruit à tout casser *ou* à tout rompre, A noise enough to wake the dead. " Wake Duncan with thy knocking ! I would thou couldst ! "—*Macbeth* II, 2.

Un bruit de tous les diables *ou* Un bruit de chien, The devil (*or* The dickens) of a noise, The devil's own row.

See also COURIR, LOIN, MENER, PENDRE, TROMPETTE.

brûler. Brûler l'étape. To pass through (*or* To run by) without stopping.

Brûler la cervelle à quelqu'un, To blow someone's brains out.

Brûler la politesse à quelqu'un, To go without saying good-bye, To take French leave. " Stand not upon the order of your going, But go at once."—*Macbeth* III, 4.

Brûler le pavé, To tear (*or* To scorch) along [the road].

Brûler les étapes, To press on (*with the work*).

Brûler les planches, To act spiritedly (*in the theatre*), To bring the house down.

Brûler ses vaisseaux (*fig.*), To burn one's boats *or* one's bridges.

C'est un cerveau brûlé, He is a hare-brained fellow *or* a madcap. " Why, what a madcap hath heaven lent us here!"—*King John* I, 1.

C'est un homme brûlé, He is done for.

L'argent lui brûle la poche, Money burns a hole in his pocket.

Le tapis brûle, Put down your stakes (*Gaming*).

Le torchon brûle, There is quarrelling in that household.

Les mains lui brûlent, He is all impatience to be up and doing.

Les pieds lui brûlent, He is itching to be off.

Sans brûler une cartouche *ou* une amorce, Without firing a shot. *Quotations under* FÉRIR.

Se brûler la cervelle, To blow one's brains out.

[Venir] se brûler à la chandelle (*fig.*), To singe one's feathers *or* one's wings, To burn one's fingers. "Thus hath the candle singed the moth. O these deliberate fools ! when they do choose, They have the wisdom by their wit to lose."—*The Merchant of Venice* II, 9.

See also ALLUMETTE, BOUT.

brun. Sur (*ou* À) la brune, At dusk, In the gloaming.

brusquer. Brusquer l'aventure *ou* la fortune, To try one's luck, To tempt fortune, To chance it, To risk it.

Brusquer les choses, une affaire, To precipitate matters, a matter.

bûche. C'est une bûche, He is a block[head] *or* a dolt. " You blocks, you stones, you worse than senseless things ! "—*Julius Caesar* I, 1.

Cet homme ne se remue non plus qu'une bûche, This man won't move a finger *or* won't bestir himself.

See also RAMASSER.

buisson. Faire (*ou* Trouver) buisson creux, To draw a blank (*find nothing*) ; To find the bird (*person*) flown.

See also SAUVER.

buissonnier. Faire l'école buissonnière, To play truant.

bureau. Cette affaire est sur le bureau, This matter is on the carpet *or* on the tapis *or* under consideration.

Un bureau d'esprit, A coterie of wits.

Un homme de bureau, A man (*who works*) in an office.

See also AIR.

Buridan. *See* ÂNE.

buse. *See* ÉPERVIER.

but. Aller droit au but, To come (*or* To go) straight to the point.

De but en blanc (*fig.*), Point-blank, Straight away.

Toucher (*ou* Frapper) au but, To reach the goal, To hit the mark.

See also MANQUER, VENIR.

C

cabaret. *See* PILIER.

caboche. C'est une bonne caboche, He has a good head.

Il a la caboche dure, He is a stubborn man.

cabriole. Il s'en est tiré par une cabriole, He laughed it off.

cacher. Cacher sa vie, To live a secluded life. " And this our life, exempt from public haunt, Finds tongues in trees, books in the running brooks, Sermons in stones, and good in everything. I would not change it."—*As You Like It* II, 1.

Un esprit caché, A secretive mind. " Dive, thoughts, down to my soul."—*King Richard III* I, 1.

Une vie cachée, A secluded life.

See also CHAIR, EAU, FEU, JEU, SERPENT.

cachet. Avoir du cachet, To have an air about one, To have the stamp of individuality.

See also COURIR.

cadavre. C'est un cadavre ambulant, He looks like a corpse, He is not long for this world.

cadet. *See* SOUCI.

cadran. Faire le tour du cadran, To come back to where one started ; To sleep the clock round. " Time is come round, And where I did begin there shall I end."—*Julius Caesar* V, 3.

Caïphe. *See* RENVOYER.
caisse. *See* BATTRE.
calcul. *See* TROMPER.
calendes. Renvoyer (*ou* Remettre) aux calendes grecques, To put off till doomsday.
caler. C'est un homme calé, He is a man of substance ; He knows what he is about ; He knows what he is talking about, He is a well-informed man.
Caler [la voile], To take in sail (*fig.*), To give in, To knuckle down *or* under, To sing small.
calice. Un calice d'amertume (*fig.*), A cup of bitterness. " Let this cup pass from me."—*Matthew* xxvi, 39.
See also AVALER, BOIRE.
calotte. La calotte des cieux (*fig.*), The vault of heaven, The welkin. " That inverted Bowl we call The Sky."—EDWARD FITZGERALD, *Rubaiyat of Omar Khayyam* LXXVIII. *Other quotations under* La VOÛTE du ciel.
camarde. La camarde, [Grim] death, The Grim Reaper. " Dusty death." —*Macbeth* V, 5. " Death, that winter."—*King Henry VIII* III, 2. " That churl Death."—SHAKESPEARE, *Sonnets* XXXII. " This fell sergeant, death."—*Hamlet* V, 2. " Invisible commander."—SHAKESPEARE, *Venus and Adonis*.
camp. Être en camp volant, To be on a flying visit.
See also ALARME.
campagne. Être en campagne, To be on the war-path.
Il a fait une belle campagne, He has given himself a lot of trouble for nothing.
Mettre ses amis en campagne, To get one's friends to lend a hand.
Se mettre en campagne, To set to work, To get going.
Son imagination est en campagne, His mind is very uneasy.
See also BATTRE, VIE.
camper. Camper là quelqu'un, To leave someone in the lurch.
Il campe, He has no fixed abode.
Me voilà bien campé, A pretty pickle I'm in.
canard. *See* MOUILLER, PLONGER.
cane. Faire la cane, To funk, To run away, To show the white feather. " There's not a piece of feather in our host.—Good argument, I hope, we will not fly."—*King Henry V* IV, 3.
See also MARCHER, POULE.
caner. Caner, To funk, To run away, To show the white feather.
canin. *See* FAIM.
canon. De la chair à canon, Cannon-fodder. " Food for powder ; they'll fill a pit as well as better."—1 *King Henry IV* IV, 2.
canonicat. C'est un canonicat, It (*the job*) is a sinecure.
canonique. Ce n'est pas canonique, It's not conventional, It's not the thing (*to say or do*), It isn't done.
cap. *See* ARMER.
capable. Prendre (*ou* Avoir) l'air capable *ou* Faire le capable, To make a pretence of being (*or* To pretend to be) (*or* To think oneself) very [cap]able *or* very clever.
See also TOUT.
cape. *See* COMÉDIE, RIRE, ROMAN.
capilotade. Mettre quelqu'un en capilotade, To pound someone to a jelly, To beat someone black and blue ; To pull someone to pieces (*fig.*).
Capitole. *See* ROCHE.
capituler. Capituler avec sa conscience, To compromise with one's conscience.
Ville qui capitule est à demi rendue, To get someone to listen to one's proposal is half the battle.
caporal. *See* QUATRE.
capot. Être (*ou* Demeurer) (*ou* Rester) capot, To be abashed, To be taken aback, To look sheepish.

caque. *See* HARENG.
caquet. Rabattre (*ou* Rabaisser) le caquet de (*ou* à) quelqu'un, To shut someone up, To sit on someone (*slang*).
Un caquet bon bec (*fig.*), A scandal-mongering gossip (*woman*).
caractère. Sortir de son caractère, To lose one's self-restraint *or* one's patience *or* one's temper (*one's usual calm demeanour*).
See also AIGRE.
carat. *See* SOT.
caravane. *See* MARCHER.
carême. Une face (*ou* Une figure) de carême, A cadaverous face.
See also HAUT, MARÉE, MARS.
carême-prenant. C'est un vrai carême-prenant, He is a regular guy (*grotesquely dressed*).
caresse. *See* MANGER.
caresser. Caresser quelqu'un des yeux *ou* du regard, To look fondly at someone.
carnaval. C'est un vrai carnaval, He is a regular guy (*grotesquely dressed*).
Caron. *See* BARQUE.
carpe. Faire des yeux de carpe pâmée, To turn up the whites of one's eyes, To look like a dying duck in a thunderstorm.
Faire la carpe pâmée, To feign illness.
carquois. Il a vidé son carquois, He has run dry (*of epigrams*), He has shot his bolt. " If Cupid have not spent all his quiver in Venice."—*Much Ado About Nothing* I, 1.
carré. C'est une tête carrée, He is a level-headed man ; He is a stubborn man.
carreau. Jeter (*ou* Coucher) (*ou* Étendre) quelqu'un sur le carreau, To stretch someone on the ground (*kill or wound severely*), To lay someone out (*slang*).
See also DEMEURER, GARDE, GARDER, RESTER.
carrément. *See* ALLER.
carrière. Donner [libre] carrière à son imagination, To give free play (*or* free scope) to one's imagination.
Il a eu une longue carrière, He had a long innings (*fig.*).
Se donner carrière, To let oneself go.
See also COURIR, FOURNIR.
carrosse. *See* CINQUIÈME, ROULER.
carte. Avoir carte blanche, To have a free hand.
C'est la carte forcée, It is Hobson's choice.
Donner (*ou* Laisser) carte blanche à quelqu'un, To give someone a free hand.
Tirer les cartes à quelqu'un, To tell someone's fortune by the cards.
See also BROUILLER, CHÂTEAU, DÉCOUVRIR, DESSOUS, JOUER, PERDRE, RETOURNER, SAVOIR.
carton. Rester dans les cartons, To be pigeon-holed, To be shelved (*as a project*).
Un personnage de carton, A figure-head.
Une maison de carton, A jerry-built house.
cartouche. *See* BRÛLER.
cas. Être dans le cas de faire une chose, To be in the position to do a thing ; To be quite likely to do a thing.
Faire cas de quelqu'un, To have a good opinion of someone.
Faire cas de quelque chose, To value (*or* To set store by) (*or* To attach importance to) something. *See also under* BOUE.
See also CONSCIENCE, LIMITE, NET, PENDABLE.
casaque. *See* TOURNER.
casaquin. Donner sur le casaquin à quelqu'un, To dust someone's jacket, To give someone a good thrashing.
On lui est tombé sur le casaquin, He got a good dressing down (*thrashing or scolding*).
caser. Cela a de la peine à se caser dans sa tête, He can't keep that in his head (*remember it*).

cassant. C'est un homme cassant, He is an overbearing man.

casse. *See* PASSER.

casser. Casser la tête à quelqu'un (*fig.*), To make a deafening noise, To split someone's ear-drums.

Casser la tête à quelqu'un de, avec, quelque chose, To drive someone crazy about (*or* over), with, something.

Casser le cou à quelqu'un (*fig.*), To break (*or* To ruin) someone.

Casser les reins à quelqu'un, To break someone['s back] (*ruin his schemes or career*).

Casser les vitres (*fig.*), Not to mince matters, To blurt out everything.

Casser sa pipe, To kick the bucket, To hop the twig *or* the stick (*slang*), To go west (*slang*) (*die*).

Il est cassé aux gages, He has been discharged (*from his employment*) ; He is in his superior's bad books.

Payer les pots cassés, To stand the racket, To face the music. " You will not pay for the glasses you have burst ? "—*The Taming of the Shrew, Induction, Scene* I.

Qui casse les verres les paie, The culprit must pay for the damage.

Se casser la tête à quelque chose, pour trouver un expédient, To puzzle (*or* To rack) (*or* To cudgel) one's brains about something, to find an expedient. " Cudgel thy brains no more about it, for your dull ass will not mend his pace with beating."—*Hamlet* V, 1.

Se casser le cou (*fig.*), To ruin oneself (*financially*), To break.

Se casser le nez, To fall on one's face ; To come a cropper (*slang*) (*fail disastrously*) ; To find nobody at home.

Se casser le nez contre quelqu'un, To run (*or* To knock up) against someone, To bump into someone.

See also APPLAUDIR, BRAS, BRUIT, CROÛTE, CRUCHE, ENCENSOIR, OMELETTE, OS, SUCRE.

casse-tête. Un casse-tête chinois, A Chinese puzzle, A regular teaser.

casseur. Un casseur d'assiettes, A brawler, A swashbuckler.

cataracte. Les cataractes du ciel, The cataracts (*or* The flood-gates) of heaven. " You cataracts and hurricanoes, spout Till you have drench'd our steeples, drown'd the cocks!"—*King Lear* III, 2.

Catherine. *See* COIFFER.

catholique. Cela n'est pas bien catholique, That is not very orthodox.

Un catholique à gros grains, An unscrupulous man.

cauchemar. C'est mon cauchemar, He (It) is my bugbear *or* my pet aversion.

cause. Avoir gain de cause *ou* Avoir cause gagnée, To win one's case, To get a decision in one's favour, To carry the day.

Donner gain de cause (*ou* Donner cause gagnée) à quelqu'un, To decide in someone's favour, To give someone best.

En tout état de cause, At all events, In any case.

Et pour cause, And for a very good reason.

Être en cause (*fig.*), To be concerned in the case *or* the matter.

Mettre quelqu'un en cause (*fig.*), To bring someone into the affair, To implicate someone.

See also COMMUN, CONDAMNER, CONNAISSANCE, DÉSESPOIR, FAIT, HORS, IGNORANCE.

causer. *See* BEC, CHIFFON, CHOSE, PLUIE.

cautère. C'est un cautère sur une jambe de bois, It is a useless remedy.

caution. Être (*ou* Se rendre) caution d'une chose, To warrant the truth of a thing, To answer for a thing.

Il est sujet à caution, He is not to be depended on, He is unreliable.

cave. Chercher quelque chose depuis

la cave jusqu'au grenier, To hunt high and low for something.

See also RAT.

caveçon. Il a besoin de caveçon, He needs restraining.

See also COUP 17.

caver. Caver au pire, To prepare for the worst.

Caver au plus fort (*fig.*), To carry things to extremes.

caverne. Cette maison est une [vraie] caverne, This house is a [regular] den of thieves.

céder. [Le] céder à quelqu'un, To yield the palm to someone, To be surpassed by someone.

See also HACHER.

cèdre. Depuis le cèdre jusqu'à l'hysope, From the greatest to the smallest (*cedar being big tree and hyssop small bush*).

ceindre. Ceindre ses reins, To gird up one's loins (*prepare for effort*).

ceinture. Il ne lui va pas à la ceinture, He is much shorter than (*or* not nearly so tall as) he; He can't hold a candle to him.

See also BON 21.

cela. N'est-ce que cela ? Is that all ? (*it is of no importance*).

See also CONNAÎTRE, DIRE, MANQUER, PARLER, VOIR.

célèbre. Du jour au lendemain il devint célèbre, He awoke to find himself famous.

céleste. *See* FLAMBEAU, LAMBRIS, PATRIE, TROUPE, VOÛTE.

célibat. *See* BONHEUR.

cendre. *See* FEU, MORT, RENAÎTRE.

cénobite. Vivre en cénobite *ou* Mener une vie de cénobite, To live in retirement *or* in seclusion, To lead a retired (*or* secluded) life.

cent. *See* CHAGRIN, COUP 32, 36, DÉESSE, DESSUS, DONNER, FOIS, MILLE, MOT, PIED, PIQUE, POINT.

cercle. *See* CHERCHER.

cercueil. *See* DESCENDRE.

cérémonie. Faire des cérémonies, To stand on ceremony; To make a fuss.

cerner. Avoir les yeux cernés, To have rings under the eyes.

cerveau. *See* BRÛLER, CREUSER, CREUX, FROID.

cervelle. *See* BON 24, BRÛLER, CREUX, PETIT, PLOMB, ROMPRE, TÊTE, TROTTER.

César. Il faut rendre à César ce qui appartient à César, Render to Caesar the things that are Caesar's (*Matthew* xxii, 21).

cesse. *See* FIN, TRAVAILLER.

chacun. *See* COUR, DÛ, GOÛT, MAÎTRE, MÉTIER, PRENDRE, TOUR.

chagrin. Cent ans (*ou* Cent heures) (*ou* Cent livres) de chagrin ne paient pas un sou de dettes, Care killed the cat [, for all its nine lives] (*therefore be cheerful*). *Quotations under* SOUCI.

chair. Avoir la chair de poule, To have one's flesh creep, To come over all creepy *or* all goosey.

C'est lui (*ou* Le voilà) **en chair et en os, It is he in flesh and blood.**

Cela fait venir la chair de poule, It makes one's flesh creep.

Entre la chair et la chemise il faut cacher le bien qu'on fait, " But when thou doest alms, let not thy left hand know what thy right hand doeth: That thine alms may be in secret."—*Matthew* vi, 3–4.

N'être ni chair ni poisson, To blow hot and cold, To fluctuate (*or* To vacillate) weakly now one way, now the other (*of persons*); To be neither fish, flesh, nor good red herring, To be neither fish nor flesh nor fowl (*of things*). " *Falstaff.* Thou art a beast, . . . an otter. *Prince Henry.* An otter, Sir John ! why an otter ? *Fal.* Why, she's neither fish nor flesh."—1 *King Henry IV* III, 3.

Voir quelqu'un en chair et en os, To see someone in the flesh.

See also CANON, HACHER, PROMPT.

chaise. *See* BÂTON.

chaleur. Supporter la fatigue de tout le jour et la chaleur *ou* Porter le poids du jour et de la chaleur, To bear the burden and heat of the day (*Matthew* xx, 12).

See also EXTINCTION, PLOMB.

chambre. Un stratège en chambre, An arm-chair strategist. " The bookish theoric, Wherein the toged consuls can propose As masterly as he: mere prattle without practice, Is all his soldiership."—*Othello* I, 1.

chameau. Rejeter le moucheron et avaler le chameau *ou* Couler un moucheron et avaler un chameau, To strain at a gnat and swallow a camel (*Matthew* xxiii, 24).

champ. Abandonner le champ de bataille, To leave one's rival in possession of the field (*after debate*).

Avoir encore du champ devant soi, To still have resources at one's command.

Avoir le champ libre, To be free to do it.

Donner du champ à quelqu'un, To give someone scope.

Donner un champ libre à son imagination, To give free play (*or* free scope) (*or* free vent) to one's imagination.

Être aux champs, To be put out (*irritated*) ; To be all at sea.

Il a bien pris (*ou* a bien choisi) son champ de bataille, He has chosen his ground (*or* laid his plans) well.

Laisser à quelqu'un le champ libre, To leave someone a clear field, To give someone free scope. " I must have liberty Withal, as large a charter as the wind, To blow on whom I please."—*As You Like It*, II, 7.

Le champ de bataille lui est demeuré *ou* Il est resté maître du champ de bataille, He was left in possession of the field (*after the debate*).

Le champ est libre, The coast is clear (*fig.*). " See the coast clear'd, and then we will depart."—1 *King Henry VI* I, 3.

Mettre quelqu'un aux champs, To put someone out, To drive someone wild. Un rien le met aux champs *ou* Il se met aux champs pour la moindre chose, The merest thing puts him out.

Prendre du champ, To give oneself plenty of room.

Se donner du champ, To give oneself elbow-room.

See also BOUT, CLEF, COURIR, GAGNER, SAUVER, VIE.

champignon. Pousser comme des champignons (*fig.*), To spring up like mushrooms.

chance. Ne pas avoir l'ombre d'une chance *ou* la moindre chance [de succès], Not to have the ghost of a chance, Not to have an earthly (*slang*).

chandelle. C'est une chandelle qui s'éteint, He (She) is sinking fast. " Here burns my candle out,—ay, here it dies."—3 *King Henry VI* II, 6. " My inch of taper will be burnt and done."—*King Richard II* I, 3. " Out, out, brief candle ! Life's but a walking shadow ; a poor player, That struts and frets his hour upon the stage, And then is heard no more."—*Macbeth* V, 5.

Le jeu ne vaut pas (*ou* n'en vaut pas) la chandelle, The game is not worth the candle.

Tenir la chandelle, To hold the candle. " For I am proverb'd with a grandsire phrase,—I'll be a candle-holder, and look on."—*Romeo and Juliet* I, 4. " *Lorenzo.* Descend, for you must be my torch-bearer. *Jessica, in boy's clothes.* What ! must I hold a candle to my shames ? They in themselves, good sooth, are too, too light."—*The Merchant of Venice* II, 6.

Voir des chandelles *ou* Voir trente-six (*ou* mille) chandelles, To see stars. " Dazzle mine eyes, or do I see three suns?"—3 *King Henry VI* II, 1. " Five moons were seen to-night ; Four fixed ; and the fifth did whirl about The other four in wondrous motion."—*King John* IV, 2.

See also BOUT, BRÛLER, DEVOIR.

change. Donner (*ou* Faire prendre) le change à quelqu'un, To lead someone astray, To put someone off the scent, To hoodwink someone.

Prendre le change, To be put off the scent, To be led astray.

See also RENDRE.

changer. Changer d'avis, To change one's mind, To alter one's opinion. " Trust ye ! With every minute you do change a mind ; And call him noble that was now your hate, Him vile that was your garland."—*Coriolanus* I, 1.

Changer de ton *ou* de note *ou* de gamme, To change one's tone *or* one's tune, To sing another tune *or* in a different key.

Changer de visage, To change colour (*turn pale or red*) ; To change countenance (*from some emotional cause*).

Plus ça change, plus c'est la même chose, The more it changes, the less it alters.

See also AVEUGLE, BATTERIE, BLANC, CHEMISE, ÉPAULE, NOURRICE, PEAU, POIDS, PROPOS, THÈSE, TOUT.

chanoine. Mener une vie de chanoine, To lead a pleasant and quiet life.

See also GRAS.

chanson. Chansons [que tout cela] ! Fiddlesticks ! Nonsense ! Bosh ! That's all my eye [and Betty Martin].

Il dit toujours la même chanson *ou* Il n'a qu'une chanson, He is always (*or* He keeps) harping on the same string. *Quotation under* MÊME.

Je ne me paie pas de chansons, I am not to be put off with words.

Voilà bien une autre chanson, That's quite another matter.

See also MÊME, TON, UN.

chant. Le chant du cygne, The swan-song : C'était le chant du cygne, It was his swan-song. " I will play the swan, And die in music."—*Othello* V, 2. " He makes a swan-like end, Fading in music."—*The Merchant of Venice* III, 2. " I am the cygnet to this pale faint swan, Who chants a doleful hymn to his own death."—*King John* V, 7.

Un chant de sirène, A siren song (*deceitful language*).

See also ALOUETTE.

chanter. C'est comme si vous chantiez, You are wasting your breath, I'm not listening (*to what you are saying*).

Chanter à quelqu'un sa gamme, To tell someone all one's grievances against him.

Chanter plus haut, To increase the amount of one's offer, To offer a better price.

Chanter sur un autre ton *ou* sur une autre note (*fig.*), To sing in a different key, To change one's tune.

Chanter victoire, To shout (*or* To cry) victory, To shout [in triumph], To halloo, To shout for joy : Il ne faut pas chanter victoire avant le temps, Don't halloo (*or* shout) till you are out of the wood. Il a réussi, il chante victoire, He has succeeded, he is shouting for joy.

Chanter victoire sur quelqu'un, To crow over someone.

Faire chanter quelqu'un, To black-mail someone.

See also ABBÉ, LOUANGE, MÊME, PALINODIE.

chanterelle. Appuyer sur la chanterelle, To draw attention to a most important point.

chanteur. Un maître chanteur, A blackmailer. *Note.* 1.—Un maître chanteur = *also* A minnesinger, A master-singer, A meistersinger.—Les Maîtres chanteurs de Nuremberg, Die Meistersinger von Nürnberg. *Note.* 2.—A singing master *is* Un professeur de chant.

chantier. Mettre, Avoir, un ouvrage sur le chantier, To put, To have, a [piece of] work in hand.

chaos. Sa tête est un chaos, His (Her) brain is (*or* thoughts are) in a whirl. " But I do love thee ! and when I love thee not Chaos is come again."—*Othello* III, 3. " My thoughts are whirled like a potter's wheel ; I know not where I am nor what I do."—1 *King Henry VI* I, 5.

chapeau. Chapeau bas (*fig.*), Hat (*or* Cap) in hand. " Go to them with this bonnet in thy hand ; . . . Thy knee bussing the stones, . . , Now humble . . ."—*Coriolanus* III, 2. (*Note.*—To buss = To kiss).

Mettre le chapeau sur l'oreille, To wear one's hat rakishly *or* on one side (*in a swaggering way*).

Mettre son chapeau de travers, To take up a threatening attitude.

chapelet. *See* DÉFILER.

chaperon. Jouer le rôle de chaperon, To play gooseberry.

chapitre. Avoir voix au chapitre, To have a say in the matter.

chaque. *See* JOUR, NID, REVERS.

charbon. D'un sac à charbon ne peut sortir blanche farine, You cannot make a silk purse out of a sow's ear.

Être sur des charbons [ardents], To be on tenterhooks *or* on pins and needles (*suspense*). " I stand on fire: Come to the matter."—*Cymbeline* V, 5.

See also MARCHER.

charbonnier. *See* FOI, MAÎTRE.

charge. À charge de revanche *ou* À charge d'autant, I would do as much for you: Rendez-moi ce service à charge de revanche, Do me this service. I would do as much for you.

Cela est à ma charge, à sa charge, That is part of my duty, of his duty.

Être à charge à quelqu'un, To be a burden on someone, To be on someone's hands.

Être à la charge de quelqu'un, To be at somebody's expense ; To be dependent on someone.

La vie lui est à charge, Life is a burden to him. " There's nothing in this world can make me joy : Life is as tedious as a twice told tale Vexing the dull ear of a drowsy man."—*King John* III, 4.

Revenir (*ou* Retourner) à la charge (*fig.*), To return to the charge.

Se rendre à charge à quelqu'un, To depend on someone for [one's] support (*means of livelihood*).

See also BÉNÉFICE.

charger. Le temps est chargé, The sky is overcast. " 'Tis a day Such as the day is when the sun is hid." —*The Merchant of Venice* V, 1.

See also COUP 13, MULET.

charité. Charité bien ordonnée commence par soi-même, Charity begins at home.

Faire la charité à quelqu'un, To give charitable aid to someone.

charme. *See* PORTER.

charpenter. Charpenter habilement son discours, To frame one's speech skilfully.

Un homme solidement charpenté, A well-built man.

charpie. Cette viande est en charpie, This meat is cooked to shreds *or* done to rags.

charretier. *See* BON 48, JURER.

charrette. *See* ATTELER.

charrue. Mettre la charrue devant les bœufs, To put the cart before the horse.

Tirer la charrue (*fig.*), To have to work like a horse (*so hard*).

See also ATTELER, MAIN.

Charybde. *See* TOMBER.

chasse. Il n'est chasse que de vieux chiens, Old men are the wisest counsellors. " Advised age."—2 *King Henry VI* V, 2.

Qui va à la chasse perd sa place, He who leaves his place loses it.

chasse-marée. Aller [d']un train de chasse-marée, To go post-haste. *Quotations under* POSTE.

chasser. Chasser sur les terres d'autrui, To poach on other people's preserves (*fig.*).

Chassez le naturel, il revient au galop *ou* Les bons chiens chassent de race *ou* Bon chien chasse de race, What's bred in the bone will come out in the flesh. " How hard it is to hide the sparks of nature ! "—*Cymbeline* III, 3. "Cowards father cowards, and base things sire base." —*Cymbeline* IV, 2.

Il chasse de race, He is a chip of the old block, It runs in his blood. " Is my name Talbot ? and am I your son ? And shall I fly ? . . . The world will say, he is not Talbot's blood That basely fled when noble Talbot stood . . . To save a paltry life, and slay bright fame."—1 *King Henry VI* IV, 5 and 6.

Leurs chiens ne chassent plus ensemble, They no longer hit it off together, They are no longer friends.

Un clou chasse l'autre, One drives away the other, One succeeds the other. " As one nail by strength drives out another."—*Two Gentlemen of Verona* II, 4.

See also FAIM, FENÊTRE.

chasseresse. Diane chasseresse (*poetic*), Diana of the chase.

chat. Acheter, Vendre, chat en poche, To buy, To sell, a pig in a poke.

Avoir un chat dans la gorge, To have a frog in the throat.

C'est le chat, The cat did it (*the naughty thing you deny having done*).

C'est une chatte, She is a very dainty eater.

Chat échaudé craint l'eau froide, A burnt child dreads [the] fire, Once bitten twice shy. " The bird that hath been limed in a bush, With trembling wings misdoubteth every bush."—3 *King Henry VI* V, 6.

Écrire comme un chat, To write an illegible scrawl.

Éveiller (*ou* Réveiller) le chat qui dort, To rouse the sleeping lion.

Il le guette comme le chat fait la souris, He watches him like a cat does a mouse. " The cat, with eyne of burning coal, Now couches fore the mouse's hole."—*Pericles, Prince of Tyre* III, 1 *Induction.*

Il n'y a pas un chat, There is not a soul (*or* There is nobody) about.

La nuit tous les chats sont gris, All cats are grey in the dark.

N'éveillez (*ou* Ne réveillez) pas (*ou* Il ne faut pas [r]éveiller) le chat qui dort, Let sleeping dogs lie. " Immortal gods, . . . Grant I may never prove so fond, To trust . . . a dog that seems a-sleeping."—*Timon of Athens* I, 2. " Wake not a sleeping wolf."—2 *King Henry IV* I, 2.

Quand les chats n'y sont pas (*ou* Le chat parti) (*ou* Absent le chat), les souris dansent, When the cat's away the mice will play. " Playing the mouse in absence of the cat."—*King Henry V* I, 2.

See also APPELER, BON 1, BOUILLIE, BRAISE, CHIEN, EMMITOUFLER, FOUETTER, FRIAND, MARCHER, MARRON, RETOMBER.

château. Bâtir (*ou* Faire) des châteaux en Espagne, To build castles in the air *or* in Spain.

Un château de cartes, A house of cards (*lit.* & *fig.*) ; A chalet, A (*lightly constructed*) rural villa.

châtier. *See* AIMER.

chatouiller. Chatouiller quelqu'un à

l'endroit le plus sensible, au bon endroit, To touch someone on the tenderest spot, on the right spot.

Se chatouiller pour se faire rire, To force oneself to (*or* To make oneself) laugh (*as at a feeble joke*).

chaud. Avoir la tête chaude, To be hot-headed.

Avoir le sang chaud, To be hot-blooded.

Cela ne fait ni chaud ni froid, It makes no difference, It won't affect (*serve or harm*) it in any way.

Cela ne me fait ni froid ni chaud, It is all the same (*or* is all one) (*or* is a matter of complete indifference) to me, It won't affect me in any way.

Il y fait chaud comme dans un four, It is as hot there as [in] an oven.

Le rendre tout chaud (*ou* Le rendre chaud comme braise) à quelqu'un, To give it back hot [and strong] to someone (*avenge oneself promptly, reply forcibly and promptly*).

Souffler le chaud et le froid, To blow hot and cold.

Tout chaud, tout bouillant, Post-haste. *Quotations under* POSTE.

See also BATTRE, GORGE, NOUVELLE, PLEURER, SERRE, TOMBER.

chauffer. Ça chauffe, Things are warming up *or* are humming *or* are beginning to hum.

See also BAIN, BOIS, FOUR.

chaume. Être né, Habiter (*ou* Vivre), sous le chaume, To be born, To live, in a cottage *or* in humble surroundings. " O knowledge ill-inhabited ! worse than Jove in a thatch'd house."—*As You Like It* III, 3.

chausser. Chausser le cothurne, To put on the buskin (*write or act tragedy*) ; To inflate one's style (*of language*).

Les cordonniers sont les plus mal chaussés, The cobbler's wife is (*or* The shoemaker's children are) the worst shod.

Se chausser une idée dans la tête *ou* Se chausser d'une idée, To get an idea (*a wrong idea*) into one's head.

See also NU.

chausses. *See* TIRER.

chaussure. Trouver chaussure à son pied, To find just what one wants *or* what one is looking for ; To find (*or* To meet) one's match.

Une chaussure à tous pieds, A formula (*serving to accommodate differences*) acceptable to all parties.

chauve. L'occasion est chauve, Opportunities are hard to seize.

chaux. Bâtir à chaux et à ciment *ou* à chaux et à sable, To build solidly.

Être bâti à chaux et à sable, To be solidly (*or* strongly) built (*of house*); To be of a strong (*or* of an iron) constitution, To be as strong as a horse (*of man*).

chef. De son chef, In one's own right (*Law*) ; On one's own account ; On one's own initiative, Off one's own bat.

Être en chef dans une affaire, To be in charge of an affair.

chemin. Chemin faisant *ou* En chemin, On the way, As I (we) went along.

Être dans (*ou* sur) le chemin de quelqu'un, To be (*or* To stand) in somebody's way.

Faire du chemin, To make headway.

Faire son chemin, To make one's way [in the world], To get on ; To gain ground (*of an idea*).

Faire voir [bien] du chemin à quelqu'un, To lead someone a [fine] dance.

Le chemin de velours, The primrose path. " The primrose path of dalliance."—*Hamlet* I, 3.

Le chemin étroit (qui mène à la vie) *ou* Le chemin du paradis, The narrow way (which leadeth unto life) *Matthew* vii, 14. *Quotations under* VOIE.

Prendre des chemins de traverse (*fig.*), To act in an underhand way.

Prendre le chemin de l'école *ou* le chemin des écoliers, To go the longest way round, To go a roundabout way. " Then the whining school-boy, with his satchel And shining morning face, creeping like snail, Unwillingly to school."—*As You Like It* II, 7.

S'arrêter en bon (*ou* en beau) chemin *ou* S'arrêter à mi-chemin (*fig.*), To stop when success seems assured *or* within sight of goal, To stop half-way *or* after a good start.

Suivre le chemin battu (*fig.*), To follow the beaten track.

Tous chemins vont à Rome *ou* Tout chemin mène à Rome, All roads lead to Rome, There are more ways than one to the wood ; There are more ways than one of killing a cat.

See also ALLER, BARRER, DEMEURER, DROIT, FRAYER, HÂTER, HERBE, HÔPITAL, PIERRE, QUATRE, RENTRER, TRACER, VIEUX, VOIE.

cheminée. *See* CROIX, MANTEAU.

cheminer. *See* DROIT.

chemise. Changer de quelque chose comme de chemise, To change something (*as domestic servants*) continually.

Donner jusqu'à sa [dernière] chemise, To give the [very] shirt [from] off one's back (*be extremely generous*).

Engager (*ou* Jouer) jusqu'à sa [dernière] chemise, To put one's shirt on it.

Manger jusqu'à sa dernière chemise, To eat one's last crust.

N'avoir pas de chemise, Not to have a shirt to one's back (*be very poor*).

Vendre jusqu'à sa dernière chemise, To sell the very shirt off one's back (*because one is so short of money*).

See also CHAIR.

chenet. Vivre les pieds sur les chenets, To live an easeful life.

chenille. *See* LAID.

cher. Il me le paiera cher, I will make him pay dearly for it.

Je le lui ferai payer (*ou* Il le paiera) plus cher qu'au marché, I'll take the change out of him (*avenge myself on him*).

Le temps est cher *ou* Les moments sont chers, Time is precious, Time presses (*therefore hasten*). " Now he weighs time Even to the utmost grain."—*King Henry V* II, 4.

Vendre bien cher (*ou* Vendre chèrement) sa vie *ou* sa peau, To sell one's life dearly.

See also MOITIÉ, TROU.

chercher. Ce trait d'esprit est cherché, This witticism is far-fetched.

Chercher femme, To look for a wife.

Chercher le mouvement perpétuel *ou* Chercher la quadrature du cercle, To attempt the impossible, To try to square the circle.

Chercher les aventures, To seek fame, fortune, by venturesome means.

Chercher quelque chose dans sa tête *ou* dans sa mémoire, To rack one's brains (*or* To ransack one's memory) for something.

Chercher sa vie, To seek a livelihood.

Chercher son malheur, To court one's misfortune.

Chercher son pain, To beg one's bread.

" Cherchez la femme " (DUMAS PÈRE, *Mohicans de Paris* vol. ii, chap. 16), Look for the woman, There's a woman in the case.

Le malheur le cherche, Misfortune dogs him.

Les plaisirs le cherchent, Pleasures seem to seek him out, He always has a good time.

Qui cherche trouve (*proverbe*) *ou* Cherchez, et vous trouverez (*Matthieu* vii, 7), Seek, and ye shall find (*Matthew* vii, 7).

Se chercher [soi-même], To search one's own heart. *Quotation under* CONNAÎTRE.

See also AIGUILLE, ÂNE, BALLE, BIEN,

CAVE, CHICANE, MIDI, NOISE, PLAIE, QUATRE, RAISON, SOLIDE, TERRE.

chère. Faire bonne chère *ou* Faire chère lie, To make good cheer.

Il n'est chère que de vilain, No feast is so good as a miser's feast.

See also AIMER, APPÉTIT.

chétif. Avoir chétive mine, To look sickly ; To look wretched.

cheval. C'est le cheval de bât, He is the drudge, He does the dirty work. " I was a pack-horse in his great affairs."—*King Richard III* I, 3.

C'est son [grand] cheval de bataille, It is his pet argument.

C'est un cheval de bât, He is a blockhead.

C'est un cheval échappé, He is a scapegrace *or* a wild and reckless young man.

C'est un cheval pour le travail *ou* un cheval à la besogne, He is a glutton for work.

Être à cheval sur quelque chose (*fig.*), To be a stickler for something.

Monter sur ses grands chevaux, To ride (*or* To mount) the high horse.

Un cheval de retour, An old offender, An old lag, A gaol (*or* jail) bird.

See also APOCALYPSE, APPÉTIT, AVEUGLE, BON 48, BRIDE, BRIDER, ÉCRIRE, ÉCURIE, ENGRAISSER, FIÈVRE, FOIN, PARLER, PAS, REMÈDE, SELLE, TRAVAILLER, TROMPETTE.

chevalier. C'est le chevalier de la triste figure, He is a most dismal man *or* (*slang*) is a Dismal Desmond *or* a dismal Jimmy. " Poor fellow ! never joyed since the price of oats rose."—1 *King Henry IV* II, 1. *Note.*—Le Chevalier de la Triste-Figure, The Knight of the Rueful Countenance (*Don Quixote*).

Se conduire en vrai chevalier, To behave like a true gentleman.

Se faire le chevalier de quelqu'un, To champion someone's cause.

Un chevalier d'industrie, An adventurer, A swindler, A crook.

chevet. C'est mon livre de chevet, It is my bedside book.

Cet argument est son épée de chevet, He always falls back on that argument.

cheveu. Cela vient comme des cheveux sur la soupe, That is irrelevant to the matter in hand, That is foreign to the subject, You are flying (*or* going) off at a tangent.

Être en cheveux, To be hatless (*of a woman*).

Il n'a tenu qu'à un cheveu *ou* Il ne s'en est fallu que de l'épaisseur d'un cheveu, It very nearly came to pass *or* came off.

Prendre (*ou* Saisir) l'occasion aux cheveux, To take time (*or* the occasion) by the forelock, To seize the opportunity. " Let's take the instant by the forward top."—*All's Well That Ends Well* V, 3. (*Note.*—forward top = forelock.)

Se prendre aux cheveux, To have a tussle *or* a set-to, To come to blows.

See also DRESSER, ÉBÈNE, QUATRE, TIRER.

cheville. Il ne lui va pas à la cheville, He is not fit to (*or* He can't) hold a candle to him.

La cheville ouvrière (*fig.*), The mainspring, The master mind, The prime mover.

See also CLOU.

cheviller. Avoir l'âme chevillée dans le (*ou* au) corps, To be hard to kill, To have nine lives *or* as many lives as a cat. *Quotation under* DUR.

chèvre. *See* BROUTER, DANSER, MÉNAGER.

chez. Avoir un chez-soi, To have a home (*or* a house) of one's own. Quand j'aurai un chez-moi, When I have a home of my own. Quand vous aurez un chez-vous, When you have a home of your own. Il a maintenant un chez-lui, He now has a home of his own.

Faire comme chez soi, To make oneself at home.

Il n'y a pas de petit chez-soi, "Be it ever so humble, there's no place like home."—J. HOWARD PAYNE.

See also MAÎTRE, POINTE.

chic. Avoir du chic, To have style, To be stylish *or* smart.

C'est un chic bonhomme, He's a real good fellow, He's a brick (*slang*); He's a sport (*slang*).

Faire de chic, To work without a model (*of an artist*).

chicane. Chercher chicane à quelqu'un, To try to pick a quarrel with someone.

Des gens (*ou* Des hommes) de chicane, Pettifogging lawyers. " Why may not that be the skull of a lawyer? Where be his quiddits now, his quillets, his cases, his tenures, and his tricks?"—*Hamlet* V, 1.

chicaner. Chicaner le terrain, To dispute every inch of the ground.

chiche. Être chiche de louanges, To be sparing (*or* chary) of praise.

chien. Autant vaut être mordu d'un chien que d'une chienne, As well be hanged for a sheep as a lamb.

C'est le chien de Jean de Nivelle, il s'enfuit quand on l'appelle, He is like a will-o'-the-wisp, he runs away when you want him.

C'est saint Roch et son chien, They are always together, They are like David and Jonathan.

C'est un bon chien couchant, He is a thorough-going toad-eater, He's a proper toady.

C'est un mauvais chien, He is a harsh man. " *Shylock*. Thou call'dst me dog . . . But, since I am a dog, beware my fangs. . . . *Salarino*. It is the most impenetrable cur That ever kept with men."—*The Merchant of Venice* III, 3.

C'est un métier de chien, It is a toilsome trade, It is an arduous profession.

Entre chien et loup, In the twilight *or* gloaming.

Faire le chien après quelqu'un, To follow someone like a dog. " Knowing naught, like dogs, but following."—*King Lear* II, 2.

Faire le chien couchant auprès de quelqu'un, To toady (*or* To cringe) to (*or* To fawn on) someone. " Dogs, easily won to fawn on any man!" —*King Richard II* III, 2. " Why, what a candy deal of courtesy This fawning greyhound then did proffer me!"—1 *King Henry IV* I, 3.

Il est comme le chien du jardinier [qui ne mange point de choux et n'en laisse point manger aux autres], He is a dog in the manger.

Il fait un temps à ne pas mettre un chien dehors, The weather is not fit for a dog to be out in. " Good my lord, enter: The tyranny of the open night's too rough For nature to endure."—*King Lear* III, 4.

Il n'en donnerait pas (*ou* Il n'en jetterait pas) sa part aux chiens, He won't abandon his claim, give up his share, without a struggle.

Il ne faut point se moquer des chiens qu'on ne soit hors du village, Don't halloo (*or* shout) till you are out of the wood.

Il vient là comme un chien dans un jeu de quilles, He is [as] welcome as a dog on a racecourse *or* as a Derby dog *or* as snow in harvest.

Jeter (*ou* Donner) sa langue aux chiens, To give it (*the riddle*) up, To buy it.

Mener une vie de chien, To lead a dog's life.

Quand on veut noyer son chien, on dit qu'il a la rage *ou* Qui veut noyer son chien, l'accuse de la rage, Give a dog a bad (*or* an ill) name and hang him. " *Cinna the Poet*. I am Cinna the poet . . . I am not Cinna the conspirator. *Citizens*. It is no matter, his name's Cinna; pluck but his name out of his heart, and turn him going. Tear him, Tear him!"—*Julius Caesar* III, 3.

Quel chien, What a miser.

Recevoir quelqu'un comme un chien [dans un jeu de quilles], To give someone a cold welcome. " Unbidden guests Are often welcomest when they are gone."—1 *King Henry VI* II, 2.

S'accorder comme chien et chat *ou* comme chiens et chats, To fight like cat and dog.

Se regarder en chiens de faïence, To stare at each other with unseeing eyes *or* with eyes looking off into space, To look at each other with a vacant stare, To pretend to take no notice of each other. " They spake not a word ; But, like dumb statuas or breathing stones, Star'd each on other."—*King Richard III* III, 7.

Un chien de temps, Wretched (*or* Rotten) weather.

Un chien regarde bien un évêque, A cat may look at a king. " Heaven is here Where Juliet lives ; and every cat, and dog, And little mouse, every unworthy thing, Live here in heaven, and may look on her ; But Romeo may not."—*Romeo and Juliet* III, 3.

Une chienne de vie, A wretched (*or* A rotten) life.

Une querelle de chien, The devil of a row, The devil among the tailors.

Vivre comme chien et chat *ou* comme chiens et chats, To lead a cat and dog life.

See also ABOYER, AIMER, ATTACHE, BON 49, BRUIT, CHASSE, CHASSER, COLÈRE, COUCHER, FOU, FOUETTER, GARDER, HARGNEUX, LOUP, MAL, MORDRE, NAGER, OS, QUATRE, ROMPRE, SAUCISSE, TRAIN, VIE.

chiendent. Voilà le chiendent, There's the rub, That is the question. *Quotation under* QUESTION.

chienlit. À la chienlit ! What a guy (*he is*) !

chiffe. Il est mou comme une chiffe *ou* C'est une chiffe, He has no backbone, He is backboneless.

Se sentir mou comme une chiffe, To feel [as] limp as a rag.

chiffon. Causer (*ou* Parler) [de] chiffons, To talk [about] dress.

Un chiffon de papier, A scrap of paper (*a document whose contents are valueless, a negligible promise*).

chiffonner. Cela le chiffonne, That ruffles him.

Une petite mine chiffonnée, Pleasing but irregular features.

chiffre. *See* ZÉRO.

chignon. *See* CRÊPER.

chinois. *See* CASSE-TÊTE.

chinoiserie. Des chinoiseries [administratives], Red tape, Complicated formalities.

choisir. Ne choisit pas qui emprunte, Beggars can't be choosers.

See also CHAMP, COURT.

choix. *See* EMBARRAS.

chopper. Il a choppé lourdement, He has put his foot in it (*blundered badly*).

chorus. Faire chorus, To [repeat in] chorus.

chose. C'est chose faite, It is an accomplished fact.

Dites-lui, Dites-leur, bien des choses de ma part, Remember me kindly to him, to them.

Faire bien les choses, To do things well (*treat guests sumptuously, or the like*).

La chose publique, The common weal, The public welfare.

Parler (*ou* Causer) de choses et d'autres, To talk of one thing and another *or* of cabbages and kings.

See also APPELER, AUTRE, BIEN, DEMI, DIRE, IDÉE, JUGER, MONDE, NOMMER, OCCUPER, PRÈS, PROMETTRE, TOUTE, VOIR.

chou. Envoyer quelqu'un planter ses choux, To rusticate someone.

Faire d'une chose comme des choux

de son jardin, To make free of a thing.

Faire ses choux gras, To feather one's nest.

Faire ses choux gras de quelque chose, To fare sumptuously on something ; To do good business (*or* To do well) with something (*as a particular commodity or line of goods*).

Faites-en des choux et des raves, Do what you like with it.

Il est allé planter ses choux [chez lui], He is living a retired life in the country, He is rusticating.

See also CHIEN, MÉNAGER, RAMER, TONNER.

chrétien. *See* PARLER.

ciel. Tomber du ciel, To come as if sent from heaven (*of persons*) ; To fall from the clouds, To come as a godsend (*of things*).

Voir les cieux ouverts (*fig.*), To have a foretaste of heaven.

See also AIDER, AIRAIN, ALOUETTE, AVERTISSEMENT, CALOTTE, CATARACTE, COUP 73, ÉLEVER, MENACER, RAVIR, REMUER, VOÛTE.

cierge. *See* DEVOIR, DROIT.

ciller. Personne n'ose ciller devant lui, One scarcely dare breathe in his presence (*everyone fears him*).

cimaise. Faire à un tableau les honneurs de la cimaise, To accord to a picture the honour of being hung on the line.

Poser un tableau sur la cimaise, To hang a picture on the line.

ciment. *See* CHAUX.

cinq. *See* PIED, SEC.

cinquième. C'est une cinquième roue à un carrosse, It (He) is the fifth wheel of a coach (*entirely unnecessary*).

circuit. Un circuit de paroles, A circumlocution.

cire. C'est une cire molle, He (She) can be moulded like wax. " Have wrought the easy-melting king like wax."—3 *King Henry VI* II, 1.

Manier quelqu'un comme de la cire, To mould someone like wax.

See also JAUNE.

ciseau. Les ciseaux de la Parque (*Mythology*), The shears of Atropos (*which cut the thread of life*). " Till the Destinies do cut his thread of life."—*Pericles, Prince of Tyre* I, 2. " Then death rock me asleep, abridge my doleful days ! Why, then, let grievous, ghastly, gaping wounds Untwine the Sisters Three ! Come, Atropos, I say ! "—2 *King Henry IV* II, 4. " O Sisters Three, Come, come to me, With hands as pale as milk ; Lay them in gore, Since you have shore With shears his thread of silk."—*A Midsummer Night's Dream* V, 1. " O fates, come, come ; Cut thread and thrum."—*A Midsummer Night's Dream* V, 1.

Un ouvrage de ciseau, A work of sculpture.

See also COUP 41.

citer. *See* ORDRE.

clair. Être clair comme eau de roche, To be [as] clear as crystal. " O Helen, goddess, nymph, perfect, divine! To what, my love, shall I compare thine eyne ? Crystal is muddy."—*A Midsummer Night's Dream* III, 2.

Être clair comme le jour *ou* comme deux et deux font quatre, To be [as] clear as the day *or* as daylight *or* as noonday, To be [as] plain as a pikestaff *or* [as] plain as the nose in your face. " As clear as is the summer's sun."—*King Henry V* I, 2. " Plain as way to parish church." —*As You Like It* II, 7. " Yet but three ? Come one more, Two of both kinds makes up four." — *A Midsummer Night's Dream* III, 2.

Gagner, clair et net, tant de francs dans une affaire, To clear so many francs out of a deal.

Mettre le sabre au clair, To draw the sword.

Parler clair et net, To speak plainly *or* frankly. " Though I cannot be said to be a flattering honest man, it must not be denied that I am a plain-dealing villain."—*Much Ado About Nothing* I, 3.

Sabre au clair, With drawn sword (*of one person*), With drawn swords (*of several or many persons*).

Tirer au clair un fait, To elicit a fact.

Tirer au clair une affaire, une difficulté, To clear up a matter, a difficulty.

Voilà qui est clair et net, It is all clear and straightforward.

Voir clair dans une affaire, To understand a matter clearly.

See also HAUT, TAUPE.

claque. *See* TÊTE.

claquer. Faire claquer son fouet, To assert one's authority, To throw one's weight about.

claques. *See* CLIQUES.

claquet. La langue lui va comme un claquet de moulin, His (Her) tongue never ceases wagging.

clarté. Avoir des clartés de tout, To have general knowledge, To be well-informed.

classe. Faire la classe, To teach (*in a school*).

Faire ses classes, To be at school.

L'esprit de classe, Class consciousness.

La lutte des classes, Class war[fare].

clef. Avoir la clef des champs, To be free to go anywhere.

C'est la clef de [la] voûte, It is the keystone (*central principle, etc., on which all depends*).

Donner la clef des champs à quelqu'un, à un oiseau, To set someone, a bird, at liberty.

Mettre la clef sous la porte, To abscond, To do a bolt *or* (*slang*) a bunk.

Prendre la clef des champs, To bolt, To skedaddle, To [do a] bunk (*slang*).

Tenir la clef de l'énigme, To have the key to the riddle.

clerc. Faire un pas de clerc, To [make a] blunder, To put one's foot in it.

cliques. Prendre ses cliques et ses claques, To clear out, bag and baggage.

cliquetis. Un cliquetis de mots, A jingle of words.

cloaque. C'est un cloaque de vices *ou* un cloaque de tous les vices *ou* un cloaque d'impureté, It (*as a town*) is a sink (*or* a cesspool) of iniquity ; He (She) is sunk in vice.

cloche. *See* DÉMÉNAGER, ÉLEVER, ENTENDRE.

clocher. Des rivalités de clocher, Petty local jealousies.

Il n'a jamais perdu de vue le clocher de son village, He is an untravelled man. " Which would be great impeachment in his age, In having known no travel in his youth."—*Two Gentlemen of Verona* I, 3.

Il n'a vu que le clocher de son village, He knows nothing of the world. " He cannot be a perfect man Not being tried and tutor'd in the world."—*Two Gentlemen of Verona* I, 3.

Il y a quelque chose qui cloche, There is a screw loose somewhere, There is something amiss.

La politique de clocher, Parish-pump politics.

See also BOITEUX.

clore. Clore la bouche (*ou* le bec) à quelqu'un, To silence someone, To shut someone up. *Cf.* Bouche close, *under* BOUCHE.

clou. C'est le clou de la fête, That is the star turn (*or* the chief attraction) [of the entertainment].

Cela ne tient ni à fer ni à clou, That is very insecure *or* rickety.

Cela ne vaut pas un clou, That is

not worth a hang *or* damn *or* a tinker's dam[n] *or* a scrap.

Être au clou, To be in clink.

Il ne manque pas un clou à cette maison, This house is perfect in every respect.

Il tient ni à clou ni à cheville, He is in very feeble health, His health is in a very rickety state.

Mettre une chose au clou, To give up using a thing ; To put something up the spout (*pawn it*).

See also CHASSER, COMPTER, MAIGRE, RIVER.

clouer. Clouer la bouche (*ou* le bec) à quelqu'un, To silence someone, To shut someone up.

See also PAVILLON.

cocagne. *See* PAYS, VIE.

coche. *See* MANQUER, MOUCHE.

cocher. *See* FOUETTER.

cochon. *See* GARDER, JOUER.

coco. C'est un vilain coco, He's a most objectionable person.

code. C'est dans le code, It is the law of the land.

Se tenir dans les marges du code, To keep within the law *or* on the windy side of the law.

cœur. Avoir à cœur de faire quelque chose, To be bent (*or* set) (*or* To have one's heart set) on doing something.

Avoir du cœur au ventre, To have plenty of courage *or* pluck. " With hearts in their bellies no bigger than pins' heads."—1 *King Henry IV* IV, 2.

Avoir [le] cœur au métier *ou* à l'ouvrage, To have one's heart in one's work.

Avoir le (*ou* un) cœur de pierre *ou* de roche *ou* de marbre *ou* d'airain *ou* d'acier, To have a heart of stone *or* a stony (*or* a marble) heart *or* a heart of steel, To be stony-hearted *or* hard-hearted. " And pluck commiseration of his state From brassy bosoms and rough hearts of flint."—*Merchant of Venice* IV, 1. " One whose hard heart is button'd up with steel."—*Comedy of Errors* IV, 2. " No doubt the murderous knife was dull and blunt Till it was whetted on thy stone-hard heart."—*King Richard III* IV, 4. " Her tears will pierce into a marble heart."—3 *King Henry VI* III, 1.

Avoir quelque chose sur le cœur, To have something on one's mind ; To harbour resentment ; To have something (*some food*) lying heavy on one's stomach : J'ai encore mon dîner sur le cœur, My dinner still lies heavy on my stomach.

Avoir un cœur de lion, To be lion-hearted. " Richard, that robb'd the lion of his heart, And fought the holy wars in Palestine."—*King John* II, 1. " Be lion-mettled, proud; and take no care Who chafes, who frets, or where conspirers are."—*Macbeth* IV, 1. " Care I for the limb, the thews, the stature, bulk, and big assemblance of a man ! Give me the spirit, Master Shallow."—2 *King Henry IV* III, 2.

Avoir un cœur de poule, To be chicken-hearted. " Lord have mercy on thee for a hen ! "—*All's Well That Ends Well* II, 3.

Avoir un cœur de tigre, To have a tiger's heart (*be very cruel*). " O tiger's heart wrapp'd in a woman's hide ! "—3 *King Henry VI* I, 4.

C'est un cœur d'or, He (She) has a heart of gold.

Elle est son amie de cœur, She is his sweetheart *or* (*slang*) his best girl. " I mean, that my heart unto yours is knit ; So that but one heart we can make of it : Two bosoms interchainèd with an oath; So then two bosoms and a single troth."—*A Midsummer Night's Dream* II, 3.

En avoir le cœur net, To get to the

bottom of it, To know the rights of it, To clear the matter up.

Être dans la joie de son cœur, To be beside oneself with joy. " More dances my rapt heart Than when I first my wedded mistress saw."—*Coriolanus* IV, 5.

Être tout cœur, To be all heart, To have a heart bigger than one's body.

Il a un grand cœur *ou* C'est un grand cœur, He is a great-hearted man. " Fare thee well, great heart !— . . . this earth that bears thee dead Bears not alive so stout a gentleman."—1 *King Henry IV* V, 4.

Il est son ami de cœur, He is her sweetheart *or* (*slang*) her best boy.

Ils sont amis de cœur, They are bosom friends. " The friends thou hast, and their adoption tried, Grapple them to thy soul with hoops of steel."—*Hamlet* I, 3. " Keep thy friend Under thy own life's key."—*All's Well That Ends Well* I, 1.

Mettre le cœur au ventre à quelqu'un, To put heart into (*or* To hearten) someone, To buck someone up (*slang*).

Remettre le cœur au ventre à quelqu'un, To put fresh heart into someone. " Give renew'd fire to our extincted spirits."—*Othello* II, 1.

S'en donner à cœur joie, To enjoy oneself to the full, To have a good time.

Savoir un homme par cœur, To know a man through and through.

Si le cœur vous en dit, If you feel like it *or* feel so inclined, If you have a mind to *or* are so minded, If it appeals to you. Le cœur vous en dit-il ? Do you feel like it ? *and so on.*

Tourner sur le cœur, To turn the stomach . Ce qu'il a mangé lui a tourné sur le cœur, What he has eaten has turned his stomach.

Une affaire de cœur, A love affair.

See also ABONDANCE, AMER, ARRACHER, BLESSER, BON 22, 43, BONDIR, BOUCHE, BRONZER, CREVER, DÉCHARGER, DEMEURER, DESSÉCHER, DÉTOUR, DILATER, DÎNER, DIRE, EFFUSION, FADE, FENDRE, FERMER, FOND, GAIETÉ, HAUT, JOLI, LÈVRE, LOIN, MAIN, MAL, MAUVAIS, ŒIL, OUVERTURE, OUVRIR, PESER, PLACER, PLI, POIGNARD, PORTER, PRENDRE, RESTER, RIRE, RONGER, SERREMENT, SERRER, TENIR, TRANSPERCER.

coffre. Avoir le coffre bon *ou* Avoir un bon coffre, To be sound in wind and stomach, To have a good wind (*breath as needed in exertion*).

cognée. Mettre la cognée à l'arbre, To set to work (*especially to demolish something*). " We set the axe to thy usurping root."—3 *King Henry VI* II, 2.

See also MANCHE.

cogner. *See* MUR.

coiffer. Coiffer sainte Catherine, To remain single (*of a woman*)

Se coiffer de quelqu'un, de quelque chose, To become (*or* To be) infatuated with someone, with something.

See also NAÎTRE.

coin. Cet homme a la mine de demander l'aumône au coin d'un bois, This man looks like a burglar.

Les quatre coins de la terre, The four corners of the earth. " By the four opposing coigns Which the world together joins."—*Pericles, Prince of Tyre* Act III (*Dumb Show*).

See also FRAPPER, MOURIR.

coincer. Être coincé (*fig.*), To be cornered.

coing. *See* JAUNE.

Colas. *See* VACHE.

colère. Être dans une colère bleue *ou* Avoir une colère de chien, To be in a towering rage *or* in the devil of a rage. " Scarce can I speak, my choler is so great: O, I could hew up rocks and fight with flint."—2 *King Henry VI* V, 1.

See also CUVER, LÂCHER, PETIT.

colique. Avoir la colique, To have the wind up, To be in a blue funk (*all slang*).

collège. Cela sent le collège, That smacks (*or* savours) of pedantry.

Il sent encore son collège, He still has school-boy ways about him.

coller. Coller quelqu'un, To floor (*or* To stump) someone.

See also OS.

collet. Être collet monté, To be prim and proper, To be strait-laced, To be starchy (*fig.*).

Prêter le collet à quelqu'un, To come forward and fight someone.

collier. Donner à plein collier dans . . ., To throw oneself [heart and soul] into (*an enterprise*); To embrace (*a doctrine, etc.*) eagerly.

Être franc du collier, To be self-reliant; To pull one's weight (*be no shirker*). *Quotation under* METTRE.

Reprendre le collier [de misère], To get back into harness, To go back to drudgery (*uncongenial work*).

See also COUP 25.

colporteur. Un colporteur de nouvelles, A newsmonger.

combat. Le combat d'intérêts, The clash of interests.

Le combat des éléments, The war of the elements.

See also FINIR, HORS, SOUTENIR.

combattre. Combattre de politesse, de générosité, etc., avec quelqu'un, To vie with someone in politeness, in generosity, etc.

See also CORPS, COURTOIS.

comble. C'est le comble [de nos maux], It is the last straw.

C'est le comble du ridicule, It is the height of absurdity.

La mesure est comble, The measure is full, The sands have run out (*punishment for his many crimes awaits him*).

Pour comble, To crown all.

Pour comble [de malheur], As a crowning misfortune, To make matters worse.

combler. C'est un homme comblé, He has all his heart's desires. " Everything lies level to our wish." —2 *King Henry IV* IV, 4.

comédie. C'est un [vrai] personnage de comédie, He (She) shouldn't be taken seriously.

C'est une [vraie] comédie, It is [altogether] ludicrous (*to speak, to act, like that*).

Donner la comédie [aux gens], To make a laughing-stock of oneself; To poke fun [at people].

Jouer la comédie à quelqu'un, To act a part before someone, To be only pretending; To poke fun at someone. *Quotation under* RIDICULE.

Tout cela est comédie, All that is pretence *or* a sham.

Une comédie de cape et d'épée, A comedy of the age of chivalry.

See also SECRET.

comédien. Il est bon comédien, He is a good actor (*is merely acting the part to serve his own interests*).

comique. Avoir du comique dans l'esprit, To have a comical turn of mind.

Avoir du comique dans la figure, To have a funny (*or* laughing) face.

Avoir le masque comique, To have the face of a comedian.

C'est le comique de la troupe, He is the funny man of the company *or* party (*persons assembled socially*).

comité. En petit comité, Informally (*without ceremony*): Se réunir, Dîner, en petit comité, To meet, To dine, informally.

commande. Un sourire de commande, A feigned (*or* A forced) smile.

commander. *See* BAGUETTE.

comme. C'est tout comme, It comes (*or* It amounts) to that.

See also ALORS, COUCHER, DIRE, ÊTRE, FAIRE, RETROUVER, RIEN, TANT.

commencement. Il y a commencement à tout, Everything has a beginning.

commencer. A moitié fait qui commence bien, Well begun is half done.

Commencer la danse *ou* le branle (*fig.*), To take the lead, To set the ball [a-]rolling, To open the ball; To be the first to suffer.

See also CHARITÉ.

comment. *See* DIRE, SAVOIR.

commentaire. Cela (*ou* Voilà qui) se passe de commentaire, Comment is needless.

Point de commentaire, No answering back (*or, slang,* No back-chat), please.

commerce. Être d'un commerce agréable *ou* d'un bon commerce, To be easy to get on with, To be pleasant to deal with.

Être d'un commerce sûr, To know how to keep a secret, To be discreet.

Faire un mauvais (*ou* un méchant) (*ou* un vilain) commerce, To be mixed up in (*or* with) shady dealings.

commercer. Commercer avec quelqu'un (*fig.*), To hold intercourse (*or* To have dealings) with someone.

commère. Une rusée commère, A knowing woman.

See also COMPÈRE.

commode. C'est un homme qui n'est pas commode, He is a man who is not easy to get on with, He is a hard nut to crack; He is a man who can't take a joke.

Être commode à vivre, To be easy to get on with, To be pleasant to deal with.

commun. Être du commun des martyrs, To be of the common run of men, To be a very ordinary person. " All the courses of my life do show I am not in the roll of common men."—1 *King Henry IV* III, 1.

Faire bourse commune, To share expenses, To pool resources.

Faire cause commune avec quelqu'un, To make common cause with someone, To join hands.

Faire vie commune, To live together and share expenses.

Vivre sur le commun, To live at the common expense (*not bearing one's share*).

See also ÂNE, ANNÉE, SOUFFLET.

compagnie. Être de bonne compagnie, de mauvaise compagnie, To be well-bred, ill-bred.

Par compagnie, on se fait pendre, You cannot touch pitch without being defiled, He must have a long spoon that sups with the devil. " There is a thing, Harry, which thou hast often heard of, and it is known to many in our land by the name of pitch: this pitch, as ancient writers do report, doth defile; so doth the company thou keepest."—1 *King Henry IV* II, 4. " Marry, he must have a long spoon that must eat with the devil."—*The Comedy of Errors* IV, 3.

See also DÉFRAYER, FAUSSER, QUITTER.

compagnon. C'est un bon compagnon, He is a jolly fellow.

C'est un hardi compagnon, He is a man of deeds.

C'est un petit compagnon, He cuts a sorry figure.

Vivre avec quelqu'un (*ou* Traiter quelqu'un) de pair à compagnon *ou* Être compère et compagnon avec quelqu'un, To be hail fellow well met with someone.

compas. Avoir le compas dans l'œil, To have an accurate (*or* a sure) eye (*for measurements*).

Faire toutes choses par règle et par compas *ou* par compas et par mesure, To do everything strictly according to rule.

compère. C'est un bon compère, He is a jolly fellow.

C'est un rusé compère, He is a knowing card.

Tout va par compère et par commère, It all goes (*in that administration*) by favouritism and recommendation.

See also COMPAGNON.

complet. *See* FOUR.

compliment. Je vous en fais mon compliment, Allow me to congratulate you on having made a prize blunder.

Sans compliment, No compliments (*please*) ; Candidly. "Come, come ; sans compliment, what news abroad ?"—*King John* V, 6.

See also DUO, RENGAINER.

composer. Une société bien composée, A select company [of people].

See also ALMANACH.

composition. Il est de bonne (*ou* de facile) composition, He is easy to deal with.

Il est de difficile composition, He is hard to deal with, He is a hard nut to crack.

compote. Avoir les yeux, la tête, etc., en compote, To have one's eyes, one's head, etc., bashed in.

comprendre. *See* GOUTTE.

comptable. Être comptable à quelqu'un de ses actions, To be accountable to someone for one's actions. " Peradventure, I stand accountant for as great a sin."—*Othello* II, 1.

comptant. Argent comptant porte médecine, Money cures all ills. " Why, nothing comes amiss, so money comes withal."—*The Taming of the Shrew* I, 2.

Avoir de l'esprit argent comptant, To be quick at repartee.

C'est de l'argent comptant, It is as good as ready money.

Payer comptant (*fig.*), To make a prompt return (*of good or bad treatment*).

Prendre quelque chose pour argent comptant, To take something for gospel [truth], To take something in.

compte. À ce compte-là, In that case, On that score, At that rate, That being so.

Cela n'entre pas en ligne de compte, That need not be taken into consideration, That has nothing to do with it *or* with the matter.

De compte fait (*fig.*) *ou* Tout compte fait, All things considered, Taking everything into account.

Donner son compte à quelqu'un, To pay someone off ; To hand someone his (her) card (*dismiss him, her*) ; To settle someone's hash.

Erreur n'est pas (*ou* ne fait pas) compte, Errors are always excepted (*can be corrected*). " Omittance is not quittance."—*As You Like It* III, 5.

Il en a [pour] son compte *ou* Il en a reçu pour son compte *ou* On lui en a donné pour son compte, He has suffered a severe blow, He has got it in the neck (*slang*).

Le prendre sur son compte de faire quelque chose, To take it upon oneself to do something.

Mettre (*ou* Faire entrer) quelque chose en ligne de compte, To take something into account *or* into consideration, To bear something in mind, To make allowances for something.

Passer sur le compte de, To set to the account of, To impute to.

Y trouver son compte, To profit by it, To do (*one*) good, To pay : N'offensez pas cet homme-là, vous n'y trouveriez pas votre compte, Do not offend that man, it would do you no good *or* it wouldn't pay.

See also APOTHICAIRE, AVOIR, BON 29, 34, 53, 67, BOUT, LAISSER, LOIN, RÉGLER, REVENIR, TENIR.

compter. Compter les clous de la porte, To cool (*or* To kick) one's heels on the doorstep.

Compter les morceaux, To watch the mouthfuls (*how much someone is eating*) ; To watch every penny someone is spending.

Compter les morceaux à quelqu'un, To allow someone only bare necessaries.

Compter ses pas, To walk slowly, To dawdle ; To go reluctantly.

Compter tous les pas de quelqu'un (*fig.*), To watch someone's every step *or* move.

Les, Nos, instants sont comptés, The, Our, sands are running out. " Now our sands are almost run ; More a little, and then done."—*Pericles, Prince of Tyre* V, 2, *Induction.* (*Note.—Some editions of Shakespeare give* " and then dumb.")

Qui compte sans son hôte, compte deux fois, Don't reckon without your host.

Sans compter ; Without stint ; Not counting . . ., Not to mention . . ., Let alone . . .

Savoir compter (*fig.*), To know how to look after number one (*oneself*).

Ses jours sont comptés, His days (*or* The sands) are numbered, His number is going up, He has not many days to live. " The sands are number'd that make up my life ; Here must I stay, and here my life must end."—3 *King Henry VI* I, 4.

Tout [bien] compté *ou* Tout compté, tout rabattu *ou* Tout bien compté et rabattu, Taking everything into account, After making every allowance, All things considered.

See also CÔTE, LOUP, MARCHER.

conclure. *See* LÉGER, MARCHÉ.

condamner. C'est un malade condamné, (*if a woman*) une malade condamnée, The patient['s life] is despaired of, It is a hopeless case.

Condamner quelqu'un sur l'étiquette [du sac] *ou* Condamner quelqu'un sans connaissance de cause, To condemn someone unheard *or* without a hearing.

Condamner un (une) malade, To give up (*or* To despair of) a sick person *or* a patient.

See also BÊTE.

condition. Entrer, Être, en condition, To go into, To be in (*domestic*) service.

conduire. *See* AVEUGLE, BARQUE, CHEVALIER, TOMBEAU, VUE.

conduite. Avoir de la conduite, To be well-behaved.

confesser. *See* DIABLE, PARDONNER.

confession. Confier quelque chose à quelqu'un sous le sceau de la confession, To confide something to someone under the seal of confession *or* of confidence *or* of silence.

On lui donnerait le bon Dieu sans confession, Butter wouldn't melt in his (her) mouth.

confirmer. *See* EXCEPTION.

confisquer. Confisquer quelqu'un, To enslave someone (*bring under dominant influence*).

connaissance. Agir en connaissance de cause, To act with full knowledge of the case, To know what one is about.

Être en âge de connaissance, To have arrived at years of discretion.

Être (*ou* Se trouver) en pays de connaissance, To be among people one knows, To feel at home ; To be on familiar ground.

Parler avec connaissance de cause, To speak with full knowledge of the facts, To know what one is talking about.

Une figure de connaissance, A familiar face.

See also BIEN, CONDAMNER, HAUTEUR, MEUBLER.

connaître. Connais-toi toi-même, Know thyself. " Once read thy own breast right, And thou hast done with fears ; Man gets no other light, Search he a thousand years. Sink in thyself! there ask what ails thee at that shrine."—MATTHEW ARNOLD, *Empedocles on Etna* I, 2.

Je ne connais cette personne ni de près ni de loin, I have not the slightest notion (*or* the foggiest idea) who that person is.

Je ne connais pas la couleur de ses paroles, He has never spoken a word to me.

Je ne connais pas la couleur de son argent, I have never seen the colour of his money.

Je ne connais que cela, And there's an end of it, And done with [it]: Il faut que vous obéissiez, je ne connais que cela, You will have to obey, and there's an end of it. Il résiste, châtiez-le, je ne connais que cela, He refuses to obey, punish him and done with [it].

Je ne m'y connais plus, I am all adrift *or* all at sea.

Ne point (*ou* Ne plus) se connaître *ou* Ne connaître plus rien, Not to know what one is doing, To lose control of oneself, To be beside oneself, To know no bounds: Il ne se connaît plus de joie, He is beside himself with joy, His joy knows no bounds. Sa fureur ne connaît plus rien, His fury knows no bounds, He is beside himself with rage.

Savoir se connaître, To know how to control oneself.

Se faire connaître, To make known (*or* To announce) one's identity, To introduce oneself; To become known, To come to the front (*as an author*).

See also AIR, ARTISAN, BESOIN, DESSOUS, ÈVE, GAGNER, LOUP, MALHEUR, MONDE, POCHE, RAISON, TERRAIN.

conquérant. Avoir l'air conquérant, To have a swaggering air; To be a lady-killer.

conquête. *See* VIVRE.

consacrer. Consacrer ses veilles au travail, To burn the midnight oil.

conscience. C'est conscience de faire telle chose, One is lo[a]th (*or* It goes against one's conscience) to do such a thing.

Mettre la main sur la conscience, To search one's conscience.

Se faire un cas de conscience (*ou* Se faire conscience) d'une chose, To scruple (*or* To be lo[a]th) to do a thing.

See also ACQUIT, ACQUITTER, CAPITULER, DÉCHARGER, DESCENDRE, ENCHÈRE, LARGE, NET, OREILLER.

conscrit. C'est un conscrit (*fig.*), He is a novice *or* a tyro.

conseil. *See* NUIT, OREILLER, PARTI.

conseilleur. Les conseilleurs ne sont pas les payeurs, Advisers run no risks.

consentir. Qui ne dit mot consent, Silence gives consent.

conséquence. C'est un homme sans conséquence, He is a man of no consequence *or* of no importance.

Tirer à conséquence, To be [taken as] a precedent.

conserver. Conserver [toute] sa tête, To retain [all] one's faculties (*in old age*); To keep one's head (*in a critical situation*).

Conserver un ressentiment contre quelqu'un de quelque chose, To harbour resentment against someone (*or* To bear someone malice) for something.

See also DISTANCE, INDIVIDU.

considérer. Tout bien considéré, All things considered, Taking everything into account.

consigner. Consigner quelqu'un à la (*ou* à sa) porte *ou* Consigner la (*ou* sa) porte à quelqu'un, To give orders that someone is not to be admitted. (*Note.*—To show someone the door *is* Mettre quelqu'un à la porte.)

Consigner sa porte, To refuse admittance to everyone.

consistance. C'est un homme sans consistance dans le monde, He is a man of no standing in the world.

Prendre (*ou* Acquérir) de la consistance (*fig.*), To be gaining credit (*as a rumour*).

consolation. *See* FICHE.

conspuer. Conspuer quelqu'un, To hiss (*or* To hoot) (*or* To boo) someone, To give someone the bird (*slang*).

Être conspué, To be hissed *or* hooted *or* booed, To get the bird (*slang*).

constellation. *See* NAÎTRE.

constituer. Se constituer prisonnier, To give oneself up.

consulter. Consulter le (*ou* son) miroir, To have a look at oneself in the glass. " It is not vainglory for a man and his glass to confer in his own chamber."—*Cymbeline* IV, 1. " But I,—that am not shap'd for sportive tricks, Nor made to court an amorous looking-glass." —*King Richard III* I, 1. " Shine out, fair sun, till I have bought a glass, That I may see my shadow as I pass."—*King Richard III* I, 2.

Consulter ses forces, To take stock of one's strength *or* resources.

See also OREILLER.

contagieux. *See* AIR.

conte. *See* BLEU, FAIRE.

contenance. *See* BON 42, 43, EMPÊCHER.

content. Avoir son content d'une chose, To have had enough of a thing.

Être content de soi, To be pleased with oneself, To be self-satisfied *or* self-complacent (*pleased with the way one has acted*).

Être content de soi *ou* Être content de sa [petite] personne, To be very pleased with one's own [sweet] self, To be self-conceited. " She cannot love, Nor take no shape nor project of affection, She is so self-endeared."—*Much Ado About Nothing* III, 1.

Il est on ne peut plus content, He is [as] pleased as can be, He is [as] pleased as Punch.

contentement. Contentement passe richesse, Contentment is better than riches. " Poor and content is rich, and rich enough; But riches fineless is as poor as winter To him that ever fears he shall be poor."—*Othello* III, 3. (*Note.*—fineless = without end). " My crown is in my heart, not on my head ; Not deck'd with diamonds and Indian stones, Nor to be seen: my crown is call'd content,—A crown it is that seldom kings enjoy."—3 *King Henry VI* III, 1.

conter. En avoir long à conter, To have a long story to tell.

En conter (*ou* Conter fleurette[s] *ou* des fleurettes) à une femme, To court (*or* To make love to) a woman, To whisper soft nothings to a woman.

En conter [de belles] à quelqu'un, To pull someone's leg ; To tell someone some fine tales *or* some tall stories, To draw the long bow.

See also AILLEURS, HISTOIRE.

contre. J'étais tout contre, I was close by *or* hard by.

contremarche. *See* EXÉCUTER.

contre-poil. Prendre quelqu'un à contre-poil, To rub someone [up] the wrong way.

convenance. Pour des raisons de convenance, On grounds of expediency.

convenir. *See* NOTE.

conversation. Être à la conversation, To attend (*or* To give heed) [to the conversation].

See also DÉ, DÉFRAYER, EMPARER (S'), RAMENER, TOMBER.

convertir. *See* PRÊCHER.

convoquer. *See* BAN.

coq. Être (*ou* Vivre) comme un coq en pâte, To live like a fighting cock.

Faire un coq-à-l'âne, To tell a cock-and-bull story.

Le coq du village *ou* de la paroisse, The cock of the walk.

Passer du coq à l'âne, To fly (*or* To go) off at a tangent (*fig.*).

See also FIER, HARDI, JAMBE, ROUGE.

coque. *See* SORTIR.

coqueluche. Être la coqueluche de toutes les femmes, To be a great favourite among the ladies.

coquille. *See* RENTRER, SORTIR.

corde. Avoir plusieurs cordes (*ou* plus d'une corde) à son arc, To have more than one string to one's bow.

Cela ne rentre pas dans mes cordes, That is not in my line.

Cet homme ne vaut pas la corde pour le pendre, This man is not worth powder and shot.

Il a de la corde de pendu dans sa poche, He has the devil's own luck.

Il ne faut pas trop tendre la corde *ou* trop tirer sur la corde, One must not carry things too far, Don't lay it on.

Il ne faut point parler de corde dans la maison d'un pendu, One must not mention hemp in the house of one who has been hanged, Do not allude to the skeleton in the cupboard.

La corde ne peut être toujours tendue, One must have some relaxation, All work and no play makes Jack a dull boy. " Nature does require Her times of preservation."—*King Henry VIII* III, 2. " Awhile to work, and after holiday."—*King Richard II* III, 1.

Les assiégés se rendirent la corde au cou, The besieged surrendered (*or* yielded) with halters on their necks. " He is fled, my lord, and all his powers do yield ; And humbly thus, with halters on their necks, Expect your highness' doom of life or death."—2 *King Henry VI* IV, 9.

Mettre la corde au cou à quelqu'un (*fig.*), To put a halter (*or* a noose) round someone's neck (*dominate him*).

Se mettre la corde au cou (*fig.*), To put a halter (*or* a noose) round one's own neck.

Tenir la corde, To have the advantage, To be in the lead, To be first favourite.

See also DANSER, SAC, TOUCHER, USER.

cordon. Il n'est pas digne de délier (*ou* de dénouer) les cordons des souliers d'un tel, He is not fit to hold a candle to so-and-so.

Un cordon bleu, A first-rate (*woman*) cook.

See also BARDER, BOURSE.

cordonnier. *See* CHAUSSER.

corne. Attaquer (*ou* Prendre) le taureau (*ou* le bœuf) (*ou* la bête) par les cornes, To take the bull by the horns.

See also MANGER, MONTRER, RENTRER.

corneille. Y aller comme une corneille qui abat des noix, To make wild shots at it, To work at it with misdirected enthusiasm.

See also BAYER.

corner. Corner quelque chose aux oreilles de quelqu'un, To din something into someone's ears.

Les oreilles ont bien dû vous corner, Your ears must have been burning *or* tingling (*we were talking about you*).

Les oreilles vous cornent, You're hearing things (*non-existent noises or remarks*).

cornu. Des visions cornues, Preposterous ideas.

corps. À corps perdu, Headlong.

À son corps défendant, In self-defence ; Against one's will, Reluctantly, Grudgingly, Under protest ; Under duress *or* coercion.

Combattre corps à corps, To fight hand to hand *or* at close quarters.

Passer sur le corps de quelqu'un, To pass over someone's head (*obtain situation to which he had automatic claim*). " 'Tis the curse of service, Preferment goes by letter and affection, And not by old gradation, where each second Stood heir to the first."—*Othello* I, 1.

Prendre corps, To take shape.

Prendre du corps, To put on flesh.

See also BOURREAU, CHEVILLER, DIABLE, DRÔLE, ESPRIT, OMBRE, RENTRER, TAILLER.

corriger. Corriger le hasard *ou* la fortune, To assist fortune (*cheat at play*).

See also TARD.

corsaire. *See* DEMI.

corser. L'affaire se corse, The plot thickens, Things (*or* Events) are taking a serious turn.

cortège. Les infirmités sont le cortège de la vieillesse, Infirmities are the accompaniment (*or* the concomitants) of old age. " Infirmity,—Which waits upon worn times."—*The Winter's Tale* V, 1. " Palsied eld."—*Measure for Measure* III, 1.

côte. Être à la côte, To be on one's beam-ends, To be on the rocks (*slang*). " Have all his ventures fail'd ? What ! not one hit ? . . . And not one vessel 'scape the dreadful touch Of merchant-marring rocks ?"—*The Merchant of Venice* III, 2.

On lui compterait les côtes, You can count his (her) (its, *animal's*) ribs, He (She) (It) is nothing but skin and bone *or* is nothing but a bag of bones.

Se tenir les côtes de rire, To hold one's sides with laughter. " Down topples she, And *tailor* cries, and falls into a cough ; And then the whole quire hold their hips and loffe."—*A Midsummer Night's Dream* II, 1. (*Note.*—And *tailor* cries : " The custom of crying tailor, at a sudden fall backwards, I think I remember to have observed. He that slips beside his chair falls as a tailor squats upon his board."—JOHNSON).

See also SERRER.

côté. Être à côté [de la question], To be beside the question.

Passer à côté d'une difficulté, To get round (*or* To evade) a difficulty.

See also BON 60, COUVERTURE, DEVOIR, LOUP, MANCHE, RANGER, RIEUR, TOURNER, VENT.

cothurne. *See* CHAUSSER.

coton. *See* ÉLEVER, FILER.

cotret. De l'huile de cotret (*fig.*), Strap oil.

See also SEC.

cou. *See* BRIDE, CASSER, CORDE, ENDETTER, PLONGER, PRENDRE, TENDRE.

couchant. Être (*ou* Toucher) à son couchant (*poetic*), To be on the decline *or* on the wane. *Quotations under* CRÉPUSCULE.

See also CHIEN.

coucher. Comme on fait son lit on se couche, One must lie in the bed one has made (*take consequences of one's acts*).

Se coucher comme les poules, To go to bed with the birds *or* with the sun (*very early*). " The marigold, that goes to bed with the sun."—*The Winter's Tale* IV, 3.

Se coucher en chien de fusil, To curl up in [one's] bed.

Un nom à coucher dehors, A crack-jaw name.

See also ALLER, CARREAU, ÉCRIT, ÉTOILE, PAILLE.

coude. De l'huile de coude (*fig.*), Elbow grease.

Se sentir (*ou* Se serrer) les coudes (*fig.*), To help one another.

See also JOUER, LEVER.

coudre. Des finesses consues de fil

blanc, Transparent artifices, Tricks easily seen through.

Être tout cousu d'or, To have one's pockets well lined, To be rolling in wealth *or* in money.

See also BOUCHE, PEAU.

coule. Être à la coule, To know the ropes *or* what's what.

couler. C'est un homme coulé, He is a ruined man.

Cela coule de source, It comes natural to him, her.

Couler des jours heureux, To pass (*or* To spend) some happy days. *Quotation under* BEAU 19.

Couler quelqu'un à fond, To silence someone ; To ruin someone utterly.

Il faut laisser couler l'eau, We must let things take their course, What cannot be cured must be endured. " What cannot be eschewed must be embraced."—*Merry Wives of Windsor* V, 5. " Things without all remedy Should be without regard."—*Macbeth* III, 2.

L'argent lui coule entre les doigts, The money runs through his fingers, He spends money like water.

See also CHAMEAU.

couleur. *See* AVEUGLE, CONNAÎTRE, DONNER, GOÛT, PARAÎTRE, PRENDRE, REVÊTIR, VOIR.

couleuvre. *See* AVALER, PARESSEUX.

coulisse. Se tenir dans la coulisse (*fig.*), To keep in the background (*while making others act*).

See also ŒIL, REGARDER.

couloir. *See* INTRIGUE, PROPOS.

coup. 1. À ce coup, This time, On this occasion.

2. À coup sûr, For a certainty. *Cf.* Jouer à coup sûr *below*.

3. À coups de cravache, By brute force.

4. À tous coups, On every possible occasion, At every opportunity.

5. Avoir du coup d'œil, To have good judgment.

6. Avoir le coup d'œil du peintre, du sculpteur, To see with an artist's eye, a sculptor's eye (*discern with his appreciation or discrimination*).

7. Avoir un coup d'œil excellent, To be able to take in the situation at a glance.

8. Avoir un coup de marteau, To be a bit touched *or* not quite all there.

9. C'est un coup de dé[s] (*fig.*), It's a toss-up (*mere chance*). " By the hazard of the spotted die."—*Timon of Athens* V, 6.

10. C'est un coup de poignard, It is a stab (*great shock, wounding or offensive remark*). " She speaks poniards, and every word stabs." —*Much Ado About Nothing* II, 1.

11. Ce fut un coup d'assommoir (*ou* un coup de massue) (*ou* un coup de foudre) (*ou* un coup de tonnerre) pour lui, This was a staggering blow (*or* a stunning blow) (*or* a crushing blow) (*or* a knock-out blow) (*or* a thunder-clap) (*or* a bolt from the blue) for him. *Cf.* En la (le) voyant, etc. *below*.

12. Cette nouvelle m'a donné un coup, The news gave me a shock *or* a turn *or* made me gasp.

13. Charger quelqu'un de coups, To belabour (*or* To thrash) someone.

14. Coup sur coup, One after (*or* on top of) the other (*in close succession*).

15. Donner (*ou* Porter) à quelqu'un le coup de grâce *ou* le dernier coup, To give someone the finishing stroke *or* his quietus.

16. Donner à quelqu'un un coup de boutoir, To give someone a stinger (*cutting remark or rebuke*).

17. Donner à quelqu'un un coup de caveçon, To take someone down a peg or two, To humiliate someone.

18. Donner à quelqu'un un (*ou* le) coup de Jarnac *ou* le coup de lapin, To stab someone in the back, To deal someone a treacherous blow,

To hit someone below the belt. " Whilst damned Casca, like a cur, behind, Struck Caesar on the neck."—*Julius Caesar* V, 1. " Durst thou have look'd upon him, being awake, And hast thou kill'd him sleeping ? O brave touch ! Could not a worm, an adder, do so much ? "—*A Midsummer Night's Dream* III, 2.

19. Donner le coup de pied de l'âne, To pluck a dead lion by the beard. " You are the hare of whom the proverb goes, Whose valour plucks dead lions by the beard."—*King John* II, 1.
20. Donner le dernier coup de lime (*ou* le [dernier] coup de pinceau) à un ouvrage, To give the finishing touch[es] to a work.
21. Donner un coup d'épaule (*fig.*), To give a lift *or* a [helping] hand.
22. Donner un coup d'œil à ce qui se passe, To have a look at what is going on.
23. Donner un coup de balai (*fig.*), To make a clean sweep.
24. Donner un coup de bec (*ou* un coup de dent) (*ou* un coup de langue) (*ou* un coup de patte) (*ou* un coup de griffe) à quelqu'un, To have a dig (*or* a fling) (*or* a slap) at someone, To give someone a slap in the face *or* a rap on the knuckles (*fig.*).
25. Donner un coup de collier (*fig.*), To put one's back into it, To make a special effort.
26. Donner un coup de main, To lend (*or* To bear) a hand.
27. Donner un coup de peigne à quelqu'un, To handle someone roughly. " We'll thwack him hence with distaffs."—*The Winter's Tale* I, 2.
28. Donner un coup de pied jusqu'à tel endroit, To just hop over to such or such a place.
29. Donner un coup de sonde, To see how the land lies, To put out a feeler, To feel one's way.
30. En la (le) voyant, il a eu (elle a eu) le coup de foudre, It was [a case of] love at first sight. " Who ever lov'd that lov'd not at first sight ?"—*As You Like It* III, 5. " So is mine eye enthralled to thy shape ; And thy fair virtue's force perforce doth move me, On the first view, to say, to swear, I love thee."—*A Midsummer Night's Dream* III, 1.
31. Encore un coup, Once again, Once more, The same again.
32. Être aux cent coups, To be in desperation.
33. Être dans son coup de feu, To be at one's busiest, To be rushed. " I have to-night despatched sixteen businesses, a month's length a-piece."—*All's Well That Ends Well* IV, 3.
34. Faire d'une pierre deux coups, To kill two birds with one stone.
35. Faire le coup de poing, To resort to fisticuffs.
36. Faire les cent coups, To be up to all sorts of tricks ; To kick up no end of a shindy, To raise Cain (*slang*) ; To paint the town red.
37. Faire un coup de main, To make a surprise attack (*Military*) ; (*Fig.*) To make a swift bold stroke *or* a lightning move.
38. Faire un coup de partie, To make a masterly move.
39. Faire un coup de tête, To act impulsively, To do something rash.
40. Faire un grand coup (*fig.*), To strike a decisive blow, To have a marked effect.
41. Faire un livre, un journal, à coups de ciseaux (*fig.*), To make a book, a [news]paper, with scissors and paste.
42. Faire un mauvais coup, To do a mischief.

43. Il a fait là un beau coup (*ironiquement*), He has made a nice mess of it, A nice mess he has made of it.
44. Il a fait un beau coup d'épée, He has committed an incredible folly.
45. Il est fait (*ou* est taillé) à coups de hache, He is a rough-hewn (*or* a ruggedly built) man.
46. Il n'y a qu'un coup de pied d'ici à tel endroit, It is only a step (*or* a short distance) from here to such place.
47. Jeter un coup d'œil sur quelque chose, To run one's eye (*or* To cast an eye *or* a glance) over something.
48. Jouer (*ou* Parier) à coup sûr, To bet on a certainty (*fig.*).
49. Juger des coups, To judge as an on-looker.
50. Monter le coup à quelqu'un, To take someone in, To have someone on. *Cf.* Un coup monté *below*.
51. Ne pas perdre un coup de dent, Not to miss a bite *or* a mouthful (*eat greedily*) ; Not to put oneself out (*take no special trouble*).
52. Ne pas se donner de coups de pied, To pat oneself on the back.
53. Porter coup (*fig.*), To tell, To take effect, To hit the mark, To go (*or* To strike) (*or* To hit) home. Le coup a porté, It struck home, That was a home-thrust.
54. Pour le (*ou* ce) (*ou* un) coup, This time, On this occasion ; For the moment, For the time being.
55. Recevoir plus de coups que de pain, To get more kicks than ha'pence.
56. Rendre coup pour coup, To hit back.
57. Risquer le coup, To chance it.
58. Sauver le premier coup d'œil, Not to betray one's first impressions, Not to give oneself away (*by one's looks*). " There is a kind of confession in your looks, which your modesties have not craft enough to colour."—*Hamlet* II, 2. " I saw his heart in his face."—*The Winter's Tale* I, 2.
59. Tenir le coup, To stand the racket, To face the music.
60. Tout d'un coup, All at once ; At one go, At one fell swoop ; In one bout, At a draught.
61. Traduire à coups de dictionnaire, To translate by looking up every other word in the dictionary.
62. Un coup d'audace, A piece of daring, A bold stroke.
63. Un coup d'autorité, An exertion of authority.
64. Un coup d'éclat, An outstanding (*or* A conspicuous) deed.
65. Un coup d'essai, A first attempt, A trial shot.
66. Un coup d'État, An unconstitutional change of government ; A bold piece of statesmanship ; An unexpected (*or* A bold) stroke of policy.
67. Un coup de filet (*fig.*), A haul, A sweep.
68. Un coup de force, A feat of strength.
69. Un coup de fouet (*fig.*), A stimulus *or* A fillip (*to the bodily system*).
70. Un coup de hasard *ou* Un coup de veine, A stroke of luck ; A mere chance, A fluke.
71. Un coup de maître, A master-stroke.
72. Un coup de théâtre, A stage trick ; A sensation[al event].
73. Un coup du ciel *ou* Un coup d'en haut *ou* Un coup de la Providence *ou* Un coup de la grâce, A special providence. " There's a special providence in the fall of a sparrow. If it be now, 'tis not to come." —*Hamlet* V, 2. " We, ignorant of ourselves, Beg often our own harms, which the wise powers Deny us for our good ; so find we profit By losing of our prayers."—*Antony and*

Cleopatra II, 1. " And that should teach us There's a divinity that shapes our ends, Rough-hew them how we will."—*Hamlet* V, 2.

74. Un coup monté, A pre-arranged affair, A put-up job.

75. Un coup raide comme balle, A blow straight from the shoulder. " O you leaden messengers, That ride upon the violent speed of fire, Fly with false aim."—*All's Well That Ends Well* III, 2.

76. Un ouvrage fait à coups de hache, A rough and ready piece of work.

77. Venir après coup, To come too late *or* after the event *or* a day after the fair. " That comfort comes too late ; 'Tis like a pardon after execution."—*King Henry VIII* IV, 2. " One day too late, . . . O, call back yesterday, bid time return, . . . To-day, to-day, unhappy day, too late."—*King Richard II* III, 2.

See also ATTENDRE, DONNER, EAU, ENCENSOIR, ENTRER, ÉPINGLE, FÉRIR, JOUER, MANQUER, MEURTRIR, PARER, PISTOLET, PREMIER, RAPPORTER, TENDRE, VENIR.

coupable. *See* AVOUER.

coupe. Être (*ou* Se trouver) sous la coupe de quelqu'un, To be under someone's thumb.

Il y a loin de la coupe aux lèvres *ou* Entre la coupe et les lèvres, There's many a slip 'twixt the cup and the lip.

See also BOIRE.

couper. Couper à quelqu'un sa journée, To upset someone's programme for the day.

Couper court, To cut it short.

Couper court à quelqu'un, à un entretien, To cut someone, an interview, short.

Couper dans le pont, To fall into the trap.

Couper la parole à quelqu'un, To cut someone short.

Couper la poire en deux, To split the difference, To meet someone half way.

Couper le sifflet à quelqu'un, To strangle (*or* To throttle) someone ; To stop someone's mouth, To shut someone up.

Il s'est coupé dans ses réponses, He contradicted himself (*or* gave himself away) in (*or* by) his replies.

On se coupe aisément quand on ne dit pas la vérité, One easily contradicts oneself (*or* gives oneself away) when one is not speaking the truth, Liars need good memories.

Se couper le nez pour faire dépit à son visage, To cut off one's nose to spite one's face.

See also BRAS, GORDIEN, HERBE, QUATRE, RACINE, TÊTE, VIF.

cour. C'est la cour du roi Pétaud [, chacun y est maître], It is bedlam let loose, It is a place of confusion [, as a household without a head *or* where everyone does as he likes, where everyone speaks at the same time].

Être bien en cour, To have friends at court (*See also* PARTI). " A friend i' the court is better than a penny in purse."—2 *King Henry IV* V, 1.

Faire sa cour aux dépens de quelqu'un, To curry favour at someone else's expense.

See also BÉNIR.

courage. *See* ARROSER, PRENDRE.

courant. Être au courant de l'affaire, To be in the know.

See also ÉCRIRE, NAGER.

courber. *See* ÉCHINE.

coureur. Un coureur de bals, A dancing man.

Un coureur de dots, A fortune hunter.

Un coureur de jetons de présence, A guinea pig (*person*).

Un coureur de prix, A pot hunter.

Un coureur de spectacles, A playgoer.

courir. Ce n'est pas le tout que de courir (*ou* Rien ne sert de courir), il faut partir de bonne heure *ou* il faut partir à point, Slow and steady (*or* and sure) wins the race, [The] more haste [the] less speed. *Quotations under* HÂTER.

Ce prédicateur est fort (*ou* est très) couru, This preacher is much sought after *or* is very popular.

Cette chanson court par la ville, This song is [all] the rage in the town.

Courir à la ruine, To be on the road to ruin.

Courir à sa fin, To be running out, To be nearing its end.

Courir après l'argent, To strive after (*making*) money.

Courir après les papillons, To amuse oneself with trifles.

Courir après son argent, To endeavour to recoup one's losses; To endeavour to collect one's money.

Courir après une ombre, To catch (*or* To clutch) at shadows. " Some there be that shadows kiss; Such have but a shadow's bliss."—*The Merchant of Venice* II, 9.

Courir comme un lapin, To run like a hare.

Courir comme un perdu, To run like mad.

Courir deux lièvres à la fois, To try to do two things at once.

Courir la fortune du pot, To take pot luck.

Courir le cachet, To give private lessons (*at pupils' homes*), To eke out a living by giving lessons.

Courir le même lièvre *ou* Courir même fortune, To be after the same thing, To have the same interests [at stake].

Courir le pays, le monde, To roam the country, the world, over.

Courir les rues, To be in everybody's mouth, To be the talk of the town, To be rife (*of news, stories, etc.*); To be found every day, To be as plentiful as blackberries.

Courir sus à quelqu'un, To fall upon (*attack*) someone, To go for someone (*slang*).

Courir une bordée, To go the round of the pubs, To go on the binge (*slang*). " Inquire at London, 'mongst the taverns there, For there, they say, he daily doth frequent, With unrestrained loose companions."—*King Richard II* V, 3.

Courir une carrière, To take (*or* To follow) a (*certain*) course (*line of conduct*).

Faire courir un bruit, To spread a rumour [abroad], To set a rumour afloat.

Il ne faut pas courir deux lièvres à la fois *ou* Qui court deux lièvres n'en prend aucun, It's no use (*or* no good) trying to do two things at once.

Je cours encore, I couldn't stand it any longer, I'm not having any more (*slang*).

La mode qui court, The present (*or* The prevailing) fashion.

Le bruit court que . . ., It is rumoured that . . ., Rumour has it that . . ., There is a report abroad that . . ., It is getting about that . . . " The bruit is, Hector's slain."—*Troilus and Cressida* V, 9. " At least, the whisper goes so."—*Hamlet* I, 1.

Maladies qui courent pendant l'hiver, Ailments that are rife in winter.

Par le temps qui court, Nowadays, As things are at present.

Son esprit court les champs, His wits are wandering.

See also BRIDE, ESPRIT, FEU, GALOP, HÔPITAL, JAMBE, POSTE, PRETENTAINE, PRESSER, VALOIR.

couronne. *See* FLEURON, PERLE, TRESSER.

couronner. La fin couronne l'œuvre, " The end crowns all."—*Troilus and Cressida* IV, 5. " *La fin couronne les œuvres.*"—2 *King Henry VI* V, 2. " All's well that ends well:

still the fine's the crown; Whate'er the course, the end is the renown." —*All's Well That Ends Well* IV, 4.

courroie. *See* ALLONGER.

courroux. Les flots en courroux (*poetic*), The raging sea, The angry waves. "As mad as the vex'd sea."—*King Lear* IV, 4. "And I have seen The ambitious ocean swell, and rage, and foam, To be exalted with the threat'ning clouds."—*Julius Caesar* I, 3. "Have I not seen the sea, puff'd up with winds, Rage like an angry boar chafed with sweat ?"—*The Taming of the Shrew* I, 2. "The chidden billow seems to pelt the clouds ; The wind-shak'd surge, with high and monstrous main, Seems to cast water on the burning Bear, And quench the guards of the ever-fixed pole : I never did like molestation view On the enchafed flood."—*Othello* II, 1.

cours. Donner [un] libre cours à sa douleur, To give free vent (*or* rein) to one's grief.

Laisser libre cours à la justice, To let justice (*or* the law) take its course.

court. Choisir une vie courte et bonne, To choose (*or* To believe in) a short life and a merry one.

Être à court [d'argent], To be short of money *or* (*slang*) of the ready, To be hard up. "I am heinously unprovided."—1 *King Henry IV* III, 3. *See also quotations under* BOURSE.

Être court de mémoire *ou* Avoir courte mémoire, To have a short memory.

Il veut la faire courte et bonne, He believes in a short life and a merry one.

La faire courte et bonne, To have a short life and a merry one. "Come, fill the Cup, and in the fire of Spring Your Winter-garment of Repentance fling : The Bird of Time has but a little way To flutter—and the Bird is on the Wing."—EDWARD FITZGERALD, *Rubaiyat of Omar Khayyam* VII.

Les plus courtes folies sont les meilleures, Short and sweet.

Pour [vous] le faire court *ou* Pour faire court, To cut a long story short, To cut it short, In a nutshell. "Short tale to make."—3 *King Henry VI* II, 1.

Prendre quelqu'un de court, To give someone too short notice, To catch someone unprepared.

Tenir quelqu'un de court, To keep a tight hold on someone, To keep someone under strict control.

Tout court, Merely, Only, Simply, That's all : Il me répondit un Non tout court, He replied "No" merely. (*See also* Demeurer [tout] court *under* DEMEURER.)

See also BRIDE, COUPER, ÉPÉE, HALEINE, HERBE, HONTE, PAILLE, PENDRE.

courtiser. *See* MOTIF.

courtois. Combattre quelqu'un à armes courtoises, To use someone with courtesy. "Let's fight with gentle words."—*King Richard II* III, 3. "I am one of those gentle ones that will use the devil himself with courtesy."—*Twelfth Night* IV, 2.

Une discussion à armes courtoises, A discussion without acrimony.

cousin. Le roi n'est pas son cousin, He thinks no small beer of himself.

couteau. Être à couteaux tirés avec quelqu'un, To be at daggers drawn with someone.

See also AIGUISER, GORGE, GUERRE.

coûter. Cela ne lui coûte guère, That is (*or* comes) easy to him.

Coûte que coûte, Cost what it may, At all costs, At any price. "What if my house be troubled with a rat, And I be pleas'd to give ten thousand ducats To have it baned ?"—*The Merchant of Venice* IV, 1. "A horse ! a horse ! my kingdom for a horse ! "—*King Richard III* V, 4.

L'argent ne lui coûte guère, He is very free with his money.

Rien ne lui coûte, He spares no effort, Nothing is too much trouble to him ; He doesn't know the meaning of the word impossible, He sticks at nothing. " Now bid me run, And I will strive with things impossible ; Yea, get the better of them."—*Julius Caesar* II, 1. (*Spoken by Caius Ligarius who was a sick man.*)

Tout lui coûte, He does nothing with a good grace.

See also GROS, ŒIL, PAS, TÊTE, TRAIN.

coutume. Une fois n'est pas coutume, Once in a way won't hurt.

See also AMENDE.

couture. *See* BATTRE.

couver. Couver des yeux, To look fondly at (*person*) ; To look longingly at (*thing*) ; To gloat over (*thing*).

Il faut laisser couver cela, That can wait, Let that sweat (*slang*).

See also FEU, POULE.

couvert. Avoir toujours son couvert mis dans une maison, chez quelqu'un, To be sure of a warm welcome in a house, at someone's house.

couverture. Tirer la couverture à soi *ou* de son côté, To take the lion's share, To look after number one.

couvrir. À mots couverts, Discreetly, With covert hints.

L'horizon se couvre (*fig.*), The horizon is clouding over, Something untoward is afoot. " Worthies, away, the scene begins to cloud."—*Love's Labour's Lost* V, 2. " Thus far our fortune keeps an upward course, And we are grac'd with wreaths of victory. But in the midst of this bright-shining day I spy a black, suspicious, threatening cloud, That will encounter with our glorious sun Ere he attain his easeful western bed."—3 *King Henry VI* V, 3.

See also FLEUR, JEU, OIGNON, PEAU.

crac. Crac ! Before you could say Jack Robinson *or* say knife. " Before you can say, Come and go, And breathe twice ; and cry, so, so."—*The Tempest* IV, 1. " Ere a man hath power to say, Behold ! " —*A Midsummer Night's Dream* I, 1.

crachat. *See* BÂTIR, NOYER.

cracher. C'est lui tout craché, You have hit him off to a T.

C'est son père tout craché, He is the very image (*or* the very spit) of his father.

Cracher en l'air[, cela vous retombera sur le nez], Curses come home to roost.

See also INJURE, PORTRAIT.

craindre. *See* CHAT.

crainte. *See* EAU.

cran. Baisser d'un cran, To have suffered somewhat *or* slightly (*in fortune, credit, health, etc.*).

Hausser d'un cran, To have improved somewhat *or* slightly (*in fortune, credit, health, etc.*).

crapaud. C'est un vilain crapaud, He is an ugly little man.

See also LAID.

crapaudière. Ce jardin est une crapaudière, This garden is a swamp.

cravache. *See* COUP 3.

créance. Avoir créance sur quelqu'un (*fig.*), To have someone in one's debt (*for some service rendered to him*).

Créateur. Recevoir son Créateur, To receive [the sacrament *or* the eucharist], To partake of the Holy Communion.

créature. *See* DERNIER.

crécelle. C'est une crécelle, He (She) is a rattle-brain *or* a rattle-head (*an empty-headed chatterer*).

Une voix de crécelle, A rasping voice.

crédit. Faire crédit à quelqu'un (*fig.*), To give someone an opportunity of proving his worth *or* time to show what he is capable of doing.

crémaillère. *See* PENDRE.

crème. C'est la crème des hommes, He is the best of men. " He . . . was the best of all Amongst the rar'st of good ones."—*Cymbeline* V, 5.

La crème de la crème, The very best *or* choicest *or* pick.

crêper. Se crêper le chignon, To tear each other's hair (*in fighting—of women*).

crépin. *See* SAINT-CRÉPIN.

crépusculaire. Une beauté crépusculaire, A beauty on the wane.

crépuscule. Le crépuscule d'un empire, de la vie, The decline (*or* The wane) (*or* The setting) of an empire, of life. " O setting sun, As in thy red rays thou dost sink to-night, So in his red blood Cassius' sun is set,—The sun of Rome is set ! "—*Julius Caesar* V, 3. " Nay then, farewell ! I have touch'd the highest point of all my greatness ; And from that full meridian of my glory I haste now to my setting."—*King Henry VIII* III, 2. " Le crépuscule de mes jours S'embellira de votre aurore."—(VOLTAIRE), Thy dawn shall blush the setting of my days.

Le crépuscule des dieux, The twilight of the gods (*Norse Mythology*).

crétin. C'est un crétin (*fig.*), He is an idiot (*utter fool*).

crétinisme. Être atteint de crétinisme (*fig.*), To be an utter fool.

creuser. Creuser sa fosse *ou* son tombeau (*fig.*), To dig one's own grave, To play ducks and drakes with one's health.

Se creuser le cerveau *ou* la tête, To rack (*or* To puzzle) one's brains (*par exemple,* à chercher . . ., *e.g.,* to find . . .).

See also ABÎME.

creux. Avoir un bon (*ou* un beau) creux, To have a fine deep bass voice.

C'est un cerveau creux *ou* Il, Elle, a le cerveau creux, He, She, is a dreamer *or* a visionary ; He, She, is empty-headed. " Unbruised youth with unstuff'd brain."—*Romeo and Juliet* II, 3.

C'est une cervelle (*ou* une tête) creuse, He (She) is empty-headed.

Il n'y en a pas pour sa dent creuse, That's only a toothful [for him to eat] (*meal is wholly insufficient*) ; There's practically nothing (*no profit*) in it for him.

Viande creuse, Unsubstantial food (*lit. & fig.*) : Il y a des livres qui sont une viande bien creuse pour l'esprit, [There are] some books [which] are [a] very unsubstantial food for the mind. Se repaître de viandes creuses, To feed on (*or* To indulge in) vain fancies, vain hopes.

See also BUISSON, RÊVER, SONGER, SONNER, VENTRE.

crève-cœur. C'est un crève-cœur de voir . . . It is heartbreaking to see . . .

crever. C'est à crever de rire, It's enough to make one split [one's sides] (*or* to make one scream) with laughter, It's a scream (*slang*).

Cela crève les yeux, That (*fact, etc.*) stares one (you) in the face.

Crever d'orgueil, de rage, etc., To be bursting with pride, with rage, etc.

Crever dans sa peau, To be bursting one's buttons (*so fat*) ; To be bursting with spite.

Crever de faim, de soif, de chaleur, To be dying of hunger, of thirst, of heat.

Crever de rire, To burst out laughing, To split [one's sides] (*or* To scream) with laughter. " O, enough Patroclus ; Or give me ribs of steel !. I shall split all In pleasure

of my spleen."—*Troilus and Cressida* I, 3.
Crever le cœur à quelqu'un, To break someone's heart. " Then burst his mighty heart."—*Julius Caesar* III, 2.
Il vous crève les yeux, It (*the thing*) is under your very nose, It stares (*or* is staring) you in the face.
Se crever de mangeaille, To burst one's buttons with food, To stuff oneself with food.
Se crever de travail, To work oneself to death.
Se crever les yeux, To ruin one's eyesight. " Light, seeking light, doth light of light beguile. So, ere you find where light in darkness lies, Your light grows dark by losing of your eyes."—*Love's Labour's Lost* I, 1.
See also ENNUI, PANSE, TYMPAN.

cri. Faire jeter les hauts cris, To raise an outcry.
Jeter (*ou* Pousser) les hauts cris, To complain bitterly, To give vent to one's indignation.
Le cri public, Public opinion.
Ne faire qu'un cri, To cry out (*in pain*) unceasingly.
Pousser des cris de paon, To utter a shrill protest.
Pousser des cris de putois, To shout like a madman.

criard. Des dettes criardes, Pressing debts.

crible. *See* PASSER.

cribler. Être criblé de dettes, To be over head and ears in debt.
See also INJURE.

crier. C'est à qui criera le plus fort, He who shouts the loudest wins.
Crier à l'aide *ou* au secours, To cry (*or* To shout) for help, To cry Help !
Crier à l'injustice, au scandale, To cry injustice, shame.
Crier [à] la faim, To cry [out] for food.
Crier au feu, au meurtre, au voleur, To shout Fire ! Murder ! Stop thief !
Crier au loup, To cry wolf [too often].
Crier au meurtre (*fig.*), To cry blue murder.
Crier comme un aigle, To screech.
Crier comme un aveugle qui a perdu son bâton, To make a fuss over a trifling inconvenience.
Crier comme un perdu *ou* comme un fou *ou* comme un enragé *ou* comme un putois *ou* comme un sourd *ou* comme un beau diable *ou* Crier à tue-tête *ou* à pleine tête *ou* à pleine gorge *ou* du haut de sa tête, To shout like a madman, To shout at the top of one's voice, To cry out lustily, To yell, To bawl.
Crier famine *ou* Crier misère, To complain of bad times.
Crier famine sur un tas de blé, To cry famine in the midst of plenty.
Crier gare, To shout Look out ! *or* Mind ! Sans crier gare, Without [a word of] warning.
Crier haro sur quelqu'un, To raise a hue and cry against someone.
Crime qui crie vengeance, Crime that cries (*or* that calls aloud) for vengeance. " Whose maiden blood, thus rigorously effus'd, Will cry for vengeance at the gates of heaven." —1 *King Henry VI* V, 4. " Foul deeds will rise, Though all the earth o'erwhelm them, to men's eyes."—*Hamlet* I, 2. " Heaven's cherubim, hors'd Upon the sightless couriers of the air, Shall blow the horrid deed in every eye, That tears shall drown the wind."—*Macbeth* I, 7. " Come, thick night, And pall thee in the dunnest smoke of hell, That my keen knife see not the wound it makes, Nor heaven peep through the blanket of the dark, To cry, ' Hold, hold ! ' "—*Macbeth* I, 5.
See also ÉCORCHER, MIRACLE, PLUMER, TOIT.

crime. Faire un crime [d'État] à quelqu'un de quelque chose *ou*

Imputer quelque chose à crime à quelqu'un, To account something (*some trifling offence*) to someone as a serious offence. " What he cannot help in his nature you account a vice in him."—*Coriolanus* I, 1.

See also CRIER, ÉCHAFAUD.

crin. À tous crins, Out and out, Thorough[-going].

Être comme un crin, To be [as] cross as two sticks.

crochet. Être (*ou* Vivre) aux crochets de quelqu'un, To live [up]on someone.

crochu. Avoir les mains crochues, To be rapacious.

crocodile. Des larmes de crocodile, Crocodile tears. " *Lodovico.* She weeps. *Othello.* O devil, devil ! If that the earth could teem with woman's tears, Each drop she falls would prove a crocodile."—*Othello* IV, 1. " And Gloster's show Beguiles him, as the mournful crocodile With sorrow snares relenting passengers."—2 *King Henry VI* III, 1. " Trust not those cunning waters of his eyes, For villany is not without such rheum."—*King John* IV, 3. " What manner o' thing is your crocodile ? . . . 'Tis a strange serpent . . . And the tears of it are wet."—*Antony and Cleopatra* II, 7.

croire. À ce que je crois, To the best of my belief.

À (*ou* S'il faut) l'en croire, If we are to believe him, According to him.

Ce n'est pas à croire *ou* C'est à ne pas y croire, It is beyond all belief.

Croire avoir trouvé la pie au nid, To find (*or* To discover) a mare's nest.

Croire tout comme l'Évangile *ou* comme article de foi, To take everything as gospel [truth], To believe everything one is told. " Think yourself a baby ; That you have ta'en these tenders for true pay, Which are not sterling."—*Hamlet* I, 3.

Il n'en sera pas cru, No one will believe him.

J'en crois à peine mes yeux, I can hardly believe my [own] eyes. " I might not this believe Without the sensible and true avouch Of mine own eyes."—*Hamlet* I, 1. " These lords . . . scarce think Their eyes do offices of truth."—*The Tempest* V, 1.

Je crois savoir que . . ., I have reason to believe that . . .

Je [le] crois bien, I should think so, I dare say, I shouldn't wonder (*if it were so*).

Je ne sais qu'en croire, I don't know what to believe.

Je vous en croirai sur parole, I will take your word for it. " I'll take thy word for faith, not ask thine oath : Who shuns not to break one will sure crack both."—*Pericles, Prince of Tyre* I, 2.

Le croira qui voudra, Believe it or not.

Ne pas en croire ses yeux, Not to believe one's eyes. " I am ready to distrust mine eyes And wrangle with my reason."—*Twelfth Night* IV, 3. " Sith yet there is a credence in my heart, An esperance so obstinately strong, That doth invert the attest of eyes and ears ; As if those organs had deceptious functions."—*Troilus and Cressida* V, 2.

S'en croire, To have the courage of one's [own] convictions ; To fancy oneself.

S'il avait voulu m'en croire, If he had taken my advice.

Se croire perdu, To give oneself up for lost.

Si vous m'en croyez, If you take my advice.

Vous pouvez m'en croire, Depend upon it, You can take it from me.

See also BON 45, ENFANT, FONDER,

GARDER, JUPITER, LIMON, MOUTARDIER, PIEUSEMENT, PRENDRE, SCIENCE, VESSIE, VOIR.

croiser. Croiser quelqu'un, To cross (*or* To thwart) someone.

Se croiser les bras *ou* Se tenir les bras croisés (*fig.*), To stand by idle.

croître. Aller croissant, To go on increasing, To be on the increase.

Ne faire que croître et embellir, To grow taller and handsomer every day (*of a young person*) ; To be on the increase. Cela ne fait que croître et embellir (*ironiquement*), The rot is spreading.

See also HERBE.

croix. Aller au-devant de quelqu'un avec la croix et la bannière, To go to receive someone in state. " The appurtenance of welcome is fashion and ceremony."—*Hamlet* II, 2.

Il a fallu pour le décider la croix et la bannière, I (We) had the deuce of a job to persuade him.

Il faut faire une croix [à la cheminée], I (We) must chalk it up (*note it as extraordinary*), Give me a piece of chalk.

N'avoir ni croix ni pile, Not to have a penny to bless oneself with.

croquer. Croquer le marmot, To cool (*or* To kick) one's heels, To be kept waiting. *Quotation under* MORFONDRE.

Croquer son patrimoine, To run through (*or* To squander) (*or* To dissipate) one's fortune. " 'Good-morrow, fool,' quoth I : 'No, sir,' quoth he, 'Call me not fool till heaven hath sent me fortune.' "—*As You Like It* II, 7.

Être [joli(e)] à croquer *ou* Être [gentil(le)] à croquer, To be perfectly sweet (*of child or young girl*).

crosse. *See* LEVER.

crotte. Être, Tomber, dans la crotte, To be in, To fall into, abject poverty.

crotter. Être crotté comme un barbet *ou* Être crotté jusqu'à l'échine, To be bespattered all over with mud.

croupière. *See* TAILLER.

croûte. Casser la (*ou* une) croûte, To have a snack, To have a bite [of something].

Casser la (*ou* une) croûte avec quelqu'un, To break bread with someone (*take a meal with him*).

croûton. C'est un [vieux] croûton, He is an old fog[e]y *or* a (*or* an old) stick-in-the-mud.

croyance. *See* PIEUX.

cru. Cette histoire est de son cru, This story is of his own invention.

Tirer de son cru, To draw on one's own imagination (*creative faculty*).

cruauté. *See* RECHERCHE.

cruche. Tant va la cruche à l'eau qu'à la fin elle se casse *ou* qu'enfin elle se brise, The pitcher goes to the well once too often, Everything has its day.

crucifier. Crucifier quelqu'un (*fig.*), To torment someone, To make someone suffer cruelly.

cruel. Ne pas trouver de cruelles, To be always lucky in love.

See also JOUER.

cueillir. Cueillir des lauriers *ou* des palmes, To win laurels.

Cueillir quelqu'un, To buttonhole someone, To take someone by the button.

Cueillir un baiser, To snatch a kiss.

cuir. Faire un cuir, To make an incorrect liaison (*in speaking French*).

cuirasse. *See* DÉFAUT.

cuirasser. Se cuirasser contre quelque chose, To steel oneself (*or* one's heart) against something. " And let his manly face . . . steel thy melting heart To hold thine own." —3 *King Henry VI* II, 2.

cuire. Cuire dans son jus, To stew in one's own juice *or* grease.

Être dur à cuire, To refuse to be beaten (*physically or morally*).

Il m'en cuit, I repent (*or* I rue) it.
Il pourrait bien vous en cuire quelque jour, You may well be sorry for it (*or* well repent, *or* rue, it) some day.
Il vous en cuira quelque jour, You will be sorry (*or* will smart) for it some day.
See also GRATTER, POMME.
cuisiner. Cuisiner quelqu'un, To draw (*or* To pump) someone (*elicit information, confession, from him*).
cuisinier. Trop de cuisiniers gâtent la sauce, Too many cooks spoil the broth.
cuisse. *See* JUPITER.
cuite. Prendre une cuite, To get tight (*drunk*).
cul. *See* SELLE.
culbute. Faire la culbute, To come to grief, To fail, To fall.
See also BOUT.
culotte. Porter la culotte, To wear the breeches *or* the trousers (*of wife*). " *Queen Margaret.* Ah, that thy father had been so resolv'd ! *Gloster.* That you might still have worn the petticoat, And ne'er have stol'n the breech from Lancaster." —3 *King Henry VI* V, 5. " I must change arms at home, and give the distaff Into my husband's hands." —*King Lear* IV, 2.
curé. *See* GROS-JEAN.
curée. *See* ÂPRE.
curiosité. Pour la curiosité du fait, As a matter of curiosity, Out of curiosity.
cuver. Cuver sa colère, To cool down.
Cuver son vin, To sleep it off.
cygne. *See* CHANT.

D

dague. *See* FIN.
dalle. *See* RINCER.
damer. Damer le pion à quelqu'un, To get the better of someone, To go one better than someone, To outwit (*or* To outdo) someone.
damner. Faire damner quelqu'un, To make someone swear, To drive someone crazy, To try someone's patience sorely. Cela me fait damner, That drives me crazy. Cela ferait (*ou* C'est à faire) damner un saint, That would (*or* It is enough to) make a saint swear.
See also ÂME.
Danaïdes. *See* TONNEAU.
Dandin. *See* VOULOIR.
danger. Il n'y a pas de danger qu'il vienne, qu'il retourne, There is no fear of his coming, of his returning *or* that he will come, that he will come back.
dans. *See* MEUBLE, POISSON.
danse. Donner une danse à quelqu'un, To give someone a good hiding. *Cf.* Faire danser quelqu'un *under* DANSER.
Gare la danse ! There will be the devil to pay. *See also* ENTRER, MENER.
danser. Danser sur la corde [raide] (*fig.*), To shoot Niagara, To be treading on dangerous ground.
Du vin à faire danser les chèvres, Wine as sour as vinegar, Rot-gut wine.
Faire danser quelqu'un, To lead someone a dance.
Il la dansera, He'll catch it, He'll get it hot *or* (*slang*) get it in the neck.
Ne savoir sur quel pied danser, Not to know which way to turn, To be all at sea.
See also ANSE, CHAT, ÉCU, VIOLON.
date. *See* PRENDRE.
dater. Dater de loin, To go back a long time, To go a long way back (*in time*), To be of long standing.
de. Ceci [est] de vous à moi, [This is] between you and me [and the gate-post *or* bedpost].
dé. À vous le dé (*fig.*), The ball is

with you, It's your turn (*or* innings) now.

Faire quitter le dé à quelqu'un, To make someone give way.

Les dés sont pipés, The dice are loaded, A trap has been laid for us.

Quitter le dé, To throw in one's hand, To give up.

Tenir le dé dans la conversation, To monopolize (*or* To engross) the conversation.

See also COUP 9, JETER.

débandade. Laisser tout aller à la débandade, To let everything go to the devil.

Mettre tout à la débandade, To throw everything into disorder, To turn everything upside down.

Vivre à la débandade, To live a disordered life.

débander. Débander l'arc ne guérit pas la plaie, To cease doing mischief does not undo the harm one has done. " What, what ? first praise me, and again say no ? . . . Where fair is not, praise cannot mend the brow."—*Love's Labour's Lost* IV, 1.

débaptiser. Débaptiser une rue, To change the name of a street. " Sir, You must no more call it York Place, that's past : . . . 'Tis now the king's, and call'd Whitehall." —*King Henry VIII* IV, 1.

débarbouiller. Laisser quelqu'un se débarbouiller, To let someone get out of it as best he can, To let someone shift for himself.

débarquer. Débarquer quelqu'un (*fig.*), To get rid of someone. Il faut le débarquer, He must go.

débarrasser. Débarrasser le plancher, To clear out, To make oneself scarce.

Se débarrasser de quelqu'un, To get rid of someone, To shake someone off ; To take someone for a ride (*kill him*).

débiter. Débiter bien sa marchandise (*fig.*), To speak with effect.

See also ATROCITÉ.

déblayer. *See* TERRAIN.

déborder. Être débordé d'ouvrage, To be overwhelmed (*or, slang,* snowed under) with work.

See also GOUTTE, INJURE.

déboulonner. Déboulonner quelqu'un, To fetch (*or* To knock) someone off his pedestal *or* his perch.

debout. Ne pas [se] tenir debout (*fig.*), Not to hold water, Not to bear examination (*as of an argument*) ; To be only half-baked (*of a scheme*).

Places debout seulement, Standing room only.

See also DORMIR, ENCORE, MOURIR, TOMBER.

déboutonner. Se déboutonner (*fig.*), To unburden (*or* To unbosom) (*or* To disburden) oneself, To get something off one's chest (*slang*).

See also MANGER, RIRE.

débrider. Sans débrider (*fig.*), Without stopping, At a stretch, Right off [the reel].

Une langue débridée, An unbridled tongue.

décerner. Décerner la palme à quelqu'un, To award the palm to someone.

déchaîner. *See* DIABLE.

déchanter. Faire déchanter quelqu'un, To make someone sing small, To take someone down a peg [or two].

décharger. Décharger son cœur, To unburden one's heart.

S'en décharger la (*ou* En décharger sa) conscience, To ease one's mind of it, To make a clean breast of it.

See also BILE.

déchirer. Déchirer l'oreille (*ou* les oreilles) à quelqu'un, To split someone's ear-drums, To make a deafening noise. " Then I'd shriek, that even your ears Should rift to hear me."—*The Winter's Tale* V, 1.

Déchirer quelqu'un à belles **dents,**

To tear someone's character to pieces *or* to rags.

See also HARGNEUX.

déchoir. Les anges déchus, The fallen angels. " Angels are bright still, though the brightest fell."—*Macbeth* IV, 3.

décider. Se décider, To come to a decision, To make up one's mind.

See also CROIX.

décision. *See* APPELER.

décocher. *See* FLÈCHE.

décorner. *See* VENT.

découpler. C'est un gaillard bien découplé, He is a strapping fellow *or* a hefty chap.

découvert. Agir, Parler, à découvert, To act, To speak, openly.

Attaquer quelqu'un à visage découvert, To attack someone openly.

découvrir. Découvrir le dessous des cartes *ou* le pot aux roses, To get to the bottom of (*or* To fathom) the mystery, To find out the secret.

Découvrir saint Pierre pour couvrir saint Paul, To rob Peter to pay Paul.

See also AVRIL, MÈCHE, VÉRITÉ.

décrier. Décrier sa marchandise, To cry stinking fish.

décrire. Ne savoir se décrire, To surpass (*or* To beggar) description. " He hath achiev'd a maid That paragons description and wild fame; One that excels the quirks of blazoning pens, And in the essential vesture of creation Does tire the ingener."—*Othello* II, 1. (*Note.*—to paragon = to surpass; ingener = engineer, originator).

décrocher. Décrocher la timbale, To carry off the prize, To bear away (*or* To carry away) the bell.

See also BÂILLER.

dedans. Donner dedans. To be taken in, To fall into the trap, To be had.

Être en dedans, To be secretive.

Mettre quelqu'un dedans, To take someone in, To have someone on (*slang*).

See also RIRE.

dédire. Ne pas pouvoir (*ou* Ne pouvoir plus) s'en dédire, Not to be able to back out (*or* to get out) of it (*fig.*).

déesse. La déesse aux cent bouches *ou* aux cent voix (*poetic*), " Lady Fame."—*Much Ado About Nothing* II, 1. " On whose bright crest Fame with her loud'st Oyes Cries, ' This is he.' "—*Troilus and Cressida* IV, 5. " See that you come Not to woo honour, but to wed it; when The bravest questant shrinks, find what you seek, That fame may cry you loud."—*All's Well That Ends Well* II, 1.

défaut. Le défaut de la cuirasse (*fig.*), The fatal joint in the armour, The vulnerable spot. " Add proof unto mine armour with thy prayers."—*King Richard II* I, 3.

défendre. *See* CORPS.

déferrer. Déferrer quelqu'un [des quatre pieds], To put someone out of countenance.

défier. Il ne faut jamais défier un fou (*ironiquement*), Confound a fool in his own folly.

défiler. Défiler son chapelet (*fig.*), To have one's say, To speak one's mind; To give vent to one's indignation.

défrayer. Défrayer la compagnie de bons mots, de plaisanteries, To keep the company amused (*or* To entertain the company) with witticisms, with jokes.

Défrayer la conversation, To be the life of the conversation; To be [one's self] the subject of the (*or* of a) conversation.

défriser. Voilà qui vous défrise, That knocks (*disconcerts*) you (*slang*).

dégommer. Dégommer quelqu'un, To sack someone, To give someone his marching orders.

dégoûter. Faire le dégoûté, To be squeamish, To turn up one's nose at it.

degré. *See* ÉCHELLE.

dégringoler. Dégringoler l'escalier quatre à quatre, To come down the stairs four (*steps*) at a time, To come tumbling (*or* rushing) down the stairs.

dehors. Être [tout] en dehors, To be [very] frank *or* outspoken.

Mettre quelqu'un dehors, To put (*or* To turn) someone out ; To sack someone.

Mettre quelqu'un dehors par les deux épaules, To throw someone out neck and crop.

See also CHIEN, COUCHER, MOUVEMENT.

déjeuner. C'est un déjeuner de soleil, It is a shoddy material (*will fade or wear out soon*), It is devil's dust (*shoddy*).

delà. *See* SOUCI.

délibérer. *See* PROPOS.

délicat. Faire le délicat, To be fastidious.

délicatesse. Être en délicatesse avec quelqu'un, To have had a slight variance with someone. Nous sommes en délicatesse, Our relations are rather strained, Our cordiality is somewhat impaired.

délier. *See* BOURSE, CORDON, ESPRIT, LANGUE.

délit. *See* PRENDRE, PROPORTIONNER.

déloger. Déloger sans [tambour ni] trompette, To slip away quietly ; To do a moonlight flit, To shoot the moon.

déluge. Après moi (nous) le déluge, After me (us) the deluge, When I am (we are) no more, let happen what may.

Passons au déluge ! Let us proceed, Get on with your story.

Remonter au déluge, To be as old as Adam *or* as the hills. " Since before Noah was a sailor."—*Twelfth Night* III, 2.

demain. À demain les affaires [sérieuses] *ou* Demain il fera jour, Time enough for business to-morrow, To-morrow is another day, Mañana. " To-morrow's tangle to itself resign."—EDWARD FITZGERALD, *Rubaiyat of Omar Khayyam* LV.

demande. Telle demande, telle réponse *ou* À sotte (*ou* À folle) demande (*ou* question), sotte (*ou* point de) réponse, A silly question deserves a silly (*or* no) answer. " What seem I that I am not ?—Wise.—What instance of the contrary ?—Your folly."—*Two Gentlemen of Verona* II, 4.

See also BEAU 3.

demander. Cela ne se demande pas, That is obvious.

Demander la lune, To cry for the moon. " Wilt thou reach stars because they shine on thee ? "—*Two Gentlemen of Verona* III, 1.

Demandez-moi pourquoi, Tell me if you can, Ask me another. " What is *pourquoy ?* do or not do ? I would I had bestowed that time in the tongues that I have in fencing, dancing, and bear-baiting."—*Twelfth Night* I, 3.

See also AMOUR, PAROLE, PLAIE, RESTE.

démanger. La langue lui démange, He is itching (*or* longing) to speak, He has cacoethes loquendi.

Le dos lui démange, He is asking for a hiding, He'll get a thrashing if he isn't careful.

Les doigts lui démangent, He is itching to write, He has the scribbling mania *or* has cacoethes scribendi, The scribbling bug has bitten him.

Les poings (*ou* Les mains) lui démangent, His fingers are itching (*or* He is spoiling) for a fight.

See also GRATTER.

démasquer. *See* BATTERIE.

démêler. Il n'est pas aisé à démêler,

He is not easy to understand, He is a dark horse.

déménager. Déménager à la cloche de bois, To do a moonlight flit, To shoot the moon.

Sa raison (*ou* Sa tête) (*ou* Il) déménage, He has taken leave of his senses, His mind is unhinged, He is off his head *or* (*slang*) off his nut, He is barmy [on the crumpet] (*slang*).

démener (se). *See* BÉNITIER.

demeurant. Les demeurants d'un autre âge, The survivors of elder days. " Why, in that elder day, to be a Roman Was greater than a king."—MARY R. MITFORD, *Rienzi* st. 4.

demeure. Il n'y a pas péril en la demeure, There is no immediate hurry.

Il y a péril en la demeure, There is danger in delay, Delay is dangerous. " Defer no time, delays have dangerous ends."—1 *King Henry VI* III, 2. " Let's away, Advantage feeds him fat while men delay."—1 *King Henry IV* III, 2.

demeurer. Demeurer en arrière *ou* en reste avec quelqu'un (*fig.*), To remain under an obligation to someone, To remain someone's debtor.

Demeurer sur la place *ou* le carreau *ou* Y demeurer, To be killed on the spot, To be left dead on the ground.

Demeurer sur le cœur, To rankle [in the mind] (*of a grievance*).

Demeurer sur le cœur *ou* sur l'estomac, To lie [heavy] on the stomach (*of food*).

Demeurer [tout] court, To stop short, To break down (*as in a speech*).

Demeurons-en là, Let us leave it at that.

En demeurer là *ou* Demeurer en chemin (*fig.*), To stay (*or* To stop) (*or* To rest) there, To leave it at that.

[En] demeurer là de quelque chose, To leave off something there, To discontinue something at that stage : Voilà où nous [en] sommes demeurés de notre lecture, That is where we left off our reading. Je reprends mon discours où j'en étais demeuré, I resume my speech where I left off.

Ne pas demeurer en reste avec quelqu'un, To give someone tit for tat, To pay someone back in his own coin, To pay someone out, To hit someone back.

See also APPÉTIT, BON 65, CAPOT, CHAMP, DIABLE, PLACE, QUATRE, SELLE.

demi. À corsaire, corsaire et demi *ou* À Normand, Normand et demi *ou* À trompeur, trompeur et demi *ou* À voleur, voleur et demi, Set a thief to catch a thief.

À malin, malin et demi, Diamond cut diamond.

Faire les choses à demi, To do things by halves.

See also BON 3, CAPITULER, ENTENDRE, PARDONNER, TOUR.

demoiselle. Il fait un temps de demoiselle, The weather is neither one thing nor the other, It is neither raining nor is the sun shining.

démon. *See* ESPRIT.

démonétiser. Démonétiser quelqu'un, To discredit (*or* To throw discredit on) someone.

démonter. Une mer démontée, A raging (*or* A boisterous) sea.

See also BÂILLER, BATTERIE.

dénicher. *See* OISEAU.

dénouer. Dénouer la langue à quelqu'un (*fig.*), To loosen someone's tongue.

See also CORDON.

dent. Avoir les dents longues, To be very hungry, To be famishing ; To be greedy *or* grasping (*of money, of honours*).

Avoir une dent contre quelqu'un, To harbour resentment (*or* To have a grudge) against someone, To bear someone malice.

Être sur les dents, To be done up *or* knocked up (*with fatigue*).

Mettre quelqu'un sur les dents, To work someone to death.

N'avoir rien à se mettre sous la dent, To have nothing to eat.

Tomber sous la dent de quelqu'un, To have got someone's knife into one. Il est tombé sous la dent d'un tel, So-and-so has got his knife into him.

See also ARMER, ARRACHER, COUP 24, 51, CREUX, DÉCHIRER, DESSERRER, GUÉRIR, LUNE, MANGER, MENTIR, MONTRER, MORDRE, MORS, ŒIL, PARLER, POULE, RIRE.

déparer. Déparer la marchandise, To pick out the best [of the goods].

départ. Être sur son départ, To be on the point of starting *or* of leaving.

dépasser. Cela dépasse la mesure, That is exceeding all bounds *or* is overstepping the line, That is coming it too strong (*slang*), That's (*or* It's) the limit (*slang*).

See also BORNE.

dépayser. Se trouver, Se sentir, dépaysé, To be, To feel, out of one's element *or* like a fish out of water, Not to feel at home.

dépendre. Un ami à pendre et à dépendre *ou* Un ami à vendre et à dépendre, A friend through thick and thin, A staunch friend. " I rather wish you foes than hollow friends."—3 *King Henry VI* IV, 1.

dépens. Apprendre une chose à ses dépens, To learn a thing to one's cost.

Faire la guerre à ses dépens, To get more kicks than ha'pence out of a thing.

Vivre aux dépens de quelqu'un, To live [up]on someone.

See also COUR, SAGE.

dépense. Faire de la dépense, To go to great expense.

Faire la dépense, To be responsible for the expenditure, To do the paying out.

Se mettre en dépense, To go to unusual expense.

See also BOUCHE, GRATTER.

dépenser. *See* GROS, PLEUVOIR.

dépit. *See* COUPER.

déplacer. Déplacer la question, To shift one's ground.

déplaire. N'en déplaise à un tel, With all due deference (*or* respect) to so-and-so.

Ne vous [en] déplaise, If you have no objection, If you don't mind, With your permission.

déployer. *See* ENSEIGNE, RIRE.

déplumer. Avoir l'air déplumé, To look shabby *or* seedy (*after having seen better days*). " For 'tis the mind that makes the body rich ; And as the sun breaks through the darkest clouds, So honour peereth in the meanest habit. What, is the jay more precious than the lark, Because his feathers are more beautiful ? Or is the adder better than the eel, Because his painted skin contents the eye ? O no, good Kate ; neither art thou the worse For this poor furniture and mean array." —*The Taming of the Shrew* IV, 3.

déposer. Déposer sa fierté, To lay aside one's pride.

dépouiller. Dépouiller le (*ou* Se dépouiller du) vieil homme (*fig.*), To put off the old man (*which is corrupt*) (*Ephesians* iv, 22).

dépourvoir. *See* PRENDRE.

déprécier. Se déprécier [soi-même], To cheapen oneself, To make oneself cheap.

déraciner. C'est un(e) déraciné(e), He (She) feels uprooted *or* feels like a fish out of water.

dérive. Aller à la dérive (*fig.*), To drift (*morally*).

Être en dérive (*fig.*), To be drifting (*morally*).

dernier. Aux derniers les bons, Last come best served.

C'est la dernière des créatures, She is the vilest of women.

C'est le dernier des hommes, He is the vilest of men.

Le dernier des derniers, The lowest of the low.

Le dernier, mais non le moindre, Last but not least.

See also CHEMISE, COUP 15, 20, ÉCHELLE, MAIN, RETRANCHEMENT, RIRE, SUCER, SUPPLICE, TOUS.

dérober. *See* PAIN.

dérouiller. Se dérouiller la mémoire, To refresh one's memory.

Se dérouiller les jambes [par la marche], To stretch one's legs [by walking].

derrière. Une pensée de derrière la tête, An ulterior motive, A mental reservation.

Une porte de derrière (*fig.*), A back-door.

See also FEU, MONTRER, RAGE.

désarçonner. Désarçonner son adversaire, To confound (*or* To floor) one's opponent.

descendre. Descendre au cercueil *ou* au tombeau (*poetic*), To go down to the grave. " And lie full low, grav'd in the hollow ground."—*King Richard II* III, 2.

Descendre en soi-même *ou* Descendre dans sa conscience, To examine one's [own] conscience.

désert. Prêcher (*ou* Parler) dans le désert, To preach in the wilderness.

désespoir. En désespoir de cause, In despair ; In desperation, In the last resort, As a last shift, When all else fails.

déshabillé. Se montrer (*ou* Paraître) dans son (*ou* en) déshabillé, To show oneself (*or* To appear) (*or* To come out) in one's true colours.

déshabiller. Déshabiller son prochain, To lay bare the faults of one's neighbour *or* of one's fellow creatures.

déshériter. Un [homme] déshérité de la fortune, de la nature, du sort, An outcast of fortune, of nature, of fate.

désir. C'est le désir qui fait naître la pensée, The wish is father to the thought, That is wishful thinking.

See also RIRE.

désirer. Se faire désirer, To make oneself sought after, To make people run after one (*desire one's acquaintance*).

désopiler. *See* RATE.

dessécher. Dessécher le cœur à quelqu'un, To make someone callous, To sear someone's heart.

dessein. À dessein, On purpose, Designedly, Intentionally, Advisedly.

desserrer. Ne pas desserrer les dents, Not to open one's lips (*be obstinately silent*), Not to utter a word.

dessiller. Dessiller les yeux à (*ou* de) quelqu'un, To open someone's eyes.

dessous. Agir en dessous, To act in an underhand way.

Avoir le dessous, To get the worst of it.

Avoir le regard (*ou* la mine) en dessous, To have a shifty look.

C'est un homme en dessous, He is a man who is underhand in his dealings.

Être au-dessous de tout, To be utterly worthless, To be trash (*as a novel*).

Être dans le troisième dessous, To be in very low water (*fig.*).

Être en dessous (*fig.*), To be underhand in one's dealings.

Faire quelque chose par-dessous [la] jambe, To do something without care *or* without exertion, To scamp something.

Il y a dans cette affaire un dessous

[de cartes], There is something underhand (*or, slang,* fishy) in this affair.

Jouer quelqu'un par-dessous [la] jambe, To get the better of someone.

Regarder quelqu'un en dessous, To look at someone furtively, To steal a glance at someone.

Traiter quelqu'un par-dessous [la] jambe, To treat someone with scant courtesy *or* in an off-hand manner.

Voir (*ou* Connaître) (*ou* Savoir) le dessous des cartes, To be in the know, To see behind the scenes.

See also BRAS, DÉCOUVRIR, PIQUE, SENS.

dessus. Avoir d'une chose [cent pieds] par-dessus la tête *ou* Avoir d'une chose par-dessus les oreilles *ou* [jusque] par-dessus les yeux, To be bored to death (*or, slang,* fed up [to the teeth]) with a thing.

Avoir des affaires par-dessus la tête *ou* [jusque] par-dessus les yeux, To be overwhelmed with (*or* snowed under by) work, To be up to one's eyes in work. " Our hands are full of business."—1 *King Henry IV* III, 2.

Avoir le dessus, To have the upper hand *or* the whip hand, To be top dog (*slang*).

Avoir le dessus du vent, To have the advantage *or* the pull.

Être au-dessus de ses affaires, To be beforehand with the world, To have money enough and to spare.

Le dessus du panier, The pick of the basket.

Par-dessus le marché (*fig.*), Into the bargain.

Par-dessus les maisons, Exorbitant, Extravagant, Excessive.

Prendre le dessus, To get the upper hand.

Regarder quelqu'un par-dessus l'épaule, To look down one's nose at someone (*in disdain*).

Reprendre le dessus, To get the upper hand again.

See also ÂNE, BONNET, BRAS, DEUX, DOIGT, ENTENDRE, NEZ, PIQUE, PLAISANTER, POCHE, SAUTER, SENS, SOUFFLER.

détacher. Détacher ses yeux d'un objet, To take one's eyes off an object : Il ne pouvait en détacher ses yeux, He couldn't take his eyes off it.

détail. C'est un détail, It's a mere detail.

déteindre. Déteindre sur quelqu'un, To leave one's mark on someone (*influence him*).

dételer. Sans dételer, Without a break (*in one's working*).

détendre. Détendre l'esprit *ou* Détendre l'arc (*fig.*), To relax, To unbend.

détente. Être dur à la détente, To be close-fisted *or* stingy.

déterrer. Avoir l'air d'un déterré *ou* un air (*ou* un visage) (*ou* une mine) de déterré, To look like a corpse *or* a death's head, To look ghastly.

détonner. Détonner, To be out of keeping (*of things*) ; To be out of place (*of persons*).

détour. Être sans détour, To be without guile.

Les détours du cœur, The innermost recesses of the heart.

détourner. *See* REPROCHE.

dette. *See* CHAGRIN, CRIARD, CRIBLER, PAYER.

deuil. Faire son deuil d'une chose, To give a thing up for lost, To say good-bye to a thing.

See also MENER.

deux. Il n'y a pas deux voix là-dessus, There are no two opinions about it.

See also ANSE, ARGUMENT, ARME, AVERTIR, AVIS, BOUT, CLAIR, COMPTER, COUP 34, COUPER, COURIR, DEHORS, DIRE, DOIGT, DORMIR, ENTRE, FEU, FOIS, GOUTTE, GRATTER,

MOT, MOUTURE, NAGER, OS, PAIRE, PAROLE, PERDRE, PIQUER, POIDS, PREMIER, PRENDRE, PROMETTRE, REGARDER, ROMAN, SELLE, SIX, UN, VALOIR.

devant. Aller au-devant du mal, To meet trouble half-way, To ask for trouble, To court disaster. " You are come to meet your trouble."—*Much Ado About Nothing* I, 1.

See also CHAMP, CROIX, GROS-JEAN, PIED, PRENDRE.

devenir. Devenir à rien, To shrink to [next to] nothing.

Ne savoir que devenir, Not to know what is to become of one.

See also CÉLÈBRE, DIABLE, FOU, RARE, ROUGE, SAGE.

déverser. Déverser le blâme sur quelqu'un, To throw (*or* To cast) the blame on someone.

deviner. Il n'y a là rien à deviner, It's obvious, It's [as] plain as a pike-staff *or* as the nose in your face. *Quotations under* CLAIR.

Vous devinez le reste, You can imagine the rest.

See also DONNER, SORCIER.

devoir. Devoir de tous côtés *ou* Devoir à Dieu et à diable *ou* Devoir au tiers et au quart, To owe money all round.

Devoir une belle (*ou* une fière) chandelle (*ou* un beau cierge) à quelqu'un, To have to thank (*or* To be beholden to) someone : Il me doit une belle chandelle pour l'avoir tiré de ce mauvais pas, He has to thank me for getting him out of this awkward situation.

See also AUTEL, BAISER, FAIRE, RESPECT, TERME.

dévolu. Jeter son dévolu sur quelque chose, To fix one's choice (*or* To set one's heart) (*or* To have designs) on something.

dévorer. Dévorer l'espace (*poetic*), To devour the way (*go very fast*). " And starting so, He seem'd in running to devour the way."—2 *King Henry IV* I, 1. " I'll put a girdle round about the earth In forty minutes."—*A Midsummer Night's Dream* II, 2. " We the globe can compass soon, Swifter than the wand'ring moon."—*A Midsummer Night's Dream* IV, 1.

Dévorer ses larmes, To stifle one's tears. " Command these fretting waters from your eyes."—*Measure for Measure* IV, 3. " I forbid my tears : but yet It is our trick ; nature her custom holds, Let shame say what it will : when these are gone, The woman will be out."—*Hamlet* IV, 7.

Le temps dévore tout, Time, consumer of things, " Tempus edax rerum."—OVID, *Metamorphoses* XV, 234. " Cormorant devouring time."—*Love's Labour's Lost* I, 1. " The cloud-capp'd towers, the gorgeous palaces, The solemn temples, the great globe itself, Yea, all which it inherit, shall dissolve, And, like this insubstantial pageant faded, Leave not a rack behind."—*The Tempest* IV, 1.

See also AFFRONT, INJURE.

dévotion. *See* TOMBER.

dia. *See* ENTENDRE, TIRER.

diable. Aller au diable [au] vert, To go a long way away. *Cf.* Demeurer au diable [au] vert *and* Être au diable [au vert] *below.*

Au (*ou* Du) diable si . . . *ou* [Je veux que] *ou* [Que] le diable m'emporte si . . ., I'll be damned (*or* hanged) (*or* blowed) (*or* blest) if . . . *Cf.* [Que] le diable l'emporte *below.*

Avoir le diable au corps, To have the devil in one, To be as if possessed, To be full of devilment (*wild spirits*), To be full of dash, of vim. " O nature, what hadst thou to do in hell When thou didst bower the spirit of a fiend In mortal paradise of such sweet flesh ? "—*Romeo and Juliet* III, 2.

C'est [là] le diable *ou* Voilà le diable, It is the devil, There's the rub, That is the question. *Quotation under* QUESTION.

C'est le diable à confesser, He (She) won't admit it ; It is a devil of a business, It is the dickens of a job, There is the deuce to pay.

C'est le diable déchaîné, It is hell let loose.

C'est le diable et son train, It is the devil and all (*everything bad*). *Cf.* Le diable et son train *below*.

C'est un diable *ou* un diable incarné *ou* un diable d'enfer *ou* un diable déchaîné *ou* un vrai diable, He (She) is a very devil *or* a devil incarnate. *Note, of a woman, one can also say* C'est une [vraie] diablesse. " We took him for a coward, but he's the very devil incardinate."—*Twelfth Night* V, 1.

C'est un grand diable, He is a big gawky fellow.

C'est un méchant diable, He is an evil fellow.

C'est un pauvre diable, He is a poor devil (*luckless or wretched fellow*).

Cela ne vaut pas le diable, That is worthless, That is not worth a damn ; That is good for nothing.

Cela se fera, ou il faudra que le diable s'en mêle *ou* à moins que le diable ne s'en mêle *ou* si le diable ne s'en mêle, That shall be done, or I'll know the reason why.

Cette affaire s'en va au diable, This business is going to the dogs.

De par tous les diables, [I'll] be damned (*or* hanged) (*or* blowed) (*or* blest) if I will, if I do, if I go, etc.

Demeurer au diable [au] vert, To live out in the wilds, To live miles from anywhere. " We lovers of your wilds Are freedom's slaves."—CECIL JOHN "*To Africa.*"

Être au diable [au vert], To be a dickens of a way off, To be miles [away] from anywhere.

Faire la part du diable, To make allowances (*for somebody's weaknesses*).

Faire le diable [à quatre], To kick up hell's delight, To raise Cain, To play Old Harry ; To try every means in one's power (*e.g.*, pour l'obtenir, to get it ; pour l'empêcher, to prevent it, him).

Faire un tapage de tous les diables, To kick up the devil of a din, To kick up hell's delight, To raise Cain.

Il est assez bon diable, He is rather a good sort [of fellow].

Il n'est pas [aus]si diable qu'il est noir, He's not as black as he's painted.

Le diable bat sa femme et marie sa fille, It is raining and the sun is shining at the same time. " You have seen Sunshine and rain at once."—*King Lear* IV, 3. " As when the sun doth light a storm."—*Troilus and Cressida* I, 1.

Le diable et son train, The whole bag of tricks, All the lot, The whole caboodle (*slang*).

Le diable n'y perd rien, Such is not really the case, It is only make-believe.

Quand le diable est (*ou* devient) vieux, il se fait ermite, " The Devil was sick, the Devil a monk would be ; The Devil was well, the devil a monk was he."—URQUHART (*Translation of Rabelais*).

Quand le diable y serait *ou* Quand ce serait le diable, For all that, In spite of all.

[Que] le diable l'emporte, The devil (*or* The deuce) take him, it, He (That) be blowed. " The devil take one party and his dam the other, and so they shall be both bestowed."—*Merry Wives of Windsor* IV, 5.

Se donner au diable, To go out of

one's way (*to do something*), To put oneself out ; To put one out of all patience : La chose est aisée, et il ne faut pas se donner au diable pour la faire, The thing is easy; it is not necessary to go out of one's way to do it. Vos sottes raisons me feraient donner au diable, Your ridiculous reasons are enough to put me out of all patience.

See also BÉNITIER, BON 23, BOURSE, BRUIT, CRIER, DEVOIR, ESPRIT, GOUTTE, JUSTICE, MANGER, MENTIR, TIRER, TORCHER.

dictionnaire. C'est un dictionnaire vivant *ou* ambulant, He is a walking encyclopaedia.

See also COUP 61.

Dieu, dieu. Jurer Dieu en vain, To take the name of God in vain.

Promettre, Jurer, ses grands dieux, To promise, To swear, by all the gods. " Now, in the names of all the gods at once."—*Julius Caesar* I, 2. " Gods and goddesses, All the whole synod of them ! "—*Antony and Cleopatra* III, 10.

See also AIDE, AIDER, AMOUR, BÊTE, BREBIS, CONFESSION, CRÉPUSCULE, DEVOIR, DOIGT, FAUTE, FEMME, MATIN, OURDIR, PLAIRE, PROPOSER, SAINT, TONDRE, VOIX, VOULOIR.

différence. *See* TOUT.

différend. *See* PARTAGER.

différent. *See* JOUR, RAPPROCHER, REPRISE.

différer. *See* JOUR.

difficile. Être difficile à vivre, To be difficult to get on with.

Faire le difficile, To be hard to please, To be very particular.

See also COMPOSITION.

difficulté. *See* CÔTÉ, TOURNER.

digérer. *See* ESTOMAC.

digue-digue. Être en digue-digue, To be all hot and bothered. " My mistress . . . is so hot because the meat is cold ; The meat is cold because you come not home."—*The Comedy of Errors* I, 2.

dilater. L'espérance dilate le cœur, Hope gladdens the heart. " True hope is swift, and flies with swallows' wings ; Kings it makes gods, and meaner creatures kings."—*King Richard III* V, 2.

See also RATE.

diligence. Faire diligence, To make haste, To hurry ; To endeavour (pour = to).

See also ACTE.

dimanche. *See* RIRE.

dindon. Envoyer quelqu'un garder les dindons (*fig.*), To rusticate someone.

Garder les dindons (*fig.*), To live a retired life in the country, To rusticate.

Il est bête comme un dindon *ou* C'est un dindon, He is a conceited booby.

Il sera le dindon [de la farce], He will be the victim [of the deception].

dîner. Dîner par cœur, To go without [one's] dinner, To dine with Duke Humphrey.

See also DORMIR, MOUTARDE, SOMMAIRE.

dire. À vrai dire, . . . *ou* Disons-le, . . ., To tell the truth, . . ., Not to mince matters, . . .

Au dire de tout le monde, By (*or* From) all accounts, By common consent.

Bien dire et bien penser ne sont rien sans bien faire *ou* Le bien-faire vaut mieux que le bien-dire, Fine words butter no parsnips. " 'Tis a kind of good deed to say well : And yet words are no deeds."—*King Henry VIII* III, 2.

C'est moi qui vous le dis ! I can tell you !

C'est tout dire, I need say no more.

C'est une chose dite *ou* C'est dit, That's settled *or* agreed.

Cela ne dit rien au cœur, That makes

no appeal to (*or* That does not touch) the heart.

Cela ne me dit rien, That conveys (*or* means) nothing to me.

[Cela] soit dit en passant, [Be it said] in passing, By the way. " It agrees well, passant."—*Merry Wives of Windsor* I, 1.

Cela vous plaît à dire, So you say (*but I don't agree with you*).

Comme qui dirait, As you might say, As who should say, So to speak.

Dire à quelqu'un une chose sur tous les tons, To put a thing before someone in every possible way.

Dire le nom et la chose, To call a spade a spade. *Quotations under* APPELER *and* NOMMER.

Disons mieux, To be more exact, Or rather, Nay.

Dites donc! Look here! I say!

Dites toujours ! Say it ! Go on ! Fire away !

Il n'y a pas à dire, There's no denying it *or* no getting away from it ; There's no getting over it, And no mistake.

J'ai dit, I have spoken (*I shall say no more*).

Je ne sais comment dire, I don't know how to put it.

Le premier venu vous dira cela, Anyone will tell you that.

Ne pas se le faire dire [deux fois], Not to wait to be told [twice] : Il ne se le fit pas dire deux fois, He didn't wait to be told twice.

On dirait [d']un fou, You would (*or* One might) think he was mad.

On dirait une barque, une voile, It looks like (*or* It might be taken for) a boat, a sail.

Pour mieux dire, To be more exact, Or rather, Nay.

Pour tout dire *ou* Pour le dire en un mot, In a word, In a nutshell, The long and the short of it is that . . . *Quotation under* MOT.

Puisque je vous le dis, You can take it from me.

Qu'en dira-t-on ? What will people say ? What will Mrs Grundy say ?

Qu'est-ce à dire ? What does this (*conduct*) mean ? What is the meaning of this ? (*in surprise or displeasure*). What does this (*e.g., word, passage*) mean ? *or* What is the meaning of this (*e.g., word, etc.*) ? = Que veut dire ceci ? *or* Qu'est-ce que ceci veut dire ? *or* Que signifie ceci ? *or* Qu'est-ce que ceci signifie ? *but all these* 4 *last-named French phrases can also mean* What does this (*conduct*) mean ?

Que dis-je ? To be more exact, Or rather, Nay.

Tenez-vous cela pour dit, Don't let me have to tell you that again.

Tout est dit *ou* Voilà qui est dit, That's settled *or* agreed.

Tout n'est pas dit, We haven't heard the last of it.

Vous dites là le mot, You've hit it, You have hit the nail on the head.

See also AINSI, AISÉ, ALLER, AUSSITÔT, AUTRE, AVENTURE, AVERTIR, AVIS, BEAU 33, BIENTÔT, BON 47, BOUT, CHANSON, CHOSE, CŒUR, CONSENTIR, COUPER, DOIGT, ENTRE, FÂCHER, FAIT, FOIS, FONTAINE, HANTER, HAUT, HISTOIRE, MERCI, MONDE, MOT, NOIRCEUR, NOUVELLE, OFFENSER, OUVRIR, PENDRE, PERSONNE, PLAISANTERIE, QUATRE, ROME, SAVOIR, SITÔT, SOUTENIR, TROUVER, TUYAU, UN, VÉRITÉ, ZUT.

directement. Aller directement à un endroit, To go straight to (*or* To make a bee-line for) a place.

discorde. *See* BRANDON, POMME.

discourir. *See* PERTE.

discours. *See* HALEINE.

discrétion. Être à la discrétion de quelqu'un, To be entirely dependent upon someone.

Se rendre à discrétion, To surrender unconditionally.

See also VIVRE.

discuter. *See* GOÛT.

diseur. Les grands diseurs ne sont pas les grands faiseurs. " Talkers are no good doers."—*King Richard III* 1, 3, Much cry and little wool.

disgracier. Être disgracié [de la nature], To be physically defective; To be ill-favoured (*ugly*).

disparaître. Disparaître de la scène du monde, To wander in the wilderness (*fig.*).

Disparaître du monde *ou* de la terre, To pass away (*die*).

disposer. *See* PROPOSER.

disposition. Une disposition particulière de la Providence, A special providence. *Quotations under* Un COUP du ciel.

disputer. *See* AIGUILLE.

distance. Conserver (*ou* Garder) ses distances, To keep one's distance (*avoid familiarity*).

Tenir quelqu'un à distance, To keep someone at a distance *or* at arm's length.

dix. *See* DOIGT, DONNER, PERDRE.

docteur. *See* TANT.

dogue. *See* HUMEUR.

doigt. Être à deux doigts de la mort, To be within an ace (*or* an inch) of death, To be at death's door.

Être à deux doigts de la ruine, To be on the brink (*or* the verge) of ruin.

Donner sur les doigts à quelqu'un, To rap someone on the knuckles (*lit. & fig.*).

Être servi au doigt et à l'œil, To be served hand and foot.

Faire marcher quelqu'un au doigt et à l'œil, To have someone at one's beck and call.

Faire toucher une chose au (*ou* du) doigt, To make a thing abundantly clear.

Il y met les quatre doigts et le pouce, He eats like a pig (*greedily and dirtily*) ; He displays great want of tact.

Ils sont comme les (*ou* Ce sont les) deux doigts de la main, They are hand in (*or* are hand and) glove with one another, They are [as] thick as thieves.

Le doigt de Dieu (*fig.*), The finger (*or* The hand) of God. " The fingers of the powers above do tune The harmony of this peace."—*Cymbeline* V, 5. " But heaven hath a hand in these events."—*King Richard II* V, 2.

Marcher au doigt et à l'œil de quelqu'un *ou* Obéir à quelqu'un au doigt et à l'œil, To be at someone's beck and call.

Mettre le doigt dessus (*fig.*), To lay (*or* To put) one's finger on it, To hit the nail on the head.

Mon petit doigt me l'a dit, A little bird told me so.

Montrer quelqu'un au doigt, To point the finger of scorn at someone. " But, alas, to make me The fixed figure of the time, for scorn To point his slow and moving finger at ! "—*Othello* IV, 2.

Ne faire œuvre de ses dix doigts, Not to do a stroke of work.

Recevoir (*ou* [En] avoir) sur les doigts, To get rapped on the knuckles.

Se mettre le doigt dans l'œil, To deceive oneself stupidly ; To be the means of one's own undoing.

See also AURORE, BAGUE, BEURRE, BOUT, COULER, DÉMANGER, ÉCORCE, LÉCHER, MORDRE, SAVOIR.

domaine. Ce n'est pas de mon domaine, It is not in my line *or* province.

don. *See* AVÈNEMENT.

donc. *See* DIRE.

donner. C'est [marché] donné, That is giving it away, It's a gift, It's dirt cheap.

Cela se donne, It can be had for the asking.

Donner dans l'œil de (*ou* à) quelqu'un,

To dazzle someone, To take someone's fancy.
Donner dans le luxe, To indulge in luxury.
Donner dans le piège *ou* dans le panneau, To fall into the trap, To be taken in, To be had.
Donner dans quelque chose, To be drawn into something.
Donner des couleurs, To advance specious pretexts. " And never yet did insurrection want Such water-colours to impaint his cause."—1 *King Henry IV* V, 1.
En donner à quelqu'un, To deceive someone ; To give someone a good hiding.
Il lui en a donné d'une [bonne], A fine trick he played on him.
Je vous donne cet homme-là pour le plus grand fourbe, I tell you that man is the worst rascal living. " A man who is the abstract of all faults."—*Antony and Cleopatra* I, 4.
Je vous le donne [à deviner] en dix *ou* en vingt *ou* en cent *ou* Je le donne au plus fin à deviner, You'll never guess it, I defy anyone to guess it.
Je vous le donne [à faire] en dix, en vingt, en cent [coups], I['ll] give you ten, twenty, a hundred strokes, tries, goes, etc., to do it, You'll never do it.
Le donner au plus habile à mieux faire, To defy anyone to do it better.
Ne savoir où donner de la tête, Not to know what is to become of one, what to do ; Not to know which way to turn (*so overworked*).
On donnera à celui qui a [déjà], Whosoever hath, to him shall be given (*Matthew* xiii, 12, *Luke* viii, 18). " The rich shall have more."—*Troilus and Cressida* I, 2. " Giving thy sum of more To that which had too much."—*As You Like It* III, 1. " A thousand pounds a year for pure respect ! . . . That promises more thousands : honour's train Is longer than his foreskirt." —*King Henry VIII* II, 3.
On ne donne rien pour rien *ou* Donnant donnant, Fair's fair, Nothing for nothing, No pay, no piper, Show me first your penny. *Quotation under* ARGENT.
Quel âge donnez-vous à cette personne ? What age do you take this person to be ? How old do you think this person is ?
Qui donne tôt donne deux fois, He gives twice who gives quickly, Bis dat qui cito dat.
Se donner au plaisir, To give oneself up to pleasure.
Se donner pour riche, To give oneself out (*or* To claim) to be rich.
Si on lui en donne long comme le doigt, il en prend long comme le bras *ou* Donnez-lui un pied, il en prendra quatre, Give him an inch and he'll take an ell.
See also AIR, ALTESSE, AVRIL, BAISER, BAISSER, BAL, BARRE, BEAU 7, 35, BESOGNE, BON 28, BRANLE, BREVET, BRIDE, CARRIÈRE, CARTE, CASAQUIN, CAUSE, CHAMP, CHANGE, CHEMISE, CHIEN, CLEF, CŒUR, COLLIER, COMÉDIE, COMPTE, CONFESSION, COUP 12, 15–29, 52, COURS, DEDANS, DIABLE, DOIGT, ENCENSOIR, ENTORSE, ESSOR, FIL, GALOP, GANT, GARDE, GARDER, GUÊPIER, JOUE, LOUP, MAIN, MAL, MERLE, MONNAIE, MOT, MUR, NERF, NEZ, ŒUF, ORDRE, PAIN, PAIX, PAQUET, PEUR, PLAT, PLI, RÉFLÉCHIR, RÉPLIQUE, RIDICULE, RIRE, SAVON, SOUFFLET, SPECTACLE, TEMPS, TÊTE, TON, TOURNURE, TRAVERS, TUER, VERGE.

dorer. Dorer la pilule, To gild the pill.
Il (Elle) a la langue dorée *ou* C'est une langue dorée, He (She) has a smooth tongue. " Helen's golden tongue."—*Troilus and Cressida* I, 2.
Le soleil dore la cime des montagnes, la cime des arbres (*poetic*), The sun gilds the mountain-tops, the

tree-tops. " Full many a glorious morning have I seen Flatter the mountain-tops with sovereign eye, Kissing with golden face the meadows green, Gilding pale streams with heavenly alchemy."—SHAKESPEARE, *Sonnets* XXXIII. " To solemnize this day the glorious sun Stays in his course, and plays the alchemist, Turning, with splendour of his precious eye, The meagre cloddy earth to glittering gold."—*King John* III, 1. " When . . . He (*the sun*) fires the proud tops of the eastern pines."—*King Richard II* III, 2. " The sun ariseth in his majesty ; Who doth the world so gloriously behold, The cedar-tops and hills seem burnish'd gold."—SHAKESPEARE, *Venus and Adonis.*

See also BON 21.

dormir. Dormez votre sommeil, Sleep sound. " Sleep give thee all his rest ! "—*A Midsummer Night's Dream* II, 2. " Sleep dwell upon thine eyes, peace in thy breast ! "—*Romeo and Juliet* II, 2. " God give you good rest ! "—*The Comedy of Errors* IV, 3. " And so, God give you quiet rest to-night ! "—*King Richard III* V, 3.

Dormir comme une souche *ou* comme un sabot *ou* comme une marmotte *ou* comme un loir *ou* Dormir à poings fermés *ou* Dormir d'un sommeil de plomb, To sleep like a log *or* like a top. " Yet all this while in a most fast sleep."—*Macbeth* V, 1. " Lest leaden slumber peise me down to-morrow." —*King Richard III* V, 3. " O murderous slumber, Lay'st thou thy leaden mace upon my boy ? "—*Julius Caesar* IV, 3. " Till o'er their brows death-counterfeiting sleep With leaden legs and batty wings doth creep."—*A Midsummer Night's Dream* III, 2.

Dormir [d']un bon somme *ou* de bon somme, To have a good sleep, To sleep sound[ly]. " Sleep she as sound as careless infancy."—*Merry Wives of Windsor* V, 5. " Sleep kill those pretty eyes, And give as soft attachment to thy senses As infants empty of all thought ! "—*Troilus and Cressida* IV, 1.

Dormir la grasse matinée, To sleep late in the morning, To lie late abed. " Was it so late, friend, ere you went to bed, that you lie so late ? "—*Macbeth* II, 1. " And make a dark night too of half the day."—*Love's Labour's Lost* I, 1. " We did sleep day out of countenance."—*Antony and Cleopatra* II, 2.

Dormir sur les deux oreilles, To have no cause for anxiety. " And sleep, that sometimes shuts up sorrow's eye, Steal me awhile from mine own company."—*A Midsummer Night's Dream* III, 2.

Dormir [tout] debout, To sleep standing up, Not to be able to keep one's eyes open. " This is a strange repose, to be asleep With eyes wide open, standing, speaking, moving, And yet so fast asleep."—*The Tempest* II, 1.

Il n'en dort pas, It keeps him awake (*he is anxious about it*). " Break not your sleeps for that."—*Hamlet* IV, 7. " *Alonso.* I wish mine eyes Would, with themselves, shut up my thoughts: They are inclined to do so. *Sebastian.* Please you, sir, Do not omit the heavy offer of it : It seldom visits sorrow ; when it doth, It is a comforter."—*The Tempest* II, 1.

Il n'y a pire eau que l'eau qui dort, Still waters run deep. " Smooth runs the water where the brook is deep."—2 *King Henry VI* III, 1.

Le bien (*ou* La fortune) lui vient en dormant, Good things come to him while asleep (*he has become rich without any effort*). " Fortune brings in some boats that are not steer'd."—*Cymbeline* IV, 3.

Ne dormir que d'un œil *ou* Dormir les yeux ouverts, To sleep with one eye open, To be on the alert.

Qui dort dîne, He who sleeps forgets his hunger. " Sleep that knits up the ravell'd sleave of care, The death of each day's life, sore labour's bath, Balm of hurt minds, great nature's second course, Chief nourisher in life's feast."—*Macbeth* II, 1.

See also CHAT, VOLCAN,

dos. Avoir plein le dos d'une personne, d'une chose, To be sick of (*or, slang*, fed up [to the teeth] with) someone, something.

Avoir (*ou* Se mettre) quelqu'un à dos, To make an enemy of someone.

Avoir toujours quelqu'un sur le dos, To be continually pestered by someone.

Renvoyer les gens dos à dos, To decide in favour of neither [side].

See also BATTRE, BON 10, DÉMANGER, GROS, LAINE, MONTRER, PORTER, SCIER, SUCRE, TENDRE, TOURNER.

dot. *See* COUREUR.

double. Mettre les bouchées doubles, To hurry through one's meal ; To hurry through one's work.

See also QUITTE.

doubler. Doubler le pas, To quicken (*or* To mend) one's pace.

Doubler ses torts d'un affront, To add insult to injury. " Ill deeds are doubled with an evil word."—*The Comedy of Errors* III, 2.

douceur. Plus fait douceur que violence, Gently does the trick. " Your gentleness shall force More than your force move us to gentleness."—*As You Like It* II, 7. " Our praises are our wages : you may ride's With one soft kiss a thousand furlongs ere With spur we heat an acre."—*The Winter's Tale* I, 2.

douche. Jeter une douche [d'eau] froide sur les projets de quelqu'un, To throw cold water on someone's plans.

douleur. *See* TRANSPERCER.

doute. Ne faire aucun doute d'une chose, To entertain no doubt about a thing. " Hang no more in doubt."—*King John* III, 1.

Révoquer (*ou* Mettre) quelque chose en doute, To cast doubts on something, To call something in question. " Doubt thou the stars are fire ; Doubt that the sun doth move ; Doubt truth to be a liar ; But never doubt I love."—*Hamlet* II, 2.

douter. À n'en pas douter, Beyond doubt, Beyond all question.

Ne douter de rien, To be full of self-confidence ; (*Ironically*) To be living in a fool's paradise. " Our doubts are traitors, And make us lose the good we oft might win By fearing to attempt."—*Measure for Measure* I, 5.

doux. Être doux comme un agneau *ou* comme un mouton, To be [as] gentle as a lamb.

See also AMER, AVALER, FILER, MARIN, ŒIL, VIOLENCE.

douzaine. À la douzaine, Very ordinary : Une personne, Un peintre, à la douzaine, A very ordinary person, painter.

On n'en trouve pas à la douzaine *ou* Il n'y en a pas treize à la douzaine, They are hard to find, They are not to be met with (*or* picked up) every day, They don't grow on blackberry bushes.

douze. *See* MOIS.

dragée. La dragée est amère, It is a bitter pill [to swallow].

Tenir la dragée haute à quelqu'un, To make someone dance to one's tune *or* to one's pipe, To keep someone dangling ; To make someone pay through the nose.

See also AVALER.

drap. Être (*ou* Se mettre) dans de

beaux (*ou* dans de vilains) draps, To be in a fine mess *or* in a pretty pickle *or* in hot water ; To be in a sorry plight *or* in a bad way. " How cam'st thou in this pickle ? "—*The Tempest* V, 1.

Il a taillé en plein drap, He was able to do just what he wanted [to do].

Il peut tailler (*ou* Il a de quoi tailler) en plein drap, He has abundant material, ample means, He has plenty to work on, to go upon.

Mettre quelqu'un dans de beaux draps, To put someone in a quandary.

On ne peut pas avoir le drap et l'argent, You can't eat your cake and have it.

See also AUNE.

drapeau. *See* POCHE.

draper. Draper quelqu'un, To pillory someone.

Se draper dans sa vertu, dans sa probité, To make a parade of one's virtue, of one's honesty.

dresser. Cela fait dresser les cheveux [sur la tête], It makes one's hair stand on end, It is a most hair-raising experience. " I could a tale unfold whose lightest word Would harrow up thy soul ; freeze thy young blood ; Make thy two eyes, like stars, start from their spheres; Thy knotted and combined locks to part, And each particular hair to stand on end, Like quills upon the fretful porcupine."—*Hamlet* I, 5.

Dresser l'oreille *ou* les oreilles, To prick up (*or* To cock up) one's ears.

Les cheveux me dressent [sur la tête], It makes my hair stand on end.

See also AUTEL, BATTERIE, ERGOT.

droguer. Droguer, To be kept waiting, To cool (*or* To kick) one's heels. *Quotation under* MORFONDRE.

droit. Aller le droit chemin, To be perfectly straight in all one's dealings, To act above-board. " There are no tricks in plain and simple faith : But hollow men . . . Sink in the trial."—*Julius Caesar* IV, 2.

Cela est de droit étroit, That must be rigidly observed *or* adhered to.

Cheminer droit, To go straight (*live uprightly*).

Être droit comme un I *ou* comme un cierge *ou* comme un jonc, To be as straight as a ramrod, To hold oneself erect, To have a fine, upstanding figure. " As upright as the cedar." —*Love's Labour's Lost* IV, 3. " Kate, like the hazel-twig, Is straight and slender."—*The Taming of the Shrew* II, 1. " Wand-like straight." —*Pericles, Prince of Tyre* V, 1.

Être droit comme un piquet *ou* comme un échalas, To be [as] stiff as a poker (*of person's carriage or manner*).

Être le bras droit de quelqu'un, To be someone's right arm (*most reliable worker*).

La droite voie (qui mène à la vie), The narrow way (which leadeth unto life) *Matthew* vii, 14. *Quotations under* VOIE.

La voie droite, The straight path *or* course (*of truth, of virtue*).

Marcher droit (*fig.*), To act straight *or* straightforwardly.

Où il n'y a rien le roi perd ses droits, You can't take the breeks off a Highlander.

Quitter le droit chemin, To swerve from the path of duty.

See also BIENSÉANCE, BON 2, 17, BUT, FIL, FORCE, MAIN, NUIRE, PRÉSENCE, TORT.

drôle. Avoir une drôle de touche, To be a queer-looking (*or* a funny-looking) individual.

C'est un drôle de corps *ou* un drôle de numéro *ou* un drôle d'oiseau *ou* un drôle de pistolet *ou* un drôle de paroissien *ou* un drôle de garçon *ou* un drôle d'individu *ou* un drôle d'homme, He's a queer customer *or* a queer fish *or* a queer card *or* a queer stick *or* a funny chap *or* man.

dû. [À] chacun son dû. Give the devil his due.

See also PROMETTRE.

duire. *See* NUIRE.

duo. Un duo d'injures, A slanging match.

Un duo de compliments, Mutual flattery (*between two persons*).

dur. Avoir l'oreille dure *ou* Être dur d'oreille, To be hard of hearing.

Avoir la main dure, To have a (*or* To rule with a) heavy hand, To be heavy-handed (*severe, oppressive*), To be a martinet.

Avoir la vie dure, To be hard to kill, To have nine lives (*of persons or animals*) ; To die hard (*as a theory*). " *Mercutio*. Tybalt, you rat-catcher, will you walk ? *Tybalt*. What wouldst thou have with me ? *Mer*. Good king of cats, nothing but one of your nine lives."—*Romeo and Juliet* III, 1.

See also CABOCHE, CUIRE, DÉTENTE, OS, PAIN.

durer. Il faut faire vie qui dure *ou* faire feu qui dure, One must husband one's resources ; One should look after one's health.

Ne pouvoir durer avec quelqu'un, To be unable to get on with someone.

See also FÊLER, JEU, PLACE.

E

eau. Battre l'eau [avec un bâton], To plough the sand[s] (*labour uselessly*). *Quotation in next entry.*

C'est un coup [d'épée] dans l'eau, It is ploughing the sand[s], It is a wasted effort. " The elements Of whom your swords are temper'd, may as well Wound the loud winds, or with bemock'd-at stabs Kill the still-closing waters, as diminish One dowle that's in my plume."—*The Tempest* III, 3. (*Note.*—dowle = filament of a feather.)

Faire venir à quelqu'un l'eau à la bouche, To make someone's mouth water.

Faire venir l'eau au moulin, To bring grist to the mill. " More sacks to the mill ! "—*Love's Labour's Lost* IV, 3.

Il ne trouverait pas de l'eau à la rivière, He cannot find what is staring him in the face.

Il passera bien de l'eau sous le pont (*ou* sous les ponts) d'ici là, Much water will flow under London Bridge (*or* Much may happen) between now and then.

L'eau lui vient à la bouche, His (Her) mouth is watering.

L'eau va toujours au moulin *ou* à la rivière, Nothing succeeds like success.

Laisser passer l'eau sous le pont, To let the world go by.

Mettre de l'eau dans son vin, To draw in one's horns, To take a back seat ; To restrain one's ardour.

Ne sentir que l'eau, To be quite tasteless (*said of food*).

Porter [de] l'eau à la mer *ou* à la rivière, To carry coals to Newcastle ; To stuff sufficiency. " What fool hath added water to the sea ? "—*Titus Andronicus* III, 1.

Revenir (*ou* Remonter) sur l'eau, To come to the surface (*or* front) again, To find one's feet again.

Se jeter (*ou* Se cacher) dans l'eau de peur de la pluie *ou* Se jeter à l'eau de peur de (*ou* à l'eau crainte de) se mouiller, To fall (*or* To jump) out of the frying pan into the fire. *Quotations under* TOMBER.

See also BAS, BEC, BÉNIR, BOUDIN, CHAT, CLAIR, COULER, CRUCHE, DORMIR, DOUCHE, FEU, FONTAINE, GOUTTE, HAUT, MAINTENIR, MARCHER,

MARIN, NAGER, NOYER, PÊCHER, POISSON, ROBINET, SUER, TEMPÊTE, TOMBER.

ébène. Des cheveux d'ébène, Raven locks.

éblouir. Une beauté qui éblouit, A dazzling beauty (*a very beautiful woman*). *Note.*—A dazzling beauty (*the quality*) *is* Une beauté éblouissante.

éborgner. Éborgner une maison, To obstruct the view from a house (*by building near it*).

ébrécher. Ébrécher son avoir, To make a hole in one's fortune (*said of large expenditure*).

écart. Les écarts de l'imagination, The freaks of the imagination, The flights of fancy. " Nature wants stuff To vie strange forms with fancy."—*Antony and Cleopatra* V, 2. " So full of shapes is fancy, That it alone is high fantastical."—*Twelfth Night* I, 1.

Les écarts de la jeunesse, Youthful indiscretions.

échafaud. " Le crime fait la honte, et non pas l'échafaud." (THOMAS CORNEILLE), To be punished for a crime of which one is innocent is no shame. " So the life, that died with shame, Lives in death with glorious fame."—*Much Ado About Nothing* V, 3. " Myself I throw, dread sovereign, at thy foot: My life thou shalt command, but not my shame: The one my duty owes; but my fair name,—Despite of death, that lives upon my grave,—To dark dishonour's use thou shalt not have. . . . My dear dear lord, The purest treasure mortal times afford Is spotless reputation; that away, Men are but gilded loam or painted clay."—*King Richard II* I, 1. *See also quotation under* BON 21.

Porter sa tête sur l'échafaud, To be guillotined.

échalas. *See* DROIT, MAIGRE.

échapper. L'échapper belle, To have a narrow escape *or* a narrow squeak *or* a close shave, To escape by (*or* with) the skin of one's teeth.

See also BROUSSAILLES, CHEVAL, PETIT, TANGENTE.

échasse. Être monté sur des échasses, To be on stilts (*pompous*); To ride the high horse.

échauder. Il s'y est (*ou* Il y a été) échaudé, He has burnt his fingers over it. *Quotation under* BRÛLER.

See also CHAT.

échauffer. C'est un échauffé, He is hot-brained *or* hot-headed (*excitable*).

Échauffer les oreilles à quelqu'un, To anger someone (*by what one says*).

See also BILE.

échec. Au jeu des échecs, les fous sont les plus près des rois, In life, the unreasonable people are often the ones in a position to make their influence felt.

Faire échec à quelqu'un *ou* Tenir quelqu'un en échec, To checkmate someone.

échelle. Après cela il faut tirer l'échelle, That's the last straw *or* (*slang*) the limit.

Après lui il faut tirer l'échelle, His performance can never be bettered.

Être au dernier degré de l'échelle, To be at the top[most rung] of the ladder. " When he once attains the utmost round."—*Julius Caesar* II, 1.

Faire monter quelqu'un à l'échelle, To take (*or* To get) a rise out of someone, To take someone in, To pull someone's leg, To lead someone up (*or* down) the garden path (*slang*).

écheveau. C'est un écheveau embrouillé, It is a tangled skein (*complicated affair, confused explanation*).

échine. Avoir l'échine souple *ou*

flexible, To have supple knees (*be submissive to one's superiors*) ; To be very accommodating *or* pliant. " For supple knees Feed arrogance, and are the proud man's fees."—*Troilus and Cressida* III, 3.

C'est une longue (*ou* une maigre) échine, He (She) is only skin and bone.

Courber (*ou* Plier) l'échine, To bow (*or* To bend) the head (*in humble submission*). " How dare thy joints forget To pay their awful duty to our presence?"—*King Richard II* III, 3.

See also CROTTER, FROTTER.

échiner. Échiner quelqu'un (*fig.*), To beat someone to within an inch of his life ; To beat someone to death ; To ill-use someone (*by word or writing*) ; To tire someone out.

S'échiner, To knock oneself up (*with overwork*).

échouer. Faire échouer les plans de quelqu'un, To wreck someone's plans.

éclair. C'est un éclair, It is a flash in the pan.

Passer comme un éclair, To be gone in a flash *or* in an instant ; To flash by. " I go, I go ; look how I go, —Swifter than arrow from the Tartar's bow."—*A Midsummer Night's Dream* III, 2.

See also PROMPT, RAPIDE.

éclat. En venir à un éclat, To resort to extreme measures.

Faire [de l']éclat, To cause a stir *or* a commotion *or* a sensation ; To cause a scandal.

See also COUP 64, RIRE.

éclater. *See* BOMBE.

éclipse, éclipser. Faire une éclipse *ou* S'éclipser, To disappear, To vanish, To make oneself scarce.

éclosion. L'éclosion d'une idée, The birth of an idea.

écluse. *See* LÂCHER.

école. Être à bonne école, To be in good hands.

Faire une école, To make a blunder, To put one's foot in it.

See also BUISSONNIER, CHEMIN.

écolier. *See* CHEMIN, PIQUET.

économie. *See* BOUT.

écorce. Entre l'arbre et l'écorce il ne faut pas mettre le doigt *ou* Il ne faut pas mettre le doigt entre le bois et l'écorce, Don't interfere in other people's quarrels.

Il ne faut pas juger de l'arbre par l'écorce, One should not judge by appearances, One should not judge a sausage by its overcoat.

écorcher. Écorcher l'anguille par la queue, To start at the wrong end, To set about it the wrong way.

Écorcher l'oreille *ou* les oreilles, To grate on the ear (*of harsh sounds*).

[Il ressemble aux anguilles de Melun,] il crie avant qu'on l'écorche, He is afraid without cause ; He cries out before he is hurt. " Cry to it, nuncle, as the cockney did to the eels when she put them i' the paste alive."—*King Lear* II, 4. (*Note.*—Cockney *here means a* squeamish or over-nice woman.)

Jamais beau parler n'écorcha la langue, Courtesy costs nothing.

See also TONDRE.

écorner. *See* VENT.

écot. Payer son écot, To pay one's score. " They say he parted well, and paid his score."—*Macbeth* V, 8. " That thou didst love her, strikes some scores away From the great compt."—*All's Well That Ends Well* V, 3.

écoute. C'est un écoute s'il pleut, He is a man who always sees a lion in the path ; It is a mere put-off, a fond delusion, a forlorn hope.

Être aux écoutes, To play the eaves-dropper. " A rat? . . . Thou wretched, rash, intruding fool."—*Hamlet* III, 4.

écouter. Écouter aux portes, To eavesdrop.

Il s'écoute [parler], He likes to hear himself talk.

Il s'écoute trop *ou* Il écoute trop son mal, He worries himself too much about his health.

See also AUTRE, OREILLE.

écraser. Écraser quelque chose au nid *ou* dans l'œuf, To nip something in the bud. *Quotation under* TUER.

Je l'écraserai comme un ver, I'll cook his goose [for him], I'll settle his hash, I'll do for him.

écrevisse. Aller [à reculons] comme les écrevisses (*fig.*), To go backward[s] (*of a person whose affairs are worsening*). " If, like a crab, you could go backward."—*Hamlet* II, 2.

See also ROUGE.

écrire. Ce qui est écrit est écrit, What is written is written. " The Moving Finger writes; and, having writ, Moves on: nor all your Piety nor Wit Shall lure it back to cancel half a Line, Nor all your Tears wash out a Word of it."—EDWARD FITZGERALD, *Rubaiyat of Omar Khayyam* LXXVI.

Écrire à quelqu'un une lettre à cheval *ou* Écrire de [la] bonne encre à quelqu'un, To write to someone in strong terms, To write someone a snorter (*slang*). " I'll write to him a very taunting letter, . . . I will be bitter with him, and passing short."—*As You Like It* III, 5. " Let there be gall enough in thy ink; though thou write with a goose-pen, no matter."—*Twelfth Night* III, 2.

Écrire au courant de la plume, To write off-hand (*without premeditation*).

Il est écrit que je ne gagnerai pas, It is fated [that] I shall not win.

See also AIRAIN, CHAT, QUATRE.

écrit. Coucher quelque chose par écrit, To set something down in writing *or* in black and white. " That . . . event that draweth from my snow-white pen the ebon-coloured ink."—*Love's Labour's Lost* I, 1.

écu. Avoir des écus, To have plenty (*or* a pot) (*or* pots) (*or* tons) of money.

Faire sauter (*ou* Faire danser) les écus, To make the money fly.

écumeur. Un écumeur d'affaires, A profit-snatcher.

Un écumeur de marmites, A cadge, A sponge.

Un écumeur de port, A land-shark.

Un écumeur des mers, A sea-rover, A pirate.

écureuil. C'est un écureuil *ou* Il est vif comme un écureuil, He is a restless person, He is always on the go, He is never still.

écurie. C'est un cheval à l'écurie, It is eating its head off (*said of thing costing money to maintain, but not being put to use*).

C'est une écurie, It is a [pig]sty (*dirty house, room*).

Fermer l'écurie quand les chevaux sont dehors, To shut the stable-door after the horse is stolen. " Shut doors after you: Fast bind, fast find—A proverb never stale in thrifty mind."—*The Merchant of Venice* II, 5.

See also NETTOYER.

effort. Faire un effort sur soi-même, To exercise self-control, To try to control oneself.

effronté. Être effronté comme un page, To be [as] cheeky as a cock sparrow, To be [as] bold as brass. *Quotation under* HARDI.

effronterie. *See* PAYER.

effusion. Des effusions de cœur, Outpourings of the heart.

Des effusions de tendresse, Demonstrations of affection.

égal. *See* BILLE, HAÏR.

égarer. Une brebis égarée (*fig.*), A lost sheep (*Psalms* cxix, 176).

église. L'Église souffrante, The souls in purgatory.

See also GUEUX, RAT.

égoïsme. *See* SUER.

Égypte. *See* REGRETTER.

éléphant. C'est l'éléphant dans les porcelaines, He is like a bull in a china shop.

See also MOUCHE.

élever. Élever quelqu'un [jusqu']aux nues *ou* jusqu'au [troisième] ciel, To laud (*or* To crack up) (*or* To cry up) someone to the skies.

Élever un enfant dans du coton *ou* Élever un enfant sous cloche, To bring up a child [wrapped] in cotton wool, To [molly-]coddle (*or* To pamper) a child.

See also AUTEL, SOUCI.

éloge. Cela fait son éloge, That speaks in his favour.

Faire son propre éloge, To sound one's own praises, To blow one's own trumpet. *Quotation under* LOUANGE.

embarras. Avoir l'embarras du choix, To have difficulty in choosing, To have more alternatives than one knows how to deal with.

Être dans l'embarras [d'argent], To be in financial difficulties *or* (*slang*) in Queer Street.

Faire de l'embarras *ou* des (*ou* ses) embarras, To give oneself airs, To make great pretence.

Un embarras de richesses, A superfluity of good things, More wealth than one knows how to deal with.

embarrasser. Être embarrassé de sa personne, To feel awkward.

embellir. *See* CROÎTRE.

emboîter. Emboîter le pas à quelqu'un, To follow (*or* To tread) in someone's [foot]steps.

emboucher. Emboucher la trompette (*fig.*), To talk in the heroic style, To adopt a high-flown style, To strike the lyre (*fig.*).

embourber. Embourber quelqu'un dans une mauvaise affaire, To involve someone in an unpleasant affair.

See also JURER.

embrasser. Qui trop embrasse mal étreint, Grasp all, lose all.

embrouiller. *See* ÉCHEVEAU.

émécher. Un homme éméché, A man slightly the worse for drink, A man who is squiffy *or* (*slang*) a bit screwed.

émissaire. *See* BOUC.

emmieller. Des paroles emmiellées, Honeyed words. " My woman's heart Grossly grew captive to his honey words."—*King Richard III* IV, 1.

Emmieller les bords du vase, To gloss [over] (*or* To explain away) the difficulties [to be overcome]. " Now to plain-dealing ; lay these glozes by."—*Love's Labour's Lost* IV, 3.

emmitoufler. Jamais chat emmitouflé ne prit souris, Too many precautions hinder, rather than help, One can be too careful. *Quotation under* PRÉCAUTION.

émoulu. *See* FRAIS.

émouvoir. *See* BILE.

emparer (s'). S'emparer de l'esprit de quelqu'un, To overrule someone's mind.

S'emparer de la conversation, To monopolize (*or* To engross) the conversation.

S'emparer de quelqu'un, To buttonhole someone, To take someone by the button.

empêcher. Être empêché de sa personne *ou* de sa contenance, To feel awkward ; To be in a quandary.

Les arbres empêchent de voir la forêt *ou* Les maisons empêchent de voir la ville, You can't see the wood for the trees.

emplette. Faire une mauvaise (*ou, ironiquement*, une belle) emplette, To make a bad bargain.

emplir. S'emplir la panse (*fig.*), To make one's pile (*of money*).

employer. Employer le vert et le sec *ou* Employer toutes les herbes de Saint-Jean, To use every possible means to succeed, To leave no stone unturned.

empocher. *See* AFFRONT.

emporte-pièce. Des mots à l'emporte-pièce, Biting (*or* Cutting) words.

emporter. Emporter la pièce *ou* le morceau, To be very cutting (*in mockery, in slander*).

Emporter une chose à la pointe de l'épée (*fig.*), To carry a thing by storm.

L'emporter de haute lutte, To carry it off with flying colours.

S'emporter comme une soupe au lait, To flare up, To fire up, To go [in] off the deep end. " Hasty as fire."—*King Richard II* I, 1.

Vous ne l'emporterez pas en paradis, You won't get away with it, You'll have to pay for it, [You wait,] I'll be even with you [yet].

See also BALANCE, DIABLE, VENT.

empresser (s'). S'empresser auprès de quelqu'un, To dance attendance on someone. " To dance attendance on their lordships' pleasures, And at the door too, like a post with packets."—*King Henry VIII* V, 2.

emprunter. *See* CHOISIR.

encaquer. *See* HARENG.

encenser. Encenser quelqu'un, To flatter someone fulsomely.

encensoir. Casser le nez à coups d'encensoir *ou* Casser l'encensoir sur le nez *ou* Donner de l'encensoir par le nez, To flatter grossly, To be profuse in compliments, To lay it on with a trowel, To lay it on thick (*slang*).

enchantement. Comme par enchantement, As if by magic.

enchère. Payer la folle enchère de quelque chose, To pay dearly for something (*e.g., one's rashness*).

Sa conscience est à l'enchère (*fig.*), His conscience is for sale.

enclume. Être (*ou* Se trouver) entre l'enclume et le marteau, To be between the devil and the deep sea, To sail (*or* To be) between Scylla and Charybdis. *Cf. quotations under* TOMBER.

Il faut être enclume ou marteau, It's either kill or be killed.

Il vaut mieux être marteau qu'enclume, Better be hunter than hunted.

Remettre un ouvrage sur l'enclume, To have another go (*or* turn) at a piece of work.

encolure. Il a l'encolure d'un sot, He has the look (*or* the appearance) of a fool.

encore. Être encore de ce monde *ou* encore sur terre *ou* encore debout, To be still in the land of the living *or* still above ground.

See also COUP 31, COURIR, NAÎTRE.

encre. *See* BOUTEILLE, ÉCRIRE.

encyclopédie. C'est une encyclopédie vivante *ou* ambulante, He is a walking encyclopaedia.

endetter. Être endetté jusqu'au cou *ou* jusqu'aux oreilles, To be over head and ears in debt, To be up to the ears (*or* up to the eyes) in debt.

endormir. Endormir la vigilance de quelqu'un, To put someone off his guard.

S'endormir du sommeil du juste, To sleep the sleep of the just.

S'endormir sur la besogne, To go to sleep over one's work (*work lazily*).

S'endormir sur le rôti, To rest on one's laurels, To leave off working.

endosser. *See* HARNOIS.

endroit. *See* CHATOUILLER, FAIBLE, HISTOIRE, SENSIBLE.

enfance. Être, Tomber, en enfance, To be in, To fall into, one's second childhood (*dotage*). (*Note.*—I was then in my childhood (*infancy*), J'étais alors dans mon enfance.) " Last scene of all, That ends this strange eventful history, Is second childishness and mere oblivion, Sans teeth, sans eyes, sans taste, sans everything."—*As You Like It* II, 7.

enfant. Faire l'enfant, To behave childishly.

Il est [bien] bon enfant de croire cela, He is very simple [indeed] to believe that. *Cf.* BON 23.

L'enfant perdu, The one set in the forefront of the battle (*fig.*). (2 *Samuel* ii, 15.)

Les enfants sont toujours les enfants, Boys will be boys.

See also BALLE, ESPRIT, INNOCENT, JEU.

enfanter. La montagne a enfanté une souris *ou* C'est la montagne qui enfante une souris, The mountain was in travail and has brought forth a mouse.

enfariner. Venir la bouche enfarinée *ou* le bec enfariné, To nurse [an] extravagant hope. " But since life teems with ill, Nurse no extravagant hope."—MATTHEW ARNOLD, *Empedocles on Etna* I, 2.

enfer. *See* DIABLE, FEU, INTENTION, JOUER, TISON, TRAIN.

enfermer. *See* LOUP.

enferrer. S'enferrer (*fig.*), To get entangled.

S'enferrer de soi-même, To be the cause of one's own undoing, To be hoist with one's own petard. *Quotations under* LACET.

enfiler. Cela ne s'enfile pas comme des perles, It is not so (*or* as) easy as it looks.

Enfiler des perles, To trifle one's time away.

enfler. Être enflé comme un ballon (*fig.*), To be bursting (*or* puffed up) with pride. " I have ventur'd, Like little wanton boys that swim on bladders, This many summers in a sea of glory ; But far beyond my depth : my high-blown pride At length broke under me."—*King Henry VIII* III, 2.

enfoncer. *See* OUVRIR, POIGNARD.

enfouir. Enfouir son talent, To hide one's talent in the earth *or* one's light (*or* candle) under a bushel *or* under a bed. (*Matthew* xxv, 25. *Mark* iv, 21. *Luke* viii, 16.) " Heaven doth with us as we with torches do, Not light them for themselves : . . . Spirits are not touch'd But to fine issues."—*Measure for Measure* I, 1.

enfuir (s'). *See* CHIEN, NU.

engager. *See* CHEMISE.

engendrer. Il n'engendre point la mélancolie, He is always merry and bright.

See also FAMILIARITÉ.

engraisser. L'œil du maître engraisse le cheval (*fig.*), There's no eye like the eye of the master (*so look after your business yourself*).

S'engraisser de la misère publique, To batten on public misfortune.

engrener. Engrener une affaire, To set an affair going.

See also BIEN.

énigme. *See* CLEF, MOT.

enjeu. Retirer son enjeu, To withdraw one's stake ; To back out (*of an undertaking*), To cry off.

enlever. Enlever les moyens à quelqu'un, To disconcert someone, To cramp someone's style.

See also PAILLE.

enluminer. Un nez enluminé, A fiery red nose. " Thou art our admiral, thou bearest the lantern in the poop,—but 'tis in the nose of thee ; thou art the Knight of the Burning Lamp."—1 *King Henry IV* III, 3. " Good Bardolph, put thy nose between his sheets, and do the office of a warming-pan."—*King Henry V* II, 1.

ennemi. *See* AUTANT, BON 43, GAGNER, MIEUX.

ennui. L'ennui de vivre, The tediousness of life, Disgust with life. " There's nothing in this world can make me joy : Life is as tedious as a twice-told tale, Vexing the dull ear of a drowsy man."—*King John* III, 4.

Périr (*ou* Crever) (*ou* Suer) d'ennui, To be bored to death *or* to tears *or* (*slang*) bored stiff.

ennuyer. S'ennuyer à périr *ou* à avaler sa langue, To be bored to death *or* to tears *or* (*slang*) bored stiff.

ennuyeux. Être ennuyeux comme la pluie, To be [as] dull as ditch-water.

enrager. *See* CRIER, MANGER, MOUTON.

enrhumer. Être enrhumé comme un loup, To have a very bad cold.

enseigne. À bon vin [il ne faut] point (*ou* pas) d'enseigne, Good wine needs no bush.

Enseignes déployées, With flying colours.

Nous sommes tous, tous les deux, logés à la même enseigne, We are all, both, in the same boat. " O, too much folly is it, well I wot, To hazard all our lives in one small boat."—1 *King Henry VI* IV, 6.

ensemble. *See* AMOUR, BIEN, CHASSER, GARDER, RIMER, TOUT, VIVRE.

entendeur. *See* BON 3.

entendre. Entendre à demi-mot, To take a hint.

Entendre [bien] la plaisanterie, To know how to take a joke.

Entendre malice à quelque chose *ou* Entendre quelque chose de travers, To put a wrong construction on something.

Entendre raison, To listen to reason.

Faire entendre raison à quelqu'un, To bring someone to reason, To make someone see reason.

Faites comme vous l'entendez, Do as you see fit *or* as you please.

Il n'entend ni à hue, ni à dia, He won't listen to reason.

Il n'entend pas de cette oreille-là, He turns a deaf ear, He won't listen to (*or* hear of) that arrangement.

Il n'entend pas raillerie *ou* plaisanterie, He cannot take a joke.

Il n'entend pas raillerie là-dessus, He is very touchy on that point.

Il n'est pire sourd que celui qui ne veut pas entendre, There are none so deaf as those that won't hear.

Ne pas (*ou* Ne point) entendre malice à quelque chose, To mean no harm in (*or* by) something, To do (*or* To say) something in all innocence : Il n'y entendait point malice, He meant no harm by it.

On aurait entendu voler une mouche *ou* On entendrait une souris trotter, You could have heard a pin drop.

Qui n'entend qu'une partie n'entend rien *ou* Qui n'entend qu'une cloche n'entend qu'un son, There are two sides to every question, One should hear both sides.

S'entendre avec quelqu'un, To come to an understanding with someone ; To conspire with someone ; To get on well with someone.

S'entendre comme larrons en foire, To be [as] thick as thieves.

See also FAIT, FIN, FINESSE, GOUTTE, NOUVELLE, RAMER.

enterrement. Avoir une figure d'enterrement, To have a woe-begone look, To look like a mute (*undertaker's man*).

enterrer. Enterrer quelqu'un (*fig.*), To outlive someone. Le malade enterra son médecin, The patient outlived his doctor. " But I consider By medicine life may be prolong'd, yet death Will seize the doctor too."—*Cymbeline* V, 5.

Enterrer sa vie de garçon, To give a

farewell bachelor party. " I will die bravely, like a smug bridegroom." —*King Lear* IV, 6.

Enterrer une fortune dans une entreprise, To sink a fortune in an undertaking.

entier. *See* MOURIR.

entonner. *See* LOUANGE.

entorse. Donner une entorse à un passage, à la vérité, à la loi, To twist (*or* To distort) a passage, the truth, the law. " Thou hast frighted the word out of his right sense, so forcible is thy wit."—*Much Ado About Nothing* V, 2.

entour. Savoir bien prendre les entours, To win over those surrounding the person whose favours one is seeking.

entournure. Être gêné dans les (*ou* aux) entournures, To feel awkward, To be ill at ease.

entre. Entre nous *ou* Entre nous soit dit *ou* Soit dit entre nous *ou* Entre vous et moi, Between ourselves, Between you and me [and the gatepost *or* bedpost].

Être entre deux âges, To be middle-aged.

Être entre deux vins, To be half-seas over, To be rather on (*slang*).

See also CHAIR, CHIEN COUPE, ÉCORCE, ENCLUME, FEU, LOUP, MARCHER, NAGER, PLANCHE, POIRE, QUATRE.

entrée. D'entrée de jeu (*fig.*), From the outset.

entrer. Entrer en coup de vent *ou* en trombe *ou* comme une trombe, To burst in(*to a room*).

Entrer en danse (*fig.*), To join in, To take an active part.

Entrer en jeu, To come into play (*of forces*) ; To come in[to the matter, the discussion], To be one's turn [to act, to speak].

Entrer en matière, To broach the subject.

Entrer en ménage, To set up house.

Entrer en scène (*fig.*), To appear on the scene (*of persons*).

Entrer en vogue, To come in[to fashion].

Maison où on entre comme dans un moulin, House with all the doors left wide open.

See also COMPTE, CONDITION, OREILLE, PEAU.

entretenir. *See* MAIN.

envelopper. *See* MANTEAU.

envers. Avoir l'esprit (*ou* la tête) à l'envers, To take a false view of things ; To have one's brain in a whirl. *Quotation under* CHAOS.

envie. Avoir bien envie de faire quelque chose, To have a good mind to do something.

Faire envie à quelqu'un, To make someone envious.

Il vaut mieux (*ou* Mieux vaut) faire envie que pitié, It is better to be envied than pitied.

Porter envie à quelqu'un de quelque chose, To envy someone something. " Lean-fac'd Envy in her loathsome cave."—2 *King Henry VI* III, 2.

See also PASSER.

envisager. On envisage un projet pour . . ., A plan is afoot to . . .

envoler. Le temps s'envole, Time is flying, Time flies.

See also OISEAU.

envoyer. Envoyer quelqu'un [se] promener *ou* Envoyer promener quelqu'un *ou* Envoyer paître quelqu'un, To send someone to the right-about *or* someone about his business *or* someone packing. *Cf.* Allez vous promener *under* ALLER *and see quotations thereunder*.

See also AD PATRES, CHOU, DINDON, MONDE, OURDIR.

épais. Il n'y en a pas épais, There's not much of it.

épaisseur. *See* CHEVEU.

épancher. *See* BILE.

épanouir. *See* RATE.

épargner. *See* POINT.

éparpiller. Éparpiller son esprit, To divide one's attention.

épatant. C'est épatant, It's ripping *or* topping *or* stunning, It's top-hole, It beats the band (*all slang*).

Ce n'est pas bien épatant, It's nothing to write home about.

épaule. Changer son fusil d'épaule (*fig.*), To change one's opinions ; To change one's tactics. " I can add colours to the cameleon ; Change shapes with Proteus for advantages ; And set the murderous Machiavel to school."—3 *King Henry VI* III, 2.

Plier (*ou* Baisser) les épaules, To bow (*or* To bend) one's head (*in humble submission*).

Prêter l'épaule à quelqu'un, To lend someone a [helping] hand.

See also COUP 21, DEHORS, DESSUS, PORTER.

épauler. Épauler quelqu'un, To back someone up.

épée. L'épée de Damoclès, The sword of Damocles.

Poursuivre (*ou* Presser) quelqu'un l'épée dans les reins, To prod someone on (*to do something*); To press someone hard (*in an argument*).

Son épée est trop courte, His arm (*influence*, *credit*) is too short *or* is not long enough. " Put forth thy hand, reach at the glorious gold :— What, is't too short ? I'll lengthen it with mine."—2 *King Henry VI* I, 2. (*Note.*—the glorious gold = the crown.)

See also BLANC, CHEVET, COMÉDIE, COUP 44, EAU, EMPORTER, FOURREAU, ROMAN.

éperon. Gagner ses éperons (*fig.*), To win one's spurs.

See also BOUCHE, BRIDE, REGIMBER.

épervier. On ne saurait faire d'une buse un épervier, You cannot make a silk purse out of a sow's ear.

épice. *See* PETIT.

épiderme. Avoir l'épiderme sensible (*fig.*), To be thin-skinned.

épine. C'est un fagot d'épines, on ne sait par où le prendre, He is so repellent in manner as to be almost unapproachable.

C'est une épine au pied, It is a thorn in one's flesh *or* in one's side.

Être sur des (*ou* sur les) épines, To be (*or* To sit) on thorns *or* on pins and needles.

[Il n'est] point de rose[s] sans épines, No rose without a thorn. " Roses have thorns, and silver fountains mud ; Clouds and eclipses stain both moon and sun, And loathsome canker lives in sweetest bud."—SHAKESPEARE, *Sonnets* XXXV.

Se tirer une épine du pied, To get out of a mess.

Tirer à quelqu'un une [grosse *ou* grande] épine du pied, To get someone out of a [bad] mess.

See also MARCHER.

épingle. Être tiré à quatre épingles, To be spick and span, To be dapper, To be dressed up to the nines, To look as if one had come (*or* stepped) out of a band-box.

Tirer son épingle du jeu, To get well out of it *or* out of a bad job.

Un coup (*ou* Une piqûre) d'épingle (*fig.*), A pin prick.

Une épingle ne tomberait pas par terre, You couldn't have got a sheet of paper between them (*the crowd was so dense*). " Among the crowd i' the abbey ; where a finger Could not be wedg'd in more. . . . No man living Could say, 'This is my wife,' there ; all were woven So strangely in one piece."—*King Henry VIII* IV, 1.

See also SOUCIER.

éponge. *See* BOIRE, PASSER.

époque. Faire époque, To mark an epoch *or* an era, To be a red-letter day. " What hath this day deserv'd ?

what hath it done, That it in golden letters should be set Among the high tides in the calendar ?"—*King John* III, 1.

Ne pas être de son époque, To be behind the times.

Un événement qui fait époque, An epoch-making event.

See also MOUVEMENTER, PAIR.

épouse. *See* MARCHER.

épouser. *See* FAIM.

épouvantail. C'est un épouvantail [à moineaux], He (She) is a fright *or* a scarecrow (*grotesquely dressed*).

ergot. Se dresser (*ou* Se tenir) (*ou* Monter) sur ses ergots, To bristle up.

ermite. *See* DIABLE.

errant. *See* JUIF.

erre. *See* ALLER, MARCHER, SUIVRE.

erreur. *See* COMPTE, REVENIR.

escalier. Avoir l'esprit de l'escalier, To think of a retort when it is too late.

L'esprit de l'escalier, After-wit, Belated wit.

See also DÉGRINGOLER.

escampette. Prendre la poudre d'escampette, To bolt, To skedaddle, To [do a] bunk (*slang*).

escarpin. Jouer de l'escarpin, To take to one's heels, To run away.

esclave. *See* PAROLE.

espace. *See* DÉVORER.

Espagne. *See* CHÂTEAU.

espagnol. *See* PARLER.

espérance. Mettre ses espérances en quelque chose, To pin one's faith on something.

Vivre d'espérance, To live on hope.

See also DILATER.

esprit. Avoir de l'esprit comme un démon *ou* un esprit de tous les diables, To have the devil's own wit. " Thou most excellent devil of wit."—*Twelfth Night* II, 5.

Avoir l'esprit présent *ou* l'esprit délié, To be quick-witted, To have a nimble wit.

Esprit de corps, Team spirit, Esprit de corps.

Faire de l'esprit *ou* Courir après l'esprit, To try to be witty *or* funny. " Look, he's winding up the watch of his wit ; By and by it will strike."—*The Tempest* II, 1.

Il a l'esprit aux talons *ou* Il a l'esprit ailleurs, He isn't thinking of what he is saying, His thoughts are elsewhere, He is wool-gathering.

Quand ils ont tant d'esprit, les enfants vivent peu, The good die young. " So wise so young, they say, do never live long."—*King Richard III* III, 1.

Recueillir (*ou* Reprendre) ses esprits (*fig.*), To pull oneself together.

Rendre l'esprit, To give up the ghost (*die*).

See also ASSAUT, BANDER, BEAU 18, 29, BIEN, BOUCHER, BOUT, BROUILLARD, BUREAU, CACHER, CLASSE, COMIQUE, COMPTANT, COURIR, DÉTENDRE, EMPARER (S'), ENVERS, ÉPARPILLER, ESCALIER, GROS, OUVERTURE, PERDRE, POINTU, PROMPT, RETOUR, SOUFFLER, TOURNER, TRAVAILLER, TRAVERS, TREMPER, TUER.

essai. *See* BALLON, COUP 65.

essor. Donner l'essor à son imagination, To give free play to one's imagination.

See also PRENDRE.

essuyer. Essuyer les plâtres, To be the first occupant of a new house ; To stand the first shocks (*in a new enterprise*).

estaminet. *See* PILIER.

estomac. Avoir de l'estomac, To have plenty of pluck ; To be always game. " If you dare fight to-day, come to the field ; If not, when you have stomachs."—*Julius Caesar* V, 1. " He which hath no stomach to this fight, Let him depart."—*King Henry V* IV, 3.

Il a (*ou* C'est) un estomac d'autruche, il digérerait du fer, He has the digestion of an ostrich *or* He has a cast-iron digestion. " I'll make thee eat iron like an ostrich."—2 *King Henry VI* IV, 10.

See also DEMEURER, TALON.

estrade. Monter sur l'estrade, To make an exhibition of oneself.

See also BATTEUR, BATTRE.

et. *See* CAUSE, FOUETTER, LYRE, RIRE, VOILÀ.

étable. *See* NETTOYER.

établir. *See* BROUILLARD.

étamine. *See* PASSER.

étape. *See* BRÛLER.

état. Faire état, To attach importance (de = to) ; To intend (de = to) ; To depend *or* To count (de = on) ; To rely (de = on).

Il y a des grâces d'état, Sufficient grace will be given, The occasion often gives one the strength to meet it ; One is often able to persuade oneself that things are not as black as they look.

Une affaire d'État (*fig.*), A matter of vital importance.

See also CAUSE, COUP 66, CRIME, MOMENT.

été. Être dans son été, To be in one's prime *or* in the prime of life.

L'été de la Saint-Martin, Saint Martin's summer, The Indian summer ; A Saint Martin's summer (*fig.*), A renewal of [the freshness of] youth. " Saint Martin's summer, halcyon days."—1 *King Henry VI* I, 2.

Se mettre en été, To put on summer clothing.

éteindre. *See* CHANDELLE.

étendard. L'étendard de la Croix (*poetic*), The standard (*or* The ensign) (*or* The banner) of the Cross. " Many a time hath banish'd Norfolk fought For Jesu Christ in glorious Christian field, Streaming the ensign of the Christian cross Against black pagans, Turks, and Saracens : And toil'd with works of war, retir'd himself To Italy ; and there at Venice, gave His body to that pleasant country's earth, And his pure soul unto his captain Christ, Under whose colours he had fought so long."—*King Richard II* IV, 1.

étendre. *See* CARREAU.

étiquette. *See* CONDAMNER, JUGER.

étoffe. Il a en lui l'étoffe d'un chef, He has in him the makings of a commander, He is cut out for a leader. " She had all the royal makings of a queen."—*King Henry VIII* IV, 1.

Il y a en lui de l'étoffe, There's something (*or* There's good stuff) in him.

étoile. Faire voir à quelqu'un des étoiles en plein midi, To have someone on (*slang*), To lead someone up (*or* down) the garden path (*slang*).

Loger (*ou* Coucher) à la belle étoile, To sleep in the open *or* out of doors. " Where ly'st o' nights, Timon ?— Under that's above me."—*Timon of Athens* IV, 3. " Without covering, save yon field of stars."—*Pericles, Prince of Tyre* I, 1.

Monsieur trois étoiles, Mr dash. (*Written or printed : in French,* Monsieur *** *or* M. *** ; *in English,* Mr —.)

See also NAÎTRE, PÂLIR.

étonner. *See* TROMPETTE.

étouffer. Étouffer le monstre au berceau, To nip the mischief in the bud. *Quotation under* TUER.

étoupe. Mettre le feu aux étoupes (*fig.*), To set a match to the fire, To set things ablaze.

étourneau. C'est un étourneau, He is a featherhead.

étrange. *See* LANGAGE.

étrangler. Étrangler un sujet, une question, To burke a subject, a question.

Étrangler une affaire, To rush a thing through.

être. Il n'y est plus du tout, He has

lost his head, He has taken leave of his senses.

N'y être pas, To lose one's bearings, To be all adrift *or* all at sea.

On ne peut pas être et avoir été, One cannot remain young for ever. " We were, fair queen, Two lads that thought there were no more behind But such a day to-morrow as to-day, And to be boy eternal."—*The Winter's Tale* I, 2.

Où en sommes-nous ? How do we stand ? (*with regard to something*) ; How far have we got ? (*in the matter, the reading, etc.*).

Toujours est-il que . . ., The fact remains that . . .

Voilà comme vous êtes, That is just like you, That is you all over.

Vous n'y êtes pas, You do not understand *or* do not catch my meaning *or* do not twig.

Vous y êtes, You've hit it, You have hit the nail on the head.

Y êtes-vous ? Do you understand ? Do you tumble [to it] ?

Y être, To be at home. Madame y est-elle ? Is Madam at home ? Je n'y suis pour personne, I am at home to nobody.

Y être pour quelque chose, To have a hand in it, To have a finger in the pie. " No man's pie is freed From his ambitious finger."—*King Henry VIII* I, 1.

See also BOMBE, DIABLE, HANTER, MONDE, NOUS, PEINE, PIED, RESTER, REVUE, RIEN, SAVOIR, TANT, TEMPS, TOUS, TRAIT, VOIR.

étreindre. *See* EMBRASSER.

étrier. Avoir le pied à (*ou* dans) l'étrier, (*Lit.*) To be ready to depart ; (*Fig.*) To have the ball at one's feet.

Faire perdre les étriers à quelqu'un, To put someone out of countenance.

On lui a mis le pied à l'étrier, They put him in a fair way to succeed.

Tenir l'étrier à quelqu'un (*fig.*), To lend someone a [helping] hand.

See also FERME.

étriller. *See* SÉRIEUX.

étroit. Être (*ou* Vivre) à l'étroit, To be in straitened circumstances, To practise strict economy.

Être logé à l'étroit, To be cramped for room, Not to have room to swing a cat.

See also CHEMIN, DROIT, VOIE.

étuve. Cette pièce est une étuve, This room is [as] hot as an oven.

évangile. C'est l'évangile du jour (*fig.*), It is the gospel (*doctrine*) of the day ; It is the topic of the day.

See also CROIRE.

évaporer. C'est une évaporée, She is a featherhead.

Ève. Je ne le connais ni d'Ève, ni d'Adam, I don't know him from Adam. " What Adam dost thou mean ?—Not that Adam that kept the paradise, but that Adam that keeps the prison."—*The Comedy of Errors* IV, 3.

éveiller. Être éveillé comme une potée de souris, To be [as] lively as a cricket *or* as a grig, To be [as] playful as a kitten (*of a child*).

See also ALOUETTE, CHAT, RÊVER.

évent, éventé. C'est une tête à l'évent *ou* une tête éventée *ou* C'est un éventé, une éventée, He (She) is a featherhead.

éventer. *See* MÈCHE, MINE, SECRET.

évêque. *See* CHIEN.

évidence. *See* REFUSER.

éviter. *See* GALEUX.

excepter. Les personnes présentes sont [toujours] exceptées, Present company [always] excepted.

exception. L'exception confirme la règle, The exception proves the rule.

See also TOUS.

excuser. Qui s'excuse s'accuse, Who excuses himself accuses himself. " And oftentimes excusing of a fault Doth make the fault the worse by the excuse,—As patches set upon a little breach Discredit more in hiding of the fault Than did the fault before it was so patch'd."—*King John* IV, 2.

exécuter. Exécuter marches et contremarches (*fig.*), To leave no stone unturned.

S'exécuter, To come up to scratch ; To pay up, To fork out *or* over (*slang*), To stump up (*slang*).

exécution. Il est homme (*ou* C'est un homme) d'exécution, He is a man of deeds. " Speaking in deeds, and deedless in his tongue."—*Troilus and Cressida* IV, 5. " Speak, hands, for me ! "—*Julius Caesar* III, 1.

exemple. *See* PRÊCHER, TOPIQUE.

existence. *See* LUTTE.

expédient. *See* VIVRE.

expédier. *See* MONDE.

expliquer. Je vous expliquerai cela en un mot, I can give it you in a nutshell.

exprès. C'est [comme] un fait exprès, It looks as if it had been done on purpose.

extase. *See* RAVIR.

extinction. Disputer, Crier, jusqu'à extinction [de chaleur naturelle], To dispute, To cry out, to the point of exhaustion *or* until one is utterly exhausted.

extraire. *See* MOELLE.

extrême. *See* TOUCHER.

F

F. *See* B.

fable. Être la fable du quartier, To be the laughing-stock (*or* the talk) of the neighbourhood.

fabrique. Cela est de sa fabrique, That is of his invention.

face. *See* CARÊME, PILE, REGARDER.

fâcher. Soit dit sans vous fâcher, If I may say so without offence.

See also RUCHE.

fâcheux. *See* RÉVEIL.

facile. *See* COMPOSITION.

façon. C'est un homme sans façon, He is easy to get on with ; He is a free and easy man.

C'est une façon de bel esprit, de peintre, etc., He is a wit, a painter, of sorts.

Faire des façons, To stand on ceremony, To make a fuss.

Sans plus de façon, Without further ado.

See also PLAT, TOUR, UN.

fade. Se sentir le cœur fade, To feel disgust, To feel one's gorge rise.

fagot. Il y a fagots et fagots, All men, All things, are not alike, There are men and men, things and things (*named in English*, *e.g.*, There are dictionaries and dictionaries).

Sentir le fagot, To savour of heresy.

See also ÉPINE.

faible. Prendre quelqu'un sur son endroit faible *ou* par son faible, To get on someone's soft side.

See also PORTER, PROMPT.

faiblesse. *See* PAYER.

faïence. *See* CHIEN.

faillir. *See* ABBAYE, AUNE, BATTRE.

faim. Avoir une faim de loup *ou* une faim canine, To be ravenously hungry, To be [as] hungry (*or* [as] ravenous) as a wolf *or* [as] hungry as a hunter.

C'est la faim et la soif (*fig.*), They (*husband and wife*) are both very poor.

C'est la faim qui épouse la soif, A poor woman is marrying a poor man.

La faim chasse (*ou* fait sortir) le loup [hors] du bois, Necessity knows no law.

Mourir de faim, To die of starvation, To starve to death ; (*Fig.*), To be dying of hunger (*very hungry*),

To die for food. " I almost die for food, and let me have it."—*As You Like It* II, 7.

See also ASSAISONNER, CRIER, SOLLICITER.

faire. C'[en] est fait de moi, It's all up (*or* all over) with me.

C'est bien fait, It serves you right.

C'est un conte fait à plaisir, It is a made-up story, It is make-up.

Cela ne se fait pas, It isn't done.

Cela vaut fait, It is as good as done *or* settled.

Comme le, vous, voilà fait ! What a sight he is, you are !

Être fait comme un voleur *ou* comme un bandit, To look like a burglar.

Faire à autrui ce que nous voudrions qu'on nous fît, To do unto others as we would be done by (*Matthew* vii, 12).

Fais ce que dois, advienne (*ou* arrive) que pourra, Do your duty, come what may *or* and leave the rest to fate.

Il est bien [fait] de sa personne, He is a fine figure of a man.

Si fait, Yes, indeed, Yes, I, he, etc., did.

Un homme fait, A full-grown man.

Voilà qui est fait, That's done *or* settled.

See also AFFAIRE, AINSI, AISÉ, AUSSITÔT, AUTRE, BEAU 33, CHOSE, COMMENCER, COMPTE, COUP 34–45, DIRE, FEU, FOIS, FORT, FOU, GALÈRE, GORGE, HOMME, JAMBE, JOUR, JUSTICE, LAISSER, MÉTIER, NEZ, NID, PAS, PLUIE, POINT, PROVISION, RIEN, SAVOIR, SIÈGE, SIEN, SITÔT, SORT, TEMPÉRATURE, TÊTE, TIEN, TÔT, TOUR, TOUT, UN, VÔTRE.

faiseur. *See* ALMANACH, DISEUR.

fait. Aller, Venir, au fait, To go, To come, to the point.

C'est un fait à part *ou* C'est un autre fait, That is another (*or* a different) matter.

Cela est de mon fait, est de votre fait, est du fait d'un tel, This (*or* That) is my doing, is your doing, is so-and-so's doing.

Dire à quelqu'un son fait, To give someone a piece of one's mind. " I mind to tell him plainly what I think."—3 *King Henry VI* IV, 1.

En venir au fait, To be about to do it *or* on the point of doing it. Il allait en venir au fait, si on ne l'eût retenu, He would have done it, if he had not been held back *or* prevented.

En venir au fait et au prendre, To come to the point, To get down to brass tacks.

Entendre bien son fait, To know one's job well, To be very good at one's job.

Mettre (*ou* Poser) quelque chose en fait, To lay something down as a fact.

Prendre fait et cause pour quelqu'un, To take up the cudgels for someone.

[Quand on en vint *ou* Quant ce fut] au fait et au prendre, When it came to the point.

See also CURIOSITÉ, EXPRÈS, INTENTION, RARETÉ, VOIE.

falloir. C'est ce qu'il faut voir, We shall see about that (*it is not likely to happen*).

Il s'en faut [de] beaucoup *ou* Tant s'en faut, Far from it, Not by a long way, Not by a long chalk.

See also AUTEL, BÉNÉFICE, BOIRE, BOITEUX, BROUTER, CÉSAR, CHAIR, CHANTER, CHAT, CHIEN, CORDE, COULER, COURIR, COUVER, CROIRE, CROIX, DÉFIER, DIABLE, DURER, ÉCORCE, ENSEIGNE, FONTAINE, GALEUX, GOÛT, JEUNESSE, JURER, JUSTICE, LANGUE, LENDEMAIN, LINGE, MANCHE, MÉDECINE, MORT, NAGER, NOURRICE, OUVRIR, PAS, PEAU, PLOMB, QUATRE, RABATTRE, SORCIER, TOMBER, TONDRE, TOUCHER, TOUT, VENDRE, VENIR.

fameux. *See* LAPIN, PLATINE.

familiarité. La familiarité engendre le

mépris, Familiarity breeds contempt.

familièrement. *See* USER.

famille. *See* AIR, BEAU 26, LINGE, TENIR.

famine. Prendre quelqu'un par la famine, To starve someone out *or* someone into surrender.

See also CRIER.

fanfaron. C'est un fanfaron de vice, He is not so naughty as he makes himself out to be. " Let me be vilely painted."—*Much Ado About Nothing* I, 1.

fange. *See* PÉTRIR.

farce. Faire ses farces, To sow one's wild oats, To have one's fling.

See also DINDON, RAPIN.

fardeau. *See* ALLER.

farine. Ce sont gens de même farine, They are birds of a feather, They are of the same kidney, They are tarred with the same brush. " For both of you are birds of self-same feather."—3 *King Henry VI* III, 3.

See also CHARBON.

fatal. *See* BARQUE.

fatigue. *See* CHALEUR.

fausser. Fausser compagnie à quelqu'un, To give someone the slip ; Not to turn up : Il m'a faussé compagnie, He gave me the slip ; He didn't turn up. *Note.*—To turn up late, Arriver en retard.

faute. Faire une faute de (*ou* contre la) grammaire, To make a slip in grammar, To scratch Priscian. " *Bone?—bone*, for *benè : Priscian* a little scratch'd ; 't will serve."—*Love's Labour's Lost* V, 1.

Il m'a fait faute, I missed him (*he didn't come*) ; I missed it (*felt the want of the object I had to do without*).

La faute en est aux dieux, Qui la firent si belle, The fault lies with the gods: She is so fair. " Si c'est un crime d'aimer, On n'en doit justement blâmer Que les beautés qui sont en elle ; La faute en est aux dieux, Qui la firent si belle, Et non pas à mes yeux."—JEAN DE LINGENDES. " Do not call it sin in me That I am forsworn for thee : Thou for whom even Jove would swear Juno but an Ethiope were ; And deny himself for Jove, Turning mortal for thy love."—*Love's Labour's Lost* IV, 3.

Ne pas se faire faute de quelque chose, Not to fail to avail oneself of something; Not to hesitate (*or* to fail) (*or* to miss) (*or* to stick at) doing something.

See also ÂNE, BOIRE, FINIR, GRIVE, PARDONNER, SOULIER.

faux. Ce raisonnement porte à faux, This reasoning is beside the point.

Être faux comme un jeton, To be false to the core. " False as dicers' oaths."—*Hamlet* III, 4. " False as water."—*Othello* V, 2. " As false As air, as water, wind, or sandy earth, As fox to lamb, as wolf to heifer's calf."—*Troilus and Cressida* III, 2. " False as hell."—*Othello* IV, 2. " As false, by heaven, as heaven itself is true."—*King Richard II* IV, 1.

Faire fausse route, To be on the wrong track *or* on the wrong tack, To go the wrong way about it.

Plaider le faux pour [savoir] le vrai, To elicit the truth by alleging a falsehood.

S'inscrire en faux contre une allégation, To deny an allegation.

See also AIR, SONNER.

faveur. Prévenir en faveur de quelqu'un, de quelque chose, To speak in someone's favour, in favour of something.

See also TOUR.

fêler. Avoir le timbre fêlé, To have a screw (*or* a tile) loose.

C'est une tête fêlée, He (She) is a bit cracked.

Un pot fêlé dure longtemps *ou* Les

pots fêlés sont ceux qui durent le plus, A creaking gate hangs long.

femme. Ce que femme veut, Dieu le veut, What woman wills, God wills.

Un homme à femmes, A ladies' (*or* lady's) man.

See also CHERCHER, DIABLE, MORCEAU, TÊTE.

fendre. Être bien fendu, To be long-legged.

Fendre l'oreille à quelqu'un, To retire someone (*pension him off*).

Fendre la tête à quelqu'un, To make a deafening noise, To split someone's ear-drums.

Fendre le cœur à quelqu'un, To break someone's heart. " Now cracks a noble heart.—Good-night, sweet prince, And flights of angels sing thee to thy rest ! "—*Hamlet* V, 2.

See also BRUIT, GELER, QUATRE.

fenêtre. Chassez-le par la porte, il rentrera par la fenêtre, He turns up again like a bad halfpenny.

Jeter son argent par les fenêtres, To play ducks and drakes with (*or* To make ducks and drakes of) (*or* To squander) one's money. " *Tubal.* Your daughter spent in Genoa, as I heard, one night, fourscore ducats. *Shylock.* Thou stick'st a dagger in me."—*The Merchant of Venice* III, 1. (*Note.*—a ducat was a gold coin worth about 9 shillings.)

fer. C'est une tête de fer, He has an iron will (*is very stubborn*).

Les fers sont au feu, Work is now going on.

Mettre les fers au feu, To set to work, To make a start.

See also BARRE, BATTEUR, BATTRE, CLOU, ESTOMAC, GANTER, POT, QUATRE, ROSEAU, VERGE.

férir. Être féru de quelqu'un *ou* Être féru d'amour pour quelqu'un, To be over head and ears in love with someone. " He was more than over shoes in love."—*Two Gentlemen of Verona* I, 1. " You are over boots in love."—*Two Gentlemen of Verona* I, 1.

Sans coup férir, Without striking a blow, Without firing a shot. " Cowardly fled, not having struck one stroke."—1 *King Henry VI* I, 1. " To part with unhack'd edges, and bear back Our targes undinted."—*Antony and Cleopatra* II, 6. (*Note.*—targe = shield.)

fermant. À jour fermant, At the close of day.

À nuit fermante, At nightfall.

ferme. De pied ferme, At the halt (*Military*) ; Without budging an inch ; Calmly, Without apprehension, Resolutely : Attendre quelqu'un de pied ferme, (*Lit.*) To wait resolutely for someone ; (*Fig.*) To sit tight.

Être ferme dans (*ou* sur) ses arçons *ou* sur ses étriers (*fig.*), To be true to one's principles.

Voir d'un œil ferme la ruine de ses espérances, To put a good (*or* a bold) face on the wreck of one's hopes.

See also TENIR.

fermer. Fermer l'oreille (*ou* les oreilles) à la médisance, To be deaf (*or* To turn a deaf ear) (*or* To shut one's ears) to slander.

Fermer la bouche à quelqu'un, To silence someone, To shut someone up. Le respect me ferme la bouche, Respect seals my lips. " Within my mouth you have engaol'd my tongue, Doubly portcullis'd with my teeth and lips."—*King Richard II* I, 3.

Fermer la marche, To bring up the rear.

Fermer les yeux à la vérité, To shut one's eyes to the truth, To blink the facts.

Fermer les yeux sur une faute, sur un

abus, To shut one's eyes to (*or* To wink at) (*or* To overlook) a fault, an abuse.

Fermer son cœur à quelqu'un, à quelque chose, To harden one's heart against someone, against something.

N'avoir pas fermé l'œil (*ou* les yeux) de toute la nuit, Not to have slept a wink all night, Not to have had a wink of sleep all night. " O sleep, O gentle sleep, Nature's soft nurse, how have I frighted thee, That thou no more wilt weigh my eyelids down, And steep my senses in forgetfulness ? "—2 *King Henry IV* III, 1. " Sleep shall neither night nor day Hang upon his pent-house lid."—*Macbeth* I, 1.

See also BOURSE, BOUTIQUE, DORMIR, ÉCURIE, NEZ, OUVRIR, PARENTHÈSE.

ferrer. Être ferré [à glace] sur un sujet, To be well versed (*or* well [posted] up) in a subject, To be perfectly at home with a subject.

See also GOSIER, GUEULE.

férule. Être sous la férule de quelqu'un, To be under someone's thumb.

fervent. *See* TAPIS.

ferveur. *See* NOVICE.

fesse. N'y aller que d'une fesse, To go about it in a half-hearted way.

festin. Il n'y avait que cela pour tout festin, That was all there was to eat, That was the only fare.

fête. Ce n'est pas tous les jours fête, Christmas comes but once a year, It's a poor heart that never rejoices. " The yearly course that brings this day about Shall never see it but a holiday."—*King John* III, 1.

Faire fête à quelqu'un, To receive someone with open arms, To give someone a hearty welcome.

Il ne s'était jamais vu à pareille fête, He had never had such a good time.

La fête passée, adieu le saint, " The Devil was sick, the Devil a monk would be ; The Devil was well, the devil a monk was he."—URQUHART (*Translation of Rabelais*).

Se faire une fête de quelque chose, To look forward to something [with much pleasure].

Troubler la fête, To spoil the fun. " Lest jealousy, that sour unwelcome guest, Should, by his stealing in, disturb the feast."—SHAKESPEARE, *Venus and Adonis*. " Let her alone, lady ; as she is now, she will but disease our better mirth."—*Coriolanus* I, 3.

See also CLOU, HÉROS, TRISTE.

feu. C'est le feu et l'eau, They (*two things, two persons*) are as opposite as the [two] poles, They are poles apart, They are as like (*or* as different) as chalk and cheese. *Quotation under* ANTIPODE.

C'est un feu caché sous la cendre, They are the embers of a dying passion.

C'est un (*ou* Ce n'est qu'un) feu de paille, It (*this passion*) will soon burn itself out ; It (*this zeal*) is only a flash in the pan. " She burn'd with love, as straw with fire flameth, She burn'd out love, as soon as straw out burneth."—SHAKESPEARE, *The Passionate Pilgrim* V. " When the blood burns, how prodigal the soul Lends the tongue vows : these blazes, daughter, Giving more light than heat, . . . You must not take for fire."—*Hamlet* I, 3. " His rash fierce blaze of passion cannot last, For violent fires soon burn out themselves ; Small showers last long, but sudden storms are short ; He tires betimes that spurs too fast betimes."—*King Richard II* II, 1.

C'est un feu qui couve sous la cendre, The smoulder will soon be a flame (*he will take his revenge*).

Être [pris] entre deux feux, To be

[caught] between two fires (*lit. & fig.*).

Être tout feu, tout flamme pour quelque chose, pour quelqu'un, To be all enthusiasm for something, for someone.

Faire feu de tribord et de bâbord, To use every means in one's power.

Faire feu des quatre pieds, To go it hammer and tongs, To go all out (*slang*).

Faire la part du feu, (*Lit.*) To circumscribe the fire ; (*Fig.*) To cut one's loss.

Faire mourir quelqu'un à petit feu, To kill someone by inches, To keep someone on tenterhooks *or* on the rack. " They'll give him death by inches."—*Coriolanus* V, 4.

Il courait comme s'il avait le feu au derrière, He ran like blazes, He ran away so fast, you couldn't see him for dust.

Il se jetterait dans le feu pour lui, He would go through fire and water for him.

Jeter feu et flamme (*fig.*), To rage and fume, To storm and rage, To breathe fire and slaughter. " Here's a large mouth, indeed, That spits forth death and mountains, rocks and seas ; Talks as familiarly of roaring lions As maids of thirteen do of puppy dogs ! What cannoneer begot this lusty blood ? He speaks plain cannon,—fire and smoke and bounce."—*King John* II, 1.

Jeter [tout] son feu, To blaze up (*in anger*) and cool down ; To have shot one's bolt.

Jouer avec le feu (*fig.*), To play with fire.

Le feu lui sort des (*ou* par les) yeux, His eyes flash fire, He is glaring with rage. " With fiery eyes sparkling for very wrath."—3 *King Henry VI* II, 5.

Les feux du firmament *ou* de la nuit, *See under* FLAMBEAU.

Mettre le feu aux poudres, To make mischief, To stir up a hornets' nest ; To start a row ; To start an argument.

Mettre un pays à feu et à sang, To put a country to fire and sword.

N'avoir ni feu ni lieu, To have neither house nor home. " Houseless poverty."—*King Lear* III, 4.

N'y voir que du feu, To be completely dazzled ; To be completely hoodwinked.

On fait feu de tout bois, Every little helps.

On y court comme au feu, Everyone is rushing (*or* They are tumbling over each other) to see it, to have a look.

Prendre feu (*fig.*), To fly into a passion, To fire up.

Un feu d'enfer, A raging inferno.

See also AIR, ARTIFICE, ATTISER, COUP 33, DURER, ÉTOUPE, FER, FUMÉE, HUILE, MAIN, MARRON, RAMPE.

feuille. Trembler comme la feuille, To shake like a leaf, To tremble (*or* To quake) like an aspen leaf.

fève. *See* GÂTEAU.

ficelle. On voit la ficelle, One can see the trick (*how it is done*).

See also TENIR.

fiche. Une fiche de consolation, Some slight consolation, A crumb of comfort ; A booby prize.

ficher. Je m'en fiche [pas mal], I don't care in the least, I don't care a brass farthing *or* a rap *or* a button *or* a fig *or* a pin *or* a straw *or* a tinker's dam[n] *or* a damn *or* two hoots.

fichu. *See* NEZ.

fier. Être fier comme un coq *ou* comme Artaban, To be [as] proud as a peacock. *Quotation under* ORGUEILLEUX.

Fiez-vous-y, You can be sure of it, You can count on it ; (*By antiphrasis*) Don't reckon on it.

Se fier au hasard, To trust to luck.

See also DEVOIR.

fierté. *See* DÉPOSER.

fièvre. Une fièvre de cheval, A raging fever.

See also TOMBER.

figer. Garder un masque figé, To keep a set face.

figue. Moitié figue, moitié raisin, Half one thing (*or* way) and half the other, *e.g.*, Half willingly, half reluctantly, Partly on friendly terms, partly on unfriendly terms, Half warm, half cold (*e.g.*, *reception*), Half in earnest, half in jest.

Ni figue, ni raisin, Neither one thing nor the other.

figure. Faire figure, To cut a figure, To keep up an appearance.

See also CARÊME, CHEVALIER, COMIQUE, CONNAISSANCE, ENTERREMENT, HUMAIN, PAPIER, PAUVRE, PRENDRE, TRISTE.

fil. Aller de droit fil, To go straight at it.

Avoir [bien] du fil à retordre, To have one's work cut out (*to do it*).

Donner [bien] du fil à retordre à quelqu'un, To give someone a lot of bother *or* a hot job ; To make it hot for someone.

See also AIGUILLE, AVRIL, COUDRE, OURDIR, QUATRE, TENIR.

file. Prendre la file, To line up, To queue up.

filer. Des jours filés d'or et de soie, A life full of happiness and achievement.

Du temps que la reine Berthe filait *ou* Du temps où Berthe filait, In the days of Good Queen Bess, In the good old days, In days of yore.

Filer doux, To sing small, To eat humble pie.

Filer le parfait amour avec quelqu'un, To live love's dream with someone.

Filer un mauvais coton, To be in a bad way (*health*, *business*, *money affairs*), To be in Queer Street (*slang*).

See also ANGLAIS, HUILE.

filet. *See* BÊTE, COUP 67.

filière. Passer par la filière, To pass through all the graduate and subordinate stages (*of an employment*), To go through the mill.

fille. *See* DIABLE, MOTIF, PLANTER, THÉORIE.

filon. Trouver un filon (*fig.*), To strike it rich, To strike oil.

fils. C'est bien le fils (*ou* Il est [bien] fils) de son père, He is his father's son, He is a chip of the old block. " And, in the closing of some glorious day, Be bold to tell you that I am your son."—1 *King Henry IV* III, 2. " Although the print be little, the whole matter And copy of the father."—*The Winter's Tale* II, 3.

Faire le beau fils, To play the fine gentleman, To live like a lord (*extravagantly—of a young man*).

Il est le fils de ses œuvres, He is a self-made man.

Un fils de la terre (*fig.*), A son of the soil (*of peasant extraction*).

See also AVARE.

fin. À la fin des fins, When all is said and done.

À telle fin que de raison, As occasion may require, To suit the occasion.

Dire le fin mot, To say the last word : Il a dit, Il n'a pas encore dit, le fin mot, He has said, He has not yet said, the last word [on the matter].

Faire une chose à bonne fin, à mauvaise fin, To do a thing with good intent[ions], with ill intent[ions].

Faire une fin, To settle down, To get fixed up, To get married.

Faire une mauvaise fin *ou* une fin malheureuse, To come to a bad end.

Il est fin comme l'ambre, He is [as] sharp as a needle.

Il est fin comme une dague de plomb,

He thinks himself very sharp, but he is a blunt-witted fellow. "*Benedick.*—Thy wit is as quick as the greyhound's mouth ; it catches. *Margaret.*—And yours as blunt as the fencer's foils, which hit, but hurt not."—*Much Ado About Nothing* V, 2.

Il est trop fin pour vous, He's one too many for you.

Il n'eut ni fin ni cesse qu'il n'eût obtenu ce qu'il demandait, He didn't stop (*or* rest) till he got what he wanted.

Je n'entends pas le fin mot de tout cela, I cannot get to the bottom of it.

La fin justifie les moyens, The end justifies the means.

Le fin du fin, The quintessence (*as of a thought*). " This little flask Contains the wonderful quintessence, The perfect flower and efflorescence, Of all the knowledge man can ask ! " — LONGFELLOW, *Golden Legend* pt i.

Le fin fond, The very back (*as of a place*) ; The very bottom (*as of the sea*).

Le mot de la fin, A parting shot.

Plus fin que lui n'est pas bête *ou* Bien fin qui l'attrapera, He's no fool, There are no flies on him (*slang*).

See also ARRIVER, BEC, BÊTE, COURIR, COURONNER, CRUCHE, DONNER, GRIBOUILLE, JOUER, LAME, MENER, MERLE, MOUCHE, NEZ, NORMAND, RENARD, TENDRE, TIRER, VENIR, VOULOIR.

final. Mourir dans l'impénitence finale (*fig.*), To die in the last ditch (*desperately defending an opinion, or the like*).

finance. *See* MAL.

finesse. Entendre finesse à quelque chose, To mean to insinuate (*or* To imply) [a malicious intention] by something, To see something (*malicious or underhand*) in something : Je ne sais pas quelle finesse vous entendez à cela, Did you mean to insinuate anything ? Je n'y entends pas finesse, I see nothing in that.

See also COUDRE.

finir. C'est un homme fini, He is done for (*enfeebled and broken down*).

Finir en queue de poisson, To fizzle (*or, slang*, To peter) out (*of an undertaking*).

Le combat finit faute de combattants, The debate, The game, The dance, etc., ended (*or, slang*, petered out) for want of debaters, of players, of dancers.

See also AUTANT, BIEN.

flagrant. *See* PRENDRE.

flambeau. Le flambeau de la nuit *ou* Le [pâle] flambeau des nuits (*poetic*), [The] queen of [the] night (*the moon*). " And thou, thrice-crowned queen of night."—*As You Like It* III, 2. " This pale queen of night." —*Two Gentlemen of Verona* IV, 2. " Goddess of the night."—*Much Ado About Nothing* V, 3.

Le flambeau du jour (*poetic*), The sun. " The god of day."—*Hamlet* I, 1. " Heaven's glorious sun."—*Love's Labour's Lost* I, 1. " The glorious planet Sol In noble eminence enthron'd."—*Troilus and Cressida* I, 3. " The beauteous eye of heaven."—*King John* IV, 2. " The flame of yonder glorious heaven." —*Troilus and Cressida* V, 6. " Lo, in the orient when the gracious light Lifts up his burning head."—SHAKESPEARE, *Sonnets* VII.

Les flambeaux célestes *ou* Les célestes flambeaux *ou* Les feux du firmament *ou* Les feux de la nuit (*poetic*), The stars. " The fires of heaven." —*Coriolanus* I, 4. " The skies are painted with unnumber'd sparks,—They are all fire."—*Julius Caesar*

III, 1. " Heaven's lights."—*Love's Labour's Lost* I, 1. " The burning tapers of the sky."—*Titus Andronicus* IV, 2. " These blessed candles of the night."—*The Merchant of Venice* V, 1. " Those gold candles fix'd in heaven's air."—SHAKESPEARE, *Sonnets* XXI. " Look, love, what envious streaks Do lace the severing clouds in yonder east : Night's candles are burnt out, and jocund day Stands tiptoe on the misty mountain tops."—*Romeo and Juliet* III, 5. " The starry welkin."—*A Midsummer Night's Dream* III, 2. " Yon fiery oes and eyes of light." —*A Midsummer Night's Dream* III, 2.

See also MONTRER.

flamberge. Mettre flamberge au vent (*par plaisanterie*), To draw one's trusty blade.

flamme. *See* FEU.

flanc. Être sur le flanc, To be quite done up (*with fatigue*).

Prêter le flanc à une accusation, à la critique, aux soupçons, To lay oneself open to an accusation, to criticism, to suspicion.

See also BATTRE.

flanelle. Faire flanelle, To have a good look round without spending any money, Not to have much money, but yet to see life.

flatter. Flatter la marotte de quelqu'un, To play up to someone.

flèche. Décocher la flèche du Parthe *ou* Lancer une flèche de Parthe, To deliver a Parthian arrow *or* a Parthian shaft *or* a Parthian shot *or* a parting thrust. " Like the Parthian, I shall flying fight."—*Cymbeline* I, 6.

Faire flèche de tout bois, To resort to any shift, To leave no stone unturned.

Ne savoir plus de quel bois faire flèche, Not to know which way to turn.

Tout bois n'est pas bon à faire flèche, You can't make a silk purse out of a sow's ear.

fleur. Couvrir quelqu'un de fleurs (*fig.*), To throw bouquets (*or* nosegays), at someone.

La fleur des pois, The pick of the bunch.

See also SERPENT.

fleurer. *See* BAUME.

fleurette. *See* CONTER.

fleuron. Le plus beau fleuron de sa couronne (*fig.*), The brightest jewel in his (her) crown ; His (Her) chief possession, His (Her) principal asset.

fleuve. Une barbe de fleuve, A long flowing beard.

See also OUBLI.

flexible. *See* ÉCHINE.

florès. Faire florès, To make a stir, To be all the go.

flot. *See* COURROUX, VENIR.

fluide. Avoir le fluide, To have the [genuine] gift of the gods (*as in play acting*), To have "it" (*slang*).

flûte. Ajuster (*ou* Accorder) vos flûtes, Make up your mind (*on what you mean to tell me*) ; Settle your differences [between yourselves].

Être monté sur des flûtes, To be spindle-shanked.

See also VENIR.

foi. La foi du charbonnier, Simple (*or* Unquestioning) faith (*in what the Church teaches*). " Play fast and loose with faith ? so jest with heaven."—*King John* III, 1.

Sur la foi de, On the testimony of (*someone*) ; On the strength of (*as a letter*).

See also ARTICLE, ATHLÈTE, BAUME, CROIRE, MANQUER, SERMENT.

foin. Avoir du foin dans ses bottes *ou, en parlant d'un paysan,* dans

ses sabots, To be well off, To have feathered one's nest.
Faire ses foins, To make money.
Mettre du foin dans ses bottes, To feather one's nest (*by fair means*).
Quand il n'y a pas de foin au râtelier, les chevaux se battent, When poverty comes in at the door, love flies out of the window. *Quotation under* AMOUR.
See also AIGUILLE, BÊTE.
foire. *See* ENTENDRE.
fois. Je vous l'ai dit vingt fois *ou* cent [et cent] fois *ou* mille [et mille] fois, I have told you so times out of number *or* a hundred times.
N'en pas faire à deux fois, Not to hesitate, To decide out of hand.
S'y prendre à deux fois, To make two bites at a cherry.
Une bonne fois *ou* Une fois pour toutes, Once [and] for all.
Une fois de temps à autre, Une fois en passant, Once in a while *or* in a blue moon.
Y regarder à deux fois, To think twice about it.
See also COMPTER, COURIR, COUTUME, DIRE, DONNER, FOUR, LANGUE.
folie. *See* GRAIN.
fond. Au fond du cœur, In one's heart of hearts ; To the core.
Faire fond sur quelqu'un, sur quelque chose, To rely (*or* To depend) on someone, on something.
Je vous ai montré le fond du sac, I have laid all my cards on the table, That is all there is to it.
Lâcher le fond du sac, To let the cat out of the bag, To reveal the secret.
Voir le fond du sac, To know the secrets of the heart, To get to the bottom of it.
See also BOURSE, BOUTEILLE, COULER, FIN.
fondation. Cela est de fondation, That is an established custom.
fonder. Être fondé à croire quelque chose, To have good reasons for believing something.
fondre. Fondre à vue d'œil, To lose flesh every day, To go down in weight rapidly.
L'argent lui fond entre les mains, The money runs through his fingers, He spends money like water.
fonds. Savoir le fonds et le tréfonds d'une affaire, To know all about a matter, To know the ins and outs of an affair.
fontaine. Il ne faut pas dire, fontaine, je ne boirai pas de ton eau, You may want it, him, some day, Some day you may be glad of it, of his help. " What our contempts do often hurl from us, We wish it ours again."—*Antony and Cleopatra* I, 2.
La fontaine de Jouvence, The fountain of Youth.
for. Le for intérieur, The conscience. Dans son for intérieur, In one's heart of hearts, In one's innermost heart.
forçat. *See* TRAVAILLER.
force. À la force du poignet, By sheer strength of arm ; By sheer hard work.
Être dans la force de l'âge, To be in the prime of life.
Être de force à, To be strong enough to, To be clever enough to, To be capable of.
Faire force de voiles, To make every effort to succeed, To leave no stone unturned.
Force m'est de, I am obliged to.
Force passe droit *ou* La force prime le droit, Might is right, The battle is to the strong.
La force du sang, The call of the blood.
Y aller de toutes ses forces, To go at it with might and main *or* hammer and tongs *or* tooth and nail.
See also APPEL, CONSULTER, COUP 68, GRÉ, RAMASSER, TOUR.
forcer. Forcer la note, To overdo it.

See also CARTE, RETRANCHEMENT, SERRURE.

forêt. Vous êtes tombé dans une vraie forêt de Bondy, You have fallen among thieves.

See also EMPÊCHER.

forger. Forger un mensonge, To forge a lie. " And then to return and swear the lie he forges."—*All's Well That Ends Well* IV, 1. " Love is all truth ; lust full of forged lies."—SHAKESPEARE, *Venus and Adonis.*

forme. *See* HUMAIN, PROCÈS.

fort. Avoir fort à faire, To have a great deal to do, To have one's work cut out, To have one's hands full.

Avoir la tête forte, To be a wrong-headed (*or* a perverse) (*or* an unruly) person ; To have a strong head (*for alcohol*), To carry one's liquor well. " I have very poor and unhappy brains for drinking."—*Othello* II, 3.

C'est une tête forte *ou* une forte tête, He is a strong[-minded] man.

Être fort comme un Turc *ou* comme un bœuf, To be [as] strong as a horse *or* as a lion.

Il n'est pas fort, He's not very brilliant.

Le plus fort est fait, The worst [part] is done *or* is over.

Recourir à la manière forte, To resort to strong measures, To show the mailed fist.

Trouver plus fort que soi, To catch a Tartar.

See also CAVER, CRIER, GUEULE, PARTIE, PORTER, POUVOIR, PROPOS, RAISON, RÉPANDRE, THÈME.

fortune. Faire fortune, To make one's fortune *or* one's pile ; To catch on (*of a word*).

Un homme à bonnes fortunes, A lady-killer.

See also BON 43, BRUSQUER, CORRIGER, COURIR, DORMIR, ENTERRER, GARDER, JEU, MENER, RIRE, TENTER.

fosse. Avoir un pied dans la fosse *ou* Être sur le bord de sa fosse, To have one foot in the grave.

See also CREUSER.

fossé. Ce qui tombe dans le fossé est pour le soldat, Findings are keepings. " Be it his that finds it."—*Twelfth Night* II, 2.

See also BOUT, SAUTER.

fou. Avoir un argent fou, To have pots (*or* tons) of money.

C'est à devenir fou, It is enough to drive one mad. " That way madness lies."—*King Lear* III, 4.

De fou juge br[i]ève sentence, A fool's bolt is soon shot.

Être fait comme un chien fou, To be in mad attire, To be fantastically dressed.

Être fou à lier, To be raving mad, To be stark staring mad, To be [as] mad as a hatter.

Il est fou comme un jeune chien, He is as mad as a March hare (*scatter-brained and frisky*).

Le fou rire, Uncontrollable laughter.

Plus on est de fous, plus on rit, The more the merrier.

See also AVISER, BLANCHIR, CRIER, DÉFIER, DEMANDE, ÉCHEC, ENCHÈRE.

foudre. *See* COUP 11, 30.

fouet. *See* CLAQUER, COUP 69.

fouetter. Avoir d'autres chiens à fouetter, To have other fish to fry.

Et puis fouette cocher, And off we go ; And off we went.

Il fait cela comme un chien qu'on fouette, He does it with a very bad grace.

Il n'y a pas là de quoi fouetter un chat, It's only a trifle, It isn't worth [while] mentioning, It's nothing to write home about ; It is only a trifling offence.

See also VERGE.

fouler. *See* RATE.

four. Ce n'est pas pour vous que le four chauffe, It's not for you, You're going to be unlucky this time.

Faire four, To fall flat, To be a failure *or* (*slang*) a frost.

On ne peut être à la fois au four et au moulin, One cannot be in two places at the same time ; One cannot do two things at once.

Un four complet *ou* Un four noir, A dead failure, An awful frost (*slang*) (*of stage play*).

See also CHAUD, NOIR.

fourbe. *See* DONNER.

fourbi. *See* TOUT.

fourcher. La langue lui a fourché, He made a slip of the tongue.

fourchette. C'est une belle fourchette, He is a good trencherman, He plays a good knife and fork. " He is a very valiant trencherman ; he hath an excellent stomach."—*Much Ado About Nothing* I, 1.

fourchu. Avoir le pied fourchu, To show the cloven hoof.

Faire l'arbre fourchu, To walk on one's hands.

fourgon. *See* PELLE.

fournir. Fournir la carrière, To stay the course, To last out the distance.

Fournir sa carrière, To finish one's course (*in life*), To live (*or* To last out) one's (*normal*) span [of life], To live one's natural age. " God, I pray him, That none of you may live your natural age, But by some unlook'd accident cut off ! "—*King Richard III* I, 3. " Rebellion's head, rise never, till the wood Of Birnam rise, and our high-plac'd Macbeth Shall live the lease of nature, pay his breath To time and mortal custom."—*Macbeth* IV, 1.

Fournir une belle carrière, To be full of years and honours.

fourreau. La lame (*ou* L'épée) use le fourreau, The mind is wearing out the body.

Remettre l'épée au fourreau (*fig.*), To sheathe the sword. " My alf-supp'd sword . . . thus goes to bed." —*Troilus and Cressida* V, 8.

Son épée ne tient pas au fourreau, He is always itching for a fight.

Tirer l'épée du fourreau (*fig.*), To unsheathe the sword. " Strip your sword stark naked."—*Twelfth Night* III, 4.

fourrer. S'en fourrer jusque là, To stuff oneself to repletion, To gorge.

See also NEZ, PAIX, SAVOIR.

foyer. Un homme de foyer, A family man.

frais. Être frais comme l'œil, To be [as] fresh as a daisy *or* as paint. " How green you are, and fresh in this old world ! "—*King John* III, 4.

Il en est frais émoulu, He has only just got to the bottom of it (*the matter*).

Un jeune homme frais [émoulu] du collège, A young man fresh from school *or* from college.

See also PRINCESSE, RECOMMENCER.

franc. Avoir son franc parler avec quelqu'un, To be outspoken with someone.

See also ALLER, COLLIER, JOUER, SOU.

français. *See* PARLER.

franchir. *See* PAS, RUBICON.

frapper. Cet ouvrage est frappé au coin du génie, This work bears the stamp (*or* the hall-mark) of genius.

Frapper quelqu'un comme un sourd, To beat someone unmercifully.

Un ouvrage frappé au bon coin, A work of the right sort, A good work.

See also BRAS, BUT, POITRINE, PORTE, TAS.

frayer. Frayer le chemin (*ou* la voie) à quelqu'un, To pave the way for someone.

frein. *See* RONGER.

frère. *See* MALHEUR.

friand. Elle est friande comme une chatte, She is [as] dainty (*or* fastidious) (*in her choice of food*) as a cat.

frime. C'est de la frime, It's all

sham, It's nothing but window-dressing *or* eye-wash.

frire. Cet homme est frit, This man is done for (*ruined*).

Il n'y a rien à frire dans cette maison, dans cette affaire, There's no money to be made here, in this affair.

N'avoir plus de quoi frire, To be at the end of one's resources (*be ruined*).

Tout est frit, It's all up.

friser. Friser l'illégalité, To sail close to the wind.

froc. Jeter le froc aux orties (*fig.*), To throw off the cowl (*renounce priesthood*), To become an ex-monk; To change one's profession.

froid. C'est une tête froide *ou* un cerveau froid, He is cool-headed.

Cette nouvelle jeta un froid dans l'assemblée, This news put a damper on the assembly. "*Douglas.* That's the worst tidings that I hear of yet. *Worcester.* Ay, by my faith, that bears a frosty sound."—1 *King Henry IV* IV, 1.

N'avoir pas froid aux yeux, To be very plucky, To be game, Not to suffer from cold feet (*slang*).

See also BATTRE, CHAT, CHAUD, DOUCHE.

fromage. *See* POIRE, RAT.

front. Faire marcher (*ou* Mener) plusieurs choses de front, To have several things on at once *or* several irons in the fire.

See also AIRAIN, UNIQUE.

frotter. Frotter l'échine à quelqu'un, To dust someone's jacket (*thrash him*).

Frotter les oreilles à quelqu'un, To give someone a flea in his ear.

Ne vous y frottez pas, Have nothing to do with it, Fight shy of it.

Qui s'y frotte, s'y pique, He is not to be defied with impunity.

Se frotter à quelqu'un, To rub shoulders (*or* To associate) with someone; To come up against someone.

fruit. Un fruit sec, A failure (*unsuccessful pupil*).

See also ARBRE, SERRE.

fuir. *See* GALEUX.

fuite. *See* BON 73.

fumée. [Il n'y a] point de fumée sans feu, [There is] no smoke without fire.

Manger son pain à la fumée du rôt, To be only a looker-on (*and not to share in the amusement*).

[S'en] aller en fumée, To end in smoke: L'entreprise est allée (*ou* s'en est allée) en fumée, The venture ended in smoke.

fumier. *See* HARDI.

fuseau. *See* JAMBE.

fusil. *See* COUCHER, ÉPAULE.

G

gages. Un homme à gages, A paid servant, A wage slave. "You shall mark Many a duteous and knee-crooking knave That, doting on his own obsequious bondage, Wears out his time, much like his master's ass, For naught but provender; and when he's old, cashier'd."—*Othello* I, 1.

See also CASSER.

gageure. Cela ressemble à une gageure *ou* Cela tient de la gageure *ou* C'est une gageure, It is stranger than fiction. "If this were played upon the stage now, I could condemn it as an improbable fiction."—*Twelfth Night* III, 4.

gagner. Gagner à être connu, To improve on acquaintance.

Gagner au pied, To take to one's heels.

Gagner haut la main, To win hands down.

Gagner le large *ou* le taillis *ou* le haut *ou* les champs, To get clear.

Gagner pays, To press on *or* forward.

Gagner quelqu'un de vitesse, To steal a march on someone.

Gagner une marche sur l'ennemi, To steal a march on the enemy.

N'est pas marchand qui toujours gagne, One cannot expect to win every time.

Qui gagne du temps gagne tout, Time is everything.

See also CAUSE, CLAIR, ÉPERON, JOUER, VILLE.

gai. Être gai comme un pinson, To be [as] blithe as a lark, To be [as] jolly as a sand-boy, To be [as] merry as a cricket *or* as a grig *or* as the day is long.

See also VIN.

gaieté. Faire quelque chose de gaieté de cœur, To do something out of sheer wantonness, To do something (*bad*) with a light heart.

gaillard. *See* DÉCOUPLER.

gain. *See* CAUSE, MATIN.

gale. Il est méchant (Elle est méchante) comme la (*ou* comme une) gale *ou* C'est une gale, He (She) is a thoroughly nasty (*or* objectionable) person. " Out, scab ! "—*Twelfth Night* II, 5.

galère. C'est une [vraie] galère, It's a hell upon earth.

Qu'allait-il faire dans cette galère ? What business was it of his ? ; What business had he to be there ? What was he doing there ?

Vogue la galère, Come what may, Here goes, Let's chance it, Let her rip.

galérien. *See* TRAVAILLER.

galeux. Fuir (*ou* Éviter) quelqu'un comme une brebis galeuse, To avoid someone like the plague.

Il ne faut qu'une brebis galeuse pour gâter tout un troupeau, One scabby sheep will taint the whole flock. " I am a tainted wether of the flock, Meetest for death."—*The Merchant of Venice* IV, 1.

Qui se sent galeux se gratte, If the cap fits, wear it ; The guilty one gives himself away by his attitude. " Guiltiness will speak Though tongues were out of use."—*Othello* V, 1. "We that have free souls, it touches us not : let the galled jade wince, our withers are unwrung."—*Hamlet* III, 2. "Why, let the stricken deer go weep, The hart ungalled play."—*Hamlet* III, 2.

Une brebis galeuse, A person to be avoided (*on account of his vices*), A black sheep : C'est une brebis galeuse qu'il faut séparer du troupeau, He is a black sheep that it is necessary to separate from the flock.

galon. Quand on prend du galon, on n'en saurait trop prendre, You can't have too much of a good thing.

galop. Aller (*ou* Courir) le [grand] galop, To go fast (*in walking or running, reading or speaking*) : Si vous courez ainsi le galop, je ne pourrai vous suivre, If you go so fast, I shall not be able to follow you.

Donner, Recevoir, un galop, To give, To get, a scolding *or* a wigging.

See also CHASSER, HÔPITAL.

gamme. *See* CHANGER, CHANTER.

gant. Aller comme un gant, To fit like a glove (*of a garment*).

Jeter le gant, To throw (*or* To fling) (*or* To hurl) down the gauntlet *or* the gage. " For I will throw my glove to death himself That there's no maculation in thy heart."—*Troilus and Cressida* IV, 4. (*Note.*—maculation = blemish, defilement.) " There I throw my gage, To prove it on thee to the extremest point Of mortal breathing : seize it, if thou dar'st."—*King Richard* II IV, 1. "And interchangeably hurl down my gage."—*King Richard II* I, 1.

Mettre (*ou* Prendre) des gants, To proceed cautiously *or* tactfully (*in handling someone*).

Ramasser (*ou* Relever) le gant, To take up (*or* To pick up) the gauntlet *or* the gage, To accept the challenge.

Se donner les gants d'une chose, To take credit for a thing (*falsely*).

Vous n'en avez pas les gants, You were not the first to think of it, to do it, to discover it.

See also SOUPLE.

gantelé. La main gantelée, The mailed fist.

ganter. Une main de fer gantée de velours (*fig.*), An iron hand in a velvet glove.

garçon. C'est un garçon manqué, She's a tomboy.

Faire le mauvais garçon, To behave in an unruly manner.

Traiter quelqu'un en petit garçon, To treat someone like a child.

See also DRÔLE, ENTERRER, PLANTER.

garde. Avoir garde à carreau, To be prepared for whatever may come.

S'en donner jusqu'à la garde, To stuff oneself to repletion, To gorge.

See also SOU.

garder. En donner à garder à quelqu'un, To impose [up]on someone.

Garder à quelqu'un un chien de sa chienne *ou* La garder bonne à quelqu'un, To have a rod in pickle for someone, To bear a grudge against someone, To owe someone a grudge.

Garder un ressentiment contre (*ou* Garder rancune à *ou* contre) quelqu'un de quelque chose, To harbour resentment against someone (*or* To bear someone malice) for something.

Il voudrait faire croire que nous avons gardé les cochons (*ou* les vaches) ensemble, He is trying to make out that we are in the same station [in life] *or* that we have the same social standing, He is taking liberties, He doesn't (*or* He fails to) keep his distance. " And now is this Vice's dagger become a squire, and talks as familiarly of John of Gaunt as if he had been sworn brother to him ; and I'll be sworn he never saw him but once in the Tilt-yard." —2 *King Henry IV* III, 2.

Se garder à carreau, To be on one's guard, To take every precaution.

Vous ne savez pas ce que la Fortune vous garde, You do not know what Fortune has in store for you.

See also APPARENCE, BON 26, 44, BOURSE, DINDON, DISTANCE, FIGER, LOUP, MESURE, MÉTIER, POIRE, PROPORTION, SANG-FROID, SÉRIEUX.

gare. *See* CRIER, DANSE, TEMPÊTE.

garnir. *See* GOUSSET.

garrotter. Garrotter quelqu'un (*fig.*), To tie someone down (*as to certain conditions by a contract*).

gâteau. Avoir part au gâteau, To share in the booty.

Partager le gâteau, To share the booty, To divide the spoil.

Trouver la fève au gâteau (*fig.*), To make a lucky dip.

gâter. Cela ne gâte rien, That is all to the good.

Cela se gâte, Events (*or* Things) are taking a serious turn.

Gâter le métier, To spoil the market, To queer the pitch.

Le temps se gâte, The weather is breaking up.

See also CUISINIER, GALEUX.

gauche. *See* MAIN, MARIER, PIED.

geai. C'est le geai paré des plumes du paon, It is a case of the jackdaw in peacock feathers *or* a case of being dressed in borrowed plumes.

géant. *See* MARCHER.

geler. Il gèle à pierre fendre, It is freezing hard.

gémir. Faire gémir la presse, To

keep the printing-press busy (*said of a writer more noted for a voluminous output than the good quality of his writings*).

gémonies. Traîner quelqu'un aux gémonies, To hold someone up to public obloquy, To heap insults on someone. " Shall they hoist me up, And show me to the shouting varletry Of censuring Rome ? "—*Antony and Cleopatra* V, 2.

gendarme. C'est un vrai gendarme, She is a regular Amazon. " Stay, stay thy hands ! thou art an Amazon, And fightest with the sword of Deborah."—1 *King Henry VI* I, 2. " The bouncing Amazon, Your buskin'd mistress." —*A Midsummer Night's Dream* II, 2.

gêner. Ne vous gênez pas (*ironiquement*), Make yourself quite at home, Don't mind me, us (*to someone inconveniencing others*).

See also ENTOURNURE.

genou. *See* PLIER.

gens. *See* CHICANE, COMÉDIE, FARINE, MOQUER, PRISE, TIRER,

gentil. *See* CROQUER.

gésir. *See* QUEUE.

geste. Unir (*ou* Joindre) le geste à la parole, To suit the action to the word.

See also BEAU 30.

gibecière. *See* TOUR.

giberne. *See* BÂTON.

gibier. Les romans ne sont point gibier de dévots, Fiction is no stuff for the pious.

Les voleurs sont le gibier de la police, Robbers are fair game to the police.

Un gibier de potence, A gallows-bird.

gifle. *See* APPLIQUER, TÊTE.

girouette. *See* TOURNER.

gîte. Un lièvre va toujours mourir au gîte, There's no place like home (*after having travelled much*). *Quotations under* RETOUR.

glace. Rompre la glace (*fig.*), To break the ice.

See also FERRER.

glissant. C'est un pas glissant, It is an awkward position.

glisser. Glissez, [glissez], Don't labour the point, Enough said, Enough of that, Let that pass.

Impossible de glisser un mot, I couldn't get a word in edgeways.

See also ORANGE.

globe. C'est à mettre sous globe, That ought to be chalked up (*noted as extraordinary*), Give me a piece of chalk.

glu. Il a de la glu aux mains, Money sticks to his fingers, He has an itching palm. " Let me tell you, Cassius, you yourself Are much condemn'd to have an itching palm ; To sell and mart your offices for gold To undeservers."—*Julius Caesar* IV, 3. " That Mowbray hath receiv'd eight thousand nobles, In name of lendings for your highness' soldiers, The which he hath detain'd for lewd employments, Like a false traitor and injurious villain."—*King Richard II* I, 1.

gober. Gober des mouches, To stand gaping, To twiddle one's thumbs.

See also MORCEAU.

gogo. Être, Vivre, à gogo, To be, To live, in clover.

gond. Être hors des (*ou* hors de ses) gonds *ou* Sortir [hors] des gonds, To be in a rage, To lose control of oneself.

Faire sortir (*ou* Mettre) quelqu'un [hors] des gonds *ou* hors de ses gonds, To exasperate someone.

gordien. Couper le nœud gordien, To cut the Gordian knot. " The Gordian knot of it he will unloose Familiar as his garter."—*King Henry V* I, 1.

gorge. Avoir le couteau (*ou* le poignard) sur la gorge (*fig.*), To have a pistol held at one's head.

En avoir menti par la gorge, To lie in one's throat. " Then, Bolingbroke, as low as to thy heart, Through the false passage of thy throat, thou liest ! "—*King Richard II* I, 1.

Faire des gorges chaudes, To poke fun. *Quotation under* RIDICULE.

Le couteau sur la gorge, Under coercion, Under duress.

Mettre (*ou* Tenir) le pistolet (*ou* le couteau) (*ou* le poignard) sur la gorge à quelqu'un (*fig.*), To hold a pistol to someone's head.

Rendre (*ou* Faire) gorge (*fig.*), To disgorge, To make restitution.

Tenir quelqu'un à la gorge *ou* Tenir le pied sur la gorge à quelqu'un (*fig.*), To have a strangle-hold on someone, To have someone [completely] at one's mercy, To have one's foot on someone's neck.

See also ARROSER, BOUTONNER, CHAT, CRIER, PAROLE, RIRE.

gosier. Avoir le gosier pavé *ou* ferré *ou* blindé, To have a cast-iron throat (*be able to eat very hot food*).

See also HUMECTER.

goulée. *See* BÊLER.

gourme. Jeter sa gourme, To sow one's wild oats, To have one's fling.

gourmette. Lâcher la gourmette à quelqu'un, To give someone freer rein.

Rompre sa gourmette, To break free *or* loose, To break away from restraint (*dissipate after being restrained*).

gousset. Avoir le gousset [bien] garni, To have one's pockets [well] lined (*with money*). " When they have lin'd their coats."—*Othello* I, 1.

Avoir le gousset vide, To be cleaned out (*have no more money*).

goût. Des goûts et des couleurs il ne faut pas discuter *ou* [À] chacun son goût, There is no accounting for tastes, Everyone to his taste, Tastes differ.

Faire passer (*ou* Faire perdre) le goût du pain à quelqu'un, To send someone to kingdom come (*slang*). " Mightst bespice a cup To give mine enemy a lasting wink."—*The Winter's Tale* I, 2.

Mettre quelqu'un en goût d'une chose (*fig.*), To whet someone's appetite for a thing.

goutte. C'est la goutte d'eau qui fait déborder le vase *ou* Une goutte d'eau suffit pour faire déborder un vase plein, It is the last straw that breaks the camel's back. " Rain added to a river that is rank, Perforce will force it overflow the bank."—SHAKESPEARE, *Venus and Adonis*.

C'est une goutte d'eau dans la mer, It is a drop in the ocean.

Ces deux personnes se ressemblent comme deux gouttes d'eau, These two persons are [as] like as two peas. " Yet they say we are Almost as like as eggs."—*The Winter's Tale* I, 2. " 'Tis (*the child is*) as like you As cherry is to cherry."—*King Henry VIII* V, 1. " Being as like As rain to water, or devil to his dam."—*King John* II, 1.

Le diable n'y verrait goutte, One cannot make head or tail of it (*it is so involved*).

Ne voir (*ou* N'y voir) goutte dans une affaire *ou* N'entendre (*ou* Ne comprendre) goutte à une affaire, Not to be able to make head or tail of an affair.

See also SUER.

gouverner. *See* BARQUE, BOURSE, VERGE.

grâce. Sacrifier aux grâces (*ironiquement*), To put on graces, To try to be graceful.

See also BON 33, COUP 15, 73, ÉTAT.

grain. Avoir un grain [de folie dans la tête], To be slightly touched (*or* cracked) [in the head], To be not quite right in the head.

Veiller au grain, To keep a sharp look-out, To look out for squalls,

To keep one's weather eye open; To practise strict economy.

See also CATHOLIQUE, IVRAIE.

graisser. Graisser la patte à quelqu'un, To grease someone's palm. "In the corrupted currents of this world Offence's gilded hand may shove by justice; And oft 'tis seen the wicked prize itself Buys out the law: but 'tis not so above; There is no shuffling,—there the action lies In his true nature; and we ourselves compell'd, Even to the teeth and forehead of our faults, To give in evidence."—*Hamlet* III, 3.

Graisser ses bottes, To prepare for a journey; To prepare for the next (*or* the other) world (*prepare for death*).

See also BEURRE.

grammaire. *See* BROUILLER, FAUTE.

grand. Au grand jour, In broad daylight, With the milk (*humorous*—Revenir d'un bal au grand jour, To come home from a dance with the milk); (*Fig.*) Openly, Publicly.

Aux grands maux les grands remèdes, Desperate ills call for desperate remedies. "Diseases desperate grown By desperate appliance are reliev'd, Or not at all."—*Hamlet* IV, 2.

Il a les yeux plus grands que le ventre, His eyes are bigger than his belly.

Il est grand temps de . . ., que . . ., It is high time to . . ., that . . .

Le grand jour [de la publicité], The limelight.

Le grand public, The general public, The man in the street.

Ouvrir de grands yeux, To open one's eyes wide (*in astonishment*).

Recourir aux grands moyens, To resort to extremes.

See also ABATTRE, AIDE, AIR, BAUDRUCHE, BOIRE, CHEVAL, CŒUR, COUP 40, DIABLE, DIEU, DISEUR, DONNER, GALOP, HAQUENÉE, HÔPITAL, MAÎTRE, MALHEUR, MENER, MOT, NAGER, ŒUVRE, OREILLE, PENDRE, PERCHE, PIED, PITIÉ, PLAT, RIRE, RIVIÈRE, SAIGNÉE, SEIGNEUR, SORCIER, TRAIN, TRAIT, TRALALA, VOYAGE.

grand-chose. Ne pas valoir grand-chose, Not to be worth (*or* up to) much, To be no great catch.

grandeur. *See* HAUT.

grappe. *See* MORDRE.

grappin. Jeter (*ou* Mettre) le grappin sur quelqu'un (*fig.*), To have dominion over someone, To drag someone at one's heels, To have someone at one's beck and call.

gras. Être gras à lard *ou* Être gras comme un moine *ou* comme un chanoine, To be [as] fat as a porpoise. "A gross fat man.—As fat as butter."—1 *King Henry IV* II, 4.

Tuer le veau gras, To kill the fatted calf (*Luke* xv, 23–27).

See also CHOU, DORMIR.

grassement. Vivre grassement, To live on the fat of the land.

gratter. Ce sont deux ânes qui se grattent, It is a mutual admiration society.

Gratter du papier, To drive a quill.

Gratter quelqu'un où cela (*ou* où il) lui démange (*fig.*), To scratch someone's back, To play up to someone.

Gratter sur la dépense, To cut down the expenses.

Trop gratter cuit, trop parler nuit *ou* Trop parler nuit, trop gratter cuit, Least said soonest mended. (*Note.—Lit.* Too much scratching smarts *or* burns, too much talking hurts *or* is prejudicial—*nuit* is 3rd person singular of present tense of *nuire.*)

See also GALEUX, MÉTIER.

gré. Bon gré, mal gré, Whether I (he) (we) (you) (they) like it or not, Willy-nilly, Will I, etc., nill I, etc. "And, will you, nill you, I will marry you."—*The Taming of the Shrew* II, 1.

De gré ou de force, By fair means or foul.

Se savoir bon gré d'avoir fait quelque chose, To congratulate oneself on having done something.

See also TAILLER.

grec. *See* CALENDES.

grègues. *See* TIRER.

grêler. Grêler sur le persil, To brow-beat someone ; To thunder against something of no consequence.

grelot. Attacher le grelot, To bell the cat.

grenadier. *See* JURER.

grenier. *See* BLÉ, CAVE.

grenouille. Manger (*ou* Faire sauter) la grenouille, To make off with the cash.

Gribouille. Fin comme Gribouille, qui se jette dans l'eau crainte de la pluie, That is falling (*or* jumping) out of the frying pan into the fire.

griffe. La griffe du lion (*fig.*), The touch of the master-hand.

See also COUP 24.

gril. Être sur le gril (*fig.*), To be on tenterhooks *or* on the rack (*suspense*). " Let me choose ; For, as I am, I live upon the rack."—*The Merchant of Venice* III, 2.

grimace. Faire des grimaces à quelqu'un, To make (*or* To pull) faces at someone. " He's a god or a painter, for he makes faces."—*Love's Labour's Lost* V, 2.

Faire la grimace à quelqu'un, To look sourly at someone.

Faire la grimace à une proposition, To pull a long face at a proposal.

See also SINGE.

grippe. Prendre quelqu'un en grippe, To take (*or* To conceive) an unaccountable dislike to (*or* for) someone.

gris. En faire voir de grises à quelqu'un, To give someone a warm time [of it]. To lead someone a dance.

En voir de grises, To have a rough (*or* a warm) time of it, To get more than one bargained for.

Faire grise mine à quelqu'un, To look anything but pleased with someone.

See also BARBE, CHAT.

grive. Faute de grives, on mange des merles, Half a loaf is better than no bread.

See also SOÛL, VALOIR.

gros. Être gros comme une barrique, To be [as] round as a barrel (*corpulent*). " A tun of man."—1 *King Henry IV* II, 4.

Faire le gros dos (*fig.*), To [fairly] squirm with pleasure.

Faire les gros yeux à quelqu'un, To look reproachfully at someone; To look reprovingly at someone.

Il a plus d'esprit qu'il n'est gros, He sparkles (*or* coruscates) with wit.

Il a plus dépensé (*ou* plus coûté) qu'il n'est gros, He has eaten his parents, his relations, out of house and home (*fig.*).

Le gros bon sens, Plain common sense, Horse sense.

Les gros poissons mangent les petits, Might overcomes right. "Humanity must perforce prey on itself, Like monsters of the deep."—*King Lear* IV, 2.

Un gros bonnet *ou* Un gros légume *ou* Une [grosse] légume, A bigwig, A big pot, A big bug. " Burgomasters and great oneyers."—1 *King Henry IV* II, 1.

See also ARBRE, BATTRE, BŒUF, BRAS, CATHOLIQUE, JOUER, MORCEAU, PAPA, PARIER, PÂTÉ, PÈRE, SUER, VÉRITÉ.

Gros-Jean. C'est Gros-Jean qui en remontre à son curé, It's like teaching your grandmother to suck eggs. " To teach a teacher ill beseemeth me."—*Love's Labour's Lost* II, 1.

Être Gros-Jean comme devant, To be no better off [than before], To be still in the same old rut (*be *disappointed in one's hopes of improvement in one's affairs, in one's position*).

grossir. *See* PEUR.

grue. Faire le pied de grue à attendre quelqu'un, To cool one's heels waiting for someone, To hang about for someone.

guêpier. Se mettre la tête dans le guêpier, To put one's head into a noose (*fig.*).

Tomber (*ou* Donner) dans le guêpier, To get badly stung (*fig.*).

guère. *See* COÛTER.

guérir. Être guéri du mal de dents, To be out of all one's troubles (*be dead*). " *Posthumus.* I am merrier to die than thou art to live. *Gaoler.* Indeed, sir, he that sleeps feels not the toothache."—*Cymbeline* V, 5.

Médecin, guéris-toi toi-même, Physician, heal thyself (*Luke* iv, 23).

See also DÉBANDER, PRÉVENIR.

guerre. À la guerre comme à la guerre, One must take things as they come.

Faire la guerre, To make (*or* To wage) war.

Faire la guerre à quelqu'un, To take someone to task.

Faire la guerre au couteau, To make war to the knife.

Faire la guerre aux mots, To criticize the wording.

Faire quelque chose de guerre lasse, To do something for the sake of peace and quietness.

La guerre sociale, Class war[fare].

Qui terre a guerre a, A landowner is never free from trouble.

See also DÉPENS, NERF, PLUME, RUSE, SENTIER.

guet. *See* ŒIL.

guetter. *See* CHAT.

gueule. Avoir la gueule de bois, To have hot coppers, To have a hangover, To have that morning after the night before feeling, To suffer from alcoholic remorse.

Avoir la gueule forte, To be loud-mouthed.

Être fort en gueule, To be full of jaw (*slang*).

Il a la gueule ferrée *ou* C'est une gueule ferrée, He has a cast-iron throat (*is able to eat very hot food*).

Laisser quelqu'un à la gueule du loup, To leave someone in a perilous position.

Mettre quelqu'un à la gueule du loup, To expose someone to certain danger.

Se mettre (*ou* Se jeter) dans la gueule du loup, To jump (*or* To rush) into the lion's mouth.

gueux. Être gueux comme un rat [d'église], To be [as] poor as a church mouse.

See also BESACE.

guide. *See* MENER.

guigne. *See* SOUCIER.

guitare. *See* MÊME.

H

habile. *See* DONNER.

habiller. Habiller quelqu'un [de toutes pièces], To speak ill of someone.

See also PEUR.

habit. L'habit ne fait pas le moine, It is not the cowl that makes the monk. " I do not like their coming. They (*Cardinals Wolsey and Campeius*) should be good men ; their affairs as righteous ; But all hoods make not monks."—*King Henry VIII* III, 1. " *Cucullus non facit monachum :* honest in nothing but in his clothes." — *Measure for Measure* V, 1.

See also ARLEQUIN, LOUP.

habiter. *See* CHAUME.

habitude. Être un animal d'habitude, To be a creature of habit.

L'habitude est une autre (*ou* une seconde) nature, Use is second nature. " How use doth breed a habit in a man."—*Two Gentlemen of Verona* V, 4.

hache. *See* COUP 45, 76.

hacher. Hacher quelqu'un menu comme chair à pâté, To make mincemeat of someone. " Mincing with his sword her husband's limbs."—*Hamlet* II, 2. " I will chop her into messes."—*Othello* IV, 1.

Il se ferait hacher plutôt que de céder, He would rather suffer anything, would rather die, than give in.

haie. *See* BORDER, MOURIR, VALOIR.

haïr. Haïr quelqu'un, quelque chose, comme la peste (*ou* à l'égal de la peste) *ou* comme la mort, To hate someone, something, like poison. " This all-hating world."—*King Richard II* V, 5.

haleine. Avoir l'haleine courte (*fig.*), To be soon at the end of one's tether (*soon short of ideas*).

Être en haleine, To be in good fettle ; To be in the right mood (*to do something*).

Faire (*ou* Tenir) des discours à perte d'haleine, To be [very] long-winded.

Tenir quelqu'un en haleine, To keep someone in suspense.

Tout d'une haleine, All in one breath, At one go ; Right off the reel.

Un travail de longue haleine, A long and exacting labour.

hallebarde. *See* PLEUVOIR.

hameçon. *See* MORDRE, PRENDRE.

hanche. *See* POING.

hanter. Dis-moi qui tu hantes, et je te dirai qui tu es, A man is known by the company he keeps.

haquenée. C'est une grande haquenée, She is a tall gawky (*or* ungainly) woman.

hardi. Être hardi comme un coq sur son fumier, To be [as] bold as a cock on his own dunghill.

Être hardi comme un page *ou* comme un pierrot, To be [as] cheeky as a cock sparrow, To be [as] bold as brass. " Bold as an oracle."—*Troilus and Cressida* I, 3.

See also COMPAGNON.

hareng. Ils sont rangés (*ou* serrés) (*ou* pressés) là comme des harengs en caque *ou* Ils sont encaqués là comme des harengs, They are packed in there like sardines.

La caque sent toujours le hareng, What's bred in the bone will come out in the flesh.

See also MAIGRE.

hargneux. Chien hargneux a toujours l'oreille déchirée, A quarrelsome man is always in the wars.

harnois. Blanchir (*ou* Vieillir) sous le harnois, To grow grey in the service.

Endosser le harnois, To don the uniform.

haro. *See* CRIER.

hasard. *See* CORRIGER, COUP 70, FIER, JEU.

hasarder. Hasarder sa tête pour le (*ou* au) service de quelqu'un, To risk one's life in someone's service.

See also PAQUET.

hâter. Qui trop se hâte reste en chemin *ou* Plus on se hâte, moins on avance, Slow and steady (*or* and sure) wins the race, [The] more haste, [the] less speed. " *Romeo.* O, let us hence ; I stand on sudden haste. *Friar Lawrence.* Wisely and slow ; they stumble that run fast."—*Romeo and Juliet* II, 3. " We may outrun, By violent swiftness, that which we run at, And lose by over-running."—*King Henry VIII* I, 1. " Too swift arrives as tardy as too slow."—*Romeo and Juliet* II, 6. " Her more than haste is mated with delays."—SHAKESPEARE, *Venus and Adonis*.

hausser. C'est un homme qui ne se hausse ni ne se baisse, He is a most unexcitable man.

Hausser le ton *ou* Hausser d'un ton, To become threatening ; To become arrogant ; To open one's mouth wider (*claim more*).

See also ACTION, CRAN.

haut. Avoir la haute main, To have the upper hand, To rule the roast *or* the roost. *Quotation under* PLUIE.

C'est du haut allemand pour moi, It's all Greek (*or* double Dutch) to me. *Quotation under* HÉBREU.

Des hauts et des bas, Ups and downs.

Être haut à la main, To be quick to chastise, To be free with one's hands ; To be overbearing.

Être haut en couleur, To have a high colour *or* a florid complexion.

Haut la main, With flying colours ; Hands down.

Haut le pied ! Off you go ! Be off !

Haut les cœurs ! Take courage ! Keep up your courage ! Pluck up your hearts *or* your spirits *or* your courage !

Haut les mains ! Hands up !

Il a dit son sentiment haut et clair, He gave his opinion frankly *or* outspokenly.

Le carême est haut cette année, Easter is late this year.

Le prendre [de] haut (*ou* de bien haut) (*ou* de très haut) avec quelqu'un, To be [very] high and mighty with (*or* towards) someone.

Le temps est haut, The clouds are high (*it will not rain*).

Les eaux sont hautes *ou* La rivière est haute, Money is plentiful, There is no dearth of funds.

Les eaux sont hautes (*ou* La rivière est haute) chez lui, He is in funds.

Parler haut, To speak loudly ; To speak firmly ; To speak insolently. " Thou haught insulting man."—*King Richard II* IV, 1.

Parler haut et clair, To speak plainly *or* frankly. " Be plain, good son, and homely in thy drift."—*Romeo and Juliet* II, 3.

Penser tout haut (*fig.*), To speak one's mind.

Prendre le carême de trop haut, To ask the impossible ; To attempt the impossible.

Prendre le haut bout, To take the best place.

Prendre le haut ton *ou* Le prendre d'un (*ou* sur un) ton haut *ou* sur le haut ton *ou* Avoir le verbe haut, To be overbearing [in manner].

Regarder quelqu'un de haut en bas *ou* du haut de sa grandeur, To look down on (*or* contemptuously at) someone.

Reprendre les choses de plus haut, To go back to general principles, to primary causes.

Tenir la main haute à quelqu'un, To keep someone in hand, To keep a tight hand (*or* hold) on someone.

Tenir le haut bout, To hold the foremost place, To be held in high esteem, To carry weight.

Tomber de son haut (*fig.*), To be very much taken aback, To be dumbfounded *or* flabbergasted.

Traiter quelqu'un du (*ou* de) haut en bas, To treat someone condescendingly *or* in a high and mighty way.

Voir les choses de haut, To take a general view (*or* a bird's-eye view) of things.

See also BÂTON, BRIDE, CHANTER, COUP 73, CRI, CRIER, DRAGÉE, EMPORTER, GAGNER, PAROLE, PAVÉ, PENDRE, PORTER, SONNER, TÊTE, VISER, VOL.

hauteur. Être à la hauteur, To be equal to the task.

Être à la hauteur de quelqu'un, To be on a level with (*or* To be a match for) someone.

Être à la hauteur du siècle *ou* des idées (*ou* des connaissances) actuelles, To be abreast of (*or*

To move with) the times, To be up to date (*slang*). " Be a child o' the time."—*Antony and Cleopatra* II, 7.

Tomber de sa hauteur, To fall flat [on the ground]; To be flabbergasted.

hébreu. Parler hébreu, To talk Greek *or* double Dutch (*unintelligibly*).

Tout cela, c'est de l'hébreu pour moi, It (*or* That) is [all] Greek (*or* double Dutch) to me. " *Cassius.* Did Ccero say anything? *Casca.* Ay, he spoke Greek. *Cassius.* To what effect? *Casca.* Nay, an I tell you that, I'll ne'er look you i' the face again . . . ; but, for mine own part, it was Greek to me."—*Julius Caesar* I, 2.

herbe. À chemin battu il ne croît point d'herbe, There are too many people [engaged] in that trade already.

Couper l'herbe sous le pied à quelqu'un, To cut the ground from under someone's feet.

Il a marché sur quelque mauvaise herbe, Something has put him out.

L'herbe sera bien courte, s'il ne trouve de quoi brouter, He can find a living where others fail to do so.

Mauvaise herbe croît toujours, Ill weeds grow apace. " Idle weeds are fast in growth."—*King Richard III* III, 1. " Small herbs have grace, great weeds do grow apace: And since, methinks, I would not grow so fast, Because sweet flowers are slow, and weeds make haste."—*King Richard III* II, 4.

Sur quelle herbe a-t-il (avez-vous) marché? What is the matter with him, you? What has put him (you) out?

See also EMPLOYER, MANGER.

hérésie. Il ne fera point d'hérésie, He is a dull-witted fellow.

héroïque. *See* REMÈDE.

héros. Le héros de la fête, The one in whose honour the dinner, etc., is being given, The guest of honour. *See also* SALON.

heur. Il n'y a qu'heur et malheur en ce monde, Life has its ups and downs, We must take the rough with the smooth.

heure. Être le maître de l'heure, To rule the roast *or* the roost. *Quotation under* PLUIE.

Un homme, Un ami, de toutes les heures, A man, A friend, one is always glad to see; A man, A friend, who is always ready to oblige.

See also BERGER, BON 6, 8, 36, BOUILLON, CHAGRIN, COURIR, MATIN, MIDI, OUBLIER, PERDRE, QUART.

heureux. Avoir la main heureuse, To be successful; To be lucky.

See also COULER, NAÎTRE, PARADE.

heurter. *See* MUR, PORTE.

hibou. C'est un hibou, He is a gloomy unsocial man; He is an unsociable man. " Society is no comfort To one not sociable."— *Cymbeline* IV, 1.

Faire le hibou, To be unsociable, Not to join in (*the conversation, the fun*), To sit out.

hic. Voilà (*ou* C'est là) le hic, There's the rub, That is the question. *Quotation under* QUESTION.

hirondelle. Une hirondelle ne fait pas le printemps, One swallow does not make a summer.

histoire. . . ., [à ce que] dit l'histoire, . . ., . . ., so goes the story, . . .

C'est mon histoire que vous contez là *ou* Voilà mon histoire, That's just what happened to me *or* what I found.

C'est toute une histoire, It's a long story.

C'est une histoire *ou* Ce sont des histoires *ou* Histoire que tout cela, That's all bunkum, That's all my eye [and Betty Martin].

Ce n'est pas le plus beau de son

histoire, It is not a thing that redounds to his credit ; It is not a thing that redounds to his advantage.

Ce n'est pas le plus bel endroit de son histoire, It is not a thing that redounds to his credit.

En voilà (*ou* Voilà bien) des histoires, Here's a pretty go *or* a pretty kettle of fish *or* a fine how-d'ye-do.

Histoire de . . ., Just to . . ., for . . . : Je l'ai fait, histoire de rire, I did it just for [the] fun [of the thing].

Le plus beau de l'histoire, The cream of the story, The best of it.

Que d'histoires ! What a fuss !

See also AUTRE, PAGE.

hiver. Mi-mai, queue d'hiver, Ne'er cast a clout till May be out.

homérique. Un rire homérique, Homeric laughter.

homicide. Être homicide de soi-même (*fig.*), To ruin one's health.

homme. C'est un homme à tout, He is a handy man.

C'est un homme à tout faire, He is a man of all work *or* a Jack of all trades ; He is a man who is capable of anything (*bad*).

Ce n'est pas être homme, It is most inhuman.

Cela sent son homme de qualité, That shows his good breeding.

Il y a (*ou* Il se mêle) toujours de l'homme dans nos actions, We are only human. " But ships are but boards, sailors but men."—*The Merchant of Venice* I, 3.

L'âge d'homme, Manhood, Man's estate.

Un homme du vieux temps *ou* du temps passé *ou* d'autrefois, A man of the old school (*old-fashioned*).

See also AFFREUX, ALLER, ANTIQUE, ARGENT, ARRIVER, AVERTIR, AVEU, BAUDRUCHE, BEAU 4, BILIEUX, BON 22, 25, BOUT, BOUTONNER, BRIN, BRÛLER, BUREAU, CALER, CASSANT, CHARPENTER, CHICANE, COMBLER, COMMODE, CONSÉQUENCE, CONSISTANCE, COULER, DÉPOUILLER, DERNIER, DESSOUS, DRÔLE, ÉMÉCHER, EXÉCUTION, FAÇON, FAIRE, FEMME, FINIR, FORTUNE, FOYER, FRIRE, GAGES, HAUSSER, HEURE, HUMEUR, JUGER, LIMON, LIVRER, MAIN, MÉMOIRE, MODE, MONDE, MORCEAU, NOUVEAU, NOYER, ŒUVRE, ORGUEIL, OUVRIR, PAILLE, PENDRE, PEU, PIÈCE, PIED, PROJET, PROPOSER, QUATRE, RACCROCHER, RETORS, ROCHE, RUE, SAC, SENS, SERRER, TANNANT, TERRE, TÊTE, TOURNER, UNIR, UNIVERSEL, VENIN, VENTRE, VISION.

honneur. Faire honneur à un repas, To do justice to a meal.

Ne jouer que [pour] l'honneur, To be only playing for love.

Piquer d'honneur une personne, To put a person on his mettle.

Sauf votre honneur, With [all] due respect (*or* deference) to you. "*Sauf vostre honneur*, me understand vell."—*King Henry V* V, 2.

Se piquer d'honneur, To be on one's honour.

See also BANQUEROUTE, BIEN, CIMAISE, HUMEUR, SEIGNEUR.

honnir. Honni soit qui mal y pense, Evil be to him who evil thinks.

honte. Revenir (*ou* S'en retourner) avec sa courte honte, To come back a sadder and a wiser man.

See also BOIRE, ÉCHAFAUD.

honteux. Il n'y a que les honteux qui perdent, Nothing venture, nothing have.

Jamais honteux n'eut belle amie, Faint heart never won fair lady. " He that perforce robs lions of their hearts May easily win a woman's."—(*said of King Richard Cœur-de-lion*)—*King John* I, 1. " Assure thyself there is no love-broker in the world can more prevail in man's commendation with woman than report of valour." —*Twelfth Night* III, 2. " She lov'd me for the dangers I had pass'd."—*Othello* I, 3.

Le morceau honteux, The last piece [left on the dish], The last bit going begging.

Les pauvres honteux, The poor who are ashamed to beg. " And his poor self, A dedicated beggar to the air, With his disease of all-shunn'd poverty, Walks, like contempt, alone."—*Timon of Athens* IV, 1.

hôpital. Mettre quelqu'un à l'hôpital (*fig.*), To beggar someone.

Prendre le chemin de l'hôpital *ou* Courir en poste à l'hôpital *ou* Aller le grand galop à l'hôpital, To be on the road to ruin, To be going to the dogs.

horloge. *See* RÉGLER.

horoscope. Tirer l'horoscope de quelqu'un, To cast someone's horoscope; To tell someone's fortune.

horreur. C'est une belle horreur, It is a fearful and wonderful sight, It is a sublime horror (*e.g., a great storm, a big fire*).

Un musée des horreurs, A chamber of horrors.

hors. Être hors d'affaire, To be out of danger (*of patient*).

Être hors de combat, To be out of action, To be disabled; To be silenced.

Être hors de service, To be unfit for use, To be done for.

Être hors de soi, To be beside oneself (*with rage, etc.*).

Être hors ligne, To be out of the common.

Mettre quelqu'un hors de cause (*fig.*), To exonerate someone.

Mettre quelqu'un hors de combat, To put someone out of action, To disable someone; To silence someone.

See also GOND, PAGE, POISSON, PROPOS.

hôte. Les hôtes des bois, The denizens of the woods (*poetic*).

See also COMPTER.

hue. *See* ENTENDRE, TIRER.

huile. Faire [la] tache d'huile, To spread [gradually *or* by degrees], To mushroom.

Filer de l'huile sur les vagues, To pour oil on troubled waters.

Il n'y a plus d'huile dans la lampe, His life is flickering out. " My oil-dried lamp and time bewasted light Shall be extinct with age and endless night."—*King Richard II* I, 3. " 'Let me not live,' quoth he, 'After my flame lacks oil.' "—*All's Well That Ends Well* I, 2.

Il tirerait de l'huile d'un mur, All is grist that comes to his mill.

Jeter de l'huile sur le feu (*fig.*), To pour oil on the flame, To add fuel to the flames. " I need not add more fuel to your fire."—3 *King Henry VI* V, 4.

On tirerait plutôt de l'huile d'un mur que de tirer de l'argent de lui, It would be easier to get blood out of a stone than money from him.

Sentir l'huile, To smell of the lamp *or* of oil (*to bear marks of study—said of author's writings*).

See also COTRET, COUDE.

humain. N'avoir pas figure (*ou* forme) humaine, Not to look like a human being; To be very much disfigured.

See also PAYER, TENDRESSE.

humanité. *See* PAYER.

humecter. S'humecter le gosier, To wet one's whistle.

humeur. C'est un homme d'humeur, He is a man of uneven temper. " You are altogether governed by humours."—1 *King Henry IV* III, 1.

C'est un homme sans humeur, He is an even-tempered man.

Être d'une humeur massacrante *ou* maussade *ou* Être d'une humeur de dogue, To be as churlish as a bear, To be like a bear with a sore head.

N'avoir ni humeur ni honneur, To take insults lying down and to be lost to all sense of honour.

humide. *See* SÉJOUR.

huppé. Les plus huppés y sont pris, The cleverest are taken in by it.

hure. Avoir une vilaine hure, To have an ugly mug (*slang*).

hurler. Hurler avec les loups, To do in Rome as Rome does *or* as Romans do.

hussarde. À la hussarde, Impetuously.

hypocrisie. *See* SUER.

hypothéquer. *See* BROUILLARD.

hysope. *See* CÈDRE.

I

i. Mettre les points sur les i (*fig.*), To dot the i's and cross the t's; To watch one's step.

See also DROIT.

ici. *See* LIEUE, VOIR.

idéal. *See* BEAU 16.

idée. L'idée et la chose, The appearance and the reality (*as opposed to each other*).

Le pays des idées, The world of fancy.

See also CHAUSSER, HAUTEUR, NOIR.

idole. C'est une [vraie] idole, She is beautiful, but has no charm or animation.

ignorance. Alléguer l'ignorance *ou* Prétendre cause d'ignorance, To plead ignorance.

See also TÉNÈBRES.

ignorer. S'ignorer soi-même, Not to know oneself; To be unconscious of one's capabilities.

illégalité. *See* FRISER.

illusion. Être dans l'illusion *ou* Nourrir [en soi] une illusion, To labour under a delusion.

Se faire illusion à soi-même, To deceive oneself (*to one's own advantage*). " O, who can hold a fire in his hand By thinking on the frosty Caucasus? Or cloy the hungry edge of appetite By bare imagination of a feast? Or wallow naked in December snow By thinking on fantastic summer's heat?"—*King Richard II* I, 3.

image. *See* SAGE.

impénitence. *See* FINAL.

imperturbable. *See* SANG-FROID.

importance. *See* ACCOMMODER.

impossible. À l'impossible nul n'est tenu, No one can do impossibilities.

See also GLISSER.

impôt. L'impôt du sang, Military service, Conscription. " Your son, my lord, has paid a soldier's debt." —*Macbeth* V, 8.

imprimer. Se faire imprimer, To see oneself in print (*have one's writing published*).

impulsion. *See* MOMENT.

incarner. *See* DIABLE.

incomber. C'est à vous qu'il incombe de . . ., It rests with you to . . .

incommoder. Être incommodé dans ses affaires, To be in financial difficulties, To be in Queer Street (*slang*).

inconnu. *See* SAUT.

index. Mettre une personne, une chose, à l'index, To black-list a person, a thing. " Ah me, what act, That roars so loud, and thunders in the index?"—*Hamlet* III, 4.

indice. *See* RAPPROCHER.

indirect. *See* REPROCHE.

individu. Avoir soin de (*ou* Conserver) (*ou* Soigner) son individu, To take great care of oneself.

See also DRÔLE.

industrie. *See* CHEVALIER, NÉCESSITÉ, VIVRE.

infirmité. *See* CORTÈGE.

influence. Faire jouer toutes sortes d'influences, To use every means in one's power.

information. *See* ALLER.

infus. *See* SCIENCE.

ingrat. L'âge ingrat, The awkward age (*of youth*).

Semer en terre ingrate, To sow on (*or* in) stony ground (*fig.*) (*Mark* iv, 5, *Matthew* xiii, 5).

ingratitude. *See* PAYER.

injure. Cracher des injures à quelqu'un *ou* Cribler quelqu'un d'injures, To shower down abuse on (*or* To hurl insults at) someone. *A notable example of a shower of abuse is the invective of* PETRUCHIO *against the* Tailor *in The Taming of the Shrew* IV, 3: " O monstrous arrogance! Thou liest, thou thread, Thou thimble, Thou yard, three-quarters, half-yard, quarter, nail, Thou flea, thou nit, thou winter cricket thou!—Brav'd in mine own house with a skein of thread? Away, thou rag, thou quantity, thou remnant." (*Note.*—nail = $2\frac{1}{4}$ inches, or $\frac{1}{16}$ of a yard, being about the distance from the end of the thumb-nail to the joint at the base of the thumb.)

Déborder en injures, To break out into abuse.

Dévorer une injure, To swallow (*or* To pocket) an insult.

See also AIRAIN, BORDÉE, DUO, RAISON.

injurier. Injurier quelqu'un, To call someone names. " *Falstaff.* Go to, you are a woman, go. *Hostess.* Who, I? no; I defy thee: God's light, I was never called so in mine own house before."—1 *King Henry IV* III, 3.

innocent. Être innocent comme (*ou* Être aussi innocent que) l'enfant qui vient de naître *ou* qui est à naître, To be [as] innocent as a new-born (*or* as an unborn) babe. " What we chang'd Was innocence for innocence; we knew not The doctrine of ill-doing, nor dream'd That any did."—*The Winter's Tale* I, 2.

L'innocent du village, The village idiot. *See also* MENSONGE.

inquiétude. *See* INSPIRER.

inscrire (s'). *See* FAUX.

insolent. Avoir un bonheur insolent, To have the devil's own luck.

insoupçonné. *See* BIENFAIT.

inspirer. Cela m'inspire des inquiétudes, I see the red light, I smell a rat.

instant. *See* COMPTER, MOINS.

instrument. C'est un bel instrument que la langue, It is easy enough to talk (*but doing is more difficult*). " O, that delightful engine of her thoughts, That blabb'd them with such pleasing eloquence."—*Titus Andronicus* III, 1.

intact. C'est un homme intact, He is a man with an unblemished (*or* a spotless) reputation. *Quotation under* ÉCHAFAUD.

intention. L'enfer est pavé de bonnes intentions, [The road to] hell is paved with good intentions *or* with good resolutions.

L'intention est réputée pour le fait, It is the intention that counts, I'll (We'll) take the will for the deed.

intérêt. S'attacher à ses intérêts *ou* Être à la recherche de son intérêt, To look (*or* To have an eye) to one's own interests *or* to the main chance.

See also COMBAT.

interprète. *See* ŒIL.

interpréter. *See* BIEN.

interroger. *See* QUOI.

intrigue. Des intrigues de couloirs, Wire-pulling (*in the lobby*).

inventer. Il n'a pas inventé la poudre, He won't set the Thames on fire.

Vous inventez, You are drawing on your imagination.

invention. *See* NÉCESSITÉ.

ivraie. Séparer l'ivraie d'avec le bon grain (*fig.*), To separate the wheat from the tares.

ivre. *See* SOBRE.

J

jaloux. *See* BESACE.

jamais. *See* ÉCORCHER, EMMITOUFLER, MALHEUR, TARD, TEMPS.

jambe. Aller, Courir, à toutes jambes, To go, To run, as fast as one's legs can carry one, To go, To run, at top speed, To go hell for leather.

Avoir des jambes de (*ou* en) fuseau *ou* Avoir des jambes de coq, To be spindle-shanked. " If my legs were two such riding-rods, My arms such eel-skins stuff'd, my face so thin."—*King John* I, 1.

Avoir les jambes rompues, To feel one's legs giving way under one, To be tired out *or* dog-tired, To be ready to drop.

En aura-t-il la jambe mieux faite ? *ou* Cela lui fait une belle jambe, A [fine *or* fat] lot of good that will do him, He is no better off than before.

Faire la belle jambe, To show one's graces, To show off, To strut about.

Jouer des jambes, To leg it (*walk or run hard*) ; To take to one's heels, To skedaddle.

N'avoir plus de jambes, To be no longer able to walk, To be tired out.

Passer la jambe à quelqu'un, To trip someone up (*lit.*) ; To play someone a dirty trick.

See also BRAS, CAUTÈRE, DÉROUILLER, DESSOUS, PARENTHÈSE, PRENDRE, QUINZE, RENTRER, SAUVER.

jardin. *See* CHOU, PIERRE.

jardinier. *See* CHIEN

Jarnac. *See* COUP 18.

jaser. *See* PIE.

jauger. Jauger quelqu'un, To size someone up, To take someone's measure (*fig.*).

jaune. Être jaune comme cire *ou* comme un coing, To have a very sallow complexion. " This companion with the saffron face."—*The Comedy of Errors* IV, 4.

See also RIRE.

Jean. *See* BOUCHE, CHIEN, EMPLOYER.

jésuite. C'est un jésuite (*fig.*), He lacks frankness and sincerity.

Jésus-Christ. *See* ATHLÈTE.

jet. D'un seul jet, At one go.

See also PREMIER.

jeter. Jeter à quelqu'un quelque chose au nez *ou* Jeter quelque chose à la tête (*ou* à la figure) de quelqu'un, To fling (*or* To cast) (*or* To throw) something in someone's teeth (*fig.*).

Le dé (*ou* Le sort) en est jeté, The die is cast. " I have set my life upon a cast, And I will stand the hazard of the die."—*King Richard III* V, 4.

Se jeter à la tête de quelqu'un, To throw oneself at someone['s head] (*fig.*).

See also BÂTON, BON 49, BONNET, CARREAU, CHIEN, COUP 47, CRI, DÉVOLU, DOUCHE, EAU, FENÊTRE, FEU, FROC, FROID, GANT, GOURME, GRAPPIN, GUEULE, HUILE, LEST, MAIN, MANCHE, MOUCHOIR, MOULE, ŒIL, OUBLIETTES, PERLE, PIERRE, PLUME, POMME, POUDRE, PROPOS, RACINE, SOURICIÈRE, TÊTE, TRAVERSE, VENIN, VOILE.

jeton. *See* COUREUR, FAUX, PRÉSENCE.

jeu. C'est un jeu de hasard, It is a matter of chance.

Cacher (*ou* Couvrir) son jeu, To be a dark horse (*fig.*).

Ce n'est pas [un] jeu d'enfant, It is no child's-play.

Ce n'est qu'un jeu, It's child's-play.

Cela n'est pas du (*ou* de) jeu, That's not fair *or* not cricket ; That's not what was agreed upon.

Jeu qui trop dure ne vaut rien, One can have too much of a good thing. " If all the year were playing holidays, To sport would be as tedious as to work ; But when they seldom come, they wish'd-for come, And nothing pleaseth but rare accidents."—1 *King Henry IV* I, 2.

Jeu[x] de main, jeu[x] de vilain, (*Let us have*) No horseplay.

Le jeu (*ou* Les jeux) de la fortune, The vicissitudes (*or* The tricks) of fortune.

Les Jeux et les Ris, Sport and Mirth (*poetic*). " Awake the pert and nimble spirit of mirth."—*A Midsummer Night's Dream* I, 1. " Frame your mind to mirth and merriment, Which bars a thousand harms and lengthens life."—*The Taming of the Shrew*, *Induction*, *Scene* 2.

Mettre quelqu'un en jeu, To bring someone into it, To mix (*implicate*) someone up in it.

Se faire un jeu de quelque chose, To make light of something ; To make sport (*or* game) of (*or* To snap one's fingers at) something.

Tenir un jeu, To keep (*or* To run) a gaming establishment.

Un jeu de la nature, A freak of nature. " Now, by two-headed Janus, Nature hath framed strange fellows in her time."—*The Merchant of Venice* I, 1.

See also ALLER, ATOUT, BEAU 1, 7, 24, 34, BON 18, 43, 51, 75, CHANDELLE, CHIEN, ÉCHEC, ENTRÉE, ENTRER, ÉPINGLE, JOUER, MENER, PASSER, PIQUER, PLAIRE, SERRER, VENANT.

jeudi. *See* SEMAINE.

jeune. Il n'est rien de tel que d'être jeune, Youth is half the battle.

See also BARBE, FOU, MOTIF, OUVRIR, THÉORIE.

jeunesse. Il faut que jeunesse se passe, Youth will have its fling, Boys will be boys, Young blood must have its course. " All's brave that youth mounts and folly guides."—*As You Like It* III, 4.

Si jeunesse savait, si vieillesse pouvait, If youth but knew, could age but do. " Seeing ignorance is the curse of God, Knowledge the wing wherewith we fly to heaven."—2 *King Henry VI* IV, 7.

See also ÉCART, PLI.

joie. *See* CŒUR, PÈRE, PLEURER, POSSÉDER.

joindre. *See* BOUT, GESTE, SAUTER.

joint. Trouver le joint, To hit upon the right plan, To find the best way, To discover the trick. " He hath the joints of everything."—*Troilus and Cressida* I, 2.

joli. Faire le joli cœur, To make oneself pleasant.

See also CROQUER.

jonc. *See* DROIT.

Josse. *See* ORFÈVRE.

joue. Donner sur la joue à quelqu'un, To slap (*or* To smack) someone's face, To give someone a clout.

See also SOUFFLET, TENDRE.

jouer. Faire quelque chose en se jouant, To do something with the utmost ease *or* (*slang*) on one's head.

Jouer à quelqu'un un mauvais tour *ou* un tour pendable *ou* un tour de cochon *ou* un coup de cochon *ou* une pièce cruelle *ou* une pièce sanglante, To play a nasty (*or* a dirty) trick on someone.

Jouer à qui perd gagne (*fig.*), To play a losing game (*to suit one's purpose*), To throw a sprat to catch a herring *or* a mackerel *or* a whale. " I follow thus a losing suit against him."—*The Merchant of Venice* IV, 1.

Jouer au [plus] fin, To finesse, To engage in a skirmish of wits.

Jouer au plus sûr (*fig.*), To play for safety.

Jouer bien son jeu (*fig.*), To play one's cards well.

Jouer cartes sur table, To put one's cards on the table (*fig.*).

Jouer des coudes *ou* des pieds *ou* des mains (*fig.*), To push oneself forward.

Jouer franc jeu, To play a straight game, To play on the square ; To mean business.

Jouer gros jeu *ou* Jouer une grosse

partie *ou* Jouer un jeu à se perdre, To play for high stakes.

Jouer le jeu *ou* Jouer beau jeu *ou* Jouer selon les règles *ou* Jouer en règle, To play the game, To play fair.

Jouer le jeu de quelqu'un (*fig.*), To play into someone's hands.

Jouer quelqu'un, To trick (*or* To fool) someone, To make a fool of someone.

Jouer un jeu d'enfer, To plunge.

Se jouer à quelqu'un, à quelque chose, To venture (*or* To make bold) to attack someone, to do something : Ne vous y jouez pas, Don't venture to do it.

See also BANQUETTE, BON 51, BONHEUR, CHAPERON, CHEMISE, COMÉDIE, COUP 48, DESSOUS, ESCARPIN, FEU, HONNEUR, INFLUENCE, JAMBE, MÂCHOIRE, MALHEUR, PARTIE, PILE, PRUNELLE, QUITTE, RESSORT, RESTE, SECONDAIRE, SERRER, TOUR, TOUT, VA-TOUT, VELOURS.

joueur. *See* BALLE.

jouir. *See* RESTE.

jour. À chaque jour suffit sa peine *ou* suffit son mal, " Sufficient unto the day is the evil thereof."—*Matthew* vi, 34. " What need the bridge much broader than the flood ! "—*Much Ado About Nothing* I, 1.

Cela se voit tous les jours, That is a daily occurrence.

Elles (c.-à-d. Ces deux personnes, Ces deux choses) ne se ressemblent pas plus que (*ou* diffèrent autant que) (*ou* sont différentes comme) le jour et la nuit *ou* C'est le jour et la nuit *ou* C'est la nuit et le jour, They are as like (*or* as different) as chalk and cheese, They are as opposite as the [two] poles, They are poles apart. *Quotation under* ANTIPODE.

Faire du jour la nuit et de la nuit le jour, To turn day into night and night into day. " When I was wont to think no harm all night, And make a dark night too of half the day."—*Love's Labour's Lost* I, 1.

Il n'est pas jour chez lui, chez elle, avant telle heure, He, She, is not up and about before such time.

Les jours se suivent et ne se ressemblent pas, Who knows what tomorrow holds *or* may bring forth ?

Mettre quelque chose au [grand] jour, To bring something to light.

Paris ne s'est pas fait en un jour, Rome was not built in a day.

Voir jour [dans une affaire], To see daylight [in a matter].

Voir le jour, To see the light (*be born, be exposed to view, be published*).

See also AGONIE, AURORE, BEAU 14, 19, 20, BON 4, 19, 28, CÉLÈBRE, CHALEUR, CLAIR, COMPTER, COULER, CUIRE, DEMAIN, ÉVANGILE, FERMANT, FÊTE, FILER, FLAMBEAU, GRAND, MERVEILLE, MONTRER, ORDRE, PAIN, PERDRE, PREMIER, PRENDRE, QUATRE, TRAIN, VÉRITÉ, VIVRE, VRAI.

journalier. *See* ARME.

journée. *See* COUPER, MENTIR, ROUGE, SAINT, VIVRE.

jouteur. C'est un rude jouteur, He is a formidable opponent (*lit. & fig.*).

Jouvence. *See* FONTAINE.

joyeux. Mener une vie joyeuse *ou* Mener joyeuse vie, To live a gay life.

See also AVÈNEMENT.

Judas. *See* BAISER.

juge. *See* FOU.

juger. C'est un homme jugé, I have taken his measure *or* have sized him up (*know how worthless, how dishonest, he is*).

Il y a chose jugée quand . . ., It is idle to discuss it when . . .

Juger quelqu'un sur l'étiquette [du sac], To pass judgement on someone unheard.

See also AVEUGLE, BALLE, COUP 49, ÉCORCE, VUE.

juif. C'est un Juif errant, He is a Wandering Jew (*never settles down*).

Le petit juif, The funny-bone.

Jupiter. Il se croit sorti de la cuisse de Jupiter, He imagines himself to be of exalted birth.

jurer. Il ne faut jurer de rien, You never can tell, One can never be sure [of anything]. *Note.*—" Swear not at all " (*Matthew* v, 34) *is* " Ne jurez pas du tout."

Jurer comme un charretier [embourbé] *ou* comme un templier *ou* comme un grenadier *ou* comme un païen, To swear like a trooper. " *Lady Percy.* Not mine, in good sooth. *Hotspur.* Not yours, in good sooth ! 'Heart, you swear like a comfit-maker's wife ! . . . Swear me, Kate, like a lady as thou art, A good mouth-filling oath ; and leave *in sooth*, And such protest of pepper-gingerbread, To velvet guards and Sunday citizens."—1 *King Henry IV* III, 1.

See also DIEU.

jus. C'est jus vert ou verjus, It is six of one and half a dozen of the other, It's as broad as it's long.

See also CUIRE, TREILLE.

juste. *See* ENDORMIR, TIRER.

justice. Il faut rendre justice au diable, Give the devil his due.

Rendre justice à quelqu'un, To do someone justice, To give someone his due.

Se faire justice à soi-même, To take the law into one's own hands.

See also BROUILLER, COURS, PRISE.

justifier. *See* FIN.

L

là. *See* ATTENDRE, CAMPER, DEMEURER, DEVINER, DIABLE, DIRE, FOUETTER, HIC, LAISSER, LOIN, ÔTER, PÉCHER, PIED, PIERRE, PLANTER, QUESTION, RECONNAÎTRE, RESTER, RIRE, SORTIR, TENIR, TOPER, VENIR.

lac. Être dans le lac, To be in difficulties *or* (*slang*) in the soup *or* (*slang*) in Queer Street.

lacet. Être pris dans ses propres lacets, To be caught in one's own toils, To be hoist with one's own petard. " I told ye all, When we first put this dangerous stone a-rolling, 'Twould fall upon ourselves."—*King Henry VIII* V, 2. " Ye blew the fire that burns ye."—*King Henry VIII* V, 2. " Let it work ; For 'tis the sport to have the engineer Hoist with his own petard." —*Hamlet* III, 4. " There's no such sport as sport by sport o'erthrown ; To make theirs ours, and ours none but our own."—*Love's Labour's Lost* V, 2.

lâcher. Lâcher la bonde à sa colère, To give vent to one's anger, To pour out the vials of one's wrath.

Lâcher la bonde à ses larmes, à ses plaintes, To let loose a flood of tears, of complaints.

Lâcher la main à quelqu'un, To loosen one's hold on someone.

Lâcher la proie pour l'ombre, To drop the substance for the shadow.

Lâcher la rampe *ou* la perche, To kick the bucket, To peg out, To lose the number of one's mess (*die*). " Their father . . . took such sorrow That he quit being."—*Cymbeline* I, 1.

Lâcher les écluses de son éloquence, To open the flood-gates of one's eloquence, To let loose a flood of eloquence.

Lâcher pied, To give ground (*retreat*); To give way (*fail to resist*).

Lâcher prise, To let go ; To give over (*desist*) ; To give in (*yield*).

See also BRIDE, FOND, GOURMETTE, MOT, SECRET.

laid. Être laid comme le péché *ou*

comme les sept péchés capitaux *ou* comme un singe *ou* comme un crapaud *ou* comme une chenille *ou* comme un pou *ou* Être laid à faire peur, To be [as] ugly as sin. " Like the toad, ugly and venomous."—*As You Like It* II, 1.

See also AMOUR.

laine. Se laisser tondre (*ou* Se laisser manger) la laine sur le dos, To sit down under (*or* To submit tamely to) injustices, vexations, etc., To allow oneself to be sat on (*slang*) ; To allow oneself to be fleeced (*by exactions*). " So first the harmless sheep doth yield his fleece, And next his throat unto the butcher's knife."—3 *King Henry VI* V, 6.

laisse. Mener (*ou* Tenir) quelqu'un en laisse, To hold (*or* To have) someone on leash, To keep a tight hand on someone.

laisser. Laisser là, To leave *or* To forsake (*someone*) ; To lay aside (*something*).

Laisser quelqu'un dans la nasse *ou* en plan, To leave someone in the lurch, To give someone the slip, To let someone down.

Laisser quelque chose en plan, To leave something unfinished, To throw up something.

Laisser tout aller, To let everything go, To let things slide.

Se laisser faire, To offer no resistance.

Un laissé pour compte (*fig.*), A back number (*person—slang*).

See also ARRACHER, BATTRE, BON 52, BOURSE, BOUT, CARTE, CHAMP, COULER, COURS, COUVER, DÉBANDADE, DÉBARBOUILLER, EAU, GUEULE, MARCHER, MITONNER, MORT, ŒIL, OS, OUBLIER, PLUME, PRENDRE, QUATRE, REPOSER, SOMMEIL, TOMBER, VIVRE.

lait. Si on lui pressait le nez, il en sortirait encore du lait, He is still very green *or* still very young and inexperienced. " One would think his mother's milk were scarce out of him."—*Twelfth Night* I, 5.

See also AVALER, EMPORTER, SUCER, TENDRESSE, VACHE.

lambris. Les célestes lambris (*poetic*), The vault (*or* The roof) (*or* The floor) of heaven, The welkin. *Quotations under* VOÛTE.

lame. C'est une fine lame, He's a sly dog *or* fox ; She's a sly minx.

See also FOURREAU.

laminoir. Passer au laminoir, To go through the mill.

lampe. *See* HUILE.

lance. Rompre une lance avec (*ou* contre) quelqu'un, To break a lance (*or* To try a fall) with someone.

Rompre une lance pour quelqu'un, To take up the cudgels for someone.

lancer. *See* BALLON, FLÈCHE, POMME.

langage. Vous tenez là un étrange langage, That is a strange way to talk. " Merry and tragical ! tedious and brief ! That is, hot ice and wondrous strange snow. How shall we find the concord of this discord ? "—*A Midsummer Night's Dream* V, 1.

langue. Avoir la langue bien pendue *ou* bien affilée *ou* Avoir la langue déliée, To have the gift of the gab *or* a glib tongue. " His tongue filed."—*Love's Labour's Lost* V, 1. " Smooth not thy tongue with filed talk."—SHAKESPEARE, *Sonnets to Sundry Notes of Music* IV. " These fellows of infinite tongue."—*King Henry V* V, 2. " A knave very voluble."—*Othello* II, 1. " Fye, what a spendthrift is he of his tongue."—*The Tempest* II, 1. " Cry, holla ! to thy tongue, I pr'ythee ; it curvets unseasonably."—*As You Like It* III, 2.

Faire aller les langues, To set people's tongues wagging.

Faire tirer la langue à quelqu'un, To keep someone waiting indefinitely (*for something he wants*).

Il faut tourner sept fois sa langue dans sa bouche avant de parler, Think before you speak.

See also ACÉRER, CHIEN, CLAQUET, COUP 24, DÉBRIDER, DÉMANGER, DÉNOUER, DORER, ÉCORCHER, ENNUYER, FOURCHER, INSTRUMENT, POCHE.

lanterne. C'est une [vraie] lanterne magique, It is [just] like a passing show (*so many people are passing and repassing*).

See also VESSIE.

lapin. C'est un rude (*ou* un fameux) lapin, He is a vigorous fellow, He's hot stuff (*slang*).

See also COUP 18, COURIR.

lard. *See* GRAS.

large. Avoir la conscience large, To be not over-scrupulous.

Avoir la main large, To have an open hand, To be open-handed (*generous*) ; To be prodigal. " He hath a tear for pity, and a hand Open as day for melting charity."—2 *King Henry IV* IV, 4.

Avoir la manche large, To be very indulgent *or* broad-minded (*on questions of morality*).

Il n'en mène pas large, He is in a tight corner, and shows it, His heart is in his boots.

See also GAGNER, PRENDRE, TIRER, VOIE.

larigot. *See* BOIRE.

larme. *See* ARROSER, CROCODILE, DÉVORER, PLEURER, RIRE, VALLÉE.

larron. *See* BOURSE, ENTENDRE, OCCASION.

las. *See* GUERRE.

latin. Tout cela, c'est du latin pour moi, It (*or* That) is [all] Greek (*or* double Dutch) to me.

See also BOUT, PERDRE.

laurier. *See* CUEILLIR, REPOSER.

laver. À laver la tête d'un More (*ou* d'un âne) on perd sa lessive, There's no washing a blackamoor white. " For all the water in the ocean Can never turn a swan's black legs to white, Although she lave them hourly in the flood."—*Titus Andronicus* IV, 2.

Je m'en lave les mains (*fig.*), I wash my hands of it.

Laver la tête à quelqu'un, To give someone a good dressing down *or* a good talking to *or* (*slang*) give someone beans *or* (*slang*) socks, To haul someone over the coals.

See also LINGE.

lécher. C'est à s'en lécher les doigts *ou* On s'en lèche les doigts, It makes one smack one's lips, It makes one's mouth water (*is so good to eat*).

Un ours mal léché, An unlicked cub ; An unmannerly fellow. " Like to a chaos, or an unlick'd bear-whelp."—3 *King Henry VI* III, 2.

lecteur. C'est un avis (*ou* un avertissement) au lecteur, Let this be a warning to you, A word [is enough] to the wise, Verb. sap., Verbum [sat] sapienti. " Yet doth he give us bold advertisement."—1 *King Henry IV* IV, 1.

lecture. À la lecture, In cold print. " Must I ravel out My weav'd-up follies ? . . . If thy offences were upon record, Would it not shame thee in so fair a troop To read a lecture of them ? "—*King Richard II* IV, 1.

léger. À la légère, Lightly (*clad, armed*) ; Without due consideration.

Conclure à la légère, To jump to conclusions.

See also PIED.

légèreté. *See* OURS.

légion. Ils s'appellent légion, Their name is legion.

légume. *See* GROS.

lendemain. Il ne faut pas remettre la partie au lendemain, To-morrow is the fool's to-day, To-morrow never comes.

See also CÉLÈBRE, TRISTE.

lessive. *See* LAVER.

lest. Jeter du lest (*fig.*), To make concessions, To come off one's perch.

leste. Avoir la main leste, To be quick to chastise, To be free with one's hands.

lettre. *See* ÉCRIRE, PIED, SOT, TUER.

leu. À la queue leu leu, In Indian file.

levant. *See* ADORER.

lever. Lever la crosse en l'air, To join (*or* To fraternize with) the rioters (*said of soldiers sent to quell riot*).

Lever le coude, To lift one's elbow (*drink heavily*).

Lever le siège (*fig.*), To take one's leave (*of the company*).

See also ALOUETTE, MATIN, NEZ, ŒIL, PAILLE, PIED, TÊTE.

lèvre. Avoir le cœur sur les lèvres, To wear one's heart upon one's sleeve. " I will wear my heart upon my sleeve For daws to peck at."—*Othello* I, 1.

See also BORD, COUPE, RIRE, SUSPENDRE.

liard. N'avoir pas un [rouge] liard, Not to have a penny (*or* a copper) to bless oneself with ; To be short of the ready (*slang*).

libre. *See* CARRIÈRE, CHAMP, COURS.

librement. *See* USER.

licence. Des licences poétiques (*fig.*), Terminological inexactitudes.

lie. *See* BOIRE, CHÈRE.

lier. *See* AMITIÉ, FOU, PARTIE.

lieu. *See* FEU.

lieue. Il n'écoute pas, il est à mille lieues d'ici, He is not listening, he is miles away.

J'étais à mille lieues de supposer (*ou* de penser) que . . ., I should never have dreamt that . . .

See also BOTTE.

lièvre. *See* COURIR, GÎTE, MÉMOIRE, PEUREUX.

ligne. *See* BAPTÊME, COMPTE, HORS, MANQUER, QUATRE, TIRER.

lime. *See* COUP 20, REPASSER.

limite. Un cas limite, A border-line case.

limon. Il se croit pétri d'un autre limon que le reste des hommes, He thinks he is made of a different clay from the rest of mankind (*is superior to them*). " *Arviragus*. Are we not brothers ? *Imogen*. So man and man should be ; But clay and clay differs in dignity Whose dust is both alike."—*Cymbeline* IV, 2.

Nous sommes tous pétris du même limon, We are all made of the same clay. " With Earth's first Clay They did the Last Man knead."—EDWARD FITZGERALD, *Rubaiyat of Omar Khayyam* LXXIX.

linge. Il faut laver son linge sale en famille, One should not wash one's dirty linen in public.

Laver son linge sale en famille, To wash one's dirty linen at home.

See also PÂLE.

linotte. C'est une tête de linotte, He (She) is an empty-headed (*or* a feather-brained) person.

lion. Se faire la part du lion, To keep (*or* To take) the lion's share.

See also CŒUR, GRIFFE, PEAU, VIE.

liquide. *See* PLAINE.

lisière. Mener (*ou* Tenir) quelqu'un en lisière[s], To keep someone in leading strings.

lit. *See* COUCHER, SAUT, SAUTER.

litanie. *See* MÊME.

livre. *See* CHAGRIN, CHEVET, CREUX, NEZ, PÂLIR, PARLER, POUCE.

livrer. Je vous livre cet homme, You will find this man very accommodating ; You can do as you like with this man.

Livrer bataille à, To join battle with.

See also BÊTE, OUBLI, VENDRE, VOIE.

loge. Être aux premières loges, To have a full view *or* a front seat.

loger. *See* BOURSE, ENSEIGNE, ÉTOILE, ÉTROIT, PAYS, TUILE.

loi. Avoir la loi pour soi, To have the law on one's side.

Faire la loi à quelqu'un, To lay down the law (*or* To dictate) to someone.

Faire loi, To be (*or* To make) (*or* To constitute) law. *Cf.* NÉCESSITÉ fait loi.

Se faire loi de faire quelque chose, To make a rule (*or* a practice) (*or* a point) of doing something.

See also PASSER, VIOLENCE.

loin. À beau mentir qui vient de loin, Travellers can lie with impunity. " A good traveller is something at the latter end of a dinner ; but one that lies three-thirds and uses a known truth to pass a thousand nothings with, should be once heard and thrice beaten."—*All's Well That Ends Well* II, 5.

Être loin de compte, To be out in one's reckoning, To be wide of the mark ; To be far from agreeing (*e.g., on the terms of a bargain*).

Loin de là, Far from it, On the contrary.

Loin des yeux, loin du cœur, Out of sight, out of mind.

Loin du bruit, Far from the madding crowd.

Voir de loin *ou* Voir bien loin, To be far-seeing *or* far-sighted (*fig.*).

See also CONNAÎTRE, COUPE, DATER, MÉNAGER, MENER, NEZ, PORTER, RENVOYER, RESSEMBLER, SENTIR.

loir. *See* DORMIR.

long. Avoir le bras long *ou* la main longue, To have a long arm (*wide influence*). " Great men have reaching hands."—2 *King Henry VI* IV, 7.

En savoir long, To know a lot about it.

En savoir trop long, To know too much about it.

See also ALLER, AUNE, CARRIÈRE, CONTER, DENT, DONNER, ÉCHINE, HALEINE, NEZ, PAIN, TROUVER.

longtemps. *See* FÊLER.

longueur. *See* TIRER.

Lorris. *See* AMENDE.

loterie. *See* TERNE.

louange. Chanter (*ou* Entonner) les louanges de quelqu'un, To sing someone's praises. " O Ferdinand, Do not smile at me, that I boast her off, For thou shalt find she will outstrip all praise, and make it halt behind her."—*The Tempest* IV, 1.

Chanter ses propres louanges, To sing one's own praises, To blow one's own trumpet. " We wound our modesty, and make foul the clearness of our deservings, when of ourselves we publish them."—*All's Well That Ends Well* I, 3.

See also CHICHE.

loup. Brebis comptées, le loup les mange, The best laid plans may come to nought. " The best laid schemes o' mice an' men Gang aft a-gley."—ROBERT BURNS, *To a Mouse*, stanza 7.

D'un côté le loup nous menace, de l'autre, le chien, We are between the devil and the deep sea. *Cf. quotations under* TOMBER.

Enfermer le loup dans la bergerie *ou* Donner la brebis à garder au loup, To set the fox to mind the geese. " *York.* Wer't not all one an empty eagle were set To guard the chicken from a hungry kite, As place Duke Humphrey for the king's protector? *Queen Margaret.* So the poor chicken should be sure of death. *Suffolk.* Madam, 'tis true; and wer't not madness, then, To make the fox surveyor of the fold ? "—2 *King Henry VI* III, 1. " Thou hast entertain'd A fox to be the shepherd of thy lambs."—*Two Gentlemen of Verona* IV, 4.

Être connu comme le loup blanc, To be known to everybody.

Les loups ne se mangent pas entre eux, Dog doesn't eat dog, There is honour among thieves. " One bear will not bite another."—*Troilus and Cressida* V, 7. " A plague upon't, when thieves cannot be true to one another !"—1 *King Henry IV* II, 2.

Quand on parle du loup on en voit la queue, Talk of the devil and he will appear, Talk of the angels and you will hear the flutter of their wings.

Qui se fait brebis, le loup le mange *ou* Faites-vous brebis, le loup vous mangera, Mugs are always fleeced.

Tenir le loup par les oreilles, To have (*or* To hold) the wolf by the ears.

Un loup de mer, A hard-bitten sailor, An old salt.

Un loup en habit de brebis, A wolf in sheep's clothing (*Matthew* vii, 15). " Thou wolf in sheep's array." —1 *King Henry VI* I, 3. " Is he a lamb ? his skin is surely lent him, For he's inclin'd as is the ravenous wolf. Who cannot steal a shape that means deceit ? "—2 *King Henry VI* III, 1.

See also APPÉTIT, CHIEN, CRIER, ENRHUMER, FAIM, GUEULE, HURLER, MANGER, MARCHER, PEAU.

lourd. Il est lourd comme un bœuf, He is [as] dull-witted as an ox. " Thou mongrel beef-witted lord ! " —*Troilus and Cressida* II, 1. " Hang nothing but a calf's-skin, most sweet lout."—*King John* III, 1.

luire. *See* SOLEIL.

lumière. *See* VEILLEUSE.

lune. Avoir des lunes, To be subject to strange fancies. " Why, woman, your husband is in his old lunes again . . . any madness I ever yet beheld seemed but tameness."—*Merry Wives of Windsor* IV, 2.

C'est vouloir prendre la lune (*ou* On prendrait plutôt la lune) avec les dents, That is attempting impossibilities.

Faire un trou à la lune, To shoot the moon, To do a moonlight flit.

See also ABOYER, DEMANDER.

luron. C'est un luron, He's one of the boys.

lutte. La lutte pour l'existence, The struggle for life.

See also CLASSE, EMPORTER.

luxe. *See* DONNER.

lyre. Et toute la lyre, And all the rest of it.

M

mâcher. Mâcher à quelqu'un sa besogne *ou* Mâcher les morceaux à quelqu'un, To cut out his work for someone.

See also PAPIER.

mâchoire. Jouer des mâchoires, To fall to (*eating*).

See also BÂILLER.

Madeleine. *See* PLEURER.

magique. *See* LANTERNE.

maigre. Être maigre comme un échalas *ou* comme un clou *ou* comme un hareng saur, To be [as] thin as a lath *or* as a stick *or* as a rake. " Let us revenge this with our pikes ere we become rakes : for the gods know I speak this in hunger for bread, not in thirst for revenge."—*Coriolanus* I, 1. " Then am I a shotten herring."—1 *King Henry IV* II, 4. " Here comes Romeo.—Without his roe, like a dried herring.—O, flesh, flesh, how art thou fishified ! "—*Romeo and Juliet* II, 4.

See also ÉCHINE, MARCHER.

maille. Avoir maille à partir avec quelqu'un, To have a bone to pick with someone.

See also SOU.

main. Avoir le cœur sur la main, To be open-hearted.

Donner (*ou* Mettre) la dernière main à un ouvrage, To give the finishing touch[es] to a work.

Donner la main, To throw in one's hand *or* one's cards, To throw up the sponge.

Donner (*ou* Prêter) la main à quelqu'un, To lend someone a [helping] hand.

Donner (*ou* Prêter) la main à une entreprise, To lend (*or* To bear) a hand in an undertaking.

Donner les mains à quelque chose, To give one's consent (*or* support) to something.

Être à toutes mains, To be ready to do anything ; To be able to do anything.

Faire la main, To get one's hand in (*to enable one to acquire skill by practice*) : Cela vous fera la main, That will get your hand in.

Faire sa main, To feather one's nest (*by unfair means*).

Il prend de toutes mains, All is grist that comes to his mill.

J'en mettrais ma (*ou* la) main au feu *ou* au billot, I would stake my life on it, I would swear to it, Honour bright. " I had rather chop this hand off at a blow."—3 *King Henry VI* V, 1.

Jeter (*ou* Verser) l'or (*ou* Répandre l'argent) à pleines mains, To throw money about, To scatter money broadcast.

Mettre aux mains deux ou plusieurs personnes, To bring two or more persons to grips.

Mettre la main à l'œuvre *ou* à l'ouvrage *ou* à la charrue *ou* à la pâte, To put one's hand to the plough, To put one's shoulder to the wheel. " Stay we no longer, dreaming of renown, But sound the trumpets and about our task."—3 *King Henry VI* II, 1.

Mettre la main à la plume, To put pen to paper.

Prendre à pleines mains *ou* à toutes mains *ou* de toutes mains (*fig.*), To be very grasping (*greedy of gain*).

" Que ta main gauche ne sache pas ce que fait ta droite." (*Matthieu* vi, 3), " Let not thy left hand know what thy right hand doeth." —*Matthew* vi, 3.

S'entretenir la main, To keep one's hand in [practice].

Se faire la main, To get one's hand in (*acquire skill by practice*) : Pour se faire la main, In order to get his hand in.

Se tenir par la main, To be in league.

Tenir la main à quelque chose, To keep an eye on something, To watch something.

Tenir une nouvelle de bonne main, To have a piece of news on good authority.

Un homme à toutes mains, A man ready (*or* able) to do anything.

See also ALLER, ARME, BAISER, BAS, BRIDE, BRÛLER, CONSCIENCE, COUP 26, 37, CROCHU, DÉMANGER, DOIGT, DUR, FONDRE, GAGNER, GANTELÉ, GANTER, GLU, HAUT, HEUREUX, JEU, JOUER, LÂCHER, LARGE, LAVER, LESTE, LONG, MALADROIT, MALHEUREUX, MANGER, MARCHÉ, MARIER, MATIN, NET, NU, OFFRIR, OLIVIER, PAYER, PLUME, POIL, PRENDRE, TOUR, VALOIR, VENIR.

maintenir. Se maintenir sur l'eau (*lit.* & *fig.*), To keep one's head above water. " His bold head 'Bove the contentious waves he kept."—*The Tempest* II, 1.

See also PAGE.

maison. Faire une bonne maison, To feather one's nest (*by fair means*).

See also BÂTIR, CARTON, CLOU, DESSUS, EMPÊCHER, MAÎTRE, MENER, NET, NEUF, OUVRIR, PETIT, VERRE.

maître. Faire le maître, To lord it.

Le charbonnier est maître dans sa maison *ou* Charbonnier (*ou* Chacun) est maître chez soi, A man's house (*or, in England :* An Englishman's house) is his castle.

Le temps est un grand maître, Time

will straighten things out. " O time, thou must untangle this."—*Twelfth Night* II, 2.

Régner en maître, To reign supreme.

Tel maître, tel valet, Like master, like man.

See also CHAMP, CHANTEUR, COUP 71, COUR, ENGRAISSER, HEURE, TROUVER.

mal. Cela lui fait (*ou* Il en a) mal au cœur, It is a shock to him, It gives him a turn: Ne pensez-vous pas qu'il a (*ou* que cela lui fait) bien mal au cœur de voir . . . ? Don't you think it is a great shock to him to see . . . ? You can imagine it gives him quite a turn to see . . .

Être mal dans les papiers de quelqu'un *ou* Être mal vu de quelqu'un, To be in someone's bad (*or* black) books. " Methinks My favour here begins to warp."—*The Winter's Tale* I, 2.

Être mal dans ses finances, To be in financial difficulties *or* (*slang*) in Queer Street.

Être mal en point, To be in a bad way.

Être mal en train, To feel queer (*of person*); To hang fire (*of a piece of business*).

Être plus mal en point, To be worse off.

Mal prendre une chose, To take a thing badly, To cut up rough about a thing. " In that you brook it ill, it makes him worse: Therefore, for God's sake, entertain good comfort, And cheer his grace with quick and merry words."—*King Richard III* I, 3.

S'y prendre mal, To go the wrong way to work.

Se donner un mal de chien, To toil [laboriously] (*or* To labour [arduously]) at one's work.

See also AISE, ÂNE, ATTELER, AUTRUI, BIEN, BON 15, BRUIT, CHAUSSER, COMBLE, DEVANT, EMBRASSER, FICHER, GRAND, GRÉ, GUÉRIR, HONNIR, JOUR, LÉCHER, MARQUER, MONTER, MONTRER, PEIGNER, PEUR, PLACER, RACINE, SOMME, TENIR, TOMBER, TORCHER, TOURNER, VENIR, VOULOIR.

malade. Être malade à mourir, To be sick to death (*very ill indeed*). " The malady That doth my life besiege."—*All's Well That Ends Well* II, 1.

Le temps est bien malade, The weather is very bad.

Par suite de ces événements, le pays est bien malade, As a result of these occurrences, the country is in a very bad way. " The present time's so sick That present medicine must be minister'd, Or overthrow incurable ensues."—*King John* V, 1.

Vous voilà bien malade ! Poor fellow ! Poor you ! " Zounds ! how has he the leisure to be sick In such a justling time."—1 *King Henry IV* IV, 1.

maladroit. Avoir la main maladroite, To have clumsy fingers. Il a la main maladroite, His fingers are all thumbs.

mâle. *See* BEAU 31.

malheur. À quelque chose malheur est bon, It is an ill wind that blows nobody good. " Ill blows the wind that profits nobody."—3 *King Henry VI* II, 5. " Sweet are the uses of adversity; Which, like the toad, ugly and venomous, Wears yet a precious jewel in his head."—*As You Like It* II, 1. " Some falls are means the happier to arise."—*Cymbeline* IV, 2.

Je le connais pour mon malheur, I know him (it) to my cost.

Jouer de malheur, To have a run of bad luck, To be unlucky (*at gaming, and otherwise, e.g., at not finding someone at home*).

Le beau (*ou* Le grand) malheur ! That's nothing much to complain about.

Par malheur, As ill luck would have it.

Quel malheur ! What a pity ! How unfortunate ! What a tragedy !

Un malheur ne vient (*ou* n'arrive) jamais seul *ou* sans un autre *ou* Un malheur en amène un autre *ou* Un malheur amène son frère, Misfortunes never come singly, It never rains but it pours. " When sorrows come, they come not single spies, But in battalions."—*Hamlet* IV, 5. " One sorrow never comes but brings an heir That may succeed as his inheritor."—*Pericles, Prince of Tyre* I, 4.

See also CHERCHER, COMBLE, HEUR.

malheureux. Avoir la main malheureuse, To be clumsy ; To be unlucky.

C'est bien malheureux pour vous, [It is] hard lines [on you], You're unlucky [this time].

Ce n'est pas malheureux, And a good job too.

Être malheureux comme les pierres (*qu'on foule sous les pieds*), To be utterly miserable ; To be extremely unfortunate. " Muddied in fortune's mood."—*All's Well That Ends Well* V, 2.

See also FIN, NAÎTRE.

malice. La belle malice ! There's nothing very clever in that.

See also ENTENDRE, SAC.

malin. Être malin comme un singe, To be as artful as a wagonload of monkeys.

Être un malin, To know a thing or two, To know what's what.

See also BÊTE.

manche. Avoir quelqu'un dans sa manche, To have someone in one's pocket (*completely under one's control*).

Être du côté du manche, To be on the winning (*or* the stronger) side. " Thou slave, thou wretch, thou coward ! Thou little valiant, great in villany ! Thou ever strong upon the stronger side ! Thou Fortune's champion that dost never fight But when her humorous ladyship is by To teach thee safety ! "—*King John* III, 1. (*Note.*—humorous = capricious.)

Il ne faut pas jeter le manche après la cognée, Don't throw the helve after the hatchet, Never say die.

Se mettre du côté du manche, To side with the stronger (*or, if more than two,* with the strongest) *or* with the party in power.

See also AUTRE, LARGE, TIRER.

manchot. Il n'est pas manchot, He's all there.

mangeaille. *See* CREVER.

manger. Avez-vous peur qu'on vous mange ? He (They) can't eat you.

Il mangerait le diable et ses cornes, He is a prodigious eater, He would eat hat and feathers and all, He is as voracious as a vulture. " Eight wild boars roasted whole at a breakfast, and but twelve persons there ; is this true ?—This was but as a fly by an eagle : we had much more monstrous matter of feasts, which worthily deserved noting."—*Antony and Cleopatra* II, 2.

Manger à plus d'un râtelier *ou* à deux (*ou* à plusieurs) râteliers, To have more than one string (*or* have two strings) to one's bow (*to derive income from more than one source*).

Manger à ventre déboutonné, To burst one's buttons with food, To eat to excess, To gorge.

Manger comme un ogre *ou* comme un loup *ou* comme quatre, To eat like a horse *or* like a wolf. " They will eat like wolves."—*King Henry V* III, 6.

Manger dans la main (*fig.*), To take liberties.

Manger de la vache enragée, To have a rough time of it (*suffer pecuniary hardship*).

Manger de toutes ses dents, To gobble [one's food].

Manger du bout des dents, To pick at one's food.

Manger [la moitié de] ses mots, To clip one's words.

Manger le morceau, To make a clean breast of it, To own up.

Manger quelqu'un de caresses, To smother someone with kisses. " He would kiss you twenty with a breath."—*King Henry VIII* I, 4. " And kiss on kiss She vied so fast."—*The Taming of the Shrew* II, 1.

Manger quelqu'un, quelque chose, des yeux, To devour someone, something, with one's eyes.

Manger son blé en herbe *ou* en vert, To anticipate one's income, To spend one's income in advance.

Se manger les yeux *ou* le blanc des yeux *ou* le nez, To fly at each other (*in quarrel*).

Se mettre à manger, To fall to.

See also APPÉTIT, BÊTE, BOIRE, CHEMISE, CHIEN, FUMÉE, GRENOUILLE, GRIVE, GROS, LAINE, LOUP, PAIN, PISSENLIT, PRISON, SOU.

manier. Manier bien la parole, To wield one's language (*or* one's words) well.

See also BEURRE, CIRE.

manière. De la bonne (*ou* belle) manière, In proper fashion, Soundly, Harshly. *See also for this phrase* ARRANGER, PRENDRE, SALER, TANCER.

Faire des manières, To act for effect, To require [much] pressing (*e.g.*, pour chanter, to sing).

Il y a la manière, There is a way of doing it (*of being diplomatic*).

See also ACQUIT, FORT, PIROUETTER, TALON, VOIR.

manigancer. Qu'est-ce qu'il manigance? What is he up to? What's his little game ?

manquer. But manqué, fût-ce d'une ligne, n'est pas atteint, A miss is as good as a mile.

Il ne manquait plus que cela, That's the last straw, That crowns all.

Il s'en manque de beaucoup, Far from it.

Manquer de foi à quelqu'un, To break faith with someone. " And I will die a hundred thousand deaths Ere break the smallest parcel of this vow."—1 *King Henry IV* III, 2. " For trust not him that hath once broken faith."—3 *King Henry VI* IV, 4.

Manquer le coche *ou* le train (*fig.*), To miss the boat, To let the opportunity slip [by] *or* go [by].

Manquer son coup, To fail [in one's object *or* purpose].

S'il me manque, je ne le manquerai pas, I'll be even with him.

See also CLOU, GARÇON, PAROLE, SOUFFLE, TAIRE.

manteau. S'envelopper de son manteau, To resign oneself to (*or* To calmly await) one's fate.

Sous le manteau, On the quiet.

Sous le manteau de la cheminée, Under the rose, Sub rosa.

marbre. *See* CŒUR.

marchand. *See* GAGNER.

marchandise. *See* BON 58, DÉBITER, DÉCRIER, DÉPARER.

marche. *See* EXÉCUTER, FERMER, GAGNER, OUVRIR.

marché. Marché conclu est marché conclu, A bargain is a bargain.

Mettre à quelqu'un le marché à la (*ou* en) main, To say to someone " Do you want it or don't you ? "

See also AMENDER, BON 11, 38, 39, 54, 58, CHER, DESSUS, DONNER.

marcher. Faire marcher l'affaire, To run the business *or* (*slang*) the show. C'est lui qui fait marcher l'affaire, He runs the show.

Faire marcher quelqu'un, To order somebody about ; To take (*or* To get) a rise out of someone, To take someone in, To pull someone's leg, To lead someone up (*or* down) the garden path (*slang*).

Il ne se laisse pas marcher sur le pied, He won't be sat on (*slang*).

Je ne marche pas, [There's] nothing doing, I'm not having any (*slang*), I've had some (*slang*). " You put me off with limber vows; but I, Though you would seek to unsphere the stars with oaths, Should yet say, 'Sir, no going.' "—*The Winter's Tale* I, 2.

Marcher à pas comptés, To walk with measured tread.

Marcher à pas de géant, To walk with giant strides ; To make astonishing progress.

Marcher à pas de loup, To walk stealthily, To creep (*or* To steal) along.

Marcher à pas de tortue, To walk at a snail's pace, To crawl along. " Come forth, thou tortoise ! when ? "—*The Tempest* I, 2. " Snail-pac'd Ajax."—*Troilus and Cressida* V, 5.

Marcher à quatre pattes, To go on all fours.

Marcher comme un Basque *ou* comme un chat maigre, To walk at a great pace *or* (*slang*) at a great lick *or* (*slang*) at a lick of a pace.

Marcher comme une cane, To waddle.

Marcher comme une épouse, To walk demurely.

Marcher d'un même pas dans une affaire, To act and think with one mind in a matter (*of two or more persons*).

Marcher dans les eaux de quelqu'un, To back someone up.

Marcher en caravane, To walk (*or* To go) in a body, To walk (*or* To go) all together.

Marcher en fête, To lead the van. " My Lord, most humbly on my knee I beg The leading of the vaward."—*King Henry V* IV, 3. (*Note.*—vaward = vanward *or* van.)

Marcher entre des précipices (*fig.*), To be treading on dangerous ground.

Marcher sur des épines *ou* sur des charbons ardents *ou* sur des œufs, To tread [as] on eggs, To walk [as] on broken glass, To go like a cat on hot bricks, To go gingerly.

Marcher sur les pas (*ou* sur les traces) (*ou* sur les erres) de quelqu'un, To follow (*or* To tread) in someone's footsteps.

Marcher sur les talons de quelqu'un, To tread on someone's heels (*follow closely after*).

Ne pas vouloir marcher, To refuse to budge, To sit tight.

On marche sur les sots, The world is full of fools.

See also BRAS, DOIGT, DROIT, FRONT, HERBE, NEZ, PAIR, PIED, PLATE-BANDE, TROUPE, VUE.

maréchal. *See* BÂTON.

marée. Arriver comme marée en carême, To come in the nick of time.

La marée n'attend personne, Time and tide wait for no man.

See also VENT.

marge. *See* CODE.

marier. Se marier de la main gauche, To jump the broomstick *or* the besom.

See also DIABLE.

marin. Un marin d'eau douce, A freshwater sailor, A landlubber.

See also PIED.

Marion. *See* VIVRE.

marmelade. Avoir les yeux, la tête, etc., en marmelade, To have one's eyes, one's head, etc., bashed in.

Être dans la marmelade, To be in difficulties *or* (*slang*) in the soup *or* (*slang*) in Queer Street.

Mettre quelqu'un en marmelade, To make mincemeat of someone, To pound someone to a jelly. *Quotations under* HACHER.

marmite. Faire bouillir (*ou* Faire aller) la marmite (*fig.*), To keep the pot boiling.

La marmite bout (*ou* est bonne) dans cette maison, One fares (*eats*) well in this house.

La marmite est renversée dans cette maison, They no longer entertain guests at dinner in this house.

See also ÉCUMEUR.

marmot. *See* CROQUER.

marmotte. *See* DORMIR.

marotte. *See* FLATTER.

marquer. Marquer mal, To give a bad impression.

See also B, PAS.

marre. J'en ai marre, I've had enough of it, I'm fed up [to the teeth] with it (*slang*).

marron. Se servir de la patte du chat pour tirer les marrons du feu, To use someone as a cat's-paw.

Tirer les marrons du feu pour quelqu'un, To be someone's cat's-paw.

mars. Arriver (*ou* Venir) comme mars en carême, To come round as regularly as clockwork ; To come in the nick of time.

marteau. *See* COUP 8, ENCLUME.

martel. Avoir martel en tête, To be uneasy in one's mind, To be anxious *or* very worried.

Ne vous mettez pas martel en tête, Don't be uneasy (*or* worried) (*or* anxious) about it.

Martin. *See* ÂNE.

martyr. *See* COMMUN.

martyre. *See* SOUFFRIR.

masque. Avoir un masque mobile, To have expressive features. " I can . . . frame my face to all occasions." —3 *King Henry VI* III, 2.

See also COMIQUE, FIGER.

massacrant. *See* HUMEUR.

massacre. C'est un massacre, What gross carelessness *or* What terrible vandalism (*when something valuable has been damaged*).

masse. *See* TOMBER.

massue. *See* COUP 11.

mater. Mater quelqu'un, To bring someone to heel.

matière. Matière à réflexion, Food for thought.

See also ENTRER.

matin. Heure du matin, heure du gain *ou* À qui se lève matin Dieu aide et prête la main, The early bird catches (*or* gets) the worm.

See also OUVRIR, QUATRE, RIRE, ROUGE.

matinée. *See* DORMIR.

maussade. *See* HUMEUR.

mauvais. Avoir mauvaise mine, Not to look up to the mark, To look white about the gills.

C'est un mauvais cœur, He has a bad heart.

C'est une mauvaise tête, He (She) is a wrong-headed (*or* a perverse) (*or* an unruly) person.

Être dans une mauvaise passe, To be in a tight corner.

Faire mauvais visage à quelqu'un, To frown on someone, To treat someone coldly.

Le mauvais œil, The evil eye.

Mauvaise tête et bon cœur, A kind heart and a light head.

Regarder (*ou* Voir) une chose d'un mauvais œil, To look unfavourably on a thing.

Regarder (*ou* Voir) une personne d'un mauvais œil, To view a person with an unfriendly eye.

Trouver mauvais que quelqu'un fasse une chose, To disapprove of someone doing a thing.

Un mauvais pas, A tight corner, An awkward situation, A scrape.

See also AMOUR, ARROI, AUGURE, BESOGNE, BIAIS, BON 16, 43, 58, 73, CHIEN, COMMERCE, COMPAGNIE, COUP 42, EMPLETTE, FILER, FIN, GARÇON, HERBE, JOUER, MÉDITER, MOYEN, NAÎTRE, NOUVELLE, OUTIL, PRENDRE, QUART, RICHE, VIN.

méchant. Faire le méchant, To be nasty, To cut up rough.

Il est méchant comme un âne rouge, He is full of spite.

Il n'est pas si méchant qu'il en a l'air, His bark is worse than his bite.

Trouver plus méchant que soi, To meet one's better.

See also COMMERCE, DIABLE, GALE, OUTIL.

mèche. Découvrir (*ou* Éventer) (*ou* Vendre) la mèche, To let the cat out of the bag, To give the show away, To blow the gaff (*slang*).

médaille. *See* REVERS.

médecin. *See* AMOUR, GUÉRIR, MORT, TANT.

médecine. Il ne faut pas prendre la médecine en plusieurs verres, It is best to get it over.

See also COMPTANT.

méditer. Méditer quelque vilenie *ou* quelque mauvais tour, To be up to some mischief.

meilleur. *See* AVIS, COURT, PIÈCE.

mélancolie. *See* ENGENDRER.

mêler. *See* DIABLE, HOMME.

méli-mélo. Un méli-mélo, An omnium gatherum.

Melun. *See* ÉCORCHER.

membre. *See* TREMBLER.

même. C'est toujours la même rengaine *ou* la même chanson *ou* la même guitare, It is always the same old story.

Chanter (*ou* Réciter) toujours la même antienne *ou* la même litanie *ou* la même chanson *ou* Rabâcher toujours les mêmes choses, To be always harping on the same string, To harp (*or* To keep harping) on one string, To chew the rag (*slang*). " *King Richard.* Harp not on that string, madam ; that is past. *Queen Elizabeth.* Harp on it still shall I till heart-strings break."—*King Richard III* IV, 4.

See also BOIS, BONNET, CHANGER, CHANSON, COURIR, ENSEIGNE, FARINE, LIMON, MARCHER, MONNAIE, MOUTURE, OCCUPER, ŒIL, PANIER, PIED, REVENIR, TUER.

mémoire. Avoir une mémoire de lièvre [, qu'on perd en courant] *ou* une mémoire comme un panier percé, To have a memory like a sieve.

De mémoire d'homme, Within living memory.

See also APOTHICAIRE, CHERCHER, COURT, DÉROUILLER, PRÉSENT, RÉCENT.

menacer. Menacer le ciel *ou* les cieux (*poetic*), To threaten the welkin, To kiss the heavens *or* the clouds (*said of seas, mountains, trees, lofty structures*). " If the winds rage, doth not the sea wax mad, Threatening the welkin with his big-swoln face ? "—*Titus Andronicus* III, 1. " The sea, mounting to the welkin's cheek."—*The Tempest* I, 2. " The chidden billow seems to pelt the clouds."—*Othello* II, 1. " Then let the pebbles on the hungry beach Fillip the stars."—*Coriolanus* V, 3. " A heaven-kissing hill."—*Hamlet* III, 4. " Your stately and air-braving towers."—1 *King Henry VI* IV, 2. " Yond towers, whose wanton tops do buss the clouds."—*Troilus and Cressida* IV, 5. (*Note.*—To buss (*archaic*) = To kiss with a smack, or rudely : " Kissing and bussing differ both in this, We buss our wantons, but our wives we kiss."—HERRICK.)

See also LOUP.

ménage. *See* AMOUR, ENTRER.

ménager. Ménager la chèvre et le chou, To hold (*or* To run) with the hare and run (*or* hunt) with the hounds, To keep in with both sides. To sit on the fence.

Ménager ses pas, To spare oneself (*save oneself from exertion, etc.*).

Qui veut voyager (*ou* aller) loin ménage sa monture, Slow and steady (*or* and sure) wins the race, [The] more haste, [the] less speed. *Quotations under* HÂTER.

Se ménager, To take care of oneself (*after illness*).

See also APPARENCE, BOUT, SORTIE, SOU, TERRAIN.

mendiant. Les quatre mendiants, Almonds, raisins, nuts, and figs (*served as dessert*).

mener. Mener grand bruit, To kick up a shindy.

Mener grand deuil de quelque chose, To be very much upset (*or* cut up) about something.

Mener la danse (*fig.*) *ou* le branle *ou* le jeu, To take the lead, To set the ball [a-]rolling, To open the ball; To be the first to suffer. " And though the devil lead the measure, such are to be followed: after them."—*All's Well That Ends Well* II, 1. (*Note.*—after them = go after them.)

Mener loin quelqu'un, To lead someone too far (*in a course of action*); To cause someone a lot of annoyance; To last someone long *or* out: Cet argent ne le mènera pas loin, This money will not last him long *or* last him out.

Mener quelqu'un tambour battant *ou* Mener quelqu'un bon (*ou* grand) train, To press (*or* To drive) someone hard; To treat someone with a high hand.

Mener rondement une affaire, To hustle a thing through.

Mener sa fortune grand train, To run through one's fortune *or* one's money.

Mener un [grand] train [de maison] *ou* Mener la vie à grandes guides, To live in grand style, To cut a dash, To go the pace.

Mener une chose à bonne fin *ou* Mener une affaire à bien, To bring a thing to a successful issue, To carry a thing through, To bring a thing off, To make a success of a thing.

Mener une chose tambour battant, To hustle a thing on.

See also AVEUGLE, BAGUETTE, BARQUE, BÂTON, CÉNOBITE, CHANOINE, CHEMIN, CHIEN, FRONT, JOYEUX, LAISSE, LARGE, LISIÈRE, NEZ, PIERRE, TOMBEAU, VOIE.

mensonge. Un mensonge innocent, A fib, A story.

Un mensonge pieux *ou* officieux, A white lie.

See also REVÊTIR, SONGE.

mentir. Mentir à la journée, To be in the habit of lying, To be an inveterate liar.

Mentir comme un arracheur de dents *ou* comme tous les diables, To lie like a gas-meter, To lie unblushingly. " You told a lie; an odious, damned lie; Upon my soul, a lie; a wicked lie."—*Othello* V, 2. " The lyingest knave in Christendom."—*The Taming of the Shrew, Induction, Scene* 2.

Sans mentir *ou* À ne point mentir, Honour bright, To tell the truth.

See also GORGE, LOIN, SANG.

menton. *See* BARBE, BOUTONNER.

menu. Le menu peuple, The humbler classes, The small fry.

Mes, Ses, menus plaisirs, My, His, occasional expenses.

See also HACHER.

mépris. *See* FAMILIARITÉ.

mépriser. *See* QU'EN-DIRA-T-ON.

mer. *See* AVALER, BOIRE, DÉMONTER, EAU, ÉCUMEUR, GOUTTE, LOUP, PAQUET, TERRE.

mercenaire. *See* TRAVAILLER.

merci. Comment vous dire merci? How can I thank you? " I have a kind soul that would give you thanks, And knows not how to do it but with tears."—*King John* V, 7.

mercier. [À] petit mercier, petit panier, Don't bite off more than you can chew.

mère. *See* NÉCESSITÉ, PRUDENCE.

mériter. *See* PEINE.

merle. Beau merle, My fine fellow, *e.g.*, Halte-là, beau merle, Hold, my fine fellow.

C'est le merle blanc, He is a strange mixture (*of qualities*).

C'est un fin merle, He is a cunning old bird.

Je vous donnerai le (*ou* un) merle blanc, I shall be very much surprised, I'll eat my hat (*if you can do that*).

See also GRIVE, PIPÉE, VILAIN.

merveille. Aller à merveille, To suit down to the ground, To suit to a T.

Une merveille d'un jour, A nine days' wonder. " *Gloster*. That would be ten days' wonder at the least. *Clarence*. That's a day longer than a wonder lasts. *Gloster*. By so much is the wonder in extremes." —3 *King Henry VI* III, 2. " I was seven of the nine days out of the wonder before you came."—*As You Like It* III, 2.

See also PROMETTRE.

mesure. Cela passe la mesure, That exceeds all bounds, That is coming it rather strong (*slang*).

Donner sa mesure, To show what one is made of.

Ne garder aucune mesure *ou* Oublier toute mesure, To go beyond all bounds, To fling aside all restraint, To lose all sense of proportion. *Quotation under* BORNE.

See also COMBLE, COMPAS, DÉPASSER, POIDS.

mesurer. Mesurer la terre *ou* le sol, To measure one's length [on the ground]. " Faintness constraineth me To measure out my length on this cold bed."—*A Midsummer Night's Dream* III, 2.

Mesurer les autres à son aune *ou* à sa toise, To judge others by oneself *or* by one's own standard[s].

Mesurer quelqu'un des yeux *ou* du regard, To eye someone up and down.

On ne mesure pas les hommes à la toise *ou* Les hommes ne se mesurent pas à l'aune, Men should not be judged by their size.

See also TONDRE.

métier. J'aimerais mieux (*ou* Mieux vaudrait) bêcher la terre (*ou* gratter la terre avec les ongles) (*ou* porter l'auge) que de faire ce métier-là, I would rather sweep the streets than be in that trade *or* than do that. " I had rather be a country servant maid Than a great queen, with this condition,—To be so baited, scorn'd, and stormed at."—*King Richard III* I, 3. " Verily, I swear, 'tis better to be lowly born, And range with humble livers in content, Than to be perk'd up in a glistering grief, And wear a golden sorrow."—*King Henry VIII* II, 3.

Quand chacun fait son métier, les vaches sont bien gardées *ou* en sont mieux gardées *ou* [À] chacun son métier[, les vaches seront bien gardées], Everyone to his trade, Let the cobbler stick to his last. " It is written that the shoemaker should meddle with his yard, and the tailor with his last, the fisher with his pencil, and the painter with his nets."—*Romeo and Juliet* I, 2.

See also CHIEN, CŒUR, GÂTER, PLAT, RECETTE, TOUR.

mettre. Le mettre à quelqu'un, To take someone in, To have someone on (*slang*).

Les mettre, To take to one's heels, To run for it, To hop it (*slang*).

Mets-y-en ! *ou* Mets-y du nerf ! Go it ! (*slang*), Put some vim into it !

Y mettre du sien, du tien, To do one's, your, share, To pull one's, your, weight ; To make concessions. "This shoulder was ordain'd so thick to heave ; And heave it shall some weight, or break my back."—3 *King Henry VI* V, 7.

See also ABOI, ALARME, ARCHIVES, BAL, BAN, BANC, BÂTON, BEAU 20, BLANC, BLOC, BON 55, BONNET, BOURBIER, BOUT, BOUTIQUE, BRANLE, BRIDE, CAMPAGNE, CAPILOTADE, CAUSE, CHAMP, CHANTIER, CHAPEAU, CHARRUE, CLAIR, CLEF, CLOU, CŒUR, COGNÉE, COMPTE, CONSCIENCE, CORDE, DÉBANDADE, DEDANS, DEHORS, DENT, DÉPENSE, DOIGT, DOS, DOUBLE, DOUTE, DRAP, EAU, ESPÉRANCE, ÉTÉ, ÉTOUPE, ÉTRIER, FAIT, FER, FEU, FLAMBERGE, GANT, GLOBE, GOND, GORGE, GOÛT, GRAPPIN, GUÊPIER, GUEULE, HÔPITAL, HORS, I, INDEX, JEU, JOUR, MAIN, MANCHE, MANGER, MARCHÉ, MARMELADE, MARTEL, MEUBLE, MILLE, MOITIÉ, NAPPE, NEZ, NOIR, NOM, ŒUVRE, ORDRE, ÔTER, OUBLIETTES, PAILLE, PAIR, PANIER, PAS, PAVÉ, PAVILLON, PEAU, PETIT, PEUR, PIED, PIQUET, PLAT, PLOMB, POCHE, POIGNARD, POIL, POINT, POUCE, PRENDRE, PRISE, PRIX, PUCE, QUANT À, QUARANTAINE, QUATRE, RANCART, RANG, RÈGLE, REMORQUE, SAC, SAUCE, SAVOIR, SCÈNE, SECRET, SELLE, SENS, SI, SOU, SOURICIÈRE, SOURIS, TAPIS, TÊTE, TOMBEAU, TON, TORT, TRAVERS, VEILLEUSE, VENTRE, VERRE, VERT.

meuble. Être dans ses meubles, To have one's own furniture.

Se mettre dans ses meubles, To furnish a house, a flat, of one's own.

meubler. Avoir la bouche bien meublée, To have a fine set of teeth.

Meubler sa tête, sa mémoire, de connaissances, To stock one's head, one's mind, with knowledge.

meule. *See* NAGER.

meurtre. C'est un meurtre, It is a shame *or* a sin (*discredit*).

See also CRIER.

meurtrir. Meurtrir quelqu'un de coups, To beat someone black and blue. *Quotations under* OS.

mi-chemin. *See* CHEMIN.

micmac. Il y a [bien] du micmac là-dedans, There's something [very] fishy about it (*slang*).

midi. C'est midi [sonné], [There's] nothing doing, I'm not having any (*slang*), I've had some (*slang*). *Quotation under* MARCHER.

Chercher midi à quatorze heures, To look for difficulties where none exist.

See also ÉTOILE.

miel. *See* MOUCHE, SUCRE.

mieux. À qui mieux mieux, In emulation of (*or* Vying with) each other. " Emulation hath a thousand sons That one by one pursue."—*Troilus and Cressida* III, 3.

Faire de son mieux, To do one's best, To put one's best foot (*or* leg) foremost. " My best endeavours shall be done herein."—*The Merchant of Venice* II, 2.

Le mieux est l'ennemi du bien, Let well alone. " Striving to better, oft we mar what's well."—*King Lear* I, 4. " When workmen strive to do better than well, They do confound their skill in covetousness."—*King John* IV, 2.

See also ARRACHER, AVIS, BON 21, 73, DIRE, DONNER, ENCLUME, ENVIE, JAMBE, MÉTIER, PARLER, PLIER, POUVOIR, PRÉVENIR, RECULER, SAINT, SAUCE, TANT, TARD, TIRER, TÔT, VALOIR, VIE.

mijoter. Il se mijote quelque chose, There is something brewing *or* something afoot *or* something in the wind, There is more here than meets the eye, I smell a rat.

milieu. *See* NEZ.

mille. Des mille et des cents, Heaps, Tons, Pots.

Mettre dans le mille, To have the devil's own luck.

See also CHANDELLE, FOIS, LIEUE, MOT, POINT.

mi-mai. *See* HIVER.

mine. Éventer la mine, To let the cat

out of the bag, To give the show away, To blow the gaff (*slang*).

Faire des mines à quelqu'un, To give someone a sign (*as to withdraw*); To grimace at someone.

Faire la mine à quelqu'un, To scowl at someone.

Faire mine de vouloir . . ., To make as if to . . .

See also ALLONGER, BON 43, CHÉTIF, CHIFFONNER, DESSOUS, DÉTERRER, GRIS, MAUVAIS, PAYER, TRISTE.

minute. Être à la minute, To have hardly a minute to oneself. (*Note.*—Être ponctuel à la minute, To be punctual to the minute.)

miracle. Crier [au] miracle, I should (One would) never have thought it of him.

Il n'y a pas de quoi crier miracle, That's nothing to boast about.

Par miracle, As if by a miracle, For a wonder.

miroir. *See* CONSULTER.

misère. *See* COLLIER, CRIER.

miséricorde. À tout péché miséricorde, Be forbearing; Hope for pardon. " Forbearing one another, and forgiving one another . . .: even as Christ forgave you."—*Colossians* iii, 13. " Forbear to judge, for we are sinners all."—2 *King Henry VI* III, 3. " How would you be If He, which is the top of judgment, should But judge you as you are? O, think on that; And mercy then will breathe within your lips, Like man new made."—*Measure for Measure* II, 2.

mission. *See* PRÊCHER.

mitonner. Laisser mitonner une affaire, To let a matter simmer.

mobile. *See* MASQUE.

mode. Un homme à la mode, A popular man.

modestie. *See* PARURE.

moelle. Extraire la moelle de l'os, To derive the best possible advantage.

Jusqu'à la moelle des os, To the marrow, To the bone; To the core. *See also* SUCER.

mœurs. *See* ANTIQUE, AUTRE.

moi. *See* DE, DIRE, ENTRE.

moindre. *See* CHAMP, CHANCE, DERNIER, PLI, SOUCI.

moine. *See* ABBAYE, ABBÉ, GRAS, HABIT.

moineau. *See* ÉPOUVANTAIL, POUDRE, VALOIR.

moins. En moins d'un instant, In less than a moment, In two shakes of a duck's tail, Before you could say Jack Robinson *or* say knife.

En moins de rien, In less than no time.

Pas le moins du monde, Not in the slightest, Not a bit of it.

See also DIABLE, HÂTER, PARLER, PLUS.

mois. On a tous les ans douze mois, We grow older every day. " Let the world slip: we shall ne'er be younger."—*The Taming of the Shrew, Induction*, Scene 2.

See also TRENTE-SIX.

moitié. Sa [chère] moitié, One's better half. " He is the half part of a blessed man, Left to be finished by such a she; And she a fair divided excellence, Whose fulness of perfection lies in him."—*King John* II, 1.

Se mettre de moitié avec quelqu'un, To go halves (*or* fifty-fifty) with someone.

See also COMMENCER, FIGUE, MANGER, PARDONNER, PARTAGER.

moment. L'état des affaires à ce moment-là, The then state of affairs.

Sous l'impulsion du moment *ou* Sur le moment, On the spur of the moment.

See also BON 8, 71, CHER, PERDRE.

monceau. *See* OR.

monde. Avoir du monde, To be accustomed to move in polite society, To know what's what.

Avoir un visage de l'autre monde, To look like a corpse, To look ghastly.

C'est un homme de l'autre monde, He belongs to another world (*is different from others*).

Connaître bien son monde, To know whom one has to deal with.

De par le monde, Somewhere in the world.

Depuis que le monde est monde, Since the world began, Since the beginning of things.

Dire des choses de l'autre monde, To draw the long bow, To tell cock-and-bull stories, To talk through one's hat (*slang*).

Envoyer quelqu'un dans (*ou* Expédier quelqu'un à) l'autre monde, To send someone to kingdom come (*slang*). " I will shortly send thy soul to heaven . . . Till George be pack'd with posthorse up to heaven." —*King Richard III* I, 1.

Être au monde, To be in the land of the living.

Il est allé dans l'autre monde, He has gone hence (*is dead*).

N'avoir pas de monde, To be unaccustomed to move in polite society, Not to know what's what.

N'être plus de ce monde, To be no longer in the land of the living.

Paris, Londres, est un monde, Paris, London, is a world of its own.

Pour rien au monde, Not for the world, Not for worlds.

Revenir de l'autre monde, To be [all] at sea (*fig.*).

See also AIR, BAS, BOUT, COURIR, DIRE, DISPARAÎTRE, ENCORE, HEUR, MOINS, MOQUER, PAQUET, PARADIS, REFUSER, RENVERSER, RÉPANDRE, SAVOIR, SOLEIL, SORTIR, SPECTACLE, TOUR, TOUT, TU, VIEUX, VOYAGE, VU.

monnaie. Ces hommes n'étaient que la monnaie d'un tel, These men were only poor substitutes for so-and-so. " So doth the greater glory dim the less : A substitute shines brightly as a king Until a king be by ; and then his state Empties itself, as doth an inland brook Into the main of waters."—*The Merchant of Venice* V, 1.

Payer quelqu'un en monnaie de singe, To let someone whistle for his money.

Rendre (*ou* Donner) à quelqu'un la monnaie de sa pièce *ou* Payer quelqu'un en (*ou* de la) même monnaie, To pay someone [back] in his own coin.

See also BATTRE.

monsieur. Faire le monsieur, To play the swell.

See also BRAS, ÉTOILE, ORFÈVRE.

monstre. *See* ÉTOUFFER, RIEN.

mont. Par monts et par vaux, Over hill and dale. " *Puck.* How now, spirit ! whither wander you ? *Fairy.* Over hill, over dale, Thorough bush, thorough briar, Over park, over pale, Thorough flood, thorough fire, I do wander everywhere, Swifter than the moon's sphere."—*A Midsummer Night's Dream* II, 1. (*Note.* —thorough = through.)

See also PROMETTRE.

montagne. Il ferait battre des montagnes, He has set everyone by the ears.

See also ENFANTER, RIEN.

monter. Être bien monté, bien mal monté, To be in a good humour, in a very bad humour.

Monter à la tête, To go to the head (*of fumes*).

Monter [la tête à] quelqu'un, To work on someone's feelings, To work someone up : Quand la tête lui est montée, When he is worked up, When his blood is up.

Se monter [la tête], To get excited. Sa tête s'est montée, He got excited. Cet homme se monte aisément, This man gets excited easily.

See also BATEAU, CHEVAL, COLLET, COUP 50, 74, ÉCHASSE, ÉCHELLE, ERGOT, ESTRADE, FLÛTE, MOUTARDE, NUE, SCIE

montre. Faire passer quelqu'un à la montre, To put someone through his paces.

Passer à la montre, To pass muster.

montrer. Montrer le dos *ou* le derrière, To turn tail.

Montrer le soleil avec un flambeau, To paint the lily, To hold a farthing rushlight to the sun. " To gild refined gold, to paint the lily, To throw a perfume on the violet, To smooth the ice, or add another hue Unto the rainbow, or with taper-light To seek the beauteous eye of heaven to garnish, Is wasteful and ridiculous excess."—*King John* IV, 2.

Montrer les dents *ou* les cornes, To show one's teeth *or* one's claws, To show fight. " 'Tis Aufidius, Who . . . Thrusts forth his horns again into the world ; Which were inshell'd when Marcius stood for Rome, And durst not once peep out."—*Coriolanus* IV, 6.

Se montrer [bien], To assert oneself, To show a bold front.

Se montrer mal, To show a want of firmness.

Se montrer sous son vrai jour *ou* tel qu'on est, To show oneself (*or* To come out) (*or* To appear) in one's true colours.

See also BOUT, DÉSHABILLÉ, DOIGT, TALON.

monture. *See* MÉNAGER.

moquer. C'est se moquer du monde *ou* des gens, It is the height of impertinence.

Je m'en moque comme de l'an quarante *ou* comme de quatre sous *ou* Je me moque du tiers comme du quart, I don't care in the least, I don't care a brass farthing *or* a rap *or* a button *or* a fig *or* a pin *or* a straw *or* a tinker's dam[n] *or* a damn *or* two hoots.

See also CHIEN, PELLE, QU'EN-DIRA-T-ON.

morceau. Aimer les bons morceaux, To like good things to eat, To be fond of good living.

C'est un gros morceau, It is a hard nut to crack.

C'est un morceau de roi, It is a dish fit for a king ; She is [perfectly] sweet *or* (*slang*) is a bit of all right. La vengeance est un morceau de roi, Vengeance is sweet.

Ce n'est qu'un morceau d'homme, He is only a [tiny] little man. *Quotation under* Un [petit] BOUT d'homme.

Ce n'est qu'un morceau de femme, She is only a slip of a woman.

Prendre (*ou* Gober) le morceau, To swallow (*or* To take) (*or* To rise to) (*or* To nibble at) the bait. *Quotations under* MORDRE.

See also AVALER, COMPTER, EMPORTER, HONTEUX, MÂCHER, MANGER, ÔTER, PAIN.

mordre. Chien mort ne mord pas, Dead men tell no tales.

Mordre à belles dents, To bite lustily.

Mordre à l'hameçon (*lit. & fig.*), To swallow (*or* To take) (*or* To rise to) (*or* To nibble at) the bait. " Bait the hook well ; this fish will bite."—*Much Ado About Nothing* II, 3. " The pleasant'st angling is to see the fish Cut with her golden oars the silver stream, And greedily devour the treacherous bait."—*Much Ado About Nothing* III, 1.

Mordre à la grappe, To jump (*or* To snatch) at the offer.

Mordre le sein de sa nourrice, To bite the hand that feeds one.

S'en mordre les pouces *ou* les doigts, To repent it, To rue it.

See also ABOYER, CHIEN, TARENTULE.

More. *See* LAVER.

morfondre. Se morfondre, To be kept waiting, To cool (*or* To kick) one's heels. " Was it discretion, lords, to let this man, This good man, . . . This honest man, wait like a lousy footboy At chamber door ?"—*King Henry VIII* V, 2.

morigéner. Morigéner quelqu'un, To take someone to task, To give someone a good talking to.

mors. Prendre le mors aux dents, To take the bit between one's teeth.

mort. Après la mort le médecin, That's shutting the stable-door after the horse is stolen. " But in this point All his tricks founder, and he brings his physic After his patient's death."—*King Henry VIII* III, 2.

Avoir (*ou* Porter) la mort sur le visage, To look like a death's head *or* like a corpse, To look ghastly.

Être mort et bien mort, To be [as] dead as a door-nail. " What ! is the old king dead ?—As nail in door."—2 *King Henry IV* V, 3.

Faire le mort, To feign death ; To be mum, To lie doggo (*slang*).

Il ne faut pas (*ou* point) remuer (*ou* troubler) les cendres des morts *ou* Il faut laisser les morts en paix, Of the dead say nothing but good, Nothing but good should be spoken of the dead, Concerning the dead let nothing but good be spoken, De mortuis nil nisi bonum. " Good friend, for Jesus' sake, forbear To dig the dust enclosed here."—*Inscription on Shakespeare's grave.* " I can't listen to you—you, who would pluck the laurels from the brow of the dead Christ."—*said by* TENNYSON *to a guest who had argued the Baconian hypothesis.*

Morte la bête, mort le venin, Dead men tell no tales, Stone dead hath no fellow. " We have scotch'd the snake, not kill'd it ; She'll close, and be herself ; whilst our poor malice Remains in danger of her former tooth."—*Macbeth* III, 2.

See also ALLER, ARTICLE, BRAS, DOIGT, HAÏR, MORDRE, MOURIR, PORTE, SOUFFRIR, TOILETTE, VIE, VOIR.

mortel. *See* PLAIE, TRANSE.

morveux. Qui se sent morveux se mouche, If the cap fits, wear it. *Quotations under* GALEUX.

See also ARRACHER.

mot. Avoir le mot de l'affaire, To be in the know.

Dire (*ou* Placer) son mot, To put in one's word, To have one's say, To chime in.

En un mot [comme en cent *ou* comme en mille], In a word, In a nutshell. The long and the short of it is that. " That is the brief and the tedious of it."—*All's Well That Ends Well* II, 3.

J'ai à lui dire quatre mots *ou* J'ai deux mots à lui dire, I have a word to say to him. " Anointed, I implore so much expense of thy royal sweet breath as will utter a brace of words."—*Love's Labour's Lost* V, 2.

Je n'ai pu placer un mot, I could not get a word in edgeways.

Le grand mot est lâché, The cat is out of the bag.

Prendre quelqu'un au mot, To take someone at his word.

Se donner le mot, To be in league.

Voilà (*ou* C'est) le mot de l'énigme, That is the answer to the riddle.

See also BON 3, CLIQUETIS, CONSENTIR, COUVRIR, DÉFRAYER, DIRE, EMPORTE-PIÈCE, EXPLIQUER, FIN, GLISSER, GUERRE, MANGER, PAYER, RIRE, SACRAMENTEL, TOUCHER, TRANCHER.

motif. Courtiser une jeune fille pour le bon motif, To court a girl with honourable intentions.

mou. *See* BESOGNE, CHIFFE, CIRE.

mouche. C'est une fine mouche, He is a knowing card *or* a sly dog, She is a sly minx.

Des pattes de mouche, Scrawl (*bad handwriting*).

Faire d'une mouche un éléphant, To make a mountain out of a molehill.

Faire la mouche du coche, To play the fly on the wheel (*overestimate one's own influence*).

On ne prend pas les mouches avec du

vinaigre *ou* On prend plus de mouches avec du miel qu'avec du vinaigre, Gently does the trick. *Quotations under* DOUCEUR.

Prendre la mouche, To take huff, To take the pet, To get one's monkey up.

Quelle mouche le pique *ou* l'a piqué ? What is the matter with him ?

See also ENTENDRE, GOBER.

moucher. Ne pas se moucher du pied, To think no small beer of oneself.

See also MORVEUX.

moucheron. *See* CHAMEAU.

mouchoir. Jeter le mouchoir, To throw the handkerchief (*express condescending preference for person*).

See also POCHE.

moue. Faire la moue, To purse one's lips, To pout.

Faire une vilaine moue, To pull a wry face.

mouiller. En mouiller, To talk nineteen to the dozen.

Être mouillé jusqu'aux os *ou* Être mouillé comme un canard, To be wet (*or* soaked) to the skin, To look like a drowned rat. " Thou think'st 'tis much that this contentious storm Invades us to the skin."—*King Lear* III, 4. " Piteous they will look, like drowned mice." —1 *King Henry VI* I, 2.

See also EAU, POULE.

moule. Cela ne se jette pas en moule, That is more easily said than done.

Le moule en est perdu, We shall not (*or* never) see his like again. *Quotations under* NAÎTRE.

moulin. Il viendra moudre à notre moulin, He will come back [to us], He will need us again.

Renvoyer quelqu'un à son moulin, To ask someone to mind his own business.

Un moulin à paroles, A chatterbox.

See also BATTRE, BONNET, CLAQUET, EAU, ENTRER, FOUR, NAGER.

mourir. Bien mourir, To die in the faith.

Mourir à la peine, To die in the attempt ; To die in harness.

Mourir à la tâche *ou* à la besogne *ou* Mourir debout, To die in harness. " At least we'll die with harness on our back."—*Macbeth* V, 5.

Mourir au coin d'un bois *ou* d'une haie, To die in neglect.

Mourir avant l'âge, To come to an untimely end. " If he be dead,—O no, it cannot be, Seeing his beauty, thou shouldst strike at it—O yes, it may ; thou hast no eyes to see, But hatefully at random dost thou hit. Thy mark is feeble age ; but thy false dart Mistakes that aim, and cleaves an infant's heart . . . The Destinies will curse thee for this stroke ; They bid thee crop a weed, thou pluck'st a flower : Love's golden arrow at him should have fled, And not Death's ebon dart, to strike him dead."—SHAKESPEARE, *Venus and Adonis.*

Mourir de sa belle mort, To die a natural death *or* die in one's bed. " Rescue those breathing lives to die in beds, That here come sacrifices for the field."—*King John* II, 2.

Mourir tout entier, To die unhonoured and unsung. " Labour not for the meat which perisheth, but for that meat which endureth unto everlasting life."—*John* vi, 27.

On ne sait qui vit ni qui meurt, We may all be dead (*before that takes place*).

See also ATTACHER, FAIM, FEU, FINAL, GÎTE, MALADE, ODEUR, PAILLE, PEAU.

mousse. *See* PIERRE.

mousser. Faire mousser un succès, To cry up (*or* To overrate) a success.

Se faire mousser, To swagger, To swank (*slang*).

moutarde. C'est de la moutarde après dîner, It is too late [to be of any use], It comes a day after the fair.

La moutarde lui monte au nez, He is

beginning to show signs of impatience.

See also AMUSER.

moutardier. Il se croit le premier moutardier du pape, He thinks no small beer of himself, He is grown too big for his boots.

mouton. C'est un mouton, He is [as] gentle as a lamb.

C'est un mouton enragé, He is a man who rarely loses his temper, but when he does . . .

Revenir à ses moutons, To come (*or* To get) back to the point, To return to one's subject *or* (*gallicism*) to one's muttons ; To be always harping on the same string.

Sauter comme les moutons de Panurge, To follow one another like sheep.

See also DOUX.

mouture. C'est une seconde mouture, It is a (*literary*) rehash.

Tirer deux moutures du même sac *ou* Tirer d'un sac deux moutures, To make a double profit.

mouvement. Allons, un bon mouvement, Come, be a sport.

Être dans le mouvement, To be in the swim, To be abreast of the times, To be up to date (*slang*).

Être toujours en mouvement, To be always on the go.

Le premier mouvement est toujours le bon *ou* le meilleur, First impressions are best.

Se sentir en dehors du mouvement, To feel out of it *or* out of the running.

See also BON 36, CHERCHER, PERPÉTUEL.

mouvementer. C'est une époque mouvementée, These are stirring times. " Why, then we shall have a stirring world again."—*Coriolanus* IV, 5. " Such a justling time." —1 *King Henry IV* IV, 1. " These most brisk and giddy-paced times." —*Twelfth Night* II, 4.

moyen. Faire quelque chose par ses propres moyens, To do something off one's own bat.

Il n'y a pas moyen [de faire cela] *ou* Il n'y a pas moyen de moyenner, It can't be done.

Par tous les moyens, bons ou mauvais, By fair means or foul.

See also ANNÉE, ENLEVER, GRAND, USAGE, VOULOIR.

moyenner. *See* MOYEN.

muet. Être muet comme la tombe, To be [as] silent as the grave.

Être muet comme un poisson, To be [as] mute as a fish.

See also TÉMOIN.

mule. *See* PAS, TÊTU.

mulet. Être chargé comme un mulet, To be loaded like a pack-horse.

See also TÊTE, TÊTU.

multiplier. Se multiplier, To be here there and everywhere, To be in half a dozen places at once, To buzz around ; To have many irons in the fire.

munir. *See* AVERTIR, PATIENCE.

mur. Battre les murs, To stagger (*or* To reel) from side to side (*of drunken man*).

Donner (*ou* Heurter) de la tête (*ou* Se battre *ou* Se cogner *ou* Se heurter la tête) contre un (*ou* le) mur *ou* contre les murs (*fig.*), To run one's head against a brick wall.

Parler à un mur, To talk to a brick wall *or* to deaf ears.

Sauter le mur, To break barracks.

See also HUILE, OREILLE, PIED, RASER.

mûr. *See* POIRE.

muraille. *See* OREILLE, PARLER.

mûrir. Mûrir une question, To thrash a matter out.

muscle. Avoir du muscle, To have plenty of beef *or* of brawn.

See also NERF.

Muse. Les neuf Muses, The nine Muses. " The thrice-three Muses mourning for the death Of learning, late deceas'd in beggary."—*A Midsummer Night's Dream* V, 1.

musée. *See* HORREUR.

musique. Faire de la musique (*fig.*), To kick up a dust *or* a row *or* a shindy.

See also AUTRE, RÉGLER.

mystifier. Mystifier quelqu'un, To have someone guessing, To have someone on, To pull someone's leg, To take (*or* To get) a rise out of someone.

N

na. Na! So much for that, And that's that. *Quotation under* VOILÀ.

nage. Être [tout] en nage, To be bathed in perspiration. *Quotations under* SUER.

nager. Il ne faut pas apprendre aux poissons à nager, Don't teach your grandmother to suck eggs.

Nager comme un chien de plomb *ou* comme une meule de moulin, Not to be able to swim a stroke. " Swims with fins of lead."—*Coriolanus* I, 1.

Nager comme un poisson, To swim like a fish *or* like a duck. " Though thou canst swim like a duck, thou art made like a goose."—*The Tempest* II, 2.

Nager contre le courant, To struggle against fate.

Nager dans l'opulence, To be rolling in wealth, To wallow in money.

Nager dans le sang, To welter (*or* To wade) in blood. " I am in blood Stept in so far that, should I wade no more, Returning were as tedious as go o'er."—*Macbeth* III, 4. " And here thy hunters stand, Sign'd in thy spoil, and crimson'd in thy Lethe."—*Julius Caesar* III, 1. (*Note.*—Lethe = death.)

Nager en grande (*ou* en pleine) eau (*fig.*), To be rolling in money ; To have golden opportunities of furthering one's interests, To be in clover.

Nager entre deux eaux (*fig.*), To run with the hare and hunt with the hounds, To sit on the fence.

See also BLEU.

naissance. *See* TENIR.

naître. Encore à naître, As yet unborn.

Être né coiffé, To be born with a silver spoon in one's mouth.

Être né pour quelque chose, To be cut out for something (*profession*). Il est né poète, né peintre, He is a born poet, a born painter.

Être né sous une bonne (*ou* heureuse) étoile *ou* sous une heureuse planète *ou* sous une heureuse constellation, To be born under a lucky star. " I find my zenith doth depend upon A most auspicious star."—*The Tempest* I, 2. " Planets of good luck."—*King Richard III* IV, 4.

Être né sous une mauvaise étoile *ou* sous une étoile malheureuse, To be born under an unlucky star. " What ! shall we curse the planets of mishap, That plotted thus our glory's overthrow ? "—1 *King Henry VI* I, 1. " Combat with adverse planets in the heavens!"—1 *King Henry VI* I, 1. " Men at some time are masters of their fates : The fault, dear Brutus, is not in our stars, But in ourselves, that we are underlings."—*Julius Caesar* I, 2.

Faire naître un sourire, To call forth a smile.

Son pareil est à naître, We shall not (*or* never) see his like again. " It is impossible that ever Rome Should breed thy fellow."—*Julius Caesar* V, 3. " He was a man, take him for all in all, I shall not look upon his like again."—*Hamlet* I, 2. " A sweeter and a lovelier gentleman,—Fram'd in the prodigality of nature, . . . The spacious world cannot again afford."—*King Richard III* I, 2.

See also CHAUME, DÉSIR, INNOCENT.

nanan. Du nanan! Yum-yum! C'est du nanan, It's exquisite.

nappe. La nappe est toujours mise dans cette maison, The kettle's always boiling in this house.

nasse. Être dans la nasse, To be in difficulties *or* (*slang*) in the soup *or* (*slang*) in Queer Street.

See also LAISSER, TOMBER.

nature. C'est plus beau que nature, Would you believe it ?

See also DISGRACIER, HABITUDE, JEU, PAYER.

naturel. *See* CHASSER.

naufrage. *See* PLANCHE, PORT.

navet. Des navets ! [There's] nothing doing, I'm not having any (*slang*), I've had some (*slang*). *Quotation under* MARCHER.

See also SANG.

néant. *See* RENTRER.

nécessaire. Faire le nécessaire, To do what is (*or* To do the) necessary, To see to it ; (*fig.*) To play the busybody, To fuss around.

nécessité. Faire de nécessité vertu, To make a virtue of necessity.

Nécessité est mère d'industrie *ou* est mère de l'invention, Necessity is the mother of invention.

Nécessité n'a point de loi *ou* Nécessité fait loi, Necessity knows no law.

négligence. *See* RÉPRIMANDER, REPROCHER.

négliger. Ne rien négliger pour . . ., To leave no stone unturned to . . .

nègre. Traiter quelqu'un comme un nègre, To treat someone like a slave.

See also TRAVAILLER.

neige. *See* BOULE.

neiger. Il a neigé sur sa tête, Silver threads among the gold. " Sable curls, all silver'd o'er with white."—SHAKESPEARE, *Sonnets* XII.

nerf. C'est un paquet de nerfs, He (She) is a bundle of nerves.

Donner (*ou* Porter) sur les nerfs de quelqu'un, To get on someone's nerves.

Être tout nerfs et tout muscles, To be all thew and sinew.

L'argent est le nerf de la guerre, Money is the sinews of war. " Money is a good soldier, sir, and will on."—*Merry Wives of Windsor* II, 2.

See also METTRE.

net. Avoir la conscience nette, To have a clear conscience. " Thrice is he armed that hath his quarrel just ; And he but naked, though lock'd up in steel, Whose conscience with injustice is corrupted."—2 *King Henry VI* III, 2.

Avoir les mains nettes, To have clean hands (*fig.*).

Être net comme un sou [neuf], To be [as] clean as a new pin.

Faire les plats nets, To lick the platter clean.

Faire maison (*ou* place) nette, To make a clean sweep.

Son cas n'est pas net, He is not blameless in this matter.

See also BRAIE, CLAIR, CŒUR, REFUSER, TRANCHER.

nettoyer. Nettoyer les écuries (*ou* les étables) d'Augias, To clean out the Augean stables.

neuf. Faire maison neuve, To engage (*or* To take on) a new staff.

Faire peau neuve, To turn over a new leaf.

Tout battant neuf, Bran[d] new. " Fire-new from the mint."—*Twelfth Night* III, 2.

Voilà qui est tout neuf pour moi, That's quite new to me, That's a new one on me.

See also BALAI, MUSE, NET, PROPRE.

nez. Avoir bon nez *ou* Avoir le nez fin *ou* Avoir du nez, To be far-seeing *or* far-sighted (*fig.*).

Avoir le nez au vent (*fig.*), To be on the look-out for a bargain, To go bargain-hunting.

Avoir quelqu'un dans le nez, Not to be able to bear the sight of someone. Not to be able to stand (*or* to stick) someone at any price (*slang*).

Avoir (*ou* En sortir avec) un pied de nez *ou* Avoir le nez long, To hang one's head, To be crestfallen (*at not having succeeded*).

Ce n'est pas pour son [fichu] nez, That's not for [the likes of] him.

Cela se voit comme le nez au milieu du visage (*et, par ironie*) Cela ne se voit pas plus que le nez au milieu du visage, It is [as] plain as the nose in your face *or* as a pikestaff, One can see it with half an eye. *Quotations under* CLAIR.

Donner du nez par terre, To come a cropper (*slang*) (*fail disastrously*).

Donner sur le nez à quelqu'un, To give someone a smack on the nose *or* (*fig.*) a smack in the eye (*humiliate him*).

Faire un nez, To pull a long face.

Faire un pied de nez à quelqu'un, To make a long nose at someone, To cock (*or* To cut) (*or* To make) a snook (*or* snooks) at someone.

Fermer la porte au nez de quelqu'un, To shut the door in someone's face.

Fourrer son nez partout, To poke (*or* To thrust) one's nose into everything, To be a regular Nosy Parker (*slang*).

Marcher (*ou* Aller) le nez au vent, To walk with one's nose in the air.

Mener quelqu'un par le [bout du] nez, To lead someone by the nose.

Mettre le nez dans les livres, To begin to study.

Mettre le nez dans une affaire, To look into a matter.

Mettre le nez dessus, To guess right.

Mettre son (*ou* le) (*ou* Fourrer son) nez où l'on n'a que faire, To poke (*or* To thrust) one's nose into other people's business.

Montrer le [bout de son] nez quelque part, To show one's face somewhere.

Ne pas lever le nez de dessus (*ou* Avoir toujours le nez sur) son ouvrage, Not to take one's eyes off one's work, To hold (*or* To keep) one's nose to the grindstone.

Ne pas voir plus loin que [le bout de] son nez, Not to be able to see farther than the end of one's nose.

Regarder quelqu'un sous le nez, To stare someone out of countenance.

Rire au nez de quelqu'un, To laugh in someone's face.

See also ARRACHER, BAISSER, CASSER, COUPER, CRACHER, ENCENSOIR, ENLUMINER, JETER, LAIT, MANGER, MOUTARDE, PENDRE, PIQUER, PLAQUER, REMUER, SAIGNER, TORDRE, VER, VUE.

nickeler. Avoir les pieds nickelés, To refuse to budge, To sit tight.

nid. À chaque oiseau son nid est beau, " Be it ever so humble, there's no place like home."—J. HOWARD PAYNE.

C'est un [vrai] nid à rats, It's a poky little room ; It's a wretched hole of a place.

Petit à petit l'oiseau fait son nid, Little strokes fell great oaks. " But Hercules himself must yield to odds ; And many strokes, though with a little axe, Hew down and fell the hardest-timber'd oak."—3 *King Henry VI* II, 1.

Trouver le nid vide, To find the bird flown. *Quotation under* OISEAU.

Vilain oiseau que celui qui salit son nid, It's an ill bird that fouls its own nest.

See also CROIRE, ÉCRASER.

nique. Faire la nique à quelqu'un, To make a long nose (*or* To cock a snook) (*or* To bite one's thumb) at someone. "I will bite my thumb at them ; which is a disgrace to them if they bear it."—*Romeo and Juliet* I, 1.

nitouche. Faire la (*ou* Être une) sainte nitouche, To look as if butter would not melt in one's mouth. Elle (Il) fait la (*ou* C'est une) sainte nitouche, Butter wouldn't melt in her (his) mouth.

Nivelle. *See* CHIEN.

noblesse. Noblesse oblige, Nobility of birth (*or* Position in life) makes a certain standard of conduct obligatory. " True noblesse would Learn him forbearance from so foul a wrong."—*King Richard II* IV, 1.

Noblesse vient de vertu, Handsome is that handsome does.

noce. Faire la noce, To be (*or* To go) on the spree, To go gay, To have one's fling *or* a high old time.

N'être pas à la noce, To have a bad time [of it]; To feel very uncomfortable.

nœud. *See* GORDIEN.

noir. Avoir des papillons noirs *ou* des idées noires *ou* Broyer du noir, To be in the dumps, To have [a fit of] the blues, To have the hip *or* the pip, To brood. " I am wrapp'd in dismal thinkings."—*All's Well That Ends Well* V, 3. " Besieged with sable-coloured melancholy."—*Love's Labour's Lost* I, 1.

Il y fait noir comme dans un four *ou* Il y fait nuit noire, It is pitch dark there. " O grim-look'd night! O night with hue so black! O night, which ever art when day is not!"—*A Midsummer Night's Dream* V, 1.

Mettre dans le noir (*fig.*), To hit the mark.

See also BÊTE, BLANC, DIABLE, FOUR, POCHER, VOIR.

noirceur. Dire des noirceurs de quelqu'un, To cast aspersions on someone, To say dreadful things about someone.

noircir. Noircir du papier, To sling ink (*slang*), To write.

noise. Chercher noise à quelqu'un, To pick a quarrel with someone.

noix. *See* CORNEILLE.

nom. Je réussirai, Je le ferai, etc., ou j'y perdrai mon nom, I shall succeed, I'll do it, etc., or my name isn't So-and-So.

Mettre un nom sur un visage, To remember a person's name on seeing him.

See also APPELER, COUCHER, NOMMER, OFFRIR.

nombre. N'être là que pour faire nombre, To be there only to help to make a crowd.

nombril. Se regarder le nombril, To be preoccupied with one's own problems.

nommer. Nommer les choses par leur nom, To call a spade a spade. " I know you what you are; And, like a sister, am most loth to call Your faults as they are nam'd."—*King Lear* I, 1. *Another quotation under* APPELER.

non. *See* SIGNE.

nord. *See* PERDRE.

normand. C'est un fin normand, He is a shrewd (*or* canny) fellow.

Faire le trou normand, To drink a glass of spirits between two courses.

Répondre en normand, To give an evasive answer.

Une réconciliation normande, A patched-up peace, A peace that is no peace.

Une réponse normande *ou* Une réponse de Normand, An evasive answer.

See also DEMI.

note. Être (*ou* Rester) dans la note [qui convient], To be doing the right thing.

N'avoir qu'une note, To be always harping on the same string, To harp (*or* To keep harping) on one string, To chew the rag (*slang*).

See also CHANGER, CHANTER, FORCER, UN.

nouer. *See* AMITIÉ.

nourrice. Il faut qu'il ait été changé en nourrice, He must have been changed in the cradle (*is unlike his parents*). " O that it could be prov'd That some night-tripping fairy had exchang'd In cradle-clothes our children where they lay, And call'd mine Percy, his Plantagenet ! Then would I have his Harry, and he mine."—1 *King Henry IV* I, 1.

See also MORDRE.

nourrir. *See* ILLUSION.

nous. Ce que c'est que de nous! Such is life !

See also ENTRE, PITIÉ.

nouveau. Rien de nouveau sous le soleil, There is nothing new under the sun.

Tout nouveau, tout beau, Anything for a change. " One touch of nature makes the whole world kin,—That all, with one consent, praise new-born gawds, Though they are made and moulded of things past ; And give to dust that is a little gilt More laud than gilt o'er-dusted."—*Troilus and Cressida* III, 3.

Un homme nouveau, An upstart, A parvenu ; A newcomer (*as to literature*) ; A new man (*Theology*) (*Ephesians* ii, 15 and iv, 24, *Colossians* iii, 10).

See also AIGUILLER, RECOMMENCER.

nouvelle. J'ai de vos nouvelles, I have heard about your goings-on.

Je puis en dire des nouvelles, I can tell you a thing or two about that.

Les mauvaises nouvelles ont des ailes, Ill news flies apace. " Nimble mischance, thou art so light of foot."—*King Richard II* III, 4.

Pas de nouvelles, bonnes nouvelles, No news is good news.

Une nouvelle toute chaude, Piping-hot news.

Vous aurez (*ou* Vous entendrez) de mes nouvelles, I'll give you something to think about, I'll make you sit up (*slang*).

Vous m'en direz des nouvelles, You'll be surprised at it *or* delighted with it : Goûtez ce vin ; vous m'en direz des nouvelles, Just you taste this wine [, how good it is] !

Vous pouvez en dire des nouvelles, You know more about that than anyone else.

See also COLPORTEUR.

novice. Avoir une ferveur de novice, To have a beginner's enthusiasm, To be a new broom.

Il n'est ferveur que de novice, A new broom sweeps clean.

noyau. *See* REMBOURRER.

noyer. C'est un homme qui se noie, He is on the road to ruin.

Se noyer dans un verre d'eau *ou* dans un (*ou* dans son) crachat, To make a mountain out of a molehill.

See also CHIEN, RACCROCHER.

nu. Être nu comme un ver *ou* comme la main, To be stark naked, To be [as] naked as his mother bore him, as my mother bore me.

Il est arrivé tout nu de sa province, He came up from the country without a rag to his back *or* without a penny to bless himself with.

S'enfuir un pied chaussé, l'autre nu, To flee half-clad.

See also SOULIER.

nuage. Se perdre dans les nuages, To be in a brown study, To be wool-gathering. " Her brother . . . Feeds on his wonder, keeps himself in clouds."—*Hamlet* IV, 5.

nue. Aller (*ou* Monter) aux nues, To be an immense success *or* a great draw, To break all box-office records.

Cette pièce a été aux nues, This play has been a huge success *or* has broken all box-office records.

Se perdre dans les nues, To lose

oneself in the clouds (*be mystical, unreal, imaginary*).

Tomber des nues, To drop from the clouds (*fig.*) ; To come as a bolt from the blue ; To be thunderstruck, To be struck all of a heap.

See also ÉLEVER, PORTER, SAUTER.

nuire. Abondance de bien[s] (*ou* Surabondance de droit) ne nuit pas, Store is no sore.

Ce qui nuit à l'un duit à l'autre, One man's meat is another man's poison.

See also GRATTER, PRÉCAUTION.

nuit. La nuit des temps (*poetic*), The mists of time. " But how is it, That this lives in thy mind ? What seest thou else In the dark backward and abysm of time ? "—*The Tempest* I, 2.

La nuit porte conseil, Sleep on it, Take counsel of your pillow.

Une nuit blanche, A sleepless night.

See also CHAT, FERMANT, FERMER, FLAMBEAU, JOUR, NOIR, OMBRE, RELEVER, SOMME, TRISTE, VOILE.

nul. *See* BIEN, PROPHÈTE.

numéro. *See* DRÔLE.

O

obéir. *See* DOIGT.

obéissance. *See* PAYER.

objet. *See* PEUR.

obligation. Avoir des obligations envers quelqu'un, To owe someone a good turn.

obliger. *See* NOBLESSE.

obstacle. Être un obstacle à quelqu'un, To be (*or* To stand) in somebody's way.

obstiner (s'). *See* VENT.

occasion. L'occasion fait le larron, Opportunity makes the thief. " How oft the sight of means to do ill deeds Makes ill deeds done ! "—*King John* IV, 2.

See also CHAUVE, CHEVEU, PROFITER, RARE, TAIRE, VOL.

occuper. S'occuper de trop de choses en même temps, To have too many things on at once *or* too many irons in the fire.

See also VEDETTE.

odeur. L'argent n'a pas d'odeur, Money has no smell.

Mourir en odeur de sainteté, To die in the odour of sanctity.

N'être pas en odeur de sainteté auprès de quelqu'un, To be in someone's bad (*or* black) books.

œil. À l'œil, Free, Without paying, *e.g.*, Dîner à l'œil, To dine free.

Avoir l'œil *ou* N'avoir pas ses yeux dans sa poche *ou* Avoir l'œil américain, To keep (*or* To have) one's eyes skinned.

Avoir l'œil à (*ou* sur) quelque chose, To keep an eye on something.

Avoir l'œil au guet, To keep a sharp look-out. " Take heed ; have open eye ; for thieves do foot by night."—*Merry Wives of Windsor* II, 2.

Avoir l'œil sur quelqu'un *ou* Avoir (*ou* Tenir) quelqu'un à l'œil, To keep an eye on someone.

Coûter les yeux de la tête, To be exorbitantly dear, To cost a mint of money.

Être tout yeux, Être tout yeux et tout oreilles, To be all eyes, To be all ears and eyes *or* all attention.

Faire de l'œil (*ou* Faire l'œil) à quelqu'un, To tip someone the wink ; To make eyes at someone, To give someone the glad eye (*slang*). " The sportive court, where thou Wast shot at with fair eyes."—*All's Well That Ends Well* III, 2.

Faire les yeux doux (*ou* les doux yeux) (*ou* les yeux en coulisse) à quelqu'un, To look lovingly (*or* To cast sheep's eyes) at someone, To ogle someone.

J'ai laissé (*ou* oublié) mes yeux chez moi, I have left my glasses at home, I have forgotten my spectacles.

Jeter les yeux sur quelqu'un, To cast one's eyes on someone.

Jeter les yeux sur une brochure, To glance through a pamphlet.

Les yeux sont les interprètes de l'âme *ou* sont les truchements du cœur, The eyes are the mirror of the soul. " Even in the glasses of thine eyes I see thy grieved heart."—*King Richard II* I, 3.

Lever les yeux sur, To aspire to, To yearn for.

N'avoir d'yeux que pour une personne, To have affection only for one person.

N'avoir fait que jeter les yeux sur quelque chose, To have only just glanced at something.

Ne pas oser lever les yeux, Not to dare to look up (*be intimidated or abashed*).

Œil pour œil, dent pour dent, An eye for an eye, and a tooth for a tooth (*Exodus* xxi, 24, *Leviticus* xxiv, 20, *Matthew* v, 38). *Note.—This is known as the* law of talion *or* lex talionis = the law of retaliation, *from Latin talio, -onis* (*talis*, such).

Où aviez-vous les yeux ? *ou* Aviez-vous les yeux aux talons ? Where were your eyes ? Couldn't you see it ?

Pas plus que dans mon œil, Not at all.

Voir du (*ou* d'un) même œil que quelqu'un, To see eye to eye with someone. " I would my father look'd but with my eyes."—*A Midsummer Night's Dream* I, 1.

Voir les choses d'un autre œil (*ou* avec d'autres yeux) qu'auparavant, To look at things in a different light than formerly.

See also ASSASSIN, ATTACHER, BASILIC, BATTRE, BEAU 25, BLESSER, BON 12, 20, 63, 64, BOUCHER, BOUT, BRILLER, CARESSER, CARPE, CERNER, COMPAS, COUP 5, 6, 7, 22, 47, 58, COUVER, CREVER, CROIRE, DESSILLER, DESSUS, DÉTACHER, DOIGT, DONNER, DORMIR, ENGRAISSER, FERME, FERMER, FEU, FRAIS, FROID, GRAND, GROS, LOIN, MANGER, MAUVAIS, MESURER, OUVRIR, PAILLE, PISTOLET, PLEURER, POCHER, POUDRE, PRUNELLE, QUATRE, QUINZE, QUITTER, REGARDER, RETRACER, RÊVER, RINCER, SAUTER, SORTIR, TAPER, TOMBER, TOURNER, VUE, ZUT.

œuf. Donner un œuf pour avoir un bœuf, To throw a sprat to catch a mackerel *or* a herring *or* a whale.

Faire d'un œuf un bœuf, To make a mountain out of a molehill.

See also ÉCRASER, MARCHER, OMELETTE, PANIER, POULE, TONDRE, TUER.

œuvre. Faire œuvre de . . ., To behave as . . . : Il a fait œuvre d'homme de bien, He has behaved like an honest man.

Le grand œuvre, The philosophers' stone.

Mettre tout en œuvre pour . . ., To leave no stone unturned to . . .

See also ARTISAN, BON 4, COURONNER, DOIGT, FILS, MAIN, REPRENDRE.

offenser. Soit dit sans vous offenser, If I may say so without offence.

See also VÉRITÉ.

officieux. *See* MENSONGE.

offrir. Offrir sa main à un homme, To propose [marriage] to a man.

Offrir son nom à une femme, To propose [marriage] to a woman.

See also PAIN, SPECTACLE.

ogre. *See* MANGER.

oie. Une petite oie blanche, A Victorian miss.

oignon. Être vêtu (*ou* couvert) comme un oignon, To be very warmly dressed *or* clad.

See also RANG, REGRETTER.

oindre. Oignez vilain, il vous poindra ; poignez vilain, il vous oindra. Treat a churl kindly and you will suffer for it ; treat him roughly and he will be ready to serve you. " *Prospero.* Thou most lying slave, Whom stripes may move, not kindness . . . *Caliban.* No, pray thee !—I must obey."—*The Tempest* I, 2.

oiseau. Être battu de l'oiseau, To be down-hearted. " My lord, wise men ne'er sit and wail their woes, But presently prevent the ways to wail."—*King Richard II* III, 2.

L'oiseau n'y est plus *ou* L'oiseau [s'en] est envolé *ou* L'oiseau est déniché (*fig.*), The bird is flown. " And Shylock, for his own part, knew the bird was fledg'd."—*The Merchant of Venice* III, 1.

See also AUGURE, BRANCHE, DRÔLE, NID, PLUME, VALOIR, VILAIN, VOL.

oison. *See* BRIDER.

olivier. Présenter le rameau d'olivier *ou* Présenter l'olivier *ou* Se présenter l'olivier à la main, To hold out the olive branch. " I hold the olive in my hand : my words are as full of peace as of matter."—*Twelfth Night* I, 5. " There is not now a rebel's sword unsheathed, But peace puts forth her olive everywhere."—2 *King Henry IV* IV, 4.

ombrage. Tout lui fait ombrage, He is in constant fear of being outdone.

ombre. À l'ombre, In the shade *or* background, *e.g.*, Se tenir à l'ombre, To keep in the background ; Under cover, *e.g.*, de la nuit, of darkness ; In prison, In quod.

C'est une ombre au tableau, It is a fly in the ointment.

Faire ombre à quelqu'un, To put someone in the shade.

N'être plus que l'ombre de soi-même, To be merely the (*or* but a) shadow of one's former self.

Prendre l'ombre pour le corps, To take the shadow for the substance. " Each substance of a grief hath twenty shadows, Which show like grief itself, but are not so."—*King Richard II* II, 2.

See also CHANCE, COURIR, LÂCHER.

omelette. On ne saurait faire une omelette sans casser des œufs, You cannot make an omelet without breaking eggs.

once. Ne pas peser une once, To carry no weight (*as an objection*).

ongle. *See* BEC, BOUT, MÉTIER, PAYER, ROGNER, RONGER, RUBIS.

onguent. *See* PETIT.

onze. Prendre le train onze (*Note.—11 = one's two legs*), To ride Shanks' mare *or* Shanks' pony. " Our steed the leg."—*Coriolanus* I, 1.

See also BOUILLON.

opiner. Opiner du bonnet, To say ditto to everything, To be a yes-man. " She says, ' 'tis so ; ' they answer all, ' 'tis so ; ' And would say after her, if she said ' no.' "—SHAKESPEARE, *Venus and Adonis*.

opiniâtrer (s'). S'opiniâtrer dans son opinion, To be wedded to one's own opinion.

opinion. *See* AUTANT, BAN, OPINIÂTRER (S'), PORTER.

opposer. S'opposer à quelque chose, To set one's face against something.

opulence. *See* NAGER.

or. Acheter quelque chose au poids de l'or, To pay through the nose for something.

C'est une affaire d'or, It is a golden opportunity, This is a real bargain.

Faire un pont d'or à quelqu'un, To make a bridge of gold (*or* a golden bridge) for someone (*easy retreat*) ; To offer someone very advantageous terms, To make it worth someone's while.

Je ne ferais cela ni pour or ni pour argent, I would not do that for love or money. " If that love or gold Can in this desert place buy entertainment."—*As You Like It* II, 4. " He would not leave it . . . for the wealth That the world masters."—*The Merchant of Venice* V, 1.

Parler d'or, To speak words of wisdom. " Her words y-clad with wisdom's majesty."—2 *King Henry VI* I, 1.

Rouler sur l'or *ou* Avoir des monceaux d'or, To be rolling in wealth *or* in money, To have tons of money.

Tout ce qui brille (*ou* reluit) n'est pas or, All that glisters is not gold, All is not gold that glitters. " All that glisters is not gold,—Often have you heard that told ; Many a man his life hath sold But my outside to behold ; Gilded tombs do worms infold."—*The Merchant of Venice* II, 7.

Valoir son pesant d'or, To be worth one's (its) weight in gold.

Vendre quelque chose au poids de l'or, To sell something at a very high price.

See also ADORER, AURORE, BARRE, BOUCHE, CŒUR, COUDRE, FILER, PAROLE, PLIER, POULE.

orage. Tenir (*ou* Faire) tête à l'orage, To face the music.

orange. Glisser sur une pelure d'orange, To make only one mistake, but that a fatal one, To make just one slip. " Some run from brakes of vice, and answer none ; And some condemned for a fault alone."—*Measure for Measure* II, 1.

ordinaire. *See* TRAIN.

ordonner. *See* CHARITÉ.

ordre. Donner ordre à quelque chose, To make provision for something.

Être aux ordres de quelqu'un, To be at someone's beck and call.

Être cité à l'ordre de l'armée, To be mentioned in dispatches.

Mettre ordre à ses affaires, To put one's affairs (*or* To set one's house) in order.

Mettre quelque chose en ordre, To put something in order *or* to rights.

Passer à l'ordre du jour, To proceed with the business of the day ; To brush aside (*or* To rule out) an objection.

Une question toujours à l'ordre du jour, An evergreen topic.

oreille. Avoir sur les oreilles, To get rapped on the knuckles (*fig.*). " She'll not stick to round me i' th' ear."—SHAKESPEARE, *Sonnets to Sundry Notes of Music* IV.

Cela lui entre par une oreille et lui sort par l'autre, It goes in at one ear and out at the other.

Être tout oreilles *ou* Écouter de toutes ses oreilles *ou* Ouvrir ses oreilles toutes grandes, To be all ears *or* all attention.

Les murs (*ou* Les murailles) ont des oreilles, Walls have ears. " Pitchers have ears, and I have many servants: Besides, old Gremio is hark'ning still."—*The Taming of the Shrew* IV, 4.

N'écouter que d'une oreille, To be only half listening.

Prêter l'oreille à quelqu'un, To lend an ear to someone. " Friends, Romans, countrymen, lend me your ears."—*Julius Caesar* III, 2. " To my unfolding lend a gracious ear."—*Othello* I, 3. " Fasten your ear to my advisings."—*Measure for Measure* III, 1.

See also BAISSER, BAS, BLESSER, BOUCHER, BOUT, CHAPEAU, CORNER, DÉCHIRER, DESSUS, DORMIR, DRESSER, DUR, ÉCHAUFFER, ÉCORCHER, ENDETTER, ENTENDRE, FENDRE, FERMER, FROTTER, HARGNEUX, LOUP, ŒIL, PENDRE, PUCE, REBATTRE, ROMPRE, SOURD, TIRER, TUYAU, VENTRE.

oreiller. Prendre conseil de (*ou* Consulter) son oreiller, To take counsel of one's pillow, To sleep on it.

Une conscience pure est un bon oreiller, A quiet conscience is a soft pillow. " I feel within me A peace above all earthly dignities, A still and quiet conscience."—*King Henry VIII* III, 2.

orfèvre. Vous êtes orfèvre, Monsieur Josse, Nothing like leather.

orgueil. Un homme pétri d'orgueil, A man eaten up with pride. " But man, proud man ! Dress'd in a little brief authority,—Most ignorant of what he's most assured, His glassy essence,—like an angry ape, Plays such fantastic tricks before high heaven As make the angels weep ; who, with our spleens, Would all themselves laugh mortal."—*Measure for Measure* II, 2.

Un orgueil de Satan, An overweening pride. " My high-blown pride."—*King Henry VIII* III, 2.

See also SUER.

orgueilleux. Être orgueilleux comme Satan, To be [as] proud as Lucifer.

Être orgueilleux comme un paon, To be [as] proud as a peacock. " Fly pride, says the peacock."—*The Comedy of Errors* IV, 3.

original. C'est un original, He is a queer customer *or* a queer fish *or* a queer card *or* a queer stick *or* a funny chap.

orme. *See* ATTENDRE.

ornière. Sortir de l'ornière, To get out of the rut *or* the ruck.

ortie. *See* FROC.

os. C'est un os bien dur à ronger, It is a hard nut to crack.

Casser (*ou* Rompre) (*ou* Briser) les os à quelqu'un, To beat someone black and blue. " *Mrs Quickly*. Mistress Ford, good heart, is beaten black and blue, that you cannot see a white spot about her. *Falstaff*. What tell'st thou me of black and blue ? I was beaten myself into all the colours of the rainbow."—*Merry Wives of Windsor* IV, 5. " I'll beat the knave into a twiggen bottle."—*Othello* II, 3. (*Note.*—twiggen = made of twigs, wicker.)

Ce sont deux chiens après un os, They are both after the same thing.

Donner un os à ronger à quelqu'un, To give someone something to go on with.

Il n'a que la peau et les os *ou* Il a la peau collée sur les os *ou* Les os lui percent la peau *ou* On lui voit les os *ou* Il n'est qu'un paquet d'os, He is nothing but skin and bone *or* nothing but a bag of bones. " Am I not fallen away vilely . . . ? do I not bate ? do I not dwindle ? Why, my skin hangs about me like an old lady's loose gown ; I am withered like an old apple-john."—1 *King Henry IV* III, 3. (*Note.*—apple-john = variety of apple, keeping two years, best eaten when shrivelled and withered.) " Meager and lank with fasting grown, And nothing left but skin and bone."—SWIFT.

Il y a trop de chiens après l'os, There are too many to share in the profit (*therefore the share of each will be very small*).

Il y laissera ses os, He'll die there. " O, father abbot, An old man, broken with the storms of state, Is come to lay his weary bones among ye ; Give him a little earth for charity ! "—*King Henry VIII* IV, 2. " Heaven take my soul, and England keep my bones ! "—*King John* IV, 3.

Voilà bien des chiens après un os, Many are claiming a share in the profit.

See also CHAIR, MOELLE, MOUILLER, PERCER, SUCER, TRANSPERCER, TREMPER, VIEUX.

oser. *See* CILLER, ŒIL.

ôter. Ôte-toi de là que je m'y mette, Get out of that and make place for me.

Ôte-toi de mon soleil (*Diogène*), Get out of my light (*Diogenes*).

Ôter le pain de la bouche à quelqu'un

(*fig.*), To take the bread out of someone's mouth.

Ôtez cela de vos papiers, You can rule (*or* cut) that out.

S'ôter les morceaux de la bouche (*fig.*), To stint oneself [to oblige others].

oubli. L'oubli de soi-même, Self-effacement.

Le fleuve d'oubli, The stream of Oblivion, Lethe. " Wash'd in Lethe, and forgotten."—2 *King Henry IV* V, 2.

Livrer à l'oubli, To consign to oblivion.

Vouer à l'oubli, To doom to oblivion.

oublier. N'oublier rien pour . . ., To leave no stone unturned to . . .

On ne nous le laissera pas oublier, We shall never hear the last of it.

Oublier les heures, To lose count of time.

See also BOIRE, MESURE, ŒIL, PASSÉ.

oubliettes. Mettre (*ou* Jeter) aux oubliettes, To consign to oblivion.

oui. *See* SIGNE.

ourdir. À toile ourdie Dieu envoie le fil, God helps those who help themselves. *Quotation under* AIDER.

ours. Avoir la légèreté d'un ours, To be [as] clumsy as an elephant.

See also LÉCHER, PAVÉ, PEAU.

ouste. Ouste ! Look sharp ! Get a move on ! (*slang*). " Go put it to the haste."—*Antony and Cleopatra* V, 2. " Incite them to quick motion."—*The Tempest* IV, 1.

outil. À méchant ouvrier point de bon outil *ou* Un mauvais ouvrier n'a jamais de bons outils, An ill workman quarrels with his tools.

outrage. L'outrage des ans *ou* Les outrages du temps, The ravages of time (*to things or persons*). " The whips and scorns of time."—*Hamlet* III, 1. " Oh ! grief hath chang'd me since you saw me last ; And careful hours, with Time's deformed hand, Have written strange defeatures in my face."—*The Comedy of Errors* V, 1. (*Note.*—careful = over-anxious.) *See also quotation under* VIEILLESSE.

outre. *See* PASSER.

ouvert, e. *See under* OUVRIR.

ouverture. Ouverture d'esprit, Readiness of mind.

Ouverture de cœur, Open-heartedness, Frankness. " I have unclasp'd To thee the book even of my secret soul."—*Twelfth Night* I, 4.

ouvrage. *See* AMOUR, BOUDER, CISEAU, CŒUR, COUP 20, 76, DÉBORDER, MAIN, NEZ, PÉNÉLOPE, REPASSER, VENTRE.

ouvrier. *See* CHEVILLE, OUTIL.

ouvrir. Avoir l'appétit ouvert de bon matin, To be in a hurry (*over-anxious to get on in the world*) : C'est un jeune homme qui a l'appétit ouvert de bon matin, He is a young man in a hurry.

Enfoncer une porte ouverte, To force an open door, To imagine difficulties that don't exist.

Il faut qu'une porte soit ouverte ou fermée, One must decide one way or the other, There is no middle course.

J'avais la bouche ouverte pour vous le dire, I was just about to tell you.

Ouvrir l'appétit, To whet (*or* To sharpen) the appetite.

Ouvrir l'œil et le bon, To keep one's weather eye open, To keep one's eyes skinned, To watch out.

Ouvrir la danse *ou* le branle, To take the lead, To open the ball, To set the ball [a-]rolling ; To be the first to suffer.

Ouvrir la marche, To lead the way.

Ouvrir les yeux sur, To become aware of.

Ouvrir sa maison, To be back in residence.

Parler à cœur ouvert, To speak open-heartedly *or* unreservedly.

See also BOURSE, CIEL, DORMIR, GRAND, OREILLE, PARENTHÈSE, PARI, RÊVER, SÉSAME, TENIR.

P

page. C'est la plus belle page de son histoire, It is the finest chapter in his life.

Être (*ou* Se maintenir) à la page, To be abreast of (*or* To move with) the times, To be up to date (*slang*).

Être hors (*ou* Sortir) de page, To be one's own master.

N'être pas à la page, To be behind the times, To be a back number (*slang*).

See also EFFRONTÉ, HARDI.

païen. *See* JURER.

paille. Cela [en]lève la paille, It's quite thrilling.

Être (*ou* Coucher) sur la paille, To be down and out. " For misery is trodden on by many, And being low never reliev'd by any."—SHAKESPEARE, *Venus and Adonis*.

Mettre quelqu'un sur la paille, To reduce someone to beggary.

Mourir sur la paille, To die in the gutter.

Rompre la paille, To cry off.

Rompre la paille avec quelqu'un, To break off [all relations] with someone.

Tirer à la courte paille, To draw straws (*lots*).

Un homme de paille, A man of straw.

Voir une paille dans l'œil de son prochain et ne pas voir la poutre qui est dans le sien, To behold the mote in another's eye, but not to consider the beam in one's own eye. (*Matthew* vii, 3–5, *Luke* vi, 41–42.)

See also ALLER, FEU, POISSON, RAT.

pain. Acheter, Donner, quelque chose pour un morceau de pain, To buy, To sell, something for a [mere] song. " I know a man that had this trick of melancholy sold a goodly manor for a song."—*All's Well That Ends Well* III, 2.

C'est du pain bien dur à manger, It is very painful to live in such straightened circumstances.

Il ne vaut pas le pain qu'il mange, He is not worth his salt.

Long comme un jour sans pain, [As] long as a wet Sunday.

Manger son pain blanc le premier, To begin with the cake.

Offrir le pain et le sel à quelqu'un, To offer hospitality to someone.

Pain dérobé réveille l'appétit, Stolen fruits are sweet.

Partager le pain et le sel avec quelqu'un, To eat salt with someone (*be his guest*).

Se vendre comme des petits pains, To sell like hot cakes.

See also ARROSER, BÉNIR, BON 46, CHERCHER, COUP 55, FUMÉE, GOÛT, ÔTER, PLANCHE, PROMETTRE.

pair. Être au pair, To have caught up, To have got level (*with arrears*).

Marcher (*ou* Aller) de pair avec, To rank with, To be on a par with.

Marcher de pair avec son époque, To keep abreast of the times.

Prendre quelqu'un au pair, To take someone on mutual terms (*give board and lodging in exchange for services*).

Se mettre au pair, To catch up, To get level (*with arrears of work*).

See also COMPAGNON.

paire. Ils sont une paire d'amis, They are good chums. " ' Tarry, dear cousin Suffolk ! My soul shall thine keep company to heaven ; Tarry, sweet soul, for mine, then fly a-breast ; As in this glorious and well-foughten field We kept together in our chivalry !' "—*King Henry V* IV, 6.

Les deux font la paire, They are two of a pair, They are both tarred with the same brush.

Se faire la paire, To hook it (*slang*), To clear out.

See also AUTRE.

paître. *See* ENVOYER.

paix. Faire la paix, To make peace, To bury the hatchet.

Ne donner ni paix ni trêve à quelqu'un, To give someone no peace.

Une paix fourrée, A hollow (*or* vain) peace.

Une paix plâtrée, A patched-up peace, A peace that is no peace. " I speak of peace, while covert enmity, Under the smile of safety, wounds the world." — 2 *King Henry IV Induction.*

Une paix telle quelle, A makeshift peace, A peace of sorts.

See also BAISER, MORT.

pâle. Être pâle comme un linge, To be [as] white as a sheet. " Pale as his shirt."—*Hamlet* II, 1. " His coward lips did from their colour fly."—*Julius Caesar* I, 2.

See also FLAMBEAU.

palinodie. Chanter la palinodie, To change (*or* To disavow) one's opinion (*about a person, a thing, from bad to good*), To retract.

pâlir. Faire pâlir, To throw into the shade (*fig.*).

Pâlir sur les livres, To be for ever poring over books, To burn the midnight oil. " What, at your book so hard ? "—3 *King Henry VI* V, 6.

Son étoile pâlit, His star is dimming. " All of us have cause To wail the dimming of our shining star ; But none can cure their harms by wailing them."—*King Richard III* II, 2.

palme. *See* CUEILLIR, DÉCERNER, REMPORTER.

pâmer. *See* CARPE.

panache. Avoir du panache, To have the magic of leadership and personality, To have dashism.

Pandore. *See* BOÎTE.

panier. C'est un panier percé, He is a spendthrift, Money burns a hole in his pocket.

Mettre tous ses œufs dans le même panier, To have all one's eggs in one basket. " My ventures are not in one bottom trusted, Nor to one place ; nor is my whole estate Upon the fortune of this present year."—*The Merchant of Venice* I, 1.

On peut les mettre dans le même panier, They are tarred with the same brush.

See also ADIEU, ANSE, DESSUS, MÉMOIRE, MERCIER, SALADE.

panne. Être dans la panne, To be in poverty.

panneau. *See* DONNER, TENDRE, TOMBER.

panse. Se faire crever la panse, To get killed.

See also A, EMPLIR.

pantoufle. En pantoufles (*fig.*), In a free and easy way.

See also RAISONNER.

Panurge. *See* MOUTON.

paon. *See* CRI, GEAI, ORGUEILLEUX, PARER.

papa. C'est un gros papa, He is a nice kind gentleman with a middle-age spread.

Faire quelque chose à la papa, To do something in a leisurely way *or* something leisurely.

pape. *See* MOUTARDIER.

papier. Avoir un visage (*ou* une figure) de papier mâché, To have a pasty (*or* a mealy) face, To be pasty-faced.

See also BARBOUILLER, BARBOUILLEUR, BIEN, CHIFFON, GRATTER, MAL, NOIRCIR, ÔTER, PETIT, RAYER, RÉGLER, SOUFFRIR.

papillon. *See* COURIR, NOIR.

papillote. Cela n'est bon qu'à faire des papillotes, That is only fit for the waste-paper basket (*of a writing*).

Pâques. *See* POISSONNIER.

paquet. Donner à quelqu'un son paquet, To give someone a piece of one's mind.

Faire son paquet, To pack up and go.

Faire son paquet (*ou* ses paquets) [pour l'autre monde], To depart this life.

Il a eu (*ou* a reçu) son paquet, I gave him a piece of my mind.

Risquer (*ou* Hasarder) le paquet, To chance it.

Un paquet de mer, A [heavy] sea.

See also NERF, OS.

par. *See* DIABLE, MONDE.

parade. Il n'est pas heureux à la parade, He is not good at repartee.

paradis. Faire son paradis en ce monde, To give oneself up to pleasure.

See also CHEMIN, EMPORTER, PORTER, SAINT.

paraître. Cela me paraît rude, That is hard to believe.

Tout lui paraît couleur de rose, He sees everything through rose-coloured spectacles.

See also DÉSHABILLÉ.

parcours. *See* SAVOIR.

par-dessous. *See under* DESSOUS.

par-dessus. *See under* DESSUS.

pardonner. Péché avoué est à demi (*ou* à moitié) pardonné *ou* Une faute confessée est à demi pardonnée, A fault confessed is half redressed.

pareil. *See* BILLE, NAÎTRE, RENDRE.

parenthèse. Avoir les jambes en parenthèses, To have legs shaped like parentheses, To be bow-legged.

Fermer la parenthèse (*fig.*), To cease digressing [and get back to the subject].

Ouvrir la parenthèse (*fig.*), To embark on a digression.

parer. Parer le coup (*fig.*), To steer clear.

Se parer des plumes du paon, To dress oneself in borrowed plumes. " His feathers are but borrow'd."—2 *King Henry VI* III, 1.

See also GEAI.

paresseux. Être paresseux comme une couleuvre, To be born tired.

pari. Le pari est ouvert *ou* Les paris sont ouverts, We shall soon know [the result].

parier. Il y a [gros] à parier que . . ., The odds are that . . . " It is lots to blanks."—*Coriolanus* V, 2.

See also COUP 48, TÊTE.

Paris. *See* JOUR, SI.

parlant. Des regards parlants, Expressive looks. " I think there's ne'er a man in Christendom Can lesser hide his love or hate than he ; for by his face straight shall you know his heart."—*King Richard III* III, 4. " Yea, this man's brow, like to a title-leaf, Foretells the nature of a tragic volume : So looks the strand, whereon the imperious flood Hath left a witness'd usurpation."—2 *King Henry IV* I, 1. " The heavenly rhetoric of thine eye,—'Gainst whom the world cannot hold argument."—*Love's Labour's Lost* IV, 3.

parler. Autant vaudrait parler à un sourd, You might as well talk to a brick wall.

Faire parler de soi, To get talked about.

Faire parler la poudre, To let the guns speak, To appeal to the arbitrament of arms. *Quotations under* SORT.

Faire parler quelqu'un, To put words into someone's mouth.

Les murailles parlent, Walls have ears. *Quotation under* OREILLE.

Moins on parle, mieux cela vaut, The less said the better.

Parler à cheval à quelqu'un, To speak in strong terms to someone. " Thrown such despite and heavy terms upon her."—*Othello* IV, 2.

Parler à tort et à travers, To talk at random.

Parler à un sourd *ou* Parler aux rochers, To talk to deaf ears. " You are not wood, you are not stones, but men ; And, being men, hearing the will of Caesar, It will inflame you."—*Julius Caesar* III, 2.

Parler comme un livre, To speak (*or* To talk) like a book (*in formal phrases*) ; To express oneself well.

Parler en l'air, To talk at random ; To talk wildly.

Parler entre ses dents, To mumble.

Parler français *ou* Parler chrétien, To talk plainly, To talk in plain French. " Discuss the same in French unto him."—*King Henry V* IV, 4.

Parler français comme une vache espagnole, To murder the French language. " Seese and putter ! have I lived to stand at the taunt of one that makes fritters of English ? " —*Merry Wives of Windsor* V, 5.

Parler pour parler, To talk for talking's sake.

Parler pour rien, To waste one's breath.

Parler sec, To rap out one's words.

Parler suivant le temps *ou* suivant les temps, To speak according to circumstances.

Voilà qui est (*ou* qui s'appelle) parler *ou* C'est parler, cela, Now you're talking.

See also ABONDANCE, AISE, AUTRE, AVEUGLE, B, BONNET, BREF, CHIFFON, CHOSE, CLAIR, CONNAISSANCE, CORDE, DÉCOUVERT, DÉSERT, ÉCORCHER, ÉCOUTER, FRANC, GRATTER, HAUT, HÉBREU, LANGUE, LOUP, MUR, OR, OUVRIR, PERSONNE, PLUIE, RESPECT, SAVOIR, SENTENCE, TOUR, TROUVER, TUYAU.

paroisse. Des ouvrages, etc., de toutes les paroisses, A miscellaneous collection of works, etc.

See also COQ.

paroissien. *See* DRÔLE.

parole. Avoir deux paroles, To be double-tongued. " Despatch :—this knave's tongue begins to double."—2 *King Henry VI* II, 4.

Avoir la parole, To be one's turn to speak, To have (*or* To get) the floor.

Avoir la parole haute, To speak peremptorily.

Demander la parole, To request leave to speak *or* to address the meeting.

Être haut en parole, To be overbearing [in manner].

Il est esclave de sa parole *ou* Sa parole vaut sa signature, His word is [as good as] his bond. " His words are bonds, his oaths are oracles ; . . . His heart as far from fraud as heaven from earth." —*Two Gentlemen of Verona* II, 7.

Il ne lui manque (*ou* Il n'y manque) que la parole, It all but speaks (*bears a lifelike resemblance*).

Je lui ferai [bien] ravaler ses paroles *ou* Je lui ferai rentrer ses paroles dans la gorge *ou* dans le ventre, I will make him eat his words. " *Beatrice*. Will you not eat your word ?—*Benedick*. With no sauce that can be devised to it."—*Much Ado About Nothing* IV, 2.

La parole est d'argent, le silence est d'or, Speech is silvern, silence is golden. " Give every man thine ear, but few thy voice."—*Hamlet* I, 3.

Nous n'avons jamais eu ensemble une parole plus haute que l'autre, A cross word has never passed between us.

Prendre la parole, To speak (*in debate*), To take the floor ; To address the meeting.

Tenir [sa] parole, To keep one's word *or* one's promise, To be as good as one's word.

See also AIR, BON 3, BREF, CIRCUIT, CONNAÎTRE, COUPER, CROIRE, EMMIELLER, GESTE, MANIER, MOULIN, PAYER, PERDRE, PORTER, RENDRE, RETIRER, SACRAMENTEL, TOUR.

Parque. *See* CISEAU.

part. Faire la part de quelque chose,

To take something into consideration *or* into account, To make allowances for something.

See also BANDE, CHIEN, CHOSE, DIABLE, FAIT, FEU, GÂTEAU, LION.

partager. Partager le différend [par la moitié], To split the difference, To meet someone half way.

See also GÂTEAU, PAIN.

parterre. Prendre un billet de parterre, To come a cropper (*fall*) (*slang*).

Parthe. *See* FLÈCHE.

parti. À parti pris point de conseil, It is no use talking to a man whose mind is made up.

Avoir un parti à la cour, dans l'armée, dans le public, To have friends at court, in the army, among the public.

C'est un parti pris, It is a foregone conclusion.

[En] prendre son parti, To resign oneself to the inevitable, To make the best of a bad job *or* of it.

Prendre son parti, To come to a decision, To make up one's mind.

Tirer parti de quelque chose, To make use of something, To turn something to account, To take advantage of something (*as a mistake*). "Alas! alas! Why, all the souls that were were forfeit once; And He that might the vantage best have took Found out the remedy." —*Measure for Measure* II, 2.

See also RANGER, TENIR.

particulier. *See* DISPOSITION.

partie. Avoir affaire à forte partie, To have a powerful opponent (*or* a tough customer) to deal with.

C'est une partie perdue *ou* La partie est jouée, The game is up.

Ce (*ou* Cela) n'est pas [de] ma partie, That is not in my line, That does not come within my province.

Il est de la partie, He's in the business (*that trade*).

Lier partie, To join forces.

Quitter (*ou* Abandonner) la partie, To throw in one's hand *or* one's cards, To throw up the sponge.

Tenir bien sa partie, To hold one's own; To carry out one's duties well, To give good account of oneself.

See also BEAU 2, COUP 38, ENTENDRE, JOUER, LENDEMAIN, PELOTER, REMETTRE.

partir. *See* ANGLAIS, BAS, CHAT, COURIR, MAILLE, PIED, RIRE, TÊTE, TRAIT, VOYAGE.

partout. *See* PRÉSENT, TÊTE.

parure. La beauté sans parure, Beauty unadorned.

La modestie est la plus belle des parures, "By my modesty,—The jewel in my dower."—*The Tempest* III, 1.

pas. C'est le premier pas, It is the first step *or* the thin end of the wedge.

Cela ne se trouve pas dans (*ou* sous) le pas d'un cheval *ou* d'une mule, That (*a thing like that, such a large sum of money*) is not easily found *or* is not to be had for the asking.

En être aux premiers pas, To be back again to where one started.

En être pour ses pas, To go on a wild-goose chase.

Franchir le pas, To take the step *or* the plunge, To cross (*or* To pass) the Rubicon.

Il lui a fallu passer le pas, I made him do it.

Il n'y a que le premier pas qui coûte, The beginning is usually the most difficult part; One slip (*in conduct*) usually leads to another. "One sin I know another doth provoke." —*Pericles, Prince of Tyre* I, 1.

Marquer le pas, To mark time (*lit. & fig.*).

Mettre quelqu'un au pas, To bring someone to heel.

Passer le pas, To kick the bucket,

To hop the twig *or* the stick (*die*) (*all slang*).

Prendre le pas sur, To take precedence over ; To outstrip, To outrun.

Voilà déjà un [grand] pas de fait, That is a [great *or* long] step forward.

See also ABÎME, ALLONGER, BAISER, CLERC, COMPTER, DOUBLER, EMBOÎTER, GLISSANT, MARCHER, MAUVAIS, MÉNAGER, PLAINDRE, QUATRE, REMETTRE, SAUTER, SEMER, SUIVRE.

passe. *See* BON 35, 50, MAUVAIS.

passé. Faire oublier son passé, To live down one's past.

Oublier le passé, To forget the past, To let bygones be bygones.

Remuer (*ou* Revenir sur) le passé, To rake up the past. " Beshrew your heart, Fair daughter, you do draw my spirits from me With new lamenting ancient oversights."—2 *King Henry IV* II, 3.

passer. Cela me passe, That passes my comprehension, That beats me.

Cela ne passe pas, That won't do, That won't wash, That cock won't fight.

Cela ne se passera pas ainsi, I (We) will not let it rest at that.

Cela passe la plaisanterie *ou* la raillerie *ou* le jeu, That (*or* It) is [going] beyond a joke.

Enfin, passe pour lui, Well, that's all right as far as he is concerned.

Passer à autre chose, To pass on to other matters ; To change the subject.

Passer au crible (*ou* à l'étamine) les preuves, les faits, To sift the evidence, the facts.

Passer l'éponge sur quelque chose, To say no more about something.

Passer outre à la loi, To set the law at defiance *or* at nought.

Passer par les baguettes *ou* par les verges, To run the gauntlet.

Passer son envie d'une chose, To get over a thing (*think of it without strong feeling*).

Passez-moi la rhubarbe (*ou* la casse), je vous passerai le séné, You let me have my way and I will let you have yours.

Passons ! Let it go at that.

Se faire passer pour . . ., To give oneself out to be . . .

See also AIGUILLE, ALAMBIC, ALMANACH, BLANC, BLEU, BORNE, BOUT, BRAISE, COMMENTAIRE, COMPTE, CONTENTEMENT, COQ, CORPS, CÔTÉ, COUP 22, DÉLUGE, DIRE, EAU, ÉCLAIR, FÊTE, FILIÈRE, FOIS, FORCE, GOÛT, HOMME, JAMBE, JEUNESSE, LAMINOIR, MESURE, MONTRE, ORDRE, PAS, POMMADE, POSTÉRITÉ, QUART, RAMPE, RUBICON, SAUCE, SECOND, VENTRE.

passion. *See* SOUFFRIR.

pâte. *See* BON 22, COQ, MAIN.

pâté. Un gros pâté, A podge of a child.

See also HACHER.

Pater. *See* SAVOIR.

paternel. *See* REMONTRANCE.

patience. S'armer (*ou* Se munir) de patience, To exercise patience, To possess one's soul in patience. " Arming myself with patience." —*Julius Caesar* V, 1. " I will be the pattern of all patience."—*King Lear* III, 2. " She sat like patience on a monument, Smiling at grief." —*Twelfth Night* II, 4.

See also BOUT.

patient. Il n'a été que le patient, He took it all lying down.

patienter. Patienter, To exercise patience, To possess one's soul in patience. *Quotations under* PATIENCE.

patrie. La céleste patrie (*poetic*), Our heavenly home.

patrimoine. *See* CROQUER.

patte. Être entre les pattes de quelqu'un, To be in someone's clutches.

Faire patte de velours, To show the velvet glove.

Se tirer des pattes de quelqu'un, To escape from someone's clutches.

Tenir quelqu'un sous sa patte, To have someone in one's clutches *or* at one's mercy.

Tomber sous la patte de quelqu'un, To fall into someone's clutches.

See also COUP 24, GRAISSER, MARCHER, MARRON, MOUCHE, REMUER, RETOMBER.

pauvre. Faire pauvre figure, To cut a sorry figure.

See also HONTEUX, SIRE.

pauvreté. Pauvreté n'est pas vice, Poverty is no vice *or* crime *or* disgrace.

See also AMOUR.

pavé. C'est le pavé de l'ours, Save me from my friends. " God keep me from false friends ! "—*King Richard III* III, 1.

Être sur le pavé, To be homeless ; To be out of work.

Mettre quelqu'un sur le pavé, To turn someone into the street ; To turn someone out of his job.

Tenir le haut du pavé, To be the big man, To boss the show (*slang*).

See also BATTEUR, BATTRE, BRÛLER.

paver. Les rues en sont pavées, They are [as] plentiful as blackberries, It is (They are) [as] common as dirt.

See also GOSIER, INTENTION.

pavillon. Baisser [le] pavillon (*ou* Mettre pavillon bas) devant quelqu'un, To give in (*or* To yield) (*or* To knuckle under) (*or* To knock under) to someone, To climb down before someone.

Clouer son pavillon, To nail one's colours to the mast.

Se ranger sous le pavillon de quelqu'un, To place oneself under someone's protection.

payer. Il ne paie pas de mine, His appearance is against him, He is not much to look at.

Je suis payé pour cela, I know what it costs (*how unpleasant it is*).

Payer d'audace, To put a bold face on it, To face the music.

Payer d'effronterie, To brazen it out.

Payer d'ingratitude, To requite with ingratitude. " Blow, blow, thou winter wind, Thou art not so unkind As man's ingratitude . . . Freeze, freeze, thou bitter sky Thou dost not bite so nigh As benefits forgot : Though thou the waters warp, Thy sting is not so sharp As friend remember'd not."—*As You Like It* II, 7.

Payer d'obéissance, To knuckle down *or* under.

Payer de sa personne, To bear the brunt of it, Not to spare oneself, To do one's bit.

Payer le tribut à la faiblesse humaine *ou* à l'humanité, To give way (*or* To yield) to some human weakness. " They say, best men are moulded out of faults ; And, for the most, become much more the better For being a little bad."—*Measure for Measure* V, 1.

Payer le tribut à (*ou* la dette de) (*ou* sa dette à) la nature *ou* Payer le tribut à l'humanité, To pay the debt of nature, To go the way of all flesh (*die*). " He's walk'd the way of nature ; And to our purpose he lives no more."—2 *King Henry IV* V, 2.

Payer quelqu'un de retour, To return [to] someone like for like.

Payer ric-à-rac *ou* ric-à-ric *ou* Payer rubis sur l'ongle, To pay to the last (*or* uttermost) farthing.

Se payer de mots *ou* de paroles, To content oneself with fine words.

Se payer par ses mains, To retain (*or*, *slang*, To freeze [on] to) a debtor's property in one's possession as a set-off against his debt.

See also AMENDE, CASSER, CHAGRIN,

CHANSON, CHER, COMPTANT, ÉCOT, ENCHÈRE, MONNAIE, TÊTE, VIOLON.

pays. De quel pays venez-vous ? Where have you been brought up ? (*how ignorant you are*).

Faire voir du pays à quelqu'un, To lead someone a dance ; To lead someone on.

Se loger en pays perdu, To live in an out-of-the-way place *or* at the back of beyond. " So removed a dwelling."—*As You Like It* III, 2.

Un pays de bénédiction *ou* Un pays de cocagne, A land of plenty, A land flowing with milk and honey, [The Land of] Cocaigne, Lubberland, Lotus-land.

Voir du pays, To see the world. " Crowns in my purse I have, and goods at home, And so am come abroad to see the world."—*The Taming of the Shrew* I, 2.

See also BATTRE, CONNAISSANCE, COURIR, GAGNER, IDÉE, PROPHÈTE, SACRIFIER, SAVOIR, VIVRE, VUE.

peau. Avoir la peau de quelqu'un, To down someone ; To do for someone, To do someone in (*slang*).

C'est l'âne couvert de la peau du lion, It's the ass in the lion's skin. " With the help of a surgeon he (*Lion, i.e., Snug the joiner*) might yet recover and prove an ass."—*A Midsummer Night's Dream* V, 1. " Thou wear a lion's hide ! doff it for shame, And hang a calf's-skin on those recreant limbs! "—*King John* III, 1.

Coudre la peau du renard à celle du lion, To add cunning to force.

Entrer (*ou* Se mettre) dans la peau d'un personnage, To put oneself in a person's shoes. " If he had been as you, And you as he, you would have slipp'd like him ; But he, like you, would not have been so stern."—*Measure for Measure* II, 2.

Il ne changera jamais sa peau *ou* Il mourra dans sa peau *ou* Dans sa peau mourra le loup *ou* le renard, He'll never alter, He's past praying for. " If I had my mouth I would bite ; if I had my liberty I would do my liking : in the mean time let me be that I am, and seek not to alter me."—*Much Ado About Nothing* I, 3. " The fiend hath pricked down Bardolph irrecoverable." 2 *King Henry IV* II, 4. " Can the Ethiopian change his skin, or the leopard his spots ? "—*Jeremiah* xiii, 23.

Il ne faut pas vendre la peau de l'ours avant de l'avoir tué *ou* avant de l'avoir mis par terre, Don't count your chickens before they are hatched. " Bid them achieve me, and then sell my bones . . . The man that once did sell the lion's skin While the beast liv'd was kill'd with hunting him."—*King Henry V* IV, 3. " But yet I run before my horse to market."—*King Richard III* I, 1.

Je ne voudrais pas être dans sa peau, I shouldn't like to be in his shoes. " I would not be in some of your coats for twopence."—*Twelfth Night* IV, 1.

Quitter sa peau, To cast off the old Adam.

Tenir à (*ou* Sauver) sa peau, To save one's skin *or* one's carcass *or* one's bacon, To think discretion the better part of valour. " To-day how many would have given their honours To have sav'd their carcasses ! "—*Cymbeline* V, 3. " The better part of valour is discretion ; in the which better part I have saved my life."—1 *King Henry IV* V, 4.

See also BON 39, CHER, NEUF, OS, TREMBLER.

pêche. *See* REMBOURRER.

péché. *See* LAID, MISÉRICORDE, PARDONNER.

pécher. Ce n'est pas par là qu'il pèche, That is not his failing.
Qui perd pèche, The loser is always in the wrong.
See also PUNIR.
pêcher. Où avez-vous pêché cela ? Where did you pick that up *or* get hold of that ?
Pêcher en eau trouble, To fish in troubled waters.
Toujours pêche qui en prend un, Every little helps.
peigne. *See* COUP 27, SALE.
peigner. Un mal peigné, An unkempt (*or* A dirty) fellow.
peindre. Achever de peindre quelqu'un, To picture someone to the life (*describe him in graphic words*).
Être à peindre, To look too funny for words ; To be a picture (*of beauty*).
See also BEAU 22, 23, ROSEAU, TRAIT.
peine. En être pour sa peine, To have had one's trouble for nothing.
Être dans la peine, To be in distress ; To be in great want, To fall on evil days.
Perdre sa peine *ou* ses peines, To waste one's time [on it].
Toute peine mérite salaire, The labourer is worthy of his hire (*Luke* x, 7).
See also BIEN, BOUT, JOUR, MOURIR, PLAINDRE, PLEURER, PROPORTIONNER.
peinture. Je ne peux pas le voir en peinture, I can't bear the sight of him. " Fellow, be gone : I cannot brook thy sight."—*King John* III, 1.
peler. Il n'y avait que (*ou* Il y avait) quatre pelés et un tondu *ou* trois teigneux et un pelé, There were only a few nobodies present.
pèlerin. *See* ROUGE.
pelle. La pelle se moque du fourgon, The pot calls the kettle black. " The raven chides blackness."—*Troilus and Cressida* II, 3. " Come, sir, you blush ; as his your case is such ; You chide at him, offending twice as much."—*Love's Labour's Lost* IV, 3.
See also RAMASSER, REMUER.
pelote. Faire sa pelote, To make one's pile, To feather one's nest (*by fair means*).
peloter. Peloter en attendant partie, To fill in time (*while waiting for something to begin*).
pelure. *See* ORANGE.
pencher. *See* AIR, BALANCE.
pendable. Un cas pendable, A hanging matter, An unforgivable act.
See also JOUER.
pendre. Aller pendre la crémaillère chez quelqu'un, To go to someone's house-warming.
Dire pis que pendre de quelqu'un, To say everything that is bad of someone.
Être pendu haut et court, To be well and truly hanged, To be strung up short, To dance on nothing at the end of a rope. "*Tamora.* Come, sirrah, you must be hang'd. *Clown.* Hang'd ! By'r lady, then I have brought up a neck to a fair end."—*Titus Andronicus* IV, 4.
Être toujours pendu à la sonnette de quelqu'un, To live on someone's doorstep.
Être toujours pendu aux basques de quelqu'un, To be always hanging on someone's coat-tails *or* always following someone about. " Hang no more about me, I am no gibbet for you."—*Merry Wives of Windsor* II, 2.
Il lui en pend autant au nez *ou* Autant lui pend à l'oreille, The same thing may happen to him again.
Il n'y a pas de quoi se pendre, That's nothing much to worry about.
Il y a de quoi se pendre, It's heart-breaking.
Le bruit pend l'homme, Give a dog a bad (*or* an ill) name and hang him. *Quotation under* CHIEN.

Les grands voleurs pendent les petits, Great offenders condemn the little ones, while escaping punishment for their own misdeeds. "See how yond justice rails upon yond simple thief... The usurer hangs the cozener. Through tatter'd clothes small vices do appear; Robes and furr'd gowns hide all. Plate sin with gold, And the strong lance of justice hurtless breaks; Arm it in rags, a pigmy's straw doth pierce it."—*King Lear* IV, 6. (*Note.*—cozener = paltry thief.) "And, soiled with all the vices of the times, Thunder damnation on their neighbour's crimes!"—JUVENAL, *Satires* tr. by GIFFORD satire ii, 1, 30.

Pendre la crémaillère, To give a house-warming.

Voilà ce qui vous pend au [bout du] nez, That is what you may expect, That (*danger, etc.*) is what is hanging over you *or* over your head.

See also AUSSITÔT, COMPAGNIE, CORDE, DÉPENDRE, LANGUE, SEC, SITÔT.

Pénélope. C'est l'ouvrage de Pénélope, It is doing it and undoing it over and over again, It is Penelopizing.

pénétrer. *See* AVENIR.

pénitence. Faire pénitence, To do penance (de = for); To fare badly (*be provided with poor food*).

pensée. *See* DERRIÈRE, DÉSIR, RAPIDE.

penser. *See* DIRE, HAUT, HONNIR, LIEUE.

pépie. Avoir la pépie, To have a perpetual thirst.

Ne pas avoir la pépie, To be fond of a drink.

percer. Être percé jusqu'aux os, To be wet (*or* soaked) to the skin, To look like a drowned rat. *Quotations under* MOUILLER.

See also BOUT, MÉMOIRE, OS, PANIER.

perche. Une grande perche, A tall, lanky individual.

See also LÂCHER, TENDRE.

perdition. *See* VOIE.

perdre. À mes heures perdues *ou* À mes moments perdus, In my spare time, In my idle moments.

C'est du bien perdu, It is casting pearls before swine.

C'est une tête perdue, He is off his head (*crazy*).

Il y a perdu son latin, He has wasted his time on it, He has laboured in vain.

Je m'y perds *ou* J'y perds mon latin *ou* L'esprit s'y perd, I cannot make head or tail of it.

Perdre la carte *ou* le nord *ou* la tramontane *ou* la boussole, To lose one's bearings *or* one's head, To be all at sea, To get flustered, To get all hot and bothered.

Perdre la parole *ou* l'usage de la parole, To lose the power (*or* the faculty) of speech; To be struck dumb (*with surprise, etc.*). "Madam, you have bereft me of all words."—*The Merchant of Venice* III, 2. "I am so attir'd in wonder I know not what to say."—*Much Ado About Nothing* IV, 1.

Perdre la tête *ou* l'esprit, To take leave of one's senses.

Perdre le jour (*poetic*), To go hence (*die*). "To die,—to sleep,—No more; and by a sleep to say we end The heart-ache."—*Hamlet* III, 1.

Perdre pied, To get out of one's depth (*lit. & fig.*).

Pour un de perdu, deux (*ou* dix) de retrouvés, There's as good fish in the sea as ever came out of it.

See also ARÇON, BALLE, BEAU 24, BÊLER, BIENFAIT, BOIRE, CHASSE, CLOCHER, CORPS, COUP 51, COURIR, CRIER, CROIRE, DIABLE, DROIT, ENFANT, ÉTRIER, GOÛT, HONTEUX, JOUER, LAVER, MOULE, NOM, NUAGE, NUE, PARTIE, PAYS, PÉCHER, PEINE, RETOUR, SAINT-CRÉPIN, TEMPS.

père. Un gros père, A rotund gentleman; A podge of a child.

Un père la joie, A jolly man, A jovial soul.

See also AVARE, FILS, TOUT.

péril. *See* DEMEURE.

périlleux. *See* SAUT.

périr. *See* ENNUI, ENNUYEUX.

perle. C'est une perle, It's a gem (*utter twaddle*) ; He (She) is a pearl. " She is a pearl, Whose price hath launch'd above a thousand ships, And turn'd crown'd kings to merchants."—*Troilus and Cressida* II, 2.

Jeter des perles devant les pourceaux, To cast pearls before swine.

Une perle à sa couronne, A feather in one's cap.

See also ENFILER.

permettre. Permis à vous de . . ., You are at liberty to . . ., You can . . ., if you like.

perpétuel. C'est le (*ou* C'est un) mouvement perpétuel, He (She) is never still (*of a child*).

See also CHERCHER.

Perrette. *See* BOÎTE.

perruque. *See* TÊTE.

persévérer. *See* VENT.

persil. *See* GRÊLER.

personnage. *See* CARTON, COMÉDIE, PEAU, PREMIER.

personne. Je le lui ai dit, parlant à sa personne, I told him so, to his face.

Je parle à ma personne, I am talking to myself.

See also BON 31, CILLER, CONTENT, EMBARRASSER, EMPÊCHER, ÊTRE, EXCEPTER, MARÉE, ŒIL, PAYER.

perte. À perte de vue, As far as the eye can reach (*said, e.g., of a plain*) ; Stretching to infinity (*said, e.g., of an avenue*). *And see next entry.*

Raisonner, Discourir, à perte de vue, To keep on arguing, To keep on holding forth (*vainly and vaguely*). " Away towards Salisbury ! while we reason here A royal battle may be won and lost."—*King Richard III* IV, 4.

See also HALEINE, PUR, TEMPS.

pesant. *See* OR.

peser. Cela lui pèse sur le cœur, That is weighing on his mind.

See also ALLER, ONCE.

peste. *See* HAÏR.

Pétaud. *See* COUR.

petit. Au petit pied (*fig. only*), In miniature, On a small scale.

C'est un échappé des Petites-Maisons, He is like an escaped lunatic.

Dans les petits pots (*ou* Dans les petites boîtes) sont les bons onguents *ou* Dans les petits sacs sont les bonnes épices, Little and good.

Être dans les petits papiers de quelqu'un, To be in someone's good books *or* good graces.

Faire la petite bouche, To be hard to please, To sniff [in disdain].

Il est à mettre aux Petites-Maisons, He ought to be put in a lunatic asylum (*is so silly, says such foolish things*).

Petite cervelle, prompte colère, A little pot is soon hot.

See also ABATTRE, ALLER, BIÈRE, BONHEUR BOUT, CHEZ, CHIFFONNER, COMITÉ, COMPAGNON, CONTENT, DOIGT, FEU, GARÇON, GROS, JUIF, MERCIER, NID, OIE, PAIN, PENDRE, PLAT, PLI, PRÊTER, RIVIÈRE, SOIN, SOMME, SOULIER, TÊTE, TROU.

pétrir. Une âme pétrie de fange *ou* de boue, A creature steeped in vice.

See also LIMON, ORGUEIL.

peu. C'est un homme comme il y en a peu, He is a man (*or* is one) in a thousand.

See also AIDE, BON 3, ESPRIT, PLOMB, PRÈS, RAIDE, SOUCI, TANT, TENIR, TOQUER.

peuple. *See* MENU, VOIX.

peur. Avoir une peur bleue *ou* Suer la peur, To be in mortal terror *or* (*slang*) in a blue funk, To be scared to death. " It harrows me with fear."—*Hamlet* I, 1. " But now I am cabin'd, cribb'd, confin'd, bound in To saucy doubts and fears."—*Macbeth* III, 4.

Être habillé (*ou* Être mis) à faire peur, To be dressed like a scarecrow. " No eye hath seen such scarecrows."—1 *King Henry IV* IV, 2.

Être transi de peur, To be in fear and trembling.

Il a eu plus de peur que de mal, He was more frightened than hurt. " She hath been then more fear'd than harm'd, my liege."—*King Henry V* I, 2.

La peur donne des ailes, Fear lends wings.

La peur grossit les objets, Fear magnifies dangers. " You, ladies, you, whose gentle hearts do fear The smallest monstrous mouse that creeps on floor."—*A Midsummer Night's Dream* V, 1.

See also EAU, LAID, MANGER.

peureux. Être peureux comme un lièvre, To be [as] timid as a hare. " More a coward than a hare."—*Twelfth Night* III, 4.

Philémon. Ils sont comme Philémon et Baucis, They are like Darby and Joan.

Philippe. *See* SOBRE.

phrase. Faire des phrases, To use high-sounding phrases. Ne faites donc pas tant de phrases, We (I) have had enough of phrases. " O dear discretion, how his words are suited ! The fool hath planted in his memory An army of good words ; and I do know A many fools that stand in better place, Garnish'd like him, that for a tricksy word Defy the matter."—*The Merchant of Venice* III, 5.

physionomie. *See* RENVERSER.

pie. Il est bavard comme une pie *ou* Il jase comme une pie [borgne], He talks nineteen to the dozen, He would talk a donkey's (*or* a horse's) hind leg off. " Chattering pies."—3 *King Henry VI* V, 6.

See also CROIRE.

pièce. C'est la meilleure pièce de son sac, It is his strongest card.

Être près de ses pièces, To be hard up *or* (*slang*) in Queer Street ; To be close-fisted.

Être tout d'une pièce, To be [as] stiff as a poker (*of person's carriage or manner*).

Faire pièce à quelqu'un, To thwart someone, To put difficulties in someone's way.

La pièce de résistance, The main dish *or* course ; The principal feature.

Un homme tout d'une pièce, A bluff (*or* a plain-spoken) man. " A plain blunt man, That love my friend."—*Julius Caesar* III, 2.

Une pièce à tiroirs, An episodic play.

See also ACCOMMODER, ACCOUTRER, ARMER, BON 74, EMPORTER, HABILLER, JOUER, MONNAIE, TOMBER.

pied. Aller (*ou* Partir) d'un pied léger, (*Lit.*) To dart (*or* To hurry) out ; (*Fig.*) To take up a thing enthusiastically.

Aller dans une affaire pied à pied, To proceed in a matter step by step.

Aller du même pied, To go hand in hand (*in agreement and alliance*).

Au pied de la lettre, To the letter, Literally ; To tell the truth.

Avoir le pied marin, To have found one's sea legs, To be a good sailor ; To keep cool *or* calm and collected.

C'est un pied de pris, It is the thin end of the wedge.

Être en pied, To be on the permanent staff.

Être mis à pied, To be suspended *or* recalled ; To be dismissed (*sacked*), To get one's marching orders.

Être (*ou* Vivre) sur un grand pied, To live in grand style.

Il aurait voulu être à cent pieds sous terre, He would have liked to sink into the earth (*was so confused, so ashamed*).

Je voudrais que cet homme fût à

cent pieds sous terre, I wish that man was dead and buried. " Would I were as deep under the earth as I am above."—*Troilus and Cressida* IV, 2.

Lever le pied, To abscond *or* To decamp (*without paying one's creditors, or with other people's money*).

Marcher sur le pied à quelqu'un (*fig.*), To tread on someone's toes *or* corns.

Mettre les pieds dans le plat, To put one's foot in it.

Mettre pied à terre, To alight ; To dismount.

Mettre quelqu'un au pied du mur, To drive someone into a corner.

Partir (*ou* Sortir) de sa maison les pieds devant, To go out of one's house feet foremost (*be carried to burial*).

Partir du pied gauche, To make a good start.

Pied à pied, Foot by foot, Inch by inch (*progression*) ; Step by step.

Prendre pied, To get a foothold, To take root.

Prendre quelqu'un au pied levé, To take someone unawares (*as by a question*) ; To catch someone unprepared (*to do something immediately*).

Se lever du pied gauche, To get out of bed on the wrong side *or* on the wrong leg.

Sur le pied où sont les choses *ou* Sur ce pied-là, That being so.

Tirer pied ou aile d'une chose, To get something (*some profit*) out of a thing somehow or other.

Un homme de cinq pieds six pouces, A 7-footer.

Un pied-à-terre, A temporary lodging *or* resting place, Somewhere to stay.

Un pied plat (*fig.*), A mean wretch.

Venir de son pied [léger], To come on foot *or* on Shanks's mare. *Quotation under* ONZE.

See also AIR, ARGILE, ARMER, BON 7, 12, 20, 37, BRÛLER, CHAUSSURE, CHENET, COUP 19, 28, 46, 52, DANSER, DÉFERRER, DESSUS, DONNER, ÉPINE, ÉTRIER, FERME, FEU, FOSSE, FOURCHU, GAGNER, GORGE, GRUE, HAUT, HERBE, JOUER, LÂCHER, MARCHER, MOUCHER, NEZ, NICKELER, NU, PERDRE, PETIT, PLAIN, QUATRE, RAGE, REMUER, RETOMBER, SAUTER, SÉCHER, TOISER, TOMBE, TOMBER, TREMBLER.

piège. *See* DONNER, PRENDRE, SEMER, TENDRE.

pierre. Ce n'est là qu'une pierre d'attente, That is only a beginning.

Je le mènerai par un chemin où il n'y aura pas de pierres, I will give him no quarter, I'll put him through it (*slang*).

Jeter des pierres (*ou* une pierre) dans le jardin de quelqu'un (*fig.*), To throw stones (*or* To cast aspersions) (*or* To throw out innuendoes) (*or* To have a dig) at someone.

Jeter la pierre à quelqu'un, To cast (*or* To throw) a stone at someone (*accuse him*) : JÉSUS-CHRIST a dit : Que celui de vous qui est sans péché lui jette la première pierre, Jesus Christ said : He that is without sin among you, let him first cast a stone at her (*John* viii, 7).

Pierre qui roule n'amasse pas mousse, A rolling stone gathers no moss.

Trouver une pierre, des pierres, dans (*ou* en) son chemin, To find an obstacle, obstacles, (*or* a lion) in one's path *or* way.

Une pierre d'achoppement, A stumbling-block. " Were I a man, a duke, and next of blood, I would remove these tedious stumbling-blocks, And smooth my way upon their headless necks."—2 *King Henry VI* I, 2.

Une pierre de scandale, A cause for scandal.

See also CŒUR, COUP 34, GELER, MALHEUREUX, TOUCHE.

pierrot. *See* HARDI.

piété. *See* SUER.

pieusement. Il croit pieusement tout ce qu'on lui raconte, He believes religiously all they tell him (*without proof*).

Je le crois pieusement, I believe it out of respect for you (*although it appears strange to me*).

pieux. Je le laissai dans sa pieuse croyance, I left him in his fond (*foolishly credulous*) belief.

See also MENSONGE.

pigeon. *See* PLUMER.

pigeonnier. Un pigeonnier (*fig.*), A loft (*an elevated dwelling, an attic room*).

pignon. Avoir pignon sur rue, To have a house of one's own ; To have property.

Pilate. *See* RENVOYER.

pile. Jouer une chose à pile ou face, To toss up for a thing.

See also CROIX.

pilier. Un pilier d'estaminet *ou* de cabaret, A public-house loafer, A bar-lounger.

pilule. *See* AVALER, DORER.

pinceau. *See* COUP 20.

pincer. Être pincée pour un homme, pincé pour une femme, To be gone (*or* stuck) on a man, gone (*or* stuck) on a woman (*slang*).

pince-sans-rire. Un pince-sans-rire, A man of dry humour.

pincettes. On ne le prendrait pas avec des pincettes, One (I) wouldn't touch it (him) with a barge-pole.

pinson. *See* GAI.

pinte. Se faire une pinte de bon sang, To have a good laugh ; To have a good time.

pion. *See* DAMER.

pipe. *See* CASSER.

pipée. On ne prend pas les vieux merles à la pipée, You can't catch an old bird with chaff.

piper. Ne pas piper, Not to say a word, To be mum.

See also DÉ.

pique. Être à cent piques au-dessous de quelqu'un, de quelque chose, To be not a patch on (*or* Not to be able to hold a candle to) (*or* Not to be fit to hold a candle to) someone, something.

Être à cent piques au-dessus de quelqu'un, de quelque chose, To be miles above (*or* far superior to) someone, something.

Vous en êtes à cent piques, You're miles out (*in guessing*).

pique-assiette. Un pique-assiette, A sponger, A dinner hunter.

piquer. Piquer des deux (*fig.*), To hurry up, To be snappy about it.

Piquer l'assiette, To make a practice of feeding at other people's expense, To be a dinner hunter.

Se piquer au jeu *ou* Être piqué au jeu (*fig.*), To warm [up] (*to one's subject or work*), To be on one's mettle.

Se piquer le nez, To get fuddled (*with drink*).

See also FROTTER, HONNEUR, MOUCHE, VER, VIF.

piquet. Être planté comme un piquet, To be standing like a post (*immobile*).

Mettre un écolier au piquet, To stand a scholar in the corner.

See also DROIT.

piqueur. Un piqueur d'assiette, A sponger, A dinner hunter.

piqûre. *See* ÉPINGLE.

pire. *See* CAVER, DORMIR, ENTENDRE.

pirouette. Répondre par des pirouettes, To laugh it off *or* away.

pirouetter. On l'a fait pirouetter d'une rude manière, They had him properly on the run (*trying to escape*).

pis. *See* PENDRE, TANT.

pissenlit. Manger les pissenlits par la racine, To be pushing up the daisies (*be dead*).

pistolet. S'en aller après avoir tiré

son coup de pistolet, To go off after having shot one's bolt.

Si ses yeux étaient des pistolets, il le tuerait, He is looking daggers at him. "Ah, gentle Clifford, kill me with thy sword, And not with such a cruel threat'ning look!"—3 *King Henry VI* I, 3.

Tirer un coup de pistolet, To make a noise (*or*, *slang*, To kick up a shine) to attract attention.

See also DRÔLE, GORGE.

pitié. C'est [une] grande pitié (*ou* C'est grand-pitié) que de nous, Life is very trying. "Man is born unto trouble, as the sparks fly upward."—*Job* v, 7.

See also ENVIE.

pivoine. *See* ROUGE.

pivoter. Faire pivoter quelqu'un, To make someone dance attendance.

place. Bien tenir sa place à table, To do justice to a meal.

Ne pas tenir en place, To pace up and down (*in agitation*).

Ne pouvoir demeurer (*ou* durer) en place, To be unable to keep still.

Tenir de la place, To take up a lot of room (*of a big person*); To overestimate one's own importance.

See also CHASSE, DEMEURER, DEBOUT, NET, PREMIER, QUITTER, RESTER.

placer. Il a le cœur bien placé, His heart is in the right place.

Il a le cœur mal placé, He is a bad-hearted man.

See also MOT.

plafond. *See* ARAIGNÉE, SAUTER.

plaider. *See* FAUX.

plaie. Ne demander (*ou* Ne chercher) (*ou* Ne rêver) que plaies et bosses, To be bent on making trouble (*to suit one's own ends*); To delight in making mischief (*for sport*). "Then will two at once woo one,—That must needs be sport alone; And those things do best please me That befall preposterously."—*A Midsummer Night's Dream* III, 2.

Plaie d'argent n'est pas mortelle, There are worse things than losing money.

See also DÉBANDER, POIGNARD, RAVIVER, SAIGNER.

plaindre. Plaindre sa peine *ou* ses pas, To spare oneself [trouble].

plaine. La plaine liquide (*poetic*), The ocean wave. *Quotations under* SÉJOUR.

plain-pied. Cela va de plain-pied, That goes without saying.

plaire. À Dieu ne plaise, God forbid. "O, forfend it, God."—*King Richard II* IV, 1.

Cela va comme il plaît à Dieu, Things are all anyhow.

Le jeu lui plaît, It amuses him [and doesn't hurt us].

Se plaire à soi-même, To be self-contented.

See also DIRE.

plaisanter. Il ne plaisante pas là-dessus, He means what he says (*won't give way*); He takes such matters seriously.

plaisanterie. Dire des plaisanteries, To crack jokes.

See also DÉFRAYER, ENTENDRE, PASSER, RAPIN, TOURNER, USER.

plaisir. L'âge des plaisirs, [The days of] youth. "For youth no less becomes The light and careless livery that it wears Than settled age his sables and his weeds, Importing health and graveness."—*Hamlet* IV, 7.

Un régime du bon plaisir, An absolute monarchy, A despotism; An order of things dependent on someone's sweet will.

See also FAIRE, MENU, PRENDRE, ROI.

plan. *See* ÉCHOUER, LAISSER, PREMIER, RESTER, SECOND.

planche. Avoir du pain sur la planche, To have some money put by (*Quotation under* POIRE); To have some work in hand *or* something to go on with.

Avoir du travail sur la planche, To have work in reserve.

C'est une planche pourrie, He is a broken reed.

C'est une planche qu'il a sauvée de son naufrage, It is a little something he has rescued from the wreck of his fortunes.

C'est une vraie planche, He (She) is just like a lath (*so thin*).

Être entre quatre planches, To be in one's coffin.

See also BRÛLER, SALUT.

plancher. Le plancher des vaches, Terra firma, Dry land.

See also DÉBARRASSER.

planète. *See* NAÎTRE.

planter. Il est planté là comme une borne *ou* comme un terme, He is standing there stock-still, He doesn't budge an inch. " I will stand stone-still."—*King John* IV, 1.

Planter là quelqu'un, To leave someone in the lurch, To give someone the slip, To let someone down.

Planter là son travail, la musique, etc., To give up one's work, music, etc.

Un garçon bien planté, Une fille bien plantée, A well set-up young man, girl.

See also CHOU, PIQUET, TENTE.

plaquer. Plaquer quelque chose au nez de quelqu'un, To cast something in someone's teeth.

See also SOUFFLET.

plat. Donner (*ou* Servir) à quelqu'un un plat de sa façon *ou* de son métier, To play someone one of one's tricks.

Mettre les petits plats dans les grands, To make a great spread (*feast, meal*).

See also BATTRE, BOURSE, NET, PIED, TOMBER, TORCHER, VENTRE.

plate-bande. Marcher sur les plates-bandes de quelqu'un, To encroach on someone's preserves (*fig.*).

platine. Avoir une [fameuse] platine, To have the gift of the gab *or* a glib tongue. *Quotations under* LANGUE.

plâtras. *See* BÂTIR.

plâtre. Battre quelqu'un comme plâtre, To beat someone to a jelly.

See also ESSUYER.

plâtrer. *See* PAIX.

plein. De plein saut, At one bound.

See also BATTRE, COLLIER, CRIER, DOS, DRAP, ÉTOILE, GOUTTE, MAIN, NAGER, VOGUER.

pleur. *See* AURORE.

pleurer. C'est un pleure-pain *ou* un pleure-misère, He is always crying poverty.

Il ne lui reste que les yeux pour pleurer, He is left with nothing but regrets (*has lost all*).

Ne pleurer que d'un œil, To onion one's eyes. " Look, they weep ; And I, an ass, am onion-ey'd."—*Antony and Cleopatra* IV, 1. " And, indeed, the tears live in an onion that should water this sorrow."—*Antony and Cleopatra* I, 2. " Mine eyes smell onions ; I shall weep anon."—*All's Well That Ends Well* V, 3. " And if the boy have not a woman's gift, To rain a shower of commanded tears, An onion will do well for such a shift."—*The Taming of the Shrew, Induction, Scene* 1.

Pleurer à chaudes larmes *ou, en parlant d'une femme*, Pleurer comme une Madeleine, To cry bitterly, To weep bitter tears, To cry one's eyes (*or* one's heart) out. " These hot tears, which break from me perforce."—*King Lear* I, 4. " Mine own tears Do scald like molten lead."—*King Lear* IV, 7. " To drain upon his face an ocean of salt tears."—2 *King Henry VI* III, 2. " Like Niobe, all tears."—*Hamlet* I, 2. " Give me thy hand, That I may dew it with my mournful tears."—2 *King Henry VI* III, 2. " And water once a day her chamber round With eye-offending brine."—*Twelfth Night* I, 1. " And she hath offer'd to the doom . . . A sea of melting pearl, which some call tears."—*Two Gentlemen of Verona* III, 1.

Pleurer comme un veau, To blubber.

Pleurer d'un œil et rire de l'autre, Not to know whether to laugh or cry. " Have we, as 'twere with a defeated joy,—With one auspicious and one dropping eye, . . . In equal scale weighing delight and dole." —*Hamlet* I. 2.

Pleurer de joie, To weep for joy. " I weep for joy To stand upon my kingdom once again . . . As a long-parted mother with her child Plays fondly with her tears and smiles in meeting, So, weeping-smiling, greet I thee, my earth."—*King Richard II* III, 2. " My plenteous joys, Wanton in fulness, seek to hide themselves In drops of sorrow."—*Macbeth* I, 4. " I am a fool To weep at what I am glad of."—*The Tempest* III, 1. " A kind overflow of kindness. There are no faces truer than those that are so washed. How much better is it to weep at joy than to joy at weeping ? "— *Much Ado About Nothing* I, 1.

Pleurer pour avoir quelque chose, To have a struggle to get something.

Pleurer sa peine, To grudge one's labour.

See also RIRE.

pleuvoir. Il dépense de l'argent comme s'il en pleuvait, He spends money like water.

Il pleut à verse *ou* à seaux *ou* à torrents *ou* des hallebardes, It is raining (*or* coming down) hard *or* in buckets *or* in torrents *or* cats and dogs *or* pitchforks, It is like a cinema rain.

See also ÉCOUTE.

pli. C'est une affaire qui ne fera pas un [petit] pli *ou* pas le moindre pli, There's not the slightest difficulty about it, It's all plain sailing.

Donner un bon pli à la jeunesse, To bring up the young in the way they should go.

Les plis et les replis du cœur, The innermost recesses of the heart.

Prendre un pli, To acquire (*or* To contract) a habit.

plier. Il vaut mieux (*ou* Mieux vaut) plier que rompre, Better bend than break.

Plier les genoux devant le veau d'or, To fawn on the rich, To grovel before the mighty (*for favours*). " Why should the poor be flatter'd ? No, let the candied tongue lick absurd pomp ; And crook the pregnant hinges of the knee Where thrift may follow fawning."—*Hamlet* III, 2. (*Note.*—thrift = success, prosperity.)

See also BAGAGE, ÉCHINE, ÉPAULE, ROSEAU.

plomb. Il lui faudrait un peu de plomb dans la tête, He lacks (*mental*) ballast.

Mettre du plomb dans la tête (*ou* dans la cervelle) à quelqu'un, To knock some sense into someone's head.

Une chaleur de plomb, An oppressive heat.

See also AILE, DORMIR, FIN, NAGER.

plongeon. Faire un plongeon, (*Lit.*) To duck ; (*Fig.*) To make oneself scarce, To make a getaway.

plonger. Être plongé jusqu'au cou dans les affaires, To be up to the eyes (*or* the elbows) in work.

Plonger, To give the court bow.

Plonger comme un canard (*fig.*), To steal off, To slip away, To make oneself scarce.

See also POIGNARD, RÊVERIE.

pluie. Après la pluie, le beau temps, Every cloud has a silver lining.

Faire la pluie et le beau temps, To be all-powerful, To rule the roast *or* the roost. " Suffolk, the new-made duke that rules the roast."—2 *King Henry VI* I, 1.

Parler (*ou* Causer) de la pluie et du beau temps, To talk about the weather *or* of nothing in particular.

See also ABATTRE, EAU, ENNUYEUX.

plume. Arracher à quelqu'un une [belle] plume de l'aile, To pluck a feather from someone's wing (*fig.*) ; To make a [fine] haul out of someone ; To do someone out of a job. " We'll pull his plumes."—1 *King Henry VI* III, 3. " These growing feathers pluck'd from Caesar's wing Will make him fly an ordinary pitch ; Who else would soar above the view of men, And keep us all in servile fearfulness."—*Julius Caesar* I, 1.

Briser sa plume, To cease writing (*in indignation*).

Faire tomber à quelqu'un la plume des mains, To make someone feel he can write no more (*in discouragement, in disgust*).

Jeter la plume au vent, To trust to luck.

La belle plume fait le bel oiseau *ou* C'est la plume qui fait l'oiseau, Fine feathers make fine birds.

Laisser des (*ou* de ses) plumes, To drop some money (*in gaming, in a venture*).

Les plumes blanches, The brass hats (*army slang*).

Tenir la plume, To act as secretary.

Tirer des plumes à quelqu'un, To pluck someone (*swindle him*).

Tirer une plume de l'aile à quelqu'un, To get something out of someone, To squeeze some money out of someone.

Une guerre de plume, A paper warfare.

See also BOUT, ÉCRIRE, GEAI, MAIN, PARER, VÉNAL.

plumer. Plumer la poule sans la faire crier, To fleece someone without his being aware of it.

Plumer quelqu'un, To pluck (*or* To fleece) someone.

Un bon pigeon à plumer, A good pigeon to rook (*dupe to swindle*).

plumet. Avoir son plumet, To be slightly elevated (*tipsy*).

plumitif. Un plumitif, A quill-driver, A pen pusher. " An inkhorn mate."—1 *King Henry VI* III, 1.

plus. Qui peut le plus peut le moins, He who can do more can do less.

See also AISÉ, BEAU 6, CHANGER, CONNAÎTRE, CONTENT, CORDE, COUP 55, COURT, DOUCEUR, ÊTRE, FAÇON, FÊLER, FIN, FORT, FOU, FRIRE, GROS, HÂTER, HAUT, HISTOIRE, JAMBE, MANQUER, MÉCHANT, MONDE, NATURE, ŒIL, PAGE, PEUR, POUVOIR, PRÈS, PRESSER, PROMETTRE, RAISON, RECONNAÎTRE, REGRETTABLE, REPRENDRE, RESSEMBLER, SOUCI, TANT, TENIR, TERRAIN, TÊTE, TÔT, TOUR, UN.

plusieurs. *See* CORDE, MÉDECINE.

poche. Avoir une affaire en poche *ou* Tenir une affaire dans sa poche, To have a matter well in hand.

Connaître quelqu'un, quelque chose, comme sa poche, To know someone, something, intimately *or* inside out.

Être toujours dans la poche de quelqu'un, To be always running about after someone.

Mettez cela dans votre poche et votre mouchoir par-dessus, Put that in your pipe and smoke it.

Mettre quelqu'un dans sa poch To outmatch someone.

Mettre son drapeau dans sa poche, To pocket one's feelings, To suppress one's opinions.

N'avoir pas sa langue dans sa poche, To be quick at repartee. "You shall never take her without her answer, unless you take her without her tongue."—*As You Like It* IV, 1.

See also CHAT, CORDE, ŒIL.

pocher. Avoir les yeux pochés [au beurre noir], To have a pair of (*or* two lovely) black eyes.

poêle. *See* QUEUE, TOMBER.

poétique. *See* LICENCE.

poids. Avoir deux poids et deux mesures *ou* Changer de poids et de mesure, To hold the scales uneven, To have one law for the rich and another for the poor.

Soutenir le poids de, To bear the brunt of.

See also CHALEUR, OR.

poignard. Avoir le poignard dans le cœur *ou* dans le sein, To have a heart-ache (*mental anguish*) ; To suffer keen vexation. " My father's rough and envious disposition Sticks me at heart."—*As You Like It* I, 2.

Mettre (*ou* Plonger) (*ou* Enfoncer) un poignard dans le cœur (*ou* dans le sein) de quelqu'un, To give someone a stab *or* a dreadful shock (*as by communicating bad news*). *Quotation under* FENÊTRE.

Retourner à quelqu'un le poignard dans le cœur *ou* dans la plaie, To rub it in.

See also COUP 10, GORGE.

poignet. *See* FORCE.

poil. Avoir un poil dans la main, To be work-shy.

De tout poil, Of all kinds.

Être à poil, Not to have a stitch on, To be (*or* To stand) in buff (*naked*).

N'avoir pas un poil de sec, To be bathed in perspiration ; To be wet (*or* soaked) to the skin. *Quotations under* SUER *and* MOUILLER.

Reprendre du poil de la bête, To get the upper hand again ; To take a hair of the dog that bit one.

Se mettre à poil, To strip to the buff (*naked*).

See also BRAVE.

poindre. *See* OINDRE.

poing. Le poing sur la hanche *ou* Les poings sur les hanches (*fig.*), In a provocative attitude ; Defiantly, Threateningly.

See also COUP 35, DÉMANGER, DORMIR, RONGER.

point. Mettre au point (*fig.*), To make clear, To narrow down, To perfect, To put (*or* To lick) into shape.

Rendre des points à quelqu'un, To give someone points.

Un point, c'est tout, So much for that, And that's that. *Quotation under* VOILÀ.

Un point fait à temps en sauve mille *ou* en épargne cent, A stitch in time saves nine.

See also ÂNE, ARGENT, ATTENDRE, COURIR, I, MAL, RASSURER, SALUT.

pointe. Avoir une pointe de vin, To have had a drop too much.

Faire une pointe jusque chez quelqu'un, To break one's journey and call on someone.

Suivre (*ou* Poursuivre) (*ou* Pousser) sa pointe, To keep pegging away, To press (*or* To push) one's suit.

See also AIGUILLE, EMPORTER.

pointu. Avoir l'esprit pointu, To have a captious mind.

Une voix pointue, A shrill voice.

poire. Entre la poire et le fromage, Over the walnuts and the wine.

Faire sa poire, To fancy oneself, To put on side.

Garder une poire pour la soif, To provide against (*or* To put something by for) a rainy day. " I have five hundred crowns, The thrifty hire I sav'd under your father, Which I did store to be my foster nurse When service should in my old limbs lie lame, And unregarded age in corners thrown."—*As You Like It* II, 3.

La poire est mûre, The opportunity is ripe to be seized.

See also AVALER, COUPER.

pois. La fleur des pois, The pick of the bunch.

poison. C'est une vraie poison, She's a most detestable woman, She's a pest.

poisson. Être comme le (*ou* comme

un) poisson dans l'eau, To be [as] snug as a bug in a rug.

Être comme le (*ou* comme un) poisson hors de l'eau, To be in a very uncomfortable situation.

Être comme un poisson sur la paille, To be like a fish out of water (*out of one's element*).

See also AVALER, AVRIL, BOIRE, CHAIR, FINIR, GROS, MUET, NAGER, SAUCE.

poissonnier. Se faire poissonnier la veille de Pâques, To open a stall the day after the fair (*be too late to profit*).

poitrine. Se battre (*ou* Se frapper) la poitrine, To cry peccavi (*I have sinned*).

Polichinelle. *See* SECRET.

politesse. *See* BRÛLER.

politique. *See* AUTRUCHE, CLOCHER.

pommade. Passer la pommade à quelqu'un, To throw bouquets (*or* nosegays) at someone.

pomme. Jeter (*ou* Lancer) des pommes cuites à quelqu'un, To give someone the bird (*slang*).

La pomme de discorde, The apple of discord, The bone of contention.

Recevoir des pommes cuites, To get the bird (*slang*).

pompon. À vous, À lui, le pompon, You come, He comes, off best, You take, He takes, the cake *or* the bun *or* the biscuit.

Avoir le pompon, To come off best, To take the cake *or* the bun *or* the biscuit.

Avoir son pompon, To be intoxicated *or* (*slang*) oiled.

pont. C'est le pont aux ânes, Everyone knows that ; Anyone can do that.

Être sur le pont (*fig.*), To be at one's post.

See also COUPER, EAU, OR.

Pont-Neuf. *See* PORTER.

porc. Être comme un porc à l'auge, To be in clover.

porcelaine. *See* ÉLÉPHANT.

port. Faire naufrage au port, To fail within sight of one's goal, To fall at the last fence.

See also BON 5, ÉCUMEUR, RESTER.

porte. Être aux portes de la mort *ou* du tombeau, To be at death's door.

Frapper (*ou* Heurter) à toutes les portes, To leave no stone unturned.

See also AIMABLE, CLEF, COMPTER, CONSIGNER, DERRIÈRE, ÉCOUTER, FENÊTRE, NEZ, OUVRIR, SORTIE.

porter. Être porté par l'opinion, To be thought highly of.

Être tout porté, To be on the spot *or* here : Restez ici à dîner, vous voilà tout porté, Stay to dinner, now you are here.

Il ne le portera pas loin *ou* Il ne le portera pas en paradis, He won't get away with it, I'll be even with him yet, He'll have to pay for it.

Je le porte dans mon cœur, He is very near to my heart.

Je ne le porte pas dans mon cœur, He is in my black books.

L'un(e) portant l'autre *ou* Le fort portant le faible, [Taking] one with the other, Taking it all round, On an average.

Le porter haut, To think no small beer of oneself, To talk big.

On s'y porte, There's no room to breathe (*the crowd is so dense*). *Quotation under* ÉPINGLE.

Porter à la tête, To go to the head (*of fumes*).

Porter beau, To carry oneself well; To be good-looking.

Porter bien le vin, To carry one's liquor well. *Quotation under* FORT.

Porter haut la tête, To carry one's head high (*be proud*). " We'll both together lift our heads to heaven ; And never more abase our sight so low As to vouchsafe one glance unto the ground."—2 *King Henry VI* I, 2.

Porter la parole, To act as spokesman, To do the talking.

Porter quelqu'un, quelque chose, [jusqu']aux nues, To laud (*or* To crack up) (*or* To cry up) someone, something, to the skies.

Porter quelqu'un sur les épaules *ou* sur son dos, To be continually pestered by someone.

Porter sa vue bien loin, To be far-seeing *or* far-sighted (*fig.*).

Porter ses vues bien haut, To aim high (*be ambitious*). "Vaulting ambition."—*Macbeth* I, 7.

Se porter comme le Pont-Neuf *ou* comme un charme, To be [as] fit as a fiddle, To be in the pink of health *or* (*slang*) in the pink.

See also BOTTE, BOUCHE, BOUT, CHALEUR, COMPTANT, COUP 15, 53, CULOTTE, EAU, ÉCHAFAUD, ENVIE, FAUX, MÉTIER, MORT, NERF, NUIT, SAINT-CRÉPIN, TRIOMPHE.

portrait. C'est son vrai portrait *ou* C'est [tout] son portrait *ou* C'est son portrait tout craché, It is his very image (*there is a strong physical or moral resemblance between them*).

poser. Faire poser quelqu'un, To keep someone waiting ; To keep someone guessing.

Poser, To pose, To put on side, To put it on.

See also CIMAISE, FAIT.

posséder. Il ne se possède pas de joie, He cannot contain himself for joy, He is beside himself with joy. "But what a joy past joy calls out on me."—*Romeo and Juliet* III, 3.

possession. Possession vaut titre, Possession is nine points of the law. "And have is have, however men do catch : Near or far off, well won is still well shot."—*King John* I, 1.

possible. *See* TIRER.

poste. Courir la poste *ou* Aller un train de poste, To go post-haste. "The mayor towards Guildford hies him in all post."—*King Richard III* III, 5. "He requires your haste-post-haste appearance Even on the instant."—*Othello* I, 2. "I from my mistress come to you in post : If I return, I shall be post indeed ; For she will score your fault upon my pate."—*The Comedy of Errors* I, 2.

See also HÔPITAL.

postérité. Passer à la postérité, To go down to posterity.

pot. C'est le pot de terre contre le pot de fer, It's the weak against the strong.

Faire bouillir le pot (*fig.*), To keep the pot boiling.

Un pot à tabac, A dumpy man, A squat[ty man].

See also ANSE, BÊTE, CASSER, COURIR, DÉCOUVRIR, FÊLER, PETIT, SOURD, TOURNER.

potage. *See* RENFORT, TOUT.

potée. *See* ÉVEILLER.

potence. *See* GIBIER.

pou. *See* LAID.

pouce. Lire un livre du pouce, To skim [through] a book.

Mettre les pouces, To knuckle down *or* under.

Se tourner les pouces, To twiddle one's thumbs (*be idle*).

See also DOIGT, MORDRE, PIED, SERRER.

poudre. Cela sent la poudre, It looks like a fight.

Jeter de la poudre aux yeux de quelqu'un, To throw dust in (*or* To pull wool over) someone's eyes, To bluff someone.

Tirer sa poudre aux moineaux, To waste one's powder and shot.

See also ESCAMPETTE, FEU, INVENTER, PARLER, TRAÎNÉE, VIF.

pouf. Faire un pouf, To go off without paying one's bill.

poule. C'est une poule mouillée, He is a milksop *or* a softie. "A milk sop, one that never in his life Felt so much cold as over shoes in snow."—*King Richard III* V, 5.

"This soft courage makes your followers faint."—3 *King Henry VI* II, 2.

Être comme une poule qui a couvé des œufs de cane, To be disconcerted, To come over all hot and bothered.

Quand les poules auront des dents, Pigs might fly.

Tuer la poule aux œufs d'or *ou* Tuer la poule pour avoir l'œuf, To kill the goose that lays the golden eggs.

See also CHAIR, CŒUR, COUCHER, PLUMER.

poulet. *See* SANG.

pouls. *See* TÂTER.

poupe. *See* VENT.

poupée. C'est un visage de poupée, She has a face like a doll, She is a doll.

C'est une vieille poupée, It is mutton dressed as lamb.

C'est une vraie poupée, She (He) is all dolled up.

pourceau. *See* PERLE.

pourquoi. *See* DEMANDER.

pourrir. *See* PLANCHE.

poursuivre. *See* ÉPÉE, POINTE.

pousser. [À la] va comme je te pousse, In a happy-go-lucky way, All anyhow.

Pousser à la roue, To lend a [helping] hand.

See also BOTTE, BOUT, CHAMPIGNON, CRI, POINTE.

poutre. *See* PAILLE.

pouvoir. Il est on ne peut plus aimable, He is as nice as can be, He could not be nicer.

Il se pourrait fort bien que . . ., It is quite on the cards that . . .

Il travaille on ne peut mieux, He could not work better.

See also ARRIVER, ATTENDRE, ATTRAPER, AVENIR, BEURRE, BROSSER, CHARBON, CONTENT, CORDE, CROIRE, CUIRE, DÉDIRE, DRAP, DURER, FAIRE, FOUR, JEUNESSE, MOT, NOUVELLE, PANIER, PEINTURE, PLACE, PLUS, RETROUVER, SANG, SAUVER, SAVOIR, SENTIR, SOUFFLER, TAPER, VIVRE, VOULOIR.

pratiquer. *See* AUTRUCHE.

précaution. Trop de précaution nuit, Too many precautions hinder, rather than help, One can be too careful. "Our doubts are traitors, And make us lose the good we oft might win By fearing to attempt."—*Measure for Measure* I, 5.

prêcher. Prêcher d'exemple, To practise what one preaches.

Prêcher pour son saint, To have an eye to one's own interest.

Prêcher sans mission, To speak (*or* To act) without authority.

Prêcher un converti, To preach to the converted.

See also DÉSERT.

précipice. *See* MARCHER.

premier. Arriver bon premier, To come in an easy first, To win in a canter.

C'est un personnage de premier plan, He is a person of the first importance.

Ce n'est pas le premier venu, He isn't a mere nobody.

Cette question est au premier plan de l'actualité, This question is the topic of the hour *or* is very much to the fore at the present time.

Dès le premier jour, From the outset.

Du premier coup *ou* Du premier jet, The very first time, Right away, Straight off, At the first attempt *or* go off.

L'arbre ne tombe pas du premier coup, Rome was not built in a day.

Le premier coup en vaut deux, The first blow is half the battle.

Premier arrivé, premier servi *ou* Premier venu, premier moulu, First come, first served.

Prendre la première place, To take the lead.

See also AMOUR, COUP 58, DIRE, LOGE,

MOUTARDIER, MOUVEMENT, PAIN, PAS, TÊTE.

prendre. C'est à prendre ou à laisser, [You may] take it or leave it, It is [a case of] Hobson's choice.

Cela ne prend pas, That won't do *or* won't wash, It's no go.

Chacun prend son plaisir où il le trouve, Everyone to his taste, There is no accounting for tastes, Tastes differ.

Être pris comme dans un blé, To be caught like a rat in a trap.

Je n'y prends ni je n'y mets, I am not overstating nor understating the case.

L'affaire prend figure *ou* prend bonne allure *ou* prend une bonne tournure *ou* prend [une bonne] couleur, The affair is taking shape *or* is shaping well, The business looks promising *or* well.

L'affaire prend une mauvaise allure *ou* une mauvaise tournure *ou* une mauvaise couleur, The business looks bad *or* is taking an ugly turn.

On ne m'y prendra pas, I know better.

Où avez-vous pris cela ? Where did you get that from ? What put that into your head ?

Prendre, To catch on (*of a play, a fashion, a word*), To be a hit (*of a play*).

Prendre de l'âge, To be getting on in years. " Your lordship, though not clean past your youth, hath yet some smack of age in you, some relish of the saltness of time."—2 *King Henry IV* I, 2.

Prendre jour *ou* Prendre date, To appoint a day, To make a date (*appointment*).

Prendre le large (*fig.*), To decamp.

Prendre les devants, To go on ahead ; To be beforehand.

Prendre les devants (*ou* le devant) sur quelqu'un, To get the start of someone, To forestall someone.

Prendre quelqu'un au dépourvu *ou* quelqu'un sans vert, To catch someone napping.

Prendre quelqu'un en flagrant délit *ou* quelqu'un sur le fait, To catch someone in the very act *or* someone red-handed (*of any offence*).

Prendre quelqu'un la main dans le sac, To catch someone in the very act *or* someone red-handed (*of stealing only*).

Prendre quelqu'un sous son aile *ou* sous sa tutelle, To take someone under one's wing.

Prendre ses jambes à son cou, To take to one's heels, To show a clean pair of heels. " Your legs did better service than your hands."—3 *King Henry VI* II, 2.

Prendre son courage (*ou* son cœur) à deux mains, To screw up one's courage, To nerve oneself to a venture, To take one's courage in both hands (*gallicism*). " Screw your courage to the sticking place, And we'll not fail."—*Macbeth* I, 7.

Prendre son vol *ou* son essor, To begin to make one's way (*succeed*).

S'y prendre de la bonne (*ou* belle) manière, To set about it in the right way.

Se laisser prendre au piège *ou* à l'hameçon, To fall into the trap.

Tel est pris qui croyait prendre, It is a case of the biter bit. " But now to task the tasker."—*Love's Labour's Lost* II, 1.

See also AIR, AUSSITÔT, AUTANT, AUTEL, BAISSER, BALLE, BEC, BÉNÉFICE, BIAIS, BIEN, BIÈRE, BON 26, 60, 61, 62, BONNET, BOUCHE, BOUT, BRAS, CAPABLE, CHAMP, CHANGE, CHEMIN, CHEVEU, CLEF, CLIQUES, COMPTANT, COMPTE, CONSISTANCE, CONTRE-POIL, CORNE, CORPS, COURIR, COURT, CUITE, DESSUS, DONNER, ENTOUR, ÉPINE, ESCAMPETTE, FAIBLE, FAIT, FAMINE, FEU, FILE, FOIS, GALON, GANT, GRIPPE, HAUT, HÔPITAL, HUPPÉ, LACET, LUNE, MAIN, MAL, MÉDECINE,

MORCEAU, MORS, MOT, MOUCHE, OMBRE, ONZE, OREILLER, PAIR, PAROLE, PARTERRE, PARTI, PAS, PÊCHER, PIED, PINCETTES, PIPÉE, PLI, PREMIER, QUATRE, RETS, RHUME, SAUT, SAVOIR, SENSIBLE, SITÔT, SOU, SOUCI, TÂCHE, TANGENTE, TEMPS, TON, TOUT, TRAGIQUE, TRAVERS, TRÉBUCHET, VAINQUEUR, VENT, VESSIE, VIN, VOL.

préparer. Il se prépare quelque chose, There is something in the wind *or* something afoot *or* something brewing, There is more here than meets the eye, I smell a rat.

See also TERRAIN.

près. À beaucoup près, By a long way, By a long chalk, By long chalks, By far, Nowhere near.

À peu de chose près, Little short of, Within a little of being . . .

En y regardant de plus près, On closer examination.

Il n'y regarde pas de si près, He is not as particular as all that.

Il y regarde de près, He looks at every penny (*is close in money matters*).

Ils se touchent de près, They are closely related (*in parentage*).

Tenir quelqu'un de près, To keep a tight hold on someone, To keep someone under strict control.

See also BONNET, CONNAÎTRE, ÉCHEC, PIÈCE, ROCHE, ROGNER, TONDRE, VOIR.

présence. Des droits (*ou* Des jetons) de présence, Fees per attendance (*at a meeting*).

See also ACTE, COUREUR.

présent. Avoir la mémoire toujours présente, To have a never-failing memory. " Why should I write this down, that's riveted, Screw'd to my memory ? "—*Cymbeline* II, 2.

Cet homme est présent à tout *ou* est présent partout, This man is everywhere at once.

See also ESPRIT, EXCEPTER.

présenter. *See* ASPECT, OLIVIER.

presse. *See* GÉMIR.

pressentir. Se faire pressentir, To cast its shadow before it (*of an event*).

presser. Aller (*ou* Courir) au plus pressé, To attend to the most pressing thing(s) first.

See also ÉPÉE, HARENG, LAIT.

prétendre. *See* IGNORANCE.

pretentaine. Courir la pretentaine, To gad about, To go on the loose.

prétention. *See* RABATTRE.

prêter. C'est un prêté [pour un] rendu, It is tit for tat, It is a Roland for an Oliver.

C'est un sujet qui prête, It is a pregnant subject *or* a subject which lends itself to interesting developments.

On ne prête qu'aux riches, Only the rich can borrow money ; People are judged by their reputation.

Prêter à la petite semaine, To make short loans at exorbitant interest.

See also COLLET, ÉPAULE, FLANC, MAIN, MATIN, OREILLE, RIDICULE, RIRE.

prétexte. Sous aucun prétexte, On no account, Not on any account, Under no circumstances.

prêtre. *See* AUTEL.

preuve. Faire ses preuves, To prove oneself, To show one's mettle.

prévenir. Mieux vaut prévenir que guérir, Prevention is better than cure.

See also FAVEUR.

prévision. Selon toute prévision, In all likelihood.

primer. *See* FORCE.

prince. Il est bon prince, He is a good fellow.

See also TÉNÈBRES.

princesse. Aux frais de la princesse, At the Government's (*or* firm's) (*or* company's) expense.

printemps. *See* HIRONDELLE.

prise. En venir aux prises, To come to grips.

Être aux prises avec la justice, To be up against the law.

Mettre les gens aux prises, To set people by the ears.

See also BEC, LÂCHER.

prisme. Voir les choses dans un prisme *ou* Regarder les choses à travers un prisme, To see things in false colours.

prison. Faire (*ou* Manger) (*ou* Tâter) de la prison, To do time.

See also AIMABLE.

prisonnier. *See* CONSTITUER.

privé. Renseignements privés, Inside information.

prix. Mettre la tête de quelqu'un à prix, To put a price on someone's head. " And he that brings his head unto the king Shall have a thousand crowns for his reward."—2 *King Henry VI* IV, 8.

See also COUREUR, SALER.

probité. *See* DRAPER.

procès. Faire le procès à (*ou* de) quelqu'un, To call someone to account, To bring someone to book.

Sans autre forme de procès, Without further ado.

See also TENDANCE.

prochain. *See* PAILLE.

prodige. Faire des prodiges, To work wonders. " You are made Rather to wonder at the things you hear Than to work any."—*Cymbeline* V, 3.

prodigue. *See* AVARE.

profiter. Profiter de l'occasion, To improve the occasion *or* the shining hour.

profusion. *See* PROVISION.

proie. *See* LÂCHER.

projet. Un homme à projets, A schemer.

promener. Promener quelqu'un (*fig.*), To bamboozle someone.

See also ALLER, ENVOYER.

promesse. *See* RUINER.

promettre. Chose promise, chose due, Promises should be kept. *Quotations under* UN.

Promettre et tenir sont deux *ou* Ce n'est pas tout de promettre, il faut tenir, It is one thing to promise, another to perform, Saying and doing are different things, Fair words butter no parsnips. " Words pay no debts, give her deeds."—*Troilus and Cressida* III, 2. *See also quotations under* UN.

Promettre monts et merveilles à quelqu'un, To promise the moon and the stars to someone.

Promettre plus de beurre que de pain, To make reckless promises.

See also DIEU.

prompt. Être prompt comme un éclair *ou* comme l'éclair, To be [as] quick (*or* [as] swift) as lightning. *Quotations under* RAPIDE.

L'esprit est prompt, mais la chair est faible, The spirit is willing, but the flesh is weak (*Matthew* xxvi, 41).

See also PETIT.

prône. Il a été bien recommandé au prône (*ironiquement*), His pitch has been queered for him.

prononcer. *See* SACRAMENTEL.

prophète. Nul n'est prophète en son pays, No man is a prophet in his own country (*Mark* vi, 4, *John* iv, 44).

proportion. [Toute] proportion gardée, Due allowance being made.

proportionner. Proportionner les peines aux délits *ou* les peines et les délits, To make the punishment fit the crime.

propos. À propos, To the point ; By the way, That reminds me.

À propos de rien *ou* À propos de bottes, For nothing at all, For no earthly reason, Without rhyme or reason.

À propos et hors de propos, In season and out of season.

À tout propos, At every turn.

Arriver fort à propos. To arrive in the nick of time.

Changer de propos, To change the subject.

De propos délibéré, On purpose, Of set purpose.

Des propos d'antichambre *ou* Des propos de valet, Back-stair gossip.

Des propos de couloirs, Lobbying.

Jeter des propos de quelque chose, To hint at something, To put out a feeler on something.

Tenir des propos sur quelqu'un, To make (*nasty*) remarks about someone.

proposer. L'homme propose et Dieu dispose, Man proposes, but God disposes.

propre. Être propre comme un sou [neuf], To be [as] clean as a new pin.

Quand on est propre à tout, on n'est propre à rien *ou* Propre à tout, propre à rien, [A] Jack of all trades and master of none.

See also ÉLOGE. LACET, LOUANGE, MOYEN, VOLER.

prose. Faire de la prose sans le savoir, To do (*or* To be doing) just the right thing without knowing it.

prouver. Qui veut trop prouver ne prouve rien, To advance too many proofs spoils one's case.

Providence. Aller contre la Providence, To fly in the face of Providence.

See also COUP 73, DISPOSITION.

province. *See* NU.

provision. Aller à la provision *ou* aux provisions, To go shopping *or* marketing.

Provision fait profusion, Superabundance leads to waste.

prudence. Prudence est mère de sûreté, Safety first. " Be wary, then ; best safety lies in fear."—*Hamlet* I, 3.

prune. Pour des prunes, For nothing.

See also VENIR.

prunelle. Jouer de la prunelle, To ogle, To cast sheep's eyes, To give the glad eye (*slang*). *Quotation under* ŒIL.

La prunelle de ses yeux, The apple of one's eye (*fig.*). *Note.*—The apple of the eye (*lit.*) *is* La prunelle de l'œil.

prunier. Secouer quelqu'un comme un prunier, To give someone a good shaking ; To give someone a good dressing down (*scolding*).

public. *See* BAN, CHOSE, CRI, GRAND.

publicité. *See* GRAND.

publier. *See* TOIT, TROMPE.

puce. Avoir la puce à l'oreille, To be very uneasy, To have grave misgivings.

Cela me met la puce à l'oreille, My suspicions are awakened, I see the red light, I smell a rat.

puiser. Puiser à la source *ou* aux sources, To go to the fountainhead. " You are the fount that makes small brooks to flow."—3 *King Henry VI* IV, 8.

puissance. Traiter de puissance à puissance, To treat on a footing of equality.

punir. Être puni par où l'on a péché, To be justly punished for one's crimes, To ask for it (*slang*).

pur. En pur don, As a free gift.

En pure perte, To no purpose, Uselessly.

La pure vérité, The unvarnished truth.

Un pur, A true blue, An out-and-outer.

See also OREILLER.

putois. *See* CRI, CRIER.

Q

quadrature. *See* CHERCHER.

qualité. *See* HOMME, SONNER.

quant à. Se mettre sur son quant-à-soi, To be stand-offish.

Tenir (*ou* Se tenir sur) (*ou* Rester sur) **son quant-à-moi** *ou* son quant-à-soi, To stand on one's dignity.

quarantaine. Mettre quelqu'un en quarantaine, To send someone to Coventry.

quarante. *See* MOQUER, SOUCIER.

quart. Avoir de bons et de mauvais quarts d'heure, To be of an uneven (*or* of a fitful) temper.

Faire passer à quelqu'un un mauvais quart d'heure, To give someone a bad time of it.

Le quart d'heure de Rabelais, The day (*or* The hour) of reckoning.

Les trois quarts du temps, Most of the time.

Passer un mauvais quart d'heure, To have a bad time of it.

Pour le quart d'heure, For the moment, For the time being.

See also DEVOIR, MOQUER, TIERS.

quartier. *See* ALARME, FABLE, QUATRE.

quatorze. *See* MIDI.

quatre. Cela ne vaut pas les quatre fers d'un chien, It's worth nothing at all, It's absolutely worthless.

Entre quatre yeux (*generally pronounced* Entre quatre-z-yeux), In close confidence.

Fendre (*ou* Couper) un cheveu en quatre *ou* (*a perversion of the correct phrase*) Couper les cheveux (*ou* les fils) en quatre, To split hairs. " The tongues of mocking wenches are as keen As is the razor's edge invisible, Cutting a smaller hair than may be seen ; Above the sense of sense."—*Love's Labour's Lost* V, 2.

Il demeure à quatre pas d'ici, He lives close by *or* a few yards away (*or* a stone's throw) from here.

Il faut le tenir à quatre, He must be restrained by force, He will have to be frog-marched.

J'écris ces quatre lignes pour vous dire . . ., I am writing these few lines to tell you . . .

Laissez-lui prendre un pied, il en prendra quatre, Give him an inch and he'll take an ell.

On vous cherche par les quatre chemins, They are looking for you all over the place.

Pour quatre jours qu'on a à vivre, For the little time one has to live.

Quatre hommes et un caporal, A handful (*small number*) of men (*military or police*).

Se mettre en quatre [quartiers] pour quelqu'un, To do anything (*or* To go through fire and water) for someone. Je me mettrais en quatre [quartiers] pour lui, pour son service, I would do anything for him, to help him, There is nothing I would not do to oblige him, to help him. Il s'est mis en quatre, He did his utmost to oblige.

Se tenir à quatre pour ne pas . . . To do one's utmost (*or* one's level best) not to . . . : Je me suis tenu à quatre pour ne pas rire, pour ne pas lui dire des vérités fort dures, It was all (*or* as much as) I could do to keep from laughing, from telling him some home truths.

Tomber les quatre fers en l'air, To fall over backwards, To go sprawling.

Un de ces [quatre] jours *ou* de ces quatre matins, One of these [fine] days.

See also ALLER, CLAIR, COIN, DÉFERRER, DÉGRINGOLER, DIABLE, DOIGT, DONNER, ÉPINGLE, FEU, MANGER, MARCHER, MENDIANT, MOQUER, MOT, PELER, PLANCHE, REPAS, SEMAINE, SIX, SOU, TRAVAILLER.

qu'en-dira-t-on. Le qu'en-dira-t-on, What people [may] say, What Mrs Grundy says : Mépriser le (*ou* Braver le) (*ou* Se moquer du) qu'en-dira-t-on, Not to care what people say.

quenouille. Tomber en quenouille, To fall to the distaff side (*i.e, the female branch of the family—said of an inheritance, of a kingdom*).

querelle. Une querelle d'Allemand, A trumped-up quarrel.

See also CHIEN, RAPPELER, VIDER.

question. C'est là la question, That is the question, There's the rub. " To be, or not to be,—that is the question . . . To sleep ! perchance to dream: ay, there's the rub."—*Hamlet* III, 1.

See also ABORDER, BEAU 3, CÔTÉ, DEMANDE, DÉPLACER, MÛRIR, ORDRE, PREMIER.

queue. À la queue gît le venin, The sting is in the tail. " Who knows not where a wasp doth wear his sting ? In his tail."—*The Taming of the Shrew* II, 1. " This body hath a tail More perilous than the head."—*Cymbeline* IV, 2.

Cela n'a ni queue ni tête, I (We) (One) cannot make head or tail of it.

Faire tête à queue, To spin round and face the other way *or* and face the way it came (*of a car*).

Il n'en reste pas la queue d'un, d'une, There is not one left.

S'en aller la queue entre les jambes, To go off with one's tail between one's legs.

Tenir la queue de la poêle, To be in charge, To run (*or* To boss) the show (*slang*).

Venir en queue, To bring up the rear.

See also BRIDER, ÉCORCHER, FINIR, HIVER, LEU, LOUP, TIRER.

qui. *See* FROTTER, MIEUX, PÉCHER, PLUS, SAUVER, SAVOIR, TEMPS, TENIR, TERME, TROUVER, VIVRE, VOULOIR.

quia. *See* À QUIA.

quille. *See* CHIEN.

quinze. Avoir ses jambes de quinze ans, To be still firm on one's pins (*although getting on in years*).

Avoir ses yeux de quinze ans, To have unimpaired eyesight.

N'avoir plus ses jambes de quinze ans, Not to be as young as one was.

quitte. Je l'en tiens quitte, I can do without his help.

Jouer [à] quitte ou double, To play double or quits ; To throw good money after bad.

See also BON 29.

quitter. Il n'est si bonne compagnie qui ne se quitte, The best of friends must part.

Je vous quitte la place (*fig.*), I give you best.

Ne pas quitter quelqu'un des yeux, Not to take one's eyes off someone, Not to let someone out of one's sight.

Quitter la vie, To depart this life (*die*).

See also AVRIL, DÉ, DROIT, PARTIE, PEAU.

quoi. À quoi bon ? What's the use *or* the good ? À quoi bon l'interroger ? What's the use (*or* the good) of asking him ?

Avoir de quoi, To be well off, To be a person of substance.

Il n'y a pas de quoi, [Pray] don't mention it.

See also DRAP, FOUETTER, FRIRE, MIRACLE, PENDRE, REMERCIER, RETOURNER, RIMER, RIRE, SAVOIR, TENIR, VANTER, VENIR.

quotidien. C'est son pain quotidien (*fig.*), It is meat and drink to him.

See also TRAIN.

R

rabâcher. *See* MÊME.

rabaisser. *See* CAQUET.

rabattre. Il faut bien en rabattre (*fig.*), That must be discounted, Allowance must be made for exaggeration.

J'en rabats beaucoup, He has gone down a good deal in my estimation.

Rabattre ses prétentions *ou* En rabattre, To climb down, To draw in one's horns.

See also CAQUET, COMPTER.

Rabelais. *See* QUART.

rabrouer. Rabrouer quelqu'un, To jump down someone's throat.

rac. *See* PAYER.

raccommoder. Se raccommoder avec quelqu'un, avec quelque chose, To become reconciled to (*or* with) someone, to something.

raccourcir. Raccourcir quelqu'un, To cut off someone's head. " The time hath been, Would you have been so brief with him, he would Have been so brief with you, to shorten you, For taking so the head, your whole head's length."—*King Richard II* III, 3.

See also BRAS.

raccrocher. Se raccrocher à quelqu'un, To fall back [up]on someone.

Se raccrocher à tout comme un homme qui se noie, To catch at a straw like a drowning man.

Se raccrocher [aux branches], To retrieve one's fortunes.

race. C'est un écrivain de race, He is a born writer.

See also CHASSER, TENIR.

racine. Couper le mal à sa racine, To strike at the root of the evil.

Jeter de profondes racines, To take deep root (*lit.* & *fig.*).

See also PISSENLIT.

raconter. En raconter [de belles], To draw the long bow, To tell some fine tales *or* some tall stories.

racornir. Un racorni, A back number (*person—slang*).

radis. N'avoir plus un radis, Not to have a bean *or* a copper, To be stony broke (*slang*).

rafle. Faire rafle, To sweep the board.

rafraîchir. Rafraîchir le sang, (*Lit.*) To cool the blood, To freshen one up (*said of a drink*) ; (*Fig.*) To cheer one up, To reassure one (*said of good news*).

rage. Faire rage, To rage, To be raging (*of a storm, a battle*) ; To storm (contre quelqu'un, against someone) ; To be all the rage (*of new thing*).

Faire rage des pieds de derrière, To go it hammer and tongs, To go all out (*slang*).

See also CHIEN.

raide. Ça, c'est un peu raide, That's a bit steep *or* stiff *or* (*slang*) a bit thick, That's coming it rather strong (*slang*).

See also BARRE, COUP 75, DANSER.

raidir. Se raidir, To harden oneself (contre = against) ; To pull oneself together.

raillerie. *See* ENTENDRE, PASSER, TOURNER.

raisin. *See* FIGUE, VERT.

raison. À plus forte raison *ou* Raison de plus, All the more [reason].

Avoir des raisons avec quelqu'un, To have words with someone.

C'est une raison comme une autre, It is a good enough reason.

Chercher des raisons à quelqu'un, To pick a quarrel with someone.

Être à l'âge de raison, To have arrived at years of discretion.

Faire raison à quelqu'un, To answer someone's toast.

Pour raison à (*ou* de) moi connue, For reasons best known to myself. " O, for two special reasons ; Which may to you, perhaps, seem much unsinew'd, But yet to me they are strong." — *Hamlet* IV, 7.

Se faire raison [à] soi-même, To take the law into one's own hands.

Se faire une raison, To make the best of a bad job *or* of it.

Tirer raison d'une injure, To get satisfaction for an insult.

See also BOUTEILLE, CONVENANCE, DÉMÉNAGER, ENTENDRE, FIN, RIME, TORT.

raisonner. Ne raisonnez pas tant, Don't be so argumentative.

Raisonner comme une pantoufle, To talk through one's hat (*slang*).

See also AIGUILLE, PERTE.

rajeunir. Cela ne nous rajeunit pas, That doesn't make us out any younger (*said when a long past event is narrated*).

ramasser. Ramasser quelqu'un, To tell someone some home truths, To tell (*or* To tick) someone off (*slang*).

Ramasser ses forces, To muster all one's strength.

Ramasser une bûche *ou* une pelle, To come a cropper, To have a spill.

See also GANT, TAPE.

rameau. *See* OLIVIER.

ramener. Ramener la conversation sur un sujet, To bring the conversation back to a subject, To hark back to a subject.

Ramener quelqu'un, To pacify someone, To calm someone down ; To bring someone back to reason.

ramer. Il s'y entend comme à ramer des choux, He hasn't the remotest idea of how it should be done.

ramollir. Se ramollir, To be getting soft-witted.

rampe. Ce dialogue, Cette pièce, ne passe pas la rampe, This dialogue, This play, fails to get across *or* to get over (*i.e., the footlights*) (*slang*).

Être sous les feux de la rampe, To be in the limelight.

See also LÂCHER.

rancart. Être au rancart (*fig.*), To be on the shelf.

Mettre au rancart, To cast aside, To put on the shelf.

rancune. Sans (*ou* Point de) rancune, Let bygones be bygones.

See also GARDER, VIEUX.

rang. Être sur les rangs, To be a candidate *or, of several,* To be candidates, To be in the field.

Se mettre en rang d'oignon, To form up in [a] line.

Se mettre sur les rangs, To enter the lists, To put in [for a post].

Sortir du rang, To rise from the ranks (*Military*) ; To get out of the ruck *or* the rut.

Tenir son rang, To keep one's position (*in relation to other persons*).

ranger. Ranger, To tidy, To set to rights.

Se ranger, To steady down, To settle down (*after having sown one's wild oats*).

Se ranger autour du feu, autour d'une table, To sit round the fire, round a table.

Se ranger du côté (*ou* du parti) (*ou* Se ranger sous la bannière) de quelqu'un, To take sides (*or* To side) with someone.

See also PAVILLON.

ranimer. Ranimer (*fig.*), To put fresh heart (*or* life) into, To pull round, To bring to.

Se ranimer, To come to life again, To come round, To look up (*improve*).

rapide. Être rapide comme un éclair *ou* comme l'éclair, To be [as] quick (*or* [as] swift) as lightning. " Be swift like lightning in the execution." —*King Richard II* I, 3.

Rapide comme la pensée, [As] swift as thought. " In motion of no less celerity Than that of thought."—*King Henry V* II, 4. " Have I, in my poor and old motion, the expedition of thought ? "—2 *King Henry IV* IV, 3. " Haste me to know't, that I, with wings as swift As meditation or the thoughts of love, May sweep to my revenge."—*Hamlet* I, 5.

rapin. Une plaisanterie (*ou* Une farce) de rapin, A student's prank *or* frolic (*good-humoured, fresh*).

rappel. *See* BATTRE.

rappeler. Rappeler une ancienne querelle, To rake up an old quarrel.

Se rappeler quelque chose, To recall something, To call something to mind, To bear something in mind.

rapport. Avoir de bons rapports avec quelqu'un, To be on good terms with someone.

Faire des rapports, To tell tales (*out of school*).

rapporter. Il n'en a rapporté que des coups, He got more kicks than halfpence [out of it].

Rapporter, To tell tales (*out of school*). " This carry-tale, dissentious Jealousy."— SHAKESPEARE, *Venus and Adonis*.

S'en rapporter à quelqu'un, To put one's faith in someone. Je m'en rapporte à vous *ou* à votre témoignage, I leave it to you ; I take your word for it.

rapprocher. Rapprocher les différents indices, To put two and two together.

Se rapprocher de quelqu'un, To become reconciled (*or* To make it up) with someone.

rare. Devenir (*ou* Se rendre) (*ou* Se faire) rare, To be [quite] a stranger, To be seldom seen.

En de rares occasions, Once in a while *or* in a blue moon.

rareté. Pour la rareté du fait, As a matter of curiosity, Out of curiosity.

ras. *See* TABLE.

raser. Raser les murs, To hug the wall ; To slip by unnoticed.

Raser quelqu'un (*fig.*), To bore someone.

See also BARBIER.

rassurer. Rassurez-vous sur ce point, Set your mind at rest on that point.

rat. Avoir des rats dans la tête, To have bats in the belfry *or* something wrong in the upper storey, To have a bee in one's bonnet *or* a screw (*or* a tile) loose.

Cette serrure a un rat, The spring of this lock doesn't work.

Être comme rat en paille *ou* comme un rat dans un fromage, To live (*or* To feed) at another's cost. " The Volsces have much corn ; take these rats thither To gnaw their garners." —*Coriolanus* I, 1. " Nor care I who doth feed upon my cost ; It yearns me not if men my garments wear." —*King Henry V* IV, 3.

Un rat d'église, A church mouse (*See* GUEUX) ; A regular church-goer ; A civilian church official.

Un rat d'hôtel, A hotel thief.

Un rat de bibliothèque, A bookworm (*person*).

Un rat de cave (*fig.*), A taper (*coiled*) ; An excise officer.

See also BON 1, NID.

rate. Dilater (*ou* Désopiler) (*ou* Épanouir) la rate, To make one shake (*or* roar) with laughter.

Ne pas se fouler la rate, To take things easy.

Se fouler la rate, To wear oneself out (*or* To kill oneself) with work, To wear one's fingers to the bone.

râtelier. Remettre les armes au râtelier (*fig.*), To leave the service, To sheathe the sword. " Our bruised arms hung up for monuments ; . . . Grim-visag'd war hath smooth'd his wrinkled front."— *King Richard III* I, 1. " His glittering arms he will commend to rust, His barbed steeds to stables." —*King Richard II* III, 3.

See also FOIN, MANGER.

rattraper. *See* TEMPS, TOURNANT.

ravaler. *See* PAROLE.

rave. *See* CHOU.

ravir. Être ravi au troisième (*ou* au septième) ciel, To be in the seventh heaven [of delight]. " O love, be moderate, allay thy ecstasy, In measure rain thy joy, scant this excess ; I feel too much thy blessing ; make it less, For fear I surfeit ! "—*The Merchant of Venice* III, 2. *Quotation also under* ANGE.

Être ravi en extase, To be lost in admiration.

raviver. Raviver une plaie, To reopen an old sore. " See, see ! dead Henry's wounds Open their congeal'd mouths and bleed afresh ! "— *King Richard III* I, 2.

rayer. Rayez cela de vos papiers *ou* de vos tablettes, You can rule (*or* cut) that out, You can dismiss that from your mind, Get that out of your mind. " And therefore will he wipe his tables clean, And keep no tell-tale to his memory."—2 *King Henry IV* IV, 1. " Yea, from the table of my memory I'll wipe away all trivial fond records."—*Hamlet* I, 5.

rayon. Ce n'est pas de mon rayon, That is not in my line *or* province.

réalité. S'en tenir aux réalités, To stick to facts.

rebattre. Être rebattu de quelque chose *ou* Avoir les oreilles [battues et] rebattues de quelque chose, To be sick [and tired] of hearing [about] something.

Rebattre les oreilles à quelqu'un de quelque chose, To din something into someone's ears.

rebiffer. Faire rebiffer quelqu'un, To set (*or* To put) (*or* To get) someone's back up.

Se rebiffer, To get one's back up.

Se rebiffer contre . . ., To be up in arms against (*a person, something*).

récent. J'en ai la mémoire récente, It is fresh in my mind.

recette. Faire recette, To be a draw (*attraction*).

Les recettes du métier, The tricks of the trade.

recevoir. *See* CHIEN, COMPTE, COUP 55, CRÉATEUR, DOIGT, GALOP, PAQUET, POMME, TAPE.

réchauffer. Réchauffer un serpent dans son sein, To warm (*or* To cherish) a serpent (*or* a snake) in one's breast *or* bosom. " I fear me you but warm the starved snake, Who, cherish'd in your breasts, will sting your hearts."—2 *King Henry VI* III, 1.

Voilà qui vous réchauffera, That will warm the cockles of your heart.

recherche. Des recherches de cruauté, The refinement of cruelty.

See also INTÉRÊT.

réciter. *See* MÊME.

réclame. Faire de la réclame, To puff one's goods.

récolter. *See* SEMER.

recommander. *See* PRÔNE, SAINT.

recommencer. C'est toujours à recommencer, There's no end to it ; One has to begin all over again.

Le voilà qui recommence, He is at it again.

Recommencer de plus belle, To begin again with renewed vigour.

Recommencer sur nouveaux frais, To begin again at the beginning.

réconciliation. *See* NORMAND.

réconcilier. Se réconcilier, To make it up, To bury the hatchet, To kiss and be friends.

Se réconcilier avec soi-même, To make peace with one's conscience.

reconnaître. Je vous reconnais là, That is just like you, That is you all over.

Ne plus s'y reconnaître, To lose one's bearings, To be all at sea.

Se reconnaître (*fig.*), To collect one's thoughts, To get one's bearings, To take it in ; To pull oneself together.

recourir. *See* FORT, GRAND.

recueillir. *See* ESPRIT.

reculer. Ne reculer devant rien, To stick at nothing.

Reculer pour mieux sauter, To stoop to conquer ; To put off the evil day.

See also SEMELLE.

reculons. *See* ÉCREVISSE.

redire. *See* TROUVER.

redonner. La pluie redonne de plus belle, The rain is coming on again worse than ever, It is raining faster than ever.

Le soleil redonne de plus belle, The sun is shining hotter (*or* is blazing with more vigour) than ever.

redorer. Redorer son blason, To restore the fortunes of his house (*said of an impecunious man of rank marrying a rich commoner*).

redresse. Être à la redresse, To be cute *or* knowing *or* (*slang*) up to snuff.

réduire. *See* ABOI.

refaire. On ne se refait pas, One can't alter one's nature. *Quotations under* PEAU.

Si c'était à refaire, If I had to do it again.

réfléchir. Donner à réfléchir à quelqu'un, To give someone food for thought, To set someone thinking, To make someone think twice.

Réfléchissez-y, Think it over.

Tout bien réfléchi, All things considered, After due consideration.

réflexion. À la réflexion *ou* Réflexion faite, On thinking it over, On second thoughts.

See also MATIÈRE.

réformer. Réformer son train, To reduce one's style of living.

Se réformer, To reform, To mend one's ways, To turn over a new leaf.

refrain. C'est le refrain de la ballade, It is the same old story.

C'est son refrain, He is always harping on the same (*or* on one) string.

refrogner (se). Se refrogner [le visage], To look black, To knit one's brows.

refus. Cela n'est pas de refus, I (We) can't say no to that.

Je n'accepte pas de refus, I won't take no for an answer. " He's fortified against any denial."—*Twelfth Night* I, 5.

refuser. Refuser du monde, To turn people away (*from theatre, etc.*).

Refuser [tout] net, To refuse point blank.

Se refuser à l'évidence, To shut one's eyes to the evidence.

Se refuser à quelque chose, To set one's face against something.

regagner. *See* TEMPS, TERRAIN.

regain. Un regain de vie, A new lease of life.

régaler. Se régaler, To do oneself well, To have a good tuck-in.

regard. *See* CARESSER, DESSOUS, MESURER, PARLANT, SAISIR, TROMPER.

regarder. Je ne veux pas seulement le regarder, I cannot bear the sight of him. *Quotation under* PEINTURE.

Regarder en coulisse, To cast sidelong glances.

Regarder quelqu'un en face *ou* dans les yeux *ou* dans le blanc des yeux *ou* entre les [deux] yeux, To look someone [full] in the face *or* squarely in the eye, To stand up to someone. " I would out-stare the sternest eyes that look."—*The Merchant of Venice* II, 1.

Se faire regarder, To attract attention, To make oneself conspicuous.

Vous ne m'avez (*ou* Tu ne m'as) pas regardé, What do you take me for ? Do you see any green in my eye ?

See also BON 63, 64, BRIDE, CHIEN, DESSOUS, DESSUS, FOIS, HAUT, MAUVAIS, NEZ, NOMBRIL, PRÈS, PRISME, TRAVERS, VENT.

regimber. Regimber [sous l'éperon *ou* sous l'aiguillon], To kick over the traces (*fig.*).

régime. *See* PLAISIR, VIVRE.

registre. Cet homme-là tient registre de tout (*fig.*), That man misses nothing (*observes and remembers everything*). " He misses not much."—*The Tempest* II, 1.

règle. Dans toutes les règles, According to all the rules ; Sheer (*stupidity, folly, knavery, etc.*).

Mettre quelque chose en règle, To put something in order *or* to rights.

See also COMPAS, EXCEPTION, JOUER.

régler. Avoir un compte à régler avec quelqu'un, To have a bone to pick with someone.

C'est réglé [comme du papier à musique], [As] sure as fate.

Être réglé comme une horloge *ou* comme un (*ou* du) papier à musique, To be [as] regular as clockwork.

"To carve out dials quaintly, point by point, Thereby to see the minutes how they run,— . . . then to divide the times,—So many hours must I tend my flock; So many hours must I take my rest; So many hours must I contemplate; So many hours must I sport myself."—3 *King Henry VI* II, 5.

Régler de vieux comptes, To pay off old scores.

Régler son compte à quelqu'un, To put paid to someone's account (*fig.*), To be even with someone, To settle someone's hash, To cook someone's goose for him.

régner. *See* MAÎTRE.

regrettable. C'est d'autant plus regrettable, The more's the pity.

regretter. Regretter les oignons d'Égypte, To sigh for the flesh-pots of Egypt (*Exodus* xvi, 3).

reins. Avoir les reins solides, To be a sturdy fellow; To have a long purse.

See also CASSER, CEINDRE, ÉPÉE, SOUPLE.

rejeter. *See* CHAMEAU.

réjouir. *See* BIENHEUREUX.

relever. Je ne m'en relèverais pas la nuit, That won't keep me awake. *Quotations under* DORMIR.

See also GANT.

reluire. *See* OR.

rembourrer. Un matelas, un coussin, rembourré de noyaux de pêches (*fig.*), A mattress, a cushion, stuffed with straw *or* with a donkey's breakfast (*knobbly and hard*). "Weariness Can snore upon the flint, when restive sloth Finds the down pillow hard."—*Cymbeline* III, 6.

remède. Un remède de cheval *ou* Un remède comme pour un cheval *ou* Un remède héroïque, A drastic remedy, A kill-or-cure remedy.

See also GRAND.

remercier. Il n'y a pas de quoi me remercier, There is no occasion to thank me, No thanks are due to me.

remettre. Je m'en remets à vous, I leave it to you.

La partie est remise *ou* C'est partie remise, We'll put it off till another time.

Remettre quelqu'un au pas, To recall someone to the paths of duty, To bring someone up with a round turn.

Se remettre, To be oneself again, To pull oneself together.

See also CALENDES, CŒUR, ENCLUME, FOURREAU, LENDEMAIN, RÂTELIER, SORT.

remiser. Remiser quelqu'un, To take someone down a peg or two.

remonter. *See* ACTION, BÊTE, DÉLUGE, EAU.

remontrance. Faire à quelqu'un une remontrance [toute] paternelle, To talk to someone like a Dutch uncle.

remontrer. *See* GROS-JEAN.

remordre. Y remordre, To try [, try, try] again.

remorque. Se mettre à la remorque de quelqu'un, To be taken in tow by someone.

remporter. Remporter la palme, To bear the palm. "Ye gods, it doth amaze me, A man of such a feeble temper should So get the start of the majestic world, And bear the palm alone."—*Julius Caesar* I, 2.

See also VESTE.

remuer. Ne remuer ni pied ni patte, Not to move hand or foot.

Remuer beaucoup d'argent, To handle a lot of money.

Remuer ciel et terre, To move heaven and earth, To leave no stone unturned.

Remuer l'argent à la pelle, To be rolling in money.

Votre nez remue, You're fibbing.

See also BÛCHE, MORT, PASSÉ.

renaître. Renaître de ses cendres, To rise again from its ashes (*of a destroyed town*).

renard. C'est un fin renard, He's a sly dog *or* fox.

See also PEAU.

rencontrer. *See* BEAU 18.

rendre. Rendre à quelqu'un sa parole, To release someone from his promise.

Rendre la pareille (*ou* le change) à quelqu'un, To give someone tit for tat, To pay someone back in his own coin, To pay someone out, To hit someone back.

See also BIEN, BON 26, CAPITULER, CAUTION, CÉSAR, CHARGE, CHAUD, CORDE, COUP 56, DISCRÉTION, ESPRIT, GORGE, JUSTICE, MONNAIE, POINT, PRÊTER, RARE, RIDICULE, SOUPLE, TABLIER.

renfort. Pour renfort de potage, As a crowning misfortune, To make matters worse.

renfrogner (se). Se renfrogner [le visage], To look black, To knit one's brows.

rengaine. *See* MÊME.

rengainer. Rengainer son compliment, To say no more, To leave it at that.

renommée. Apprendre quelque chose par la voix de la renommée, To have something on common report, To learn (*or* To know) something by hearsay.

See also BON 21.

renoncer. Y renoncer, To throw up the sponge, To throw in one's hand *or* one's cards.

renseignement. *See* ALLER, PRIVÉ.

renter. Être bien renté, To be well-off *or* well-to-do.

rentrer. Faire rentrer quelqu'un sous terre, To send someone away with a flea in his ear.

Les jambes me rentrent dans le corps, I am too tired to stand, I am dog-tired.

Rentrer dans le bon chemin, To mend one's ways, To turn over a new leaf.

Rentrer dans le néant, To lapse into obscurity.

Rentrer dans sa coquille (*fig.*), To retire into one's shell.

Rentrer en danse, To return to the fray.

Rentrer en soi[-même], To retire into oneself, To search one's own heart. " Go to your bosom; Knock there; and ask your heart what it doth know That's like my brother's fault."—*Measure for Measure* II, 2.

Rentrer les cornes, To draw in one's horns.

See also CORDE, FENÊTRE, SENS, SOURIS.

renverser. Avoir la physionomie renversée, To look very much upset.

C'est le monde renversé, The like was never seen.

Renverser les rôles, To turn the tables on someone.

See also MARMITE.

renvoyer. Être renvoyé de Caïphe à Pilate, To be driven from pillar to post.

Renvoyer quelqu'un bien loin, To send someone about his business *or* someone packing.

See also BALLE, CALENDES, DOS, MOULIN.

repaître. *See* CREUX.

répandre. Être fort répandu dans le monde, To go about a good deal, To move in society circles.

See also MAIN, TRAÎNÉE.

réparer. *See* TEMPS.

repas. Faire ses quatre repas, To live well.

See also BREBIS, HONNEUR, SUCCINCT, TRISTE.

repasser. Repasser la lime sur un ouvrage (*fig.*), To touch up a piece of work.

répéter. Cela se répète souvent, That is continually happening.

See also TUER.

repli. *See* PLI.

replier. Se replier sur soi-même, To fall back upon one's own thoughts.

réplique. Se donner la réplique, To engage in a skirmish of wits with each other.

répondre. Je vous en réponds, I assure you, I can tell you, Take my word for it, I'll be bound, And no mistake, You bet !

Répondre à ses visées, To suit one's book. " This weaves itself perforce into my business."—*King Lear* II, 1.

See also ABBÉ, NORMAND, PIROUETTE, TAC, TÊTE.

réponse. *See* BERGER, COUPER, DEMANDE, NORMAND, TAPER.

repos. Soyez en repos sur mes affaires, Don't worry your head about my affairs.

reposer. À tête reposée, At leisure, After thinking it over. Laissez-moi y songer à tête reposée, Give me time to think it over.

N'avoir pas où reposer sa tête, To have nowhere to lay one's head, To be down and out.

Se reposer sur ses lauriers, To rest on one's laurels.

reprendre. On ne m'y reprendra plus, You won't catch me at it again.

Reprendre sous œuvre un projet, To resume a project, but on different lines.

Se reprendre, To pull oneself together, To collect one's thoughts.

See also COLLIER, DESSUS, ESPRIT, HAUT, POIL.

réprimander. Réprimander quelqu'un pour sa négligence, To take someone to task for his negligence.

reprise. À différentes reprises, At various times, Off and on.

reproche. Un reproche détourné *ou* Un reproche indirect, An innuendo.

reprocher. Reprocher à quelqu'un sa négligence, To take someone to task for his negligence.

réprouver. Avoir un visage de réprouvé, To have an evil (*or* a sinister) face *or* a gallows look.

réputer. *See* INTENTION.

résistance. *See* BOUT, PIÈCE, VAINCRE.

respect. Sauf (*ou* Avec) le respect que je vous dois *ou* Parlant avec respect *ou* Sauf [votre] respect, With [all] due respect (*or* deference) to you. " Saving your worship's reverence."—*The Merchant of Venice* II, 2. " No, my lord, my humble duty remembered, I will not be your suitor."—2 *King Henry IV* II, 1.

respirer. Respirer la santé, To look the picture of health.

ressaisir. Se ressaisir, To regain one's self-control, To pull oneself together.

ressembler. Cela ne vous ressemble pas, It's not a bit like you (*to do such or such a thing*).

On se ressemble de plus loin, There is a strong resemblance between them.

Qui se ressemble s'assemble, Birds of a feather flock together.

See also ÂNE, ÉCORCHER, GAGEURE, GOUTTE, JOUR, RIEN, TROMPER.

ressentiment. *See* CONSERVER, GARDER.

ressort. Ce n'est pas de mon ressort, That is not in my line *or* province.

Faire jouer tous les ressorts, To use every means in one's power, To leave no stone unturned.

reste. Être en reste, To be in arrears (de tant = by so much) ; To be behindhand (*e.g.*, de générosité = in generosity).

Jouer son reste, To play one's last stake.

Jouir de son reste, To make the most of what is left to one.

Ne pas demander son reste, To have had enough of it, Not to wait for any[thing] more.

See also DEMEURER, DEVINER, LIMON.

rester. J'y suis, j'y reste, Here I am and here I stick, Possession is nine points of the law. *Quotation under* POSSESSION.

Rester au port d'armes, To proceed no further (*in a matter*).

Rester en plan, To be left in the lurch.

Rester sur la place *ou* sur le carreau, To be killed on the spot, To be left dead on the ground.

Rester sur le cœur, To rankle [in the mind] (*of a grievance*).

Restons-en là, Let us leave it at that.

See also APPÉTIT, BON 65, CAPOT, CARTON, CHAMP, HÂTER, NOTE, PLEURER, QUANT À, QUEUE, SELLE, SOUCHE.

retarder. Il retarde [sur son temps], He is behind the times, He is a back number (*slang*).

retenir. Je vous retiens, I'll be even with you.

retirer. Retirer sa parole, To go back on one's word.

See also BON 66, ENJEU, TENTE.

retomber. Retomber sur ses pieds *ou* Retomber [comme un chat] sur ses pattes, To fall on one's feet.

See also CRACHER.

retordre. *See* FIL.

retors. C'est un [homme] retors, He is a deep customer.

retour. Avoir l'esprit de retour, To hope to return home (*to one's own country*), To hope to go back to Blighty (*army slang*). " Every tedious stride I make Will but remember me what a deal of world I wander from the jewels that I love."—*King Richard II* I, 3. " And sigh'd my English breath in foreign clouds, Eating the bitter bread of banishment." — *King Richard II* III, 1. " There is no world without Verona's walls, But purgatory, torture, hell itself. Hence-banished is banish'd from the world, And world's exile is death."—*Romeo and Juliet* III, 3. *See also 1st quotation under* PLEURER de joie.

Être perdu sans retour, To be past praying for.

Être sur le retour, To be on the decline ; To be getting on in years. *Quotation under* PRENDRE de l'âge.

Être sur son retour, To be on the point of returning ; To be on the decline ; To be getting on in years.

Faire un retour sur soi-même, To bring oneself to book.

Retour à la terre, Back to the land (*as a slogan*).

Sans esprit de retour, Never to return, For good [and all]. " The sly-slow hours shall not determinate The dateless limit of thy dear exile ; The hopeless word of ' never to return ' Breathe I against thee."—*King Richard II* I, 3.

Sans retour, For ever, For good [and all].

See also BÂTON, BEAU 1, CHEVAL, PAYER.

retourner. De quoi retourne-t-il ? (*fig.*) What is it all about ? What's up ?

On ne sait jamais avec lui de quelle carte il retourne, You never know where you are with him.

Retourner en arrière, To beat a retreat (*abandon an undertaking*), To turn back.

Retourner la situation, To turn the tables.

Retourner quelqu'un, To make someone change his mind; To upset someone, To give someone a turn.

See also BEAU 13, CHARGE, HONTE, POIGNARD, SAVOIR, VENIR.

retracer. Tout le retrace à mes yeux, Everything reminds (*or* serves to remind) me of it.

rétracter. Se rétracter, To retract, To eat one's words.

retraite. *See* BATTRE.

retranchement. Être acculé dans ses derniers retranchements, To be fighting with one's back to the wall.

Forcer quelqu'un dans ses [derniers] retranchements, To leave someone without a leg to stand on.

retrouver. Comme on se retrouve ! How small the world is !

Je ne puis m'y retrouver, I cannot make it out.

See also PERDRE, TEMPS, VACHE.

rets. Prendre quelqu'un dans ses rets, To catch someone in one's toils, To ensnare someone. "The net That shall enmesh them all."—*Othello* II, 3.

réussir. *See* BON 35.

revanche. En revanche, In return, To make up for it.

See also CHARGE.

rêve. *See* BEAU 10.

réveil. Avoir un fâcheux réveil, To have a rude awakening.

réveiller. *See* CHAT, PAIN.

revendre. Avoir de quelque chose à revendre, To have enough and to spare of something.

revenir. Cela revient au même, It comes to the same thing, It's all the same, It's all one, It's as broad as it's long.

Je n'en reviens pas, I am lost in astonishment, I can't get over it, That beats me.

Revenir à soi (*fig.*), To recover one's self-possession.

Revenir de ses erreurs, To mend one's ways, To turn over a new leaf.

Revenir sur le compte de quelqu'un, To change one's opinion about someone.

Revenir sur un sujet, To hark back to a subject.

Y revenir, To go back on it ; To cut and come again.

See also AMOUR, CHARGE, CHASSER, EAU, GRAND, HONTE, MONDE, MOUTON, PASSÉ, TEXTE.

rêver. Rêver tout éveillé *ou* Rêver les yeux ouverts *ou* Rêver creux, To have day-dreams, To day-dream.

See also PLAIE.

révérence. Tirer sa révérence à quelqu'un, To make one's bow to someone, To bow oneself out. (*Fig.*) Je vous tire ma révérence, ne comptez pas sur moi, I wish you good day (*or* I'm through) do not count on me.

rêverie. Être plongé dans de vagues rêveries, To be in a brown study, To be wool-gathering.

revers. Le revers de la médaille, The reverse of the medal, The dark side of the picture, The seamy side.

Toute (*ou* Chaque) médaille a son revers, No rose without a thorn.

revêtir. Revêtir un mensonge de belles couleurs, To colour a lie with a smooth pretence, To gloze over (*or* To gloss over) (*or* To explain away) a lie. "Your painted gloss."—*King Henry VIII* V, 2.

révolu. Quand le temps sera révolu, In the fulness of time.

révoquer. *See* DOUTE.

revue. Je suis de la revue ! Just my (*bad*) luck !

rhubarbe. *See* PASSER.

rhume. Prendre quelque chose pour son rhume, To get hauled over the coals.

ric. *See* PAYER.

riche. Le mauvais riche, Dives.

Un mauvais riche, An uncharitable rich man.

See also DONNER, PRÊTER.

richesse. *See* CONTENTEMENT, EMBARRAS.

ricochet. Par ricochet (*fig.*), Indirectly, In a roundabout way.

rideau. C'est une chose sur laquelle il faut tirer le rideau, It is a thing over which a veil should be drawn, It is a skeleton in the cupboard.

ridicule. Donner (*ou* Tomber) dans le ridicule *ou* Se rendre ridicule, To make oneself ridiculous, To make a fool of oneself.

Donner (*ou* Prêter) des ridicules à quelqu'un, To poke fun (*or* To gird) at someone. "Men of all sorts take a pride to gird at me :

the brain of this foolish-compounded clay, man, is not able to invent anything that tends to laughter, more than I invent or is invented on me."—2 *King Henry IV* I, 2.

Tourner quelqu'un en ridicule, To hold someone up to ridicule.

See also COMBLE.

rien. Cela ne ressemble à rien, It's like nothing on earth ; There is no sense in that.

Comme si de rien n'était, As if nothing had happened.

Il n'en est rien, Nothing of the kind.

N'être pour rien dans une affaire, To have no hand in a matter.

Ne savoir rien de rien, To know nothing whatever *or* absolutely nothing.

On ne fait rien de rien, One cannot make bricks without straw (*Exodus* v, 7–19).

Qui ne risque rien n'a rien, Nothing venture, nothing have. " Things out of hope are compass'd oft with venturing."—SHAKESPEARE, *Venus and Adonis*. "What pleasure, sir, find we in life, to lock it From action and adventure ?"—*Cymbeline* IV, 4.

Rien n'y fit, It was all of no use, Nothing availed.

Se faire une montagne (*ou* un monstre) d'un rien, To make a mountain out of a molehill.

Un rien qui vaille *ou* Un rien du tout, A man of no account, A nobody.

See also BALAI, BRUIT, CHAMP, CONNAÎTRE, COURIR, COÛTER, DENT, DEVENIR, DEVINER, DIABLE, DIRE, DONNER, DROIT, ENTENDRE, FRIRE, GÂTER, JEU, JEUNE, JURER, MOINS, MONDE, NÉGLIGER, NOUVEAU, OUBLIER, PARLER, PROPOS, PROPRE, PROUVER, RECULER, RIMER, SEMBLANT, TENIR, TERME, TRAIN, TROP, TROUVER, VENTRE, VOIR.

rieur. Avoir les rieurs de son côté *ou* Avoir les rieurs pour soi, To have the laugh on one's side.

riflard. Un riflard, A gamp, A brolly.

rigueur. À la rigueur, Rigorously, Strictly, To the letter ; If need be, At a pinch, If the worst comes to the worst.

Tenir rigueur à quelqu'un, To refuse to relent towards someone.

rime. Il n'y a ni rime ni raison à ce qu'il dit, There is neither rhyme nor reason in what he says.

Sans rime ni raison, Without rhyme or reason, For no earthly reason.

rimer. À quoi cela rime-t-il ? What sense is there in that ? What can you make of that ?

Cela ne rime à rien, There is no sense in that.

Ces deux choses ne riment pas ensemble, These two things do not go together *or* have no connexion with each other.

rincer. Être rincé, To be drenched *or* wet through *or* wet to the skin. *Quotations under* MOUILLER.

Il est rincé, He has lost all, He hasn't got a bean left (*slang*).

Se rincer l'œil, To have a good look, To feast one's eyes (avec = on).

Se rincer la dalle, To wet one's whistle.

riposter. *See* TAC.

rire. Avoir le mot pour rire, To be ever ready with a joke, To be full of fun (*of a person*).

Donner (*ou* Prêter) à rire, To make oneself a laughing-stock, To make oneself ridiculous ; To give occasion (*or* To afford food) for laughter. Cela ne donne (*ou* ne prête) pas à rire, That is no laughing matter.

Et de rire, Laugh [, please] (*over what I have just told you*).

Il a ri [jusqu']aux larmes, He laughed till he cried. " More merry tears The passion of loud laughter never shed." — *A Midsummer Night's Dream* V, 1.

Il n'y a pas de quoi rire, It is no laughing matter.

La fortune (*ou* Tout) lui rit *ou* Tout rit à ses désirs, Fortune (*or* Everything) smiles on him, Everything good comes his way. " Fortune is merry, And in this mood will give us anything."—*Julius Caesar* III, 2.

Partir d'un [grand] éclat de rire, To burst out laughing.

Rira bien qui rira le dernier, He laughs best who laughs last. " They laugh that win."—*Othello* IV, 1.

Rire à gorge déployée, To roar with laughter. " I will laugh like a hyen."—*As You Like It* IV, 1.

Rire à ventre déboutonné, To laugh immoderately, To heave with laughter.

Rire aux anges, To wear an ecstatic smile ; To laugh to oneself (*without apparent cause*) ; To smile sweetly in its sleep (*of a baby*).

Rire de bon cœur, To laugh heartily.

Rire du bout des lèvres *ou* du bout des dents *ou* Ne rire que du bout des lèvres *ou* des dents, To give a forced laugh. " And some that smile have in their hearts, I fear, Millions of mischief." — *Julius Caesar* IV, 1. " Why, I can smile, and murder whiles I smile."—3 *King Henry VI* III, 2.

Rire jaune, To give a sickly smile. " Seldom he smiles ; and smiles in such a sort As if he mock'd himself, and scorn'd his spirit That could be mov'd to smile at anything."—*Julius Caesar* I, 2.

Rire sous cape *ou* Rire dans sa barbe *ou* Rire en dedans, To laugh in one's sleeve, To chuckle, To snigger.

Tel qui rit vendredi, dimanche pleurera *ou* Tel rit le matin qui le soir pleurera, Laugh on Friday, cry on Sunday, Laughter is akin to tears. " Where joy most revels grief doth most lament ; Grief joys, joy grieves, on slender accident."—*Hamlet* III, 2.

Vous voulez rire, You're joking, aren't you ? You are not serious [, are you] ?

See also CHATOUILLER, CÔTE, CREVER, FOU, HOMÉRIQUE, NEZ, PLEURER, TORDRE, TRAIN.

Ris. *See* JEU.

risquer. *See* COUP 57, PAQUET, RIEN, TOUT.

rivalité. *See* CLOCHER.

river. River à quelqu'un son clou, To give someone a clincher, To leave someone without a leg to stand on, To score off someone.

rivière. Les petits ruisseaux font les grandes rivières, Many a little (*or* Many a pickle) makes a mickle, Many mickles make a muckle.

See also EAU, HAUT.

robe. *See* TAILLER.

Robin. *See* VIVRE.

robinet. C'est un robinet d'eau tiède, He is as dull as ditch-water.

Roch. *See* CHIEN.

roche. C'est un homme de la vieille roche, He is a man of the good old stock *or* of the good old school. " The world is grown so bad, That wrens may prey where eagles dare not perch : Since every Jack became a gentleman, There's many a gentle person made a Jack."—*King Richard III* I, 3.

La roche Tarpéienne est près du Capitole, Downfall sometimes follows closely on the heels of triumph. " Bear him to the rock Tarpeian, and from thence Into destruction cast him."—*Coriolanus* III, 1. " Then, in a moment, see How soon this mightiness meets misery."—*King Henry VIII Prologue.* " O mighty Caesar ! dost thou lie so low ? Are all thy conquests, glories, triumphs, spoils, Shrunk to this little measure ?"—*Julius Caesar* III, 1. " But yesterday the word of Caesar might Have stood against the world: now lies he there, And none so poor to do him reverence."—*Julius Caesar* III, 2.

See also ANGUILLE, CLAIR, CŒUR.

rocher. *See* PARLER.

Roger-Bontemps. Un Roger-Bontemps, A happy-go-lucky fellow, A jovial soul.

rogne. Être en rogne, To be cross *or* (*slang*) ratty.

rogner. Rogner les ailes à quelqu'un, To clip someone's wings.

Rogner les ongles à quelqu'un [de bien près], To cut (*or* To pare) someone's claws.

See also TAILLER.

roi. C'est un plaisir de roi, It is a pleasure fit for a king.

See also AVEUGLE, COUR, COUSIN, DROIT, ÉCHEC, MORCEAU.

rôle. *See* CHAPERON, RENVERSER, SECONDAIRE.

rôlet. Ceci n'est pas sur mon rôlet, This is not part of my duty.

Romain. C'est un Romain, He is a man of Roman honesty and patriotism. " One in whom The ancient Roman honour more appears Than any that draws breath in Italy."—*The Merchant of Venice* III, 2.

C'est un travail de Romain, It is a huge undertaking.

roman. Un roman à deux sous, A penny dreadful.

Un roman à tiroirs, An episodic novel.

Un roman de cape et d'épée, A novel of the age of chivalry.

Un roman vécu, A novel true to life *or* of real life.

Rome. J'irai le dire à Rome, I shall be very much surprised, I'll eat my hat (*slang*) (*if that happens*).

See also CHEMIN.

rompre. Rompre en visière à quelqu'un (*fig.*), To come to open hostilities with someone.

Rompre la cervelle à quelqu'un, To give someone a headache, To make someone tired (*with importunities*).

Rompre la tête (*ou* les oreilles) à quelqu'un, To make a deafening noise, To split someone's ear-drums. *Quotation under* DÉCHIRER.

Rompre la tête à quelqu'un de, avec, quelque chose, To drive someone crazy about (*or* over), with, something.

Rompre les chiens, To change the subject.

Se rompre la tête à quelque chose, pour trouver un expédient, To cudgel one's brains over something, to find an expedient.

See also APPLAUDIR, BÂTON, BRAS, BRUIT, GLACE, GOURMETTE, JAMBE, LANCE, OS, PAILLE, PLIER, TYMPAN.

rondement. *See* ALLER, MENER.

ronger. Ronger son frein, To be ready to burst with impatience, with annoyance, with anger.

Se ronger [le cœur] de chagrin, d'impatience, To eat one's heart out (*or* To pine away) from vexation, from impatience.

Se ronger les ongles, To burn with impatience.

Se ronger les poings, To fume with rage.

See also OS.

rongeur. *See* VER.

ronron. Le ronron tragique, Dull pompous oratory.

rose. Tout n'est pas rose dans la vie, Life is not all beer and skittles. " O, how full of briars is this working day world! "—*As You Like It* I, 3. " The web of our life is of a mingled yarn, good and ill together."—*All's Well That Ends Well* IV, 3. " What's yet in this That bears the name of life? Yet in this life Lie hid more thousand deaths: yet death we fear, That makes these odds all even."—*Measure for Measure* III, 1.

See also AURORE, DÉCOUVRIR, ÉPINE, PARAÎTRE, VOIR.

roseau. C'est un roseau peint en fer, He is no pillar of strength, At heart he is a coward, no matter how consistently he plays the role of the strong, fearless man. " How many cowards, whose hearts are all as false As stairs of sand, wear yet upon their chins The beards of Hercules and frowning Mars ; Who, inward search'd, have livers white as milk !"—*The Merchant of Venice* III, 2.

C'est un roseau qui plie à tout vent, He is a reed shaken with the wind (*Matthew* xi, 7, *Luke* vii, 24).

S'appuyer sur un roseau (*fig.*), To lean on a broken reed. " What shalt thou expect, To be depender on a thing that leans ?"—*Cymbeline* I, 5.

rosée. *See* TENDRE.

rôt. *See* FUMÉE.

rôti. *See* ENDORMIR.

rôtir. *See* ALOUETTE, BALAI, BON 57.

roue. Être à la roue, To know the ropes *or* what's what.

Faire la roue, To show off. " He stalks up and down like a peacock."—*Troilus and Cressida* III, 3.

See also BÂTON, CINQUIÈME.

rouge. C'est comme le rouge pour les taureaux, It is like a red rag to a bull.

Devenir rouge comme une pivoine, To turn [as] red as a turkey-cock.

Être rouge comme un coq, To be [as] red as a turkey-cock.

Être rouge comme une écrevisse, To be [as] red as a lobster.

Rouge [au] soir et blanc [au] matin, c'est la journée du pèlerin, Evening red and morning grey Sets the traveller (*or* the pilgrim) on his way *or* Red at night is the shepherd's delight, Red in the morning is the shepherd's warning. "The weary sun hath made a golden set, And by the bright track of his fiery car Gives token of a goodly day to-morrow."—*King Richard III* V, 3. " How bloodily the sun begins to peer Above yon bosky hill ! . . . The southern wind . . . Foretells a tempest and a blustering day."—1 *King Henry IV* V, 1. " Like a red morn, that ever yet betoken'd Wreck to the seaman, tempest to the field, Sorrow to shepherds, woe unto the birds, Gusts and foul flaws to herdmen and to herds."—SHAKESPEARE, *Venus and Adonis*.

See also BOULET, LIARD, MÉCHANT, TALON.

rouleau. *See* BOUT.

rouler. L'argent roule dans ce pays, Money circulates freely in this country.

L'argent roule dans cette maison, They are not short of money in this house.

Rouler carrosse, To keep a carriage ; To live in great style.

Rouler quelqu'un, To beat (*or* To surpass) someone (*in a discussion*) ; To do (*or* To diddle) someone.

Rouler sa bosse, To knock about the world. " I rather would entreat thy company To see the wonders of the world abroad, Than, living dully sluggardiz'd at home, Wear out thy youth with shapeless idleness."—*Two Gentlemen of Verona* I, 1.

Tout roule là-dessus, Everything turns on that.

See also OR, PIERRE.

roulette. Cela va comme sur des roulettes, Things are going like clockwork.

rouspétance. Faire de la rouspétance, To kick over the traces.

rouspéter. Il n'a pas rouspété, He went like a lamb.

route. *See* FAUX.

routier. Un vieux routier, An old stager.

routine. Travail de routine, Routine (*or* Donkey) work.

royaume. *See* AVEUGLE.

Rubicon. Passer (*ou* Franchir) le Rubicon, To pass (*or* To cross) the Rubicon, To take the plunge *or* the step.

rubis. Faire rubis sur l'ongle, To drink supernaculum *or* to the last drop.

See also PAYER.

ruche. Fâcher une ruche (*fig.*), To stir up a hornets' nest, To bring a hornets' nest about one's ears. " If I be waspish, best beware my sting."—*The Taming of the Shrew* II, 1. " Seek not a scorpion's nest."—2 *King Henry VI* III, 2.

rude. *See* BOTTE, JOUTEUR, LAPIN, PARAÎTRE, PIROUETTER, SAIGNÉE.

rudesse. Traiter quelqu'un avec rudesse, To browbeat someone, To ride roughshod over someone.

rue. L'homme de la rue, The man in the street.

See also COURIR, DÉBAPTISER, PAVER, PIGNON, VIEUX.

ruine. N'être plus qu'une ruine, To be merely the (*or* but a) shadow of one's former self. " O ruin'd piece of nature!"—*King Lear* IV, 6. " This wither'd brawn."—*Troilus and Cressida* I, 3. " The ruin speaks that sometime It was a worthy building."—*Cymbeline* IV, 2.

See also COURIR, DOIGT, FERME.

ruiner. Se ruiner en promesses, To make reckless promises.

See also BON 54, TRAIN.

ruisseau. *See* RIVIÈRE.

ruse. En amour la ruse est de bonne guerre, All's fair in love and war. " At lovers' perjuries They say Jove laughs."—*Romeo and Juliet* II, 2. " As waggish boys in game themselves forswear, So the boy Love is perjur'd everywhere."—*A Midsummer Night's Dream* I, 1. " It is war's prize to take all 'vantages."—3 *King Henry VI* I, 4.

See also APACHE.

rusé. *See* COMMÈRE, COMPÈRE.

S

sable. *See* AIRAIN, CHAUX.

sabot. Il est venu à Londres en sabots, He came up to London destitute *or* without a penny to bless himself with, He was a Dick Whittington.

See also DORMIR, FOIN.

sabre. *See* CLAIR.

sac. Avoir le sac, To be well off; To have a big dowry.

Être au sac, To be well off.

L'affaire (Votre affaire) est dans le sac, It (Your matter) is as good as done *or* settled.

Mettez cela dans votre sac, Put that in your pipe and smoke it.

Un homme de sac et de corde, A regular ruffian, A downright villain, A thorough-paced scoundrel, A gallows-bird.

Un sac à malices, A knowing person.

Un sac à vin, A toper, A booser. " That huge bombard of sack."—1 *King Henry IV* II, 4. " There's a whole merchant's venture of Bordeaux stuff in him."—2 *King Henry IV* II, 4. " Peace, good pint-pot."—1 *King Henry IV* II, 4.

Un sot a bientôt vidé son sac, A fool's bolt is soon shot.

Vider son sac, To say one's say.

See also CHARBON, CONDAMNER, FOND, JUGER, MOUTURE, PETIT, PIÈCE, PRENDRE, TOUR.

sacramentel. Prononcer les paroles sacramentelles *ou* les mots sacramentels, To give formal assent.

sacrifier. Sacrifier sa vie pour son pays, To lay down one's life for one's country.

See also GRÂCE.

sage. Devenir sage à ses dépens, To pay dearly for one's experience, To be wise after the event.

Être sage comme une image, To be [as] good as gold (*of a child*).

See also AVISER.

saignée. C'est une grande (*ou* une

rude) saignée qu'on a faite à sa bourse, A big hole has been made in his purse (*fig.*).

saigner. La plaie saigne encore (*fig.*), The wound still rankles.

Saigner du nez (*fig.*), To show the white feather (*Quotation under* CANE) ; To fail to carry out an engagement. "And my reliances on his fracted dates Have smit my credit."—*Timon of Athens* II, 1.

See also BLANC.

saint. Il vaut mieux s'adresser à Dieu qu'à ses saints, [If you want something done,] go to the man at the top.

Ne savoir à quel saint se vouer, Not to know to whom, which way, to turn, To be at one's wit's end.

Se recommander à tous les saints [et saintes] du paradis *ou* Se vouer à tous les saints, To try every means of escape, To beg assistance from anybody and everybody.

Toute la sainte journée, All (*or* The whole [of]) the blessed day, The livelong day.

See also ARCHE, DAMNER, FÊTE, PRÊCHER.

saint-crépin. Perdre son saint-crépin, To lose one's belongings.

Porter tout son saint-crépin avec soi, To carry all one's belongings with one.

sainte Catherine. *See* COIFFER.

sainte nitouche. *See* NITOUCHE.

sainteté. *See* ODEUR.

Saint-Glinglin. [Jusqu']à la Saint-Glinglin, To-morrow come never, When two Sundays come in a week, Till the cows come home. " Not till a hot January."—*Much Ado About Nothing* I, 1.

saint Jean. *See* BOUCHE, EMPLOYER.

Saint-Martin. *See* ÉTÉ.

saint Paul, saint Pierre. *See* DÉCOUVRIR.

saint Roch. *See* CHIEN.

saisir. Être saisi, To be staggered.

Saisir une chose du regard, To take a thing in at a glance.

See also BRAS, CHEVEU, VOL.

salade. Le panier à salade, The black Maria (*prison van*).

salaire. *See* PEINE.

sale. Être sale comme un peigne, To be filthy [dirty].

See also LINGE.

saler. Le prix en est salé, The price is very stiff *or* steep *or* exorbitant.

Saler quelqu'un [de la belle manière], To give someone a [good] trouncing, To trounce someone (*lit.* & *fig.*).

salir. *See* NID.

salon. Un héros de salon, A carpet-knight. " He is a knight, dubbed with unhacked rapier, and on carpet consideration." — *Twelfth Night* III, 4.

salut. C'est notre ancre (*ou* notre planche) de salut, It is our sheet-anchor (*fig.*).

Point de salut (*fig.*), There is no hope [of salvation, of success].

See also BON 3.

sandwich. Faire sandwich, To play gooseberry.

sang. Avoir du sang de poulet *ou* du sang de navet, To be chicken-hearted, To be lily-livered. " Go, prick thy face, and over-red thy fear, Thou lily-liver'd boy. What soldiers, patch ? Death of thy soul ! those linen cheeks of thine Are counsellors of fear. What soldiers, whey-face ? " — *Macbeth* V, 3.

Bon sang ne peut mentir, Blood will tell.

Cela est dans le sang, It runs in the blood.

Tout mon sang n'a fait qu'un tour, It gave me such a turn, I was struck all of a heap, My heart leapt into my mouth.

See also CHAUD, FEU, FORCE, IMPÔT, NAGER, PINTE, RAFRAÎCHIR, SIGNER, SUER.

sang-froid. Garder un sang-froid imperturbable, To keep [as] cool as a cucumber.

sanglant. *See* JOUER.

santé. *See* RESPIRER.

sapin. Sentir le sapin, To smell of the churchyard (*of feared fatal illness*). Un toux qui sent le sapin, A churchyard cough.

Satan. *See* ORGUEIL, ORGUEILLEUX, SUPPÔT.

sauce. Être bon à toutes les sauces, To be able to do anything.

La sauce fait passer le poisson, What advantages there are enable us to overlook the drawbacks.

La sauce vaut mieux que le poisson, The trimmings are the best part of it.

On le met à toutes les sauces, He is put to all kinds of jobs.

On ne sait à quelle sauce le mettre, There is no knowing what to do with him (*he is unemployable*).

See also APPÉTIT, CUISINIER.

saucer. Être saucé, To be drenched *or* wet through. *Quotations under* MOUILLER.

saucisse. Il n'attache par son chien avec des saucisses, He doesn't throw his money about (*is not prodigal*).

sauf. *See* AVIS, HONNEUR, RESPECT.

saur. *See* MAIGRE.

saut. Faire le saut [périlleux] (*fig.*), To take the plunge, To cross (*or* To pass) the Rubicon.

Faire un saut dans l'inconnu, To take a leap in the dark (*fig.*).

Par sauts et par bonds, By leaps and bounds ; By fits and starts, Spasmodically, Disjointedly, Jerkily.

Prendre quelqu'un au saut du lit, To call for someone betimes.

See also PLEIN.

sauter. Cela saute aux yeux, That is obvious, That is [as] clear as noonday, One can see it with half an eye, It is [as] plain as a pikestaff. *Quotations under* CLAIR.

Sauter à bas de son lit, To jump out of bed.

Sauter à picds joints par-dessus une chose, To go straight at something (*do it in spite of opposition*).

Sauter aux nues *ou* au plafond, To go wild with joy, indignation, etc., To jump out of one's skin.

Sauter le fossé *ou* le pas, To take the plunge *or* the step, To cross (*or* To pass) the Rubicon.

Se sauter aux yeux, To fly at each other (*in quarrel*).

See also ÉCU, GRENOUILLE, MOUTON, MUR, RECULER.

sauver. Sauve qui peut, Every man for himself [and the devil take the hindermost], Run for your lives.

Se sauver à toutes jambes, To make off [at great speed], To cut and run, To skedaddle.

Se sauver à travers champs *ou* à travers les buissons, To shirk the issue (*in a discussion*).

See also APPARENCE, BROUSSAILLES, COUP 58, PEAU, PLANCHE, POINT.

savoir. Je suis tout je ne sais comment, I feel all-overish.

Ne pas savoir ce qu'on veut, Not to know one's own mind.

Ne savoir où se mettre *ou* où se fourrer, To wish oneself a hundred miles away.

Ne savoir que faire *ou* Ne savoir où (*ou* à quoi) se prendre, Not to know (*or* To be at a loss to know) what to do.

Savoir [bien] son monde, To know how matters stand *or* what is going on ; To be accustomed to move in polite society, To know what's what.

Savoir, c'est pouvoir, Knowledge is power. " Knowledge the wing wherewith we fly to heaven."—2 *King Henry VI* IV, 7.

Savoir ce que parler veut dire, To be able to take a hint.

Savoir de quoi il retourne, To know

how matters stand *or* what is going on.

Savoir la carte [du pays] *ou* Savoir le parcours, To know the ropes.

Savoir une chose sur le bout du doigt *ou* Savoir une chose comme son Pater, To have a thing at one's finger-tips *or* finger-ends, To know a thing inside out *or* by heart.

Un je ne sais qui, Some one or other, A perfect stranger.

Un je ne sais quoi, An indescribable something.

See also AUNE, AUTRE, BEURRE, BOIS, CŒUR, COMPTER, CONNAÎTRE, CROIRE, DANSER, DÉCRIRE, DESSOUS, DEVENIR, DONNER, ENTOUR, ÉPERVIER, ÉPINE, FAUX, FLÈCHE, FONDS, GRÉ, JEUNESSE, LONG, MOURIR, OMELETTE, PROSE, RETOURNER, RIEN, SAINT, SAUCE, SOU, TENANT, TENIR, TOURNER, UN, VENT, VENTRE.

savon, savonner. Donner un savon à (*ou* Savonner) quelqu'un, To give someone a good dressing down *or* a good talking to, *or* (*slang*) give someone beans *or* (*slang*) socks, To haul someone over the coals.

scandale. Faire [du] scandale, To flutter the dovecotes.

See also PIERRE.

sceau. *See* CONFESSION.

scène. Il est toujours en scène, He never unbends.

Se mettre en scène, To thrust oneself forward.

See also DISPARAÎTRE, ENTRER.

scie. Monter une scie à quelqu'un, To play a stock practical joke on someone.

science. Il croit avoir la science infuse, He thinks he knows more than those who have studied.

See also ABÎME, BIEN.

scier. Scier [le dos à] quelqu'un, To bore someone to death *or* (*slang*) someone stiff.

Scylla. *See* TOMBER.

seau. *See* PLEUVOIR.

sec. Être à sec, To run dry (*have no more money or no more to say*).

Être sec comme un cotret *ou* comme [un] pendu, To be gaunt *or* rawboned *or* scrawny.

Être sec comme une allumette, To be [as] dry as a bone.

Faire quelque chose en cinq sec, To do something in a jiffy *or* in double-quick time.

See also BOIRE, EMPLOYER, FRUIT, PARLER, POIL.

sécher. Sécher sur pied, To wilt, To wither away (*of plant*) ; To stamp up and down (d'impatience = with impatience) ; To eat one's heart out ; To pine away.

second. Passer au second plan (*fig.*), To take a back seat.

See also BALLE, HABITUDE.

secondaire. Jouer un rôle secondaire, To play second fiddle. " An two men ride of a horse, one must ride behind."—*Much Ado About Nothing* III, 5. " I am too high-born to be propertied, To be a secondary at control."—*King John* V, 2.

secouer. Se secouer, To bestir oneself, To be up and doing, To pull oneself together.

See also PRUNIER.

secret. C'est le secret de la comédie *ou* de Polichinelle, It is an open secret.

C'est le tombeau des secrets, You can trust him implicitly, Wild horses wouldn't drag it from him. " When you have spoken it, 'tis dead, and I am the grave of it."—*All's Well That Ends Well* IV, 3. " A team of horse shall not pluck that from me."—*Two Gentlemen of Verona* III, 1.

Être dans le secret, To be in the secret *or* in the know.

Lâcher (*ou* Éventer) un secret, To let out a secret.

Le secret est éventé, The secret is out, The cat is out of the bag.

Mettre quelqu'un dans le secret, To let someone into the secret. " By and by thy bosom shall partake The secrets of my heart: All my engagements I will construe to thee, All the charactery of my sad brows." —*Julius Caesar* II, 1.

seigneur. À tous seigneurs tous honneurs *ou* À tout seigneur tout honneur, Honour to whom honour is due.

Faire le (*ou* Trancher du) grand seigneur, To put on (*or* To give oneself) lordly airs.

Vivre en grand seigneur, To live like a lord.

See also ARCHE, VIGNE.

sein. *See* MORDRE, POIGNARD, RÉCHAUFFER.

Seine. *See* BROUILLARD.

séjour. L'humide séjour (*poetic*), " The transparent bosom of the deep."—*Love's Labour's Lost* IV, 3. " The wat'ry kingdom."—*The Merchant of Venice* II, 7.

sel. *See* PAIN.

selle. Être bien en selle, To be well in the saddle, To be firmly established.

Mettre quelqu'un en selle, To put someone in the saddle (*in office or control*).

Se trouver (*ou* Être) (*ou* Demeurer) (*ou* Rester) [le cul] entre deux selles, To fall between two stools.

Une selle à tous chevaux, A commonplace, A platitude.

sellette. Être sur la sellette, To be under cross-examination, To be up on the carpet (*summoned for a reprimand*).

Tenir quelqu'un sur la sellette, To cross-examine someone, To call someone to account, To have someone on the carpet.

selon. *See* BESOGNE, BOURSE.

semblable. *See* VOIR.

semaine. La semaine des quatre jeudis, When two Sundays come in a week, To-morrow come never.

See also PRÊTER.

semblant. Ne faire semblant de rien, Not to appear to take any notice.

semelle. Ne pas reculer d'une semelle, Not to give way an inch.

semer. Qui sème le vent récolte la tempête, He who sows the wind shall reap the whirlwind (*Hosea* viii, 7).

Semer de l'argent, To scatter money [broadcast]; To spend money recklessly.

Semer des pièges sous les pas de quelqu'un, To lay traps for someone.

Semer quelqu'un, To shake off (*or* To shed) someone (*undesirable companion*).

See also INGRAT.

séné. *See* PASSER.

sens. Être dans son bon sens, To be in one's senses.

Être sens dessus dessous, To be upside down *or* topsy turvy, To be in confusion, To be at sixes and sevens. " All is uneven, And everything is left at six and seven." —*King Richard II* II, 2.

Il tombe sous le[s] sens que . . . *ou* Le bon sens veut que . . ., It stands to reason that . . .

Mettre quelqu'un sens dessus dessous (*fig.*), To upset someone very much.

Rentrer dans son bon sens, To recover one's senses (*fig.*).

Tout homme qui est dans son bon sens . . ., Any man in his senses . . .

See also ABONDER, ANTIPODE, BROUILLER, GROS, SOU, SOUFFLET.

sensible. Être profondément (*ou* très) sensible à quelque chose, To be fully alive to something.

Prendre quelqu'un sur son endroit sensible, To touch someone on his sore spot *or* on the raw.

See also CHATOUILLER, ÉPIDERME.

sentence. Ne parler que par sentences, To be sententious. " A sentence

(= *pithy saying*) is but a cheveril glove to a good wit. How quickly the wrong side may be turned outward ! "—*Twelfth Night* III, 1.

See also APPELER, FOU.

sentinelle. Faire sentinelle, To mount guard ; To be on the watch.

sentier. Être sur le sentier de la guerre, To be on the war-path.

sentir. Cela ne sent pas bon, Things (*the matter*, *the business*) look none too good.

Je ne peux pas le sentir, I cannot bear the sight of him. *Quotation under* PEINTURE.

Sentir quelqu'un venir de loin, To see through someone.

Sentir quelque chose de loin, To see through something.

See also CHIFFE, COUDE, DÉPAYSER, EAU, FADE, FAGOT, GALEUX, HARENG, HOMME, HUILE, MORVEUX, MOUVEMENT, POUDRE, SAPIN, TERROIR.

séparer. *See* IVRAIE.

sept. *See* BOTTE, LAID, LANGUE.

septième. *See* RAVIR.

sépulcre. *See* BLANCHIR.

sérieux. Être sérieux comme un âne qu'on étrille, To be [as] solemn as a judge.

Garder (*ou* Tenir) son sérieux, To keep a straight face.

serin. C'est un serin, He is a simpleton *or* a ninny *or* a [Simple] Simon. *Quotation under* ARGENT.

Il est un peu serin, He is a bit silly.

seriner. Seriner [quelque chose à] quelqu'un, To drum (*or* To din) something into someone.

serment. Être sur la foi du serment, To be on oath.

sermonner. Sermonner quelqu'un, To take someone to task, To give someone a talking to. " Come, sermon me no further."—*Timon of Athens* II, 2.

serpent. Le serpent est caché sous les fleurs, There is a snake in the grass. " To beguile the time, Look like the time ; bear welcome in your eye, Your hand, your tongue: look like the innocent flower, But be the serpent under 't."—*Macbeth* I, 5. " And when they from thy bosom (*i.e., the earth of England*) pluck a flower, Guard it, I pray thee, with a lurking adder, Whose double tongue may with a mortal touch, Throw death upon thy sovereign's enemies."—*King Richard II* III, 2.

See also RÉCHAUFFER.

serre. C'est un fruit de serre chaude, It is a hothouse plant (*hastily developed intellect*).

serrement. Un serrement de cœur, A pang, A tug at one's heartstrings.

serrer. Avoir le cœur serré, To be sad at heart, To be down-hearted. " 'Tis all men's office to speak patience To those that wring under the load of sorrow."—*Much Ado About Nothing* V, 1.

Cela serre le cœur, That wrings the heart. " Let me wring your heart : for so I shall, If it be made of penetrable stuff."—*Hamlet* III, 4.

Jouer serré *ou* Avoir le jeu serré, To play a cautious game, To act cautiously, To leave nothing to chance.

Serrer la vis (*ou* le bouton) (*ou* les pouces) à quelqu'un (*fig.*), To put the screw (*or* To put pressure) on someone.

Serrer les côtes à quelqu'un, To keep someone up to scratch.

Un homme serré, A close-fisted man.

See also BOURSE, COUDE.

serrure. L'amour force toutes les serrures, Love laughs at locksmiths *or* at barriers. " Were beauty under twenty locks kept fast, Yet love breaks through, and picks them all at last."—SHAKESPEARE, *Venus and Adonis*. " With love's light wings did I o'erperch these walls ; For stony limits cannôt hold love out."—*Romeo and Juliet* II, 2.

servante. Je suis votre servante (*ironiquement*), Not likely, No fear, So there, Nothing doing. *Quotation under* SERVITEUR.

service. *See* HORS.

servir. *See* AUTEL, COURIR, DOIGT, MARRON, PLAT, PREMIER, SPECTACLE, TURC.

serviteur. [Je suis votre] serviteur, Je suis son serviteur (*ironiquement*), Not likely, No fear, So there, Nothing doing, I'll see myself, him, her, further (*or* damned) first. " After a few compliments, she asked him if he did not intend to pay her. ' No indeed, I shan't, I shan't ; your servant, your servant.' "— HORACE WALPOLE. " *Page.* Pray thee, go down. *Pistol.* I'll see her damned first ;— To Pluto's damned lake, by this hand, to the infernal deep, with Erebus and tortures vile also."— 2 *King Henry IV* II, 4.

Sésame. Sésame, ouvre-toi, Open sesame.

seul. *See* ALLER, ATTENDRE, JET, MALHEUR.

si. Avec des si, on mettrait Paris dans une bouteille, If ifs and ans were pots and pans, there'd be no use for tinkers, If wishes were horses, beggars would ride. " If to do were as easy as to know what were good to do, chapels had been churches, and poor men's cottages princes' palaces."—*The Merchant of Venice* I, 2. " Much virtue in *If.*"—*As You Like It* V, 4.

See also DIABLE, FAIRE.

siècle. *See* AIRAIN, HAUTEUR.

siège. Mon siège est fait, What I have written I have written (*I will not alter it*) ; I refuse to reconsider the matter. " Then said the chief priests of the Jews to Pilate, Write not, The King of the Jews ; but that he said, I am King of the Jews. Pilate answered, What I have written I have written."—*John* xix, 21–22.

See also LEVER.

sien. Il fait des siennes, He is up to his tricks.

See also METTRE, PAILLE, TRAHIR.

siffler. Être sifflé, To be hissed *or* hooted *or* booed, To get the bird (*slang*).

Siffler, To hiss, To hoot, To boo, To give the bird to (*actor, play*) (*slang*). " *Mrs Ford.* Mrs Page, remember you your cue. *Mrs Page.* I warrant thee ; if I do not act it, hiss me."—*Merry Wives of Windsor* III, 3.

sifflet. *See* COUPER.

signature. *See* PAROLE.

signe. Faire signe que non, To shake one's head (*in dissent*).

Faire signe que oui, To nod assent.

signer. Cette manœuvre est signée *ou* C'est signé, It is pretty obvious who did it.

Je vous le signerais de mon sang, I would swear to it on my life, I would stake my life on it.

silence. *See* PAROLE.

sillon. Faire (*ou* Tracer) son sillon, To perform one's allotted task.

simple. C'est simple comme bonjour, It is [as] easy as A B C (*to understand*) ; It is [as] easy as kissing your hand *or* as shelling peas *or* as pat *or* as lying (*Hamlet* III, 2) (*to do*).

simplesse. *See* AMOUR.

singe. On n'apprend pas à un vieux singe à faire des grimaces, Don't teach your grandmother how to suck eggs. *Quotation under* GROS-JEAN.

See also LAID, MALIN, MONNAIE.

sire. C'est un pauvre sire, He is a poor specmien of humanity.

sirène. *See* CHANT.

sitôt. Sitôt dit, sitôt fait *ou* Sitôt pris, sitôt pendu, No sooner said than done.

situation. *See* RETOURNER.

six. À la six-quatre-deux, In a slapdash manner.

See also PIED.

smalah. Une smalah, A tribe (*numerous family, set or number of persons*) : Il est venu avec toute sa smalah, He came with all his tribe.

sodre. En appeler de Philippe ivre à Philippe sobre, To appeal from Philip drunk to Philip sober (*to suggest that opinion, etc., represents only passing fancy*). " Was the hope drunk Wherein you dress'd yourself ? hath it slept since ? And wakes it now, to look so green and pale At what it did so freely ? "—*Macbeth* I, 7.

social. *See* GUERRE.

soi. Être à soi, To be independent *or* one's own master ; To be by oneself *or* alone.

See also ALLER, CHEZ, COUVERTURE, FORT, HORS, LOI, MAÎTRE, MÉCHANT, PARLER, RENTRER, REVENIR, RIEUR, TÊTE.

soie. *See* FILER.

soif. *See* ÂNE, BOIRE, FAIM, POIRE, SOLLICITER.

soigner. *See* INDIVIDU.

soin. Être aux petits soins auprès de (*ou* pour) quelqu'un, To be full of attentions for someone, To wait on someone hand and foot.

See also INDIVIDU.

soir. *See* BON 28, RIRE, ROUGE.

sol. *See* MESURER.

soldat. *See* FOSSÉ, SOUPE.

solde. Être à la solde de quelqu'un, To be in someone's pay.

soleil. Le soleil luit pour tout le monde, The sun shines on all alike. " He maketh his sun to rise on the evil and on the good, and sendeth rain on the just and on the unjust."—*Matthew* v, 45. " The self-same sun that shines upon his court Hides not his visage from our cottage, but Looks on alike."—*The Winter's Tale* IV, 3.

See also ADORER, BIEN, DÉJEUNER, MONTRER, NOUVEAU, ÔTER.

solide. Avoir la tête solide, To have a good head [on one's shoulders] (*have ability*).

S'attacher (*ou* Songer) (*ou* Viser) au (*ou* Chercher le) solide, To look (*or* To have an eye) to the main chance.

See also REINS.

solliciter. Être sollicité par la faim, la soif, à (*ou* de) faire quelque chose, To be driven by hunger, thirst, to do something.

Solliciter un texte, To garble a text.

sommaire. Un dîner sommaire, A scratch dinner.

Une tenue sommaire, A scanty (*or* sketchy) costume.

sommairement. Être sommairement vêtu, To be scantily (*or* sketchily) clad *or* attired.

somme. Faire un petit somme, To have forty winks.

Faire un somme, To have (*or* To take) a nap.

Ne faire qu'un somme toute la nuit, To sleep the whole night through.

Somme toute *ou* En somme, [Up]on the whole, After all is said and done. Ce n'est pas trop mal en somme, It isn't half bad, It's not so dusty (*slang*).

See also DORMIR.

sommeil. Laisser une affaire en sommeil, To leave a matter in abeyance.

See also ENDORMIR.

son. *See* ÂNE, ENTENDRE, TROMPE.

sonde. *See* COUP 29.

sonder. *See* TERRAIN.

songe. Songe, mensonge, Dreams go by contraries. " And think no more of this night's accidents But as the fierce vexation of a dream."—*A Midsummer Night's Dream* IV, 1. " Now o'er the one-half world

Nature seems dead, and wicked dreams abuse The curtain'd sleep." —*Macbeth* II, 1. " Let not our babbling dreams affright our souls." —*King Richard III* V, 3. " I talk of dreams, Which are the children of an idle brain, Begot of nothing but vain fantasy ; Which is as thin of substance as the air, And more inconstant than the wind."—*Romeo and Juliet* I, 4. " Man is but an ass if he go about to expound this dream . . . it shall be called Bottom's Dream, because it hath no bottom." —*A Midsummer Night's Dream* IV, 1.

See also AUTRUI.

songer. Songer creux, To day-dream.

See also BESOGNE, REPOSER, SOLIDE.

sonner. Faire sonner bien haut sa qualité, To vaunt one's excellence.

Sonner creux *ou* Sonner faux (*fig.*), To sound hollow, To ring false, Not to ring true.

See also MIDI, TOCSIN.

sonnette. *See* PENDRE.

sonneur. *See* BOIRE.

sorcier. Cela n'est pas sorcier, That is not difficult [to guess, to do].

Il ne faut pas être grand sorcier pour faire cela, pour deviner cela, One doesn't have to be very clever to do that, to guess that.

sort. Faire un sort à quelqu'un, To provide for someone.

Faire un sort à une chose (*fig.*), To rescue a thing from oblivion.

Il y a un sort sur tout ce qu'il fait, Nothing he does goes right, He is unlucky in everything, He seems doomed to failure. " Alack, when once our grace we have forgot, Nothing goes right."—*Measure for Measure* IV, 4. " How sour sweet music is When time is broke and no proportion kept ! So is it in the music of men's lives."—*King Richard II* V, 5.

S'en remettre au sort des armes, To resort to the arbitrament of arms *or* of war. " There shall your swords and lances arbitrate The swelling difference of your settled hate."—*King Richard II* I, 1. " Put thy fortune to the arbitrement Of bloody strokes and mortal-staring war."—*King Richard III* V, 3.

See also AVEUGLE, JETER.

sorte. *See* INFLUENCE.

sortie. Faire une sortie à quelqu'un, To take someone severely to task.

Faire une sortie contre quelqu'un, To lash out at (*or* To pitch into) someone (*fig.*).

Se ménager une porte de sortie, To leave a loophole (*to escape or evade the intent of a contract or obligation*).

sortir. D'où sortez-vous ? Where have you been all this time ? ; Where do you come from [that you don't know that] ?

Les yeux lui sortent de la tête (*fig.*), His eyes are starting out of their sockets. *Quotation under* DRESSER.

Ne faire que sortir de la coque *ou* de la coquille, To be only a fledg[e]-ling (*of person—very young and inexperienced*). " Unbaked and doughy youth."—*All's Well That Ends Well* IV, 5.

Ne pas sortir de là, To stick to that (*to the point*), To take one's stand on that. Il n'y a pas à sortir de là, There is no getting away from that.

Sortez-le ! Chuck him out !

Sortir du monde, To depart this life, To go hence.

See also BOÎTE, BRAIE, CARACTÈRE, FAIM, FEU, GOND, JUPITER, LAIT, NEZ, OREILLE, ORNIÈRE, PAGE, PIED, RANG, VENT.

sot. C'est un sot à vingt-quatre (*ou* à trente-six) carats *ou* C'est un sot en trois lettres, He is an out-and-out (*or* a downright) fool, In plain language, he's an ass. " What a thrice-double ass Was I . . . ! "—*The Tempest* V, 1.

See also DEMANDE, ENCOLURE, MARCHER, SAC.

sou. Cela vaut cent mille francs comme un sou, That is worth a hundred thousand francs if it's worth a penny.

Il n'a pas de bon sens pour un sou, He hasn't a ha'p'orth of sense. " Thou halfpenny purse of wit, thou pigeon egg of discretion."—*Love's Labour's Lost* V, 1.

Le sou du franc, The market-penny.

Manger ses quatre sous, To spend (*squander*) (*or* To lose) what little one has.

Mettre sou sur sou, To save every penny one can.

N'avoir pas le sou *ou* N'avoir pas un sou [vaillant] *ou* N'avoir ni sou ni maille, To be penniless, Not to have a penny to bless oneself with, Not to have a copper *or* a bean, To be stony broke (*slang*). " Such a house broke ! . . . All gone ! "—*Timon of Athens* IV, 1.

Prendre garde à un sou, To look twice at every penny.

Savoir ménager les sous, To make a penny go a long way.

Un sou est un sou, A penny is a penny (*therefore don't waste one*).

See also CHAGRIN, MOQUER, NET, PROPRE, ROMAN, SUCER.

soubresaut. Cette nouvelle m'a donné un [violent] soubresaut, The news gave me [quite] a shock *or* a turn *or* made me gasp.

souche. Faire souche, To found a family.

Rester là comme une souche, To stand there like a stuffed monkey.

See also DORMIR.

souci. C'est là le moindre (*ou* le cadet) de mes soucis, That is the least of my worries *or* troubles.

Le souci de l'au-delà, Fear of the beyond. " The dread of something after death."—*Hamlet* III, 1. " To die,—to sleep ;—To sleep ! perchance to dream : ay, there's the rub ; For in that sleep of death what dreams may come, When we have shuffled off this mortal coil, Must give us pause."—*Hamlet* III, 1. " So when at last the Angel of the drink Of Darkness finds you by the river-brink, And, proffering his Cup, invites your Soul Forth to your Lips to quaff it—do not shrink."—EDWARD FITZGERALD, *Rubaiyat of Omar Khayyam* XLVI.

" Plus on est élevé, plus on a de soucis" (N. J. L. GILBERT), " Uneasy lies the head that wears a crown."—2 *King Henry IV* III, 1.

Vous vivrez peu, vous prenez trop de souci, Care killed the cat[, for all its nine lives] (*therefore be cheerful*). " What though care killed a cat, thou hast mettle enough in thee to kill care."—*Much Ado About Nothing* V, 1. " I am sure care's an enemy to life."—*Twelfth Night* I, 3.

soucier. Je m'en soucie comme d'une guigne *ou* comme d'une épingle *ou* comme de l'an quarante, I don't care in the least, I don't care a brass farthing *or* a rap *or* a button *or* a fig *or* a pin *or* a rap *or* a straw *or* a tinker's dam[n] *or* a damn *or* two hoots.

souffle. Manquer de souffle, To lack inspiration (*of a writer*).

See also TENIR.

souffler. L'esprit souffle où il veut, There is no accounting for inspiration, for genius.

Souffler à quelqu'un une chose, To trick (*or* To cheat) (*or* To jockey) (*or* To do) someone out of a thing.

Souffler comme un bœuf, To blow like a grampus.

Tu peux souffler dessus, You may whistle for it.

See also CHAUD, TEMPÊTE.

soufflet. Donner un soufflet à

quelqu'un sur la joue d'un autre, To give someone a backhander (*fig.*) (*make an indirect attack on him*).

Donner un soufflet au sens commun, To fly in the face of common sense.

Plaquer un soufflet [sur la joue] à quelqu'un, To smack (*or* To slap) someone's face, To give someone a clout.

See also APPLIQUER.

souffrant. *See* ÉGLISE.

souffrir. Le papier souffre tout, Paper is long-suffering.

Souffrir mort et passion *ou* Souffrir le martyre, To suffer cruelly, To suffer agonies, To go through hell.

souhaiter. *See* BON 28.

soûl. Être soûl comme une grive, To be [as] drunk as a fiddler *or* as a lord. " Swine-drunk."—*All's Well That Ends Well* IV, 3.

soulier. Être dans ses petits souliers, To squirm (*as under a censure or reproach*).

Faute de souliers, on va nu-pieds, Beggars can't be choosers.

See also BLESSER, BOUE, CORDON.

soupape. Une soupape de sûreté, A safety-valve (*fig.*).

soupe. La soupe fait le soldat, An army marches on its belly.

See also CHEVEU, EMPORTER, TREMPER.

souper. Avoir soupé de quelque chose, de quelqu'un, To be sick [to death] of something, of someone, To be fed up [to the teeth] with something, with someone (*slang*).

soupir. *See* TALON.

souple. Il est souple comme un gant *ou* Il a les reins souples, One can do anything one likes with him.

Rendre quelqu'un souple comme un gant, To make someone supple *or* tractable. " I will knead him, I'll make him supple."—*Troilus and Cressida* II, 3.

See also ÉCHINE.

source. *See* COULER, PUISER, TENIR.

sourd. Cela n'est pas tombé dans l'oreille d'un sourd, That remark did not pass unnoticed.

Être sourd comme un pot, To be [as] deaf as a post.

Faire la sourde oreille *ou* Faire le sourd, To turn a deaf ear.

See also CRIER, ENTENDRE, FRAPPER, PARLER.

souricière. Se mettre (*ou* Se jeter) dans la souricière, To fall into the trap (*fig.*). " *King.* What do you call the play ? *Hamlet.* The Mouse-trap. Marry, how ? Tropically."—*Hamlet* III, 2. (*Note.*—tropically = of the nature of a trope, metaphorically.)

sourire. *See* COMMANDE, NAÎTRE.

souris. Il l'aurait fait mettre dans un trou de souris, He put the fear of God into him.

On le ferait rentrer dans un trou de souris, He was in mortal terror *or* (*slang*) in a blue funk, He simply collapsed *or* (*slang*) curled up. " And peep about To find ourselves dishonourable graves." — *Julius Caesar* I, 2.

See also CHAT, EMMITOUFLER, ENFANTER, ENTENDRE, ÉVEILLER.

soutenir. Soutenir le bon combat, To fight the good fight (*to fight for a good cause*). " Fight the good fight of faith."—1 *Timothy* vi, 12.

Soutenir son dire, To maintain one's assertion.

See also POIDS.

souvent. *See* RÉPÉTER.

souvenir. *See* APPEL.

souvenir (se). Autant que je m'en souvienne, To the best of my recollection.

spectacle. Être en spectacle à tout le monde, To be in the public eye. " I love the people, But do not like to stage me to their eyes."—*Measure for Measure* I, 1. " O place and greatness, millions of false eyes Are stuck upon thee ! volumes of report

Run with these false and most contrarious quests Upon thy doings! thousand 'scapes of wit Make thee the father of their idle dream, And rack thee in their fancies!"—*Measure for Measure* IV, 1.

Se donner (*ou* S'offrir) en spectacle, To attract (*public*) attention (*to oneself*). "O, contain yourself; Your passion draws ears hither."—*Troilus and Cressida* V, 2.

Servir de spectacle, To make an exhibition (*or* an ass) of oneself.

See also COUREUR.

spectre. C'est un spectre, He looks like a ghost (*haggard and emaciated*). "Poor mortal-living ghost, . . . grave's due by life usurp'd."—*King Richard III* IV, 4.

statue. C'est une belle statue, She is a fine statue. "She shows a body rather than a life, A statue than a breather."—*Antony and Cleopatra* III, 3.

See also ARGILE.

stratège. *See* CHAMBRE.

su. *See* VU.

succès. *See* CHANCE, MOUSSER.

succession. Par succession de temps, In process of time.

succinct. Un repas succinct, A light repast, A scanty meal.

succomber. Succomber (*fig.*), To be worsted, To go to the wall.

sucer. Sucer avec le lait une doctrine, des principes, To imbibe a doctrine, principles, in early years.

Sucer quelqu'un jusqu'à la moelle [des os] *ou* jusqu'aux os *ou* jusqu'au dernier sou, To suck someone dry, To bleed someone white, To take someone's last farthing. "I will drain him dry as hay."—*Macbeth* I, 3.

sucre. Casser du sucre sur la tête (*ou* sur le dos) de quelqu'un, To speak ill of (*or* To backbite) someone, To run someone down.

Être tout sucre et tout miel, To be all honey (*of persons*).

sucrer. Elle fait la sucrée, She is demure, Butter wouldn't melt in her mouth.

sucrerie. Aimer les sucreries, To have a sweet tooth.

suer. Suer à grosses gouttes, To sweat profusely. "Beads of sweat have stood upon thy brow, Like bubbles in a late disturbed stream."—1 *King Henry IV* II, 3. "When he was brought again to the bar to hear His knell rung out, his judgment.—he was stirr'd With such an agony, he sweat extremely."—*King Henry VIII* II, 1.

Suer d'ahan *ou* Suer sang et eau, To toil and moil, To strain every nerve. "This sweaty haste Doth make the night joint labourer with the day."—*Hamlet* I, 1.

Suer l'égoïsme, To be steeped in selfishness.

Suer l'orgueil, l'hypocrisie, To stink of pride, of hypocrisy.

Suer la piété, To ooze piety.

See also ENNUI, PEUR.

sueur. *See* ARROSER.

suffire. *See* BON 3, GOUTTE, JOUR.

suisse. *See* ARGENT.

suite. Dans la suite des temps, In process of time.

See also ALLER.

suivre. Suivre les pas (*ou* les brisées) (*ou* les traces) (*ou* les erres) de quelqu'un, To follow (*or* To tread) in someone's footsteps, To follow someone's lead *or* example.

See also BARBET, CHEMIN, JOUR, POINTE.

supplice. Être au supplice, To be on the rack *or* on thorns *or* on tenterhooks (*in physical or moral torment*).

Le dernier supplice, The extreme penalty, Capital punishment.

Le supplice de Tantale (*fig.*), The punishment of Tantalus. "That worse than Tantalus' is her annoy, To clip Elysium, and to lack her joy."—SHAKESPEARE, *Venus and Adonis.*

supporter. *See* CHALEUR.

supposer. *See* LIEU.

suppôt. C'est un suppôt de Satan, He is a hell-hound *or* a fiend.

sûr. *See* COMMERCE, COUP 2, 48, JOUER.

surabondance. *See* NUIRE.

sûreté. *See* PRUDENCE, SOUPAPE.

surprendre. Surprendre la vigilance de quelqu'un, To catch someone napping.

sursomme. *See* ABATTRE.

sus. *See* COURIR.

suspendre. Être suspendu aux lèvres de quelqu'un, To hang on someone's lips, To listen to someone with rapt attention.

T

tabac. *See* POT.

table. Faire table rase, To make a clean sweep.

Une table d'attente *ou* Une table rase, (*Lit.*) A tablet for inscription (*ready to receive an inscription*) ; (*Fig.*) A blank (*a mind ready to receive impressions*). " Idleness offers up the soul as a blank to the Devil, for him to write what he will upon it."—R. SOUTH.

See also AIMER, JOUER, PLACE, TENIR.

tableau. *See* CIMAISE, OMBRE.

tablette. *See* RAYER.

tablier. Rendre son tablier, To leave (*one's employment*), To give notice, To resign.

tac. Répondre (*ou* Riposter) du tac au tac, To give as good as one gets, To give a Roland for an Oliver.

tache. Faire tache (*fig.*), To be a stain *or* a blemish, To mar ; To be out of place.

See also HUILE.

tâche. Prendre à tâche de faire une chose, To make it one's business to do a thing, To make a point of doing a thing.

See also MOURIR.

taille. Être de taille à faire quelque chose, To be big, strong, enough to do something ; To be [quite] able to do (*or* capable of doing) something.

tailler. Tailler des croupières à quelqu'un, To put difficulties in someone's way, To give someone a lot of bother.

Tailler et rogner à son gré *ou* comme on veut, To do just as one pleases.

Tailler la robe selon le corps, To cut one's coat according to one's cloth.

Tailler une bavette, Tailler des bavettes, To have a gossip, To gossip.

See also BESOGNE, COUP 45, DRAP, VIF.

taillis. *See* GAGNER.

taire. Il a manqué une belle occasion de se taire, He had better by half have held his tongue.

talent. *See* ENFOUIR.

talon. Avoir des ailes aux talons, To make off at great speed. " Be Mercury, set feathers to thy heels, And fly like thought."—*King John* IV, 2.

Avoir l'estomac dans les talons, To have an aching void, To be famished.

Des manières talon rouge, Genteel manners.

Il est très talon rouge, He is very genteel.

Montrer les talons, To take to one's heels, To show a clean pair of heels, To cut and run.

Tirer des soupirs de ses talons, To heave a sigh. " He rais'd a sigh so piteous and profound That it did seem to shatter all his bulk And end his being."—*Hamlet* II, 1.

Tourner les talons, To turn on one's heels and go.

See also ESPRIT, MARCHER, ŒIL.

tambour. Faire une chose tambour battant, To hustle a thing on.

Sans tambour ni trompette, On the quiet, On the q.t. (*slang*). *See also* DÉLOGER.

See also MENER, VENIR.

tancer. Tancer quelqu'un de la belle (*ou* bonne) manière *ou* Tancer quelqu'un vertement, To give someone a good dressing down *or* a good talking to *or* a good blowing up *or* a lick with the rough side of one's tongue *or* (*slang*) give someone beans *or* (*slang*) socks, To haul someone over the coals.

tangente. S'échapper par (*ou* Prendre) la tangente, To slip away ; To get out of it (*the difficulty*) nicely. (*Cf.* Passer du coq à l'âne *under* COQ.)

tannant. Un homme tannant, A wearisome (*or* boring) man.

tanner. Tanner quelqu'un, To weary (*or* To bore) someone.

tant. Comme il y en a tant, Like any other, Like so many more.

Tant et tant *ou* Tant et plus, Ever so much, Ever so many, Enough and to spare.

Tant s'en faut, Far from it.

Tant soit peu. Ever so little, Somewhat.

Un docteur (*ou* Un médecin) Tant mieux, An optimist. " I see some sparkles of a better hope, Which elder days may happily bring forth." —*King Richard II* V, 3.

Un docteur (*ou* Un médecin) Tant pis, A pessimist. " Here's a farmer that hanged himself on the expectation of plenty."—*Macbeth* II, 1.

See also AVOIR, BIEN, BOND, CRUCHE, RAISONNER, TERRE, TOUS.

Tantale. *See* SUPPLICE.

tapage. *See* DIABLE.

tape. Ramasser (*ou* Recevoir) une tape, To get the bird (*slang*).

taper. Taper dans l'œil à quelqu'un, To take someone's fancy.

Tu peux te taper, t'en auras pas, You may whistle for it.

Une réponse tapée, A smart answer, A ready retort.

See also TAS, VENTRE.

tapis. Amuser le tapis, To keep the company amused (*while waiting for entertainment to commence*) ; To beat about the bush.

C'est un(e) fervent(e) du tapis vert, He, She, is a devotee of the card table, of the gaming table.

Être sur le tapis, To be on the carpet *or* on the tapis (*of matter under consideration*).

Mettre une affaire sur le tapis, To bring something up (*or* forward) for discussion *or* for consideration.

Tenir quelqu'un sur le tapis, To discuss someone.

See also BRÛLER.

tapisserie. Faire tapisserie, To be a wallflower.

tard. Il est trop tard pour qu'il se corrige, He is past praying for, He'll never alter. *Quotations under* PEAU.

Il n'est jamais trop tard pour se corriger, It is never too late to mend.

Mieux vaut tard que jamais, Better late than never.

See also VÉRITÉ.

tarentule. Être mordu de la tarentule, To be very jumpy.

Tarpéienne. *See* ROCHE.

tas. Taper (*ou* Frapper) (*ou* Tirer) dans le tas, To pitch into the crowd (*strike right and left*).

See also CRIER.

tasse. *See* BOIRE.

tasser. Cela se tassera, Things will settle down *or* will turn out all right.

tâter. Se tâter le pouls, To take stock of one's position ; To be over-anxious.

Tâter le pouls à quelqu'un, To feel someone's pulse (*sound his intentions*).

See also PRISON, TERRAIN.

taupe. Être aveugle comme une taupe

ou Ne voir pas plus clair qu'une taupe, To be [as] blind as a bat *or* as a mole. " Pray you, tread softly, that the blind mole may not Hear a footfall."—*The Tempest* IV, 1.

taureau. *See* CORNE, ROUGE.

teigneux. *See* PELER.

tel. *See* ARBRE, DEMANDE, FIN, MAÎTRE, MONTRER, PAIX, PRENDRE, RIRE, VOIR.

témoignagc. *Scc* RAPPORTER.

témoin. Un témoin muet, Circumstantial evidence. " Who finds the heifer dead and bleeding fresh, And sees fast by a butcher with an axe, But will suspect 'twas he that made the slaughter ? Who finds the partridge in the puttock's nest, But may imagine how the bird was dead Although the kite soar with unbloodied beak ? "—2 *King Henry VI* III, 2. (*Note.*—puttock = kite.)

tempérament. Avoir du tempérament, To be of an amorous disposition.

température. Faire de la température, To have a temperature (*Medical*).

tempête. Gare la tempête ! Look out for squalls ! " But, lords, we hear this fearful tempest sing, Yet seek no shelter to avoid the storm." —*King Richard II* II, 1.

Le vent souffle en tempête, The wind is blowing a gale, It is blowing great guns. *Quotations under* VENT.

Une tcmpête dans un verre d'eau, A storm in a teacup.

See also SEMER.

templier. *See* BOIRE, JURER.

temps. Avant [tous] les temps *ou* Avant le temps, Before time was.

De tout temps il en a été ainsi, It was ever thus.

Être de son temps, To move with (*or* be abreast of) the times, To be up to date (*slang*).

Faire son temps, To serve one's time (*of a person*) ; To serve its time (*of a thing*).

Il y a temps pour tout, All in good time.

Le temps est (*ou* Le temps, c'est) de l'argent, Time is money.

Le temps perdu ne se retrouve jamais, Time wasted is lost for ever, Procrastination is the thief of time. " I wasted time, and now doth time waste me."—*King Richard II* V, 5.

Ne pas être de son temps, To be behind the times, To be a back number (*slang*).

Ne pas perdre de temps, To lose no time, Not to let the grass grow under one's feet.

Prendre le temps comme il vient, To take things as they come.

Qui a temps a vie, While there is life, there is hope.

Rattraper (*ou* Regagner) le temps perdu *ou* Réparer une perte de temps, To make up for lost time.

Se donner du bon temps, To have a good time.

See also AIR, AUTRE, BEAU 13, 14, CHANTER, CHER, CHIEN, COURIR, DEMOISELLE, DÉVORER, ENVOLER, FILER, FOIS, GAGNER, GRAND, HOMME, MAÎTRE, MALADE, NUIT, OCCUPER, OUTRAGE, PARLER, PLUIE, POINT, QUART, RETARDER, RÉVOLU, SUCCESSION, SUITE, TROMPER, TROUVER, TUER, VÉRITÉ.

tenant. Savoir tous les tenants et aboutissants d'une affaire, To know [all] the ins and outs (*or* the full details) of an affair.

tendance. Faire un procès de tendance à quelqu'un (*fig.*), To [call in] question (*or* To throw doubt upon) someone's motives.

tendre. Avoir du tendre pour quelqu'un, To have a soft spot (*or* place) in one's heart for someone.

Cette viande est tendre comme [la] rosée, This meat is [as] tender as a chicken.

Tendre à ses fins, To pursue one's purpose.

Tendre l'autre joue, To turn (*or* To offer) the other cheek (*in humility*). (*Luke* vi, 29.)

Tendre la perche, To help someone out (*of a difficulty, an embarrassment*).

Tendre le cou (*fig.*), To take it lying down. " Yield not thy neck To fortune's yoke, but let thy dauntless mind Still ride in triumph over all mischance."—3 *King Henry VI* III, 3.

Tendre le dos aux coups (*fig.*), To give one's back to the smiters (*Isaiah* l, 6).

Tendre un piège (*ou* un panneau) à quelqu'un, To lay a trap for someone.

See also CORDE, VIN.

tendresse. Le lait de la tendresse humaine, The milk of human kindness. " Yet do I fear thy nature ; It is too full o' the milk of human kindness To catch the nearest way."—*Macbeth* I, 5.

See also EFFUSION.

ténèbres. Le prince des ténèbres, The prince of darkness. " *Clown.* Why, sir, if I cannot serve you, I can serve as great a prince as you are.—*Lafeu.* Who's that ? a Frenchman ? —*Clown.* Faith, sir, 'a has an English name ; but his phisnomy is more hotter in France than there.—*Lafeu.* What prince is that ? —*Clown.* The black prince, sir ; *alias*, the prince of darkness ; *alias*, the devil."—*All's Well That Ends Well* IV, 5.

Les ténèbres de l'ignorance, The darkness of ignorance. " I say there is no darkness but ignorance ; in which thou art more puzzled than the Egyptians in their fog."—*Twelfth Night* IV, 2.

tenir. Cela tient de famille, It runs in the family.

Cette affaire lui tient au cœur, He has set his heart on this thing.

Cette injure lui tient au cœur, He has taken this insult to heart.

En tenir pour quelqu'un, To be fond of someone, To be in love with someone.

Il tient (Ils tiennent) [cela] de race *ou* de naissance, It runs in the (*or* in his, in their) blood.

Je le tiens, I've got (*cornered*) him.

Je vous tiendrai compte de cela, I shall not forget your kindness to me in this matter.

N'y plus tenir, Not to be able to bear (*or* stand) (*or, slang,* stick) it any longer.

Ne tenir à rien, To count for nothing (*be of no consideration*).

Ne tenir [aucun] compte de quelqu'un, de quelque chose, To take no notice of someone, of something.

Ne tenir qu'à un fil (*fig.*), To hang by a thread (*as of a momentous issue*).

Sa vie ne tient qu'à un fil *ou* un souffle, His life hangs by a thread. " The tackle of my heart is crack'd and burn'd ; And all the shrouds, wherewith my life should sail, Are turned to one thread, one little hair : My heart hath one poor string to stay it by."—*King John* V, 7. " The incessant care and labour of his mind Hath wrought the mure, that should confine it in, So thin, that life looks through, and will break out."—2 *King Henry IV* IV, 4. (*Note.*—mure = wall.)

Savoir à quoi s'en tenir, To know what to believe *or* where one is *or* how one stands.

Se tenir à peu [de chose] *ou* Se tenir à rien, To hold out for (*not to give way on*) a trifle, a mere trifle.

Se (*ou* S'en) tenir à quelque chose, To abide by something ; To stick to something ; To be content (*or* satisfied) with something.

Se tenir bien, mal, To behave oneself well, badly.

Tenez bon ! *ou* Tenez ferme ! Hold tight *or* fast ! ; Never say die !

Tenez-vous bien, Look out, I give you fair warning, You have been warned.

Tenir à faire quelque chose, To be bent (*or* keen) on doing something, To be anxious to do something.

Tenir à quelqu'un, To be beholden to someone ; To value someone highly, To prize someone.

Tenir bon *ou* Tenir ferme, To stand fast, To hold on, To hold one's own.

Tenir compte (*à quelqu'un*) d'une chose, To take something into account *or* into consideration, To bear something in mind, To make allowances for something : Dieu nous tiendra compte des moindres actes de charité, God will take into account our most trivial good deeds. Je lui tiens compte de sa bonne volonté, I take into consideration (*or* I bear in mind) his good will.

Tenir de quelqu'un, To take after (*or* To be like) someone : Il tient de son père, He takes after his father. Il est brave, il a de qui tenir, He is brave, he comes of good stock.

Tenir la vie de quelqu'un, To owe one's life to someone.

Tenir le fil d'une intrigue, d'un raisonnement, To catch the drift of a plot, of an argument.

Tenir le parti de quelqu'un, To take sides (*or* To side) with someone.

Tenir les fils *ou* les ficelles, To pull the strings (*fig.*).

Tenir pour quelqu'un, pour une opinion, To stand up (*or* To be all) for someone, for an opinion.

Tenir quelqu'un en tutelle, To keep someone under one's thumb.

Tenir quelque chose de bonne source, To have something on good authority.

Tenir table ouverte *ou* Tenir auberge (*fig.*), To keep open house *or* doors.

Tenons-nous-en là, Let it go at that.

See also ARBRE, ASSISE, AVERTIR, BATTRE, BEC, BON 13, BRASSIÈRE, BRIDE, CHANDELLE, CHEVEU, CLEF, CLOU, CODE, CORDE, CÔTE, COULISSE, COUP 59, COURT, CROISER, DÉ, DEBOUT, DIRE, DISTANCE, DRAGÉE, ÉCHEC, ERGOT, ÉTRIER, FOURREAU, GAGEURE, GORGE, HALEINE, HAUT, IMPOSSIBLE, JEU, LAISSE, LANGAGE, LISIÈRE, LOUP, MAIN, ŒIL, OMBRE, ORAGE, PAROLE, PARTIE, PATTE, PAVÉ, PEAU, PLACE, PLUME, POCHE, PRÈS, PROMETTRE, PROPOS, QUANT À, QUATRE, QUEUE, QUITTE, RANG, RÉALITÉ, REGISTRE, RIGUEUR, SELLETTE, SÉRIEUX, TAPIS, TÊTE, VALOIR.

tente. Planter sa tente, To pitch one's tent, To take up one's abode.

Se retirer sous sa tente (*fig.*), To sulk in one's tent (*like Achilles*—HOMER's *Iliad*). " *Agamemnon.* Where is Achilles ? *Patroclus.* Within his tent, but ill-dispos'd, my lord."—*Troilus and Cressida* II, 3.

tenter. Tenter l'aventure *ou* [la] fortune, To try one's luck, To tempt fortune, To chance it, To risk it.

tenue. Le temps n'a point de tenue, The weather is very unsettled.

See also SOMMAIRE.

terme. Qui a terme ne doit rien, A debt cannot be claimed before it is due.

See also BOUGER, PLANTER.

terne. C'est un terne à la loterie, It is a piece of pure luck, One chance in a thousand (*or* in a million) has come off.

terrain. Connaître bien le terrain, To be sure of one's ground, To know the ropes.

Déblayer le terrain (*fig.*), To clear the ground.

Être sur son terrain, To be on one's own ground *or* in one's element.

Ménager le terrain, To make the most of one's resources.

N'être pas (*ou* plus) sur son terrain, To be out of one's depth.

Préparer le terrain, To prepare the ground, To pave the way.

Regagner du terrain, To regain lost ground.

Sonder (*ou* Tâter) le terrain, To feel one's way, To see how the land lies, To put out a feeler.

See also CHICANER.

terre. Chercher quelqu'un par terre et par mer, To look up hill and down dale for someone.

Être [très] terre à terre, To be of the earth, earthy (1 *Corinthians* xv, 47).

Tant vaut l'homme, tant vaut la terre, The better the labour, the better the reward.

See also BATTRE, BOUT, CHASSER, COIN, DISPARAÎTRE, ENCORE, ÉPINGLE, GUERRE, INGRAT, MESURER, MÉTIER, NEZ, PEAU, PIED, POT, REMUER, RENTRER, RETOUR, VENTRE, VER.

terroir. Sentir le terroir, To smack of the soil; To be racy of the soil.

tête. Aller partout [la] tête levée *ou* [la] tête haute, To face the world with a clear conscience.

Avoir de la tête, To have one's head screwed on the right way, To have a good head on one's shoulders *or* a good head-piece; To be self-assertive.

Avoir la tête de plus que quelqu'un, To be a head taller than someone.

Avoir sa petite tête à soi, To have a will of one's own.

Avoir une tête à gifles *ou* à claques, To have an irritating (*or* impudent) face [, that one would like to smack].

C'est un homme, une femme, de tête, He, She, is a capable man, woman.

C'est une tête à perruque, He is an old fogey *or* an old fossil.

C'est une tête de mulet, He (She) is a mulish person.

C'est une tête sans cervelle, He is a brainless individual, She is a hen-witted woman. " What a lack-brain is this!"—1 *King Henry IV* II, 3.

Faire une tête, To pull a long face.

Il a encore toute sa tête, He still has all his faculties.

Il lui en coûta la tête *ou* Il le paya de sa tête, It cost him his head *or* life.

Il s'y est jeté la tête la première *ou* s'y est jeté tête baissée, He threw himself into it (*a dangerous undertaking*) headlong.

Il y va de votre tête, Your life is at stake.

J'en donnerais (*ou* J'en mettrais) (*ou* J'en parie) ma tête à couper *ou* J'en mettrais ma tête sur le billot, I would stake my life on it, I would swear to it, Honour bright. " If you and I do not rob them, cut this head from my shoulders." —1 *King Henry IV* I, 2. " I will take my death, I never meant him any ill."—2 *King Henry VI* II, 3. " Lay down my soul at stake."—*Othello* IV, 2. " *Gadshill.* Sirrah, if they meet not with Saint Nicholas' clerks, I'll give thee this neck. *Chamberlain.* No, I'll none of it: I pr'ythee, keep that for the hangman."—1 *King Henry IV* II, 1.

N'en faire qu'à sa tête, To do just as one pleases, To take nobody's advice.

Sa tête n'y est plus *ou* La tête est partie, He (She) is off his (her) head.

Tenir (*ou* Faire) tête à quelqu'un, To stand up to someone.

Tomber la tête la première, To fall headlong *or* head foremost *or* head first.

Vous en répondrez sur votre tête, You shall answer for it with your life.

See also AUTANT, BAISSER, BLANCHIR, BON 14, 25, BONNET, BRUIT, CARRÉ, CASER, CASSER, CHAOS, CHAUD,

CHAUSSER, CHERCHER, CONSERVER, COUP 39, CREUSER, CREUX, CRIER, DÉMÉNAGER, DERRIÈRE, DESSUS, DONNER, DRESSER, ÉCHAFAUD, ENVERS, ÉVENT, FÊLER, FENDRE, FER, FORT, FROID, GRAIN, GUÊPIER, HASARDER, JETER, LAVER, LINOTTE, MARCHER, MARTEL, MAUVAIS, MONTER, MUR, NEIGER, ŒIL, ORAGE, PERDRE, PLOMB, PORTER, PRIX, QUEUE, RAT, REPOSER, ROMPRE, SOLIDE, SORTIR, SUCRE, TOISER, TOMBER, TOURNER, TRAVAILLER, TREMBLER, TUILE, TURC.

têtu. Être têtu comme un mulet *ou* comme une mule *ou* comme un âne, To be [as] stubborn as a mule.

texte. Revenir à son texte, To get (*or* To come) back to the point, To return to one's subject.

See also SOLLICITER, TOILETTE, VIOLENCE.

théâtre. *See* COUP 72.

Thébaïde. Maison située dans une vraie Thébaïde, House situated in the back of beyond.

thème. Être fort en thème, To be good at book-learning (*but lacking originality and personality*). " Why, universal plodding prisons up The nimble spirits in the arteries."—*Love's Labour's Lost* IV, 3.

théorie. Une théorie de jeunes filles, A crocodile (*girls' school walking two and two*).

thèse. Cela change la thèse, That alters the case *or* puts a different complexion on the matter.

tiède. *See* ROBINET.

tien. Tu fais des tiennes, You are up to your tricks.

See also METTRE.

tiers. Le tiers et le quart, Anybody and everybody, All and sundry, All the world and his wife, Right and left.

See also DEVOIR, MOQUER.

tigre. *See* CŒUR.

timbale. *See* DÉCROCHER.

timbre. *See* FÊLER.

tirage. Il y a du tirage dans cette affaire, Things are not going smoothly in this matter.

tire-larigot. *See* BOIRE.

tirer. Cette comparaison est tirée par les cheveux, That comparison is far-fetched.

Il ne se fera pas tirer l'oreille *ou* Il ne se fera pas tirer [par] la manche, He won't want much pressing *or* won't want to be asked twice.

L'un tire à hue et l'autre à dia, They are pulling different ways *or* are not pulling together.

S'en tirer tout juste, To escape by (*or* with) the skin of one's teeth.

Se tirer d'affaire, To get over the difficulty, To save one's bacon.

Se tirer d'affaire le mieux possible, To make the best of a bad job *or* of it.

Tirer à la ligne, To pad (*lengthen literary production by inserting unnecessary matter*).

Tirer à sa fin, To draw to a (*or* its) close, To come to an end, To be nearly over ; To run low *or* out ; To be nearing one's end, To be on one's last legs.

Tirer au large, To run away, To make off, To skedaddle, To beat it (*slang*).

Tirer [en longueur], To drag [on].

Tirer le diable par la queue, To pull the devil by the tail, To struggle constantly against adversity, To struggle hard for a living.

Tirer les oreilles à quelqu'un, To give someone a flea in his ear.

Tirer ses chausses *ou* ses grègues, To make oneself scarce, To take to one's heels, To cut and run.

Tirer sur l'âge, To be growing old.

Tirer sur quelqu'un, To abuse (*or* To slang) someone.

Tirer une chose en longueur, To spin a thing out.

Vous tirez sur vos troupes *ou* sur vos gens, You are barking up the wrong tree. "There was an excellent command! to charge in with our horse upon our own wings, and to rend our own soldiers."—*All's Well That Ends Well* III, 6.

See also AVANTAGE, BOIRE, BON 29, BOUE, BOULET, BOUT, BRAIE, BRAS, CABRIOLE, CARTE, CHARRUE, CLAIR, CONSÉQUENCE, CORDE, COUTEAU, COUVERTURE, CRU, ÉCHELLE, ÉPINE, ÉPINGLE, FOURREAU, HOROSCOPE, HUILE, LANGUE, MARRON, MOUTURE, PAILLE, PARTI, PATTE, PIED, PISTOLET, PLUME, POUDRE, RAISON, RÉVÉRENCE, RIDEAU, TALON, TAS, VANITÉ, VER.

tiroir. *See* PIÈCE, ROMAN.

tison. Un tison d'enfer, A hell-hound (*man*); A hell-cat (*woman*).

titre. *See* POSSESSION.

tocsin. Sonner le tocsin contre (*ou* sur) quelqu'un, To raise a hue and cry against someone.

toi. *See* ATTENDRE, TU.

toile. *See* OURDIR.

toilette. Faire la toilette d'un mort, To lay out a corpse.

Faire la toilette d'un texte, To revise a text.

toise. *See* MESURER.

toiser. Toiser quelqu'un [de la tête aux pieds], To look someone up and down, To eye someone all over.

toit. Crier (*ou* Publier) quelque chose sur les toits, To proclaim something from the house-tops.

tombe. Avoir un pied dans la tombe, To have one foot in the grave.

See also MUET.

tombeau. Mettre (*ou* Conduire) (*ou* Mener) quelqu'un au tombeau (*fig.*), To be the death of one (*of a cause, as an illness*).

See also CREUSER, DESCENDRE, PORTE, SECRET.

tomber. Cela m'est tombé sous les yeux, I chanced to notice that.

Faire tomber la conversation sur quelque sujet, To bring the conversation round to some subject.

Faire tomber la tête de quelqu'un, To strike off someone's head. "Thy sale of offices and towns in France, —... Would make thee quickly hop without thy head."—2 *King Henry VI* I, 3.

Il faut laisser tomber cela, Let that drop, [Appear to] take no notice of that.

La pièce est tombée [à plat], The play has fallen flat *or* is a failure *or* is a flop.

Laisser tomber la conversation, To let the conversation flag.

Tomber comme une masse, To fall like a log.

Tomber dans (*ou* à) l'eau (*fig.*), To fall flat, Not to come to pass, Not to come off.

Tomber dans la dévotion, To take to religion.

Tomber dans la nasse *ou* dans le panneau, To fall into the trap.

Tomber de la poêle dans la braise *ou* Tomber de fièvre en chaud mal *ou* Tomber de Charybde en Scylla, To fall (*or* To jump) out of the frying pan into the fire, To avoid Scylla and fall into Charybdis. "Thus must I from the smoke into the smother."—*As You Like It* I, 2. "Thus have I shunn'd the fire, for fear of burning, And drench'd me in the sea, where I am drown'd."—*Two Gentlemen of Verona* I, 3. "Thou'dst shun a bear; But if thy flight lay toward the roaring sea, Thou'dst meet the bear i' the mouth."—*King Lear* III, 4. "Thus when I shun Scylla, your father, I fall into Charybdis, your mother."—*The Merchant of Venice* III, 5.

Tomber sur quelqu'un, To pitch into someone (*lit. & fig.*).

Tomber sur ses pieds *ou* Tomber debout (*fig.*), To fall on one's feet.

Un auteur tombé, An author whose play has fallen flat.

See also ALOUETTE, ARME, BIEN,

BOMBE, BRANLER, BRAS, CASAQUIN, CIEL, CROTTE, DENT, ENFANCE, ÉPINGLE, FOSSÉ, GUÊPIER, HAUT, HAUTEUR, NUE, PATTE, PLUME, PREMIER, QUATRE, QUENOUILLE, RIDICULE, SENS, SOURD, TÊTE, TUILE.

ton. C'est le ton qui fait la chanson, It isn't what one (he) (she) says, it's the way one (he) (she) says it.

Donner le ton, To set the fashion.

Le prendre avec quelqu'un sur un certain ton, To take up a certain attitude towards someone.

Prendre un ton, To put on airs.

Se mettre au ton de quelqu'un, To adapt oneself to someone's ways.

See also BAISSER, CHANGER, CHANTER, DIRE, HAUSSER, HAUT.

tondre. À brebis tondue Dieu mesure le vent, God tempers the wind to the shorn lamb.

Il faut tondre les brebis et non pas les écorcher, Don't open your mouth too wide (*don't ask for too much*).

Il tondrait un œuf, He would skin a flint.

Tondre la brebis de trop près, To overtax the people, To bleed the nation white.

Tondre quelqu'un (*fig.*), To fleece someone.

See also LAINE, PELER.

tonneau. C'est le tonneau des Danaïdes, It is like pouring water down a drain (*the expenditure is endless*), It is a Danaidean task. " As profitless as water in a sieve." *Much Ado About Nothing* V, 1.

C'est un tonneau, He is a drunkard. " A tun of man is thy companion." —1 *King Henry IV* II, 4.

tonner. Tonner sur les choux, To break a butterfly on the wheel.

See also BRUIT, TONNERRE.

tonnerre. Toutes les fois qu'il tonne, le tonnerre ne tombe pas, Threats are not always carried out.

See also COUP 11.

toper. Tope [là] *ou* Topez là, Agreed, Done, Let us shake hands on it. " *Martius*. Yonder comes news :— a wager they have met. *Lartius*. My horse to yours, no. *Mar*. 'Tis done. *Lart*. Agreed."—*Coriolanus* I, 4.

topique. Un exemple topique, A case in point.

toquer. Il est un peu toqué, He's not quite all there, He isn't all there.

torcher. Cela est mal torché *ou* est torché à la diable, That (*work*) has been scamped *or* botched.

Torcher le plat, To lick the platter clean.

torchon. *See* BRÛLER.

tordre. Tordre le nez, To show annoyance.

Tordre le nez sur quelque chose, To turn up one's nose at something.

Se tordre de rire, To be convulsed with laughter.

torrent. *See* PLEUVOIR.

tort. À tort ou à droit, Justly or unjustly, Fair or foul.

À tort ou à raison, Rightly or wrongly.

Mettre quelqu'un dans son tort, To put someone in the wrong.

See also DOUBLER, PARLER.

tortue. *See* MARCHER.

tôt. Ce sera tôt fait, It won't take long.

Le plus tôt sera le mieux, The sooner the better.

See also DONNER, VÉRITÉ.

touche. La pierre de touche (*fig.*), The touchstone. " They have all been touch'd and found base metal." —*Timon of Athens* III, 3. " Ah, Buckingham, now do I play the touch, To try if thou be current gold indeed."—*King Richard III* IV, 2.

See also DRÔLE.

toucher. C'est une corde qu'il ne faut pas toucher, It is a sore point.

Il n'a pas l'air d'y toucher, He is a dark horse.

Je lui en ai touché quelques mots, I just mentioned it to him, her.

Les extrêmes se touchent, Extremes meet.

Ne touchez pas cette corde[-là], Do not speak of that (*sore point*), Keep off that subject.

See also BARRE, BOUT, BUT, COUCHANT, DOIGT, PRÈS.

toujours. *See* AUTANT, DIRE, ENFANT, ÊTRE, GAGNER, HARENG, HERBE, MÊME, NEZ, ORDRE, PÊCHER, PRÉSENT, RECOMMENCER, SCÈNE.

toupet. Avoir du toupet, To have plenty of (*or, slang,* some) cheek.

tour. [À] chacun son tour, Turn and turn about.

Avoir le tour de main, To have the knack of it.

Avoir plus d'un tour dans son [bis]sac *ou* dans sa gibecière, To have more than one trick up one's sleeve, To have other tricks in one's locker.

En un tour de main, In a jiffy.

Faire demi-tour, To turn back (*retire from a place*).

Faire le tour du monde, To go round the world.

Fait au tour, Shapely (*limb*) ; Graceful (*with pleasing harmony of outline*) (*person*).

Jouer un tour [de sa façon *ou* de son métier] à quelqu'un, To play someone one of one's tricks.

Le tour est joué, It has come off (*the ruse has succeeded*).

Un tour de faveur, Preferential treatment.

Un tour de force, A feat of strength ; A feat of skill.

Vous parlerez à votre tour [de parole], You will speak in your turn.

See also BABEL, BÂTON, BRAS, CADRAN, JOUER, MÉDITER, SANG.

tournant. Je le rattraperai au tournant, I'll be even with him, I'll pay him out.

tourner. C'est un esprit mal tourné, He has a perverse (*or* a cross-grained) mind.

C'est un homme bien tourné, He is a well set-up, handsome man.

Faire tourner et virer quelqu'un, To twist (*or* To turn) someone round one's [little] finger. *Cf.* Tourner et virer quelqu'un *below*.

La tête lui a tourné, It has turned his, her, brain (*made him, her, a lunatic*) ; It has turned his, her, head (*excited him, her, beyond self-control*).

La tête lui tourne, His (Her) head is turning *or* going round, He (She) feels giddy, His (Her) head is swimming, He (She) has a swimming in the head.

Ne savoir de quel côté se tourner, Not to know where (*or* which way) to turn, To see no way out of it.

Tourner à tous vents *ou* Tourner comme une girouette, To turn one's face with every wind, To turn like a weathercock. "As a wedercock that turneth his face with every wind."—CHAUCER. "I am a feather for each wind that blows."—*The Winter's Tale* II, 3.

Tourner autour du pot, To beat about the bush. *Quotation under* ALLER.

Tourner bien, To take a good turn, To turn out well.

Tourner casaque, To turn tail ; To turn one's coat, To change sides.

Tourner de l'œil, To turn up one's toes (*die*) (*slang*) ; To feel ill ; To faint.

Tourner du côté de quelqu'un, To take sides (*or* To side) with someone.

Tourner et virer quelqu'un, To sound someone.

Tourner le dos à ses assaillants, To turn tail.

Tourner mal, To take a bad turn, To turn out badly, To go to the dogs *or* (*semi-humorous*) to the bow-wows. Cela tournera mal, Evil will come of it.

Tourner quelqu'un en bourrique, To drive someone crazy, To daze someone.

Tourner tout en bien, en mal, To put a good, a bad, construction (*or* complexion) on everything.

Tourner une chose en plaisanterie *ou* en raillerie, To laugh a thing off.

Tourner une difficulté, To get over a difficulty.

See also CŒUR, LANGUE, POUCE, RIDICULE, VIDE.

tournure. Donner une autre tournure à une chose, To put a different complexion on a matter.

See also PRENDRE.

tous. Tous sans exception *ou* Tous jusqu'au dernier, One and all, Every man jack of them.

Tous tant que nous sommes, All of us.

See also BRUIT, CHAUSSURE, CHEMIN, COMPTER, COUP 4, CRIN, DIABLE, DIRE, FÊTE, JOUR, LIMON, MENTIR, MOIS, SAINT, SEIGNEUR, SELLE, TEMPS, TOURNER, TOUT, TREMBLER, TRENTE-SIX, USAGE, VU.

tout. À tout prendre, [Up]on the whole, Everything considered.

Changer du tout au tout, To change (*or* To alter) completely.

Être capable de tout, To be capable of anything (*useful or bad*), To stop (*or* To stick) at nothing (*bad*).

Il en fait son tout, He (She) is everything to him.

Il y a une différence du tout au tout, There is all the difference in the world.

Le tout ensemble, The general effect.

Pour tout potage, All told.

Risquer (*ou* Jouer) le tout pour le tout, To risk all to win all. Il faut risquer le tout pour le tout, It's neck or nothing.

Se faire tout à tous, To make oneself all things to all men (1 *Corinthians* ix, 22).

Tout le fourbi *ou* Tout le tremblement, Lock, stock, and barrel, Every blessed thing, The whole bag of tricks, The whole boiling, The whole caboodle (*slang*).

Tout le monde et son père, All the world and his wife, All and sundry.

Tout taillé *ou* Tout fait, Cut and dried *or* dry.

See also ALLER, APPRENDRE, ARME, ATTENDRE, AUNE, BESOGNE, BIEN, BON 68, BOUT, BRANLER, BROCHER, BRUIT, CAUSE, CHAUD, CHEMIN, CŒUR, COMME, COMMENCEMENT, COMPTE, COMPTER, CONSIDÉRER, CONTRE, COUP 60, COURIR, COURT, COÛTER, DEMEURER, DÉVORER, DIRE, ÊTRE, FLÈCHE, FRIRE, GAGNER, HALEINE, HAUT, HISTOIRE, LAISSER, MISÉRICORDE, MOURIR, NERF, NEUF, NOUVEAU, NU, ŒIL, ŒUVRE, OR, OREILLE, PIÈCE, POIL, POINT, PORTRAIT, PRÉSENT, PROMETTRE, PROPOS, PROPRE, RACCROCHER, RÉFLÉCHIR, REFUSER, REGISTRE, RETRACER, RIEN, RIRE, ROSE, ROULER, SANG, SAVOIR, SEIGNEUR, SENS, SOLEIL, SORT, SOUFFRIR, SPECTACLE, SUCRE, TEMPS, TIRER, TOURNER, TRIOMPHER, TROTTE, UN, UNIR, VENANT, VENT, VENUE, VOIR.

toute. Pour toute chose, All told.

See also BRIDE, HISTOIRE, MESURE, NOUVELLE, PEINE, PRÉVISION, PROPORTION, REVERS, SAINT, SOMME, TÊTE.

toutes. *See* ACCOMMODER, ACCOUTRER, ARMER, FOIS, FORCE, HABILLER, HEURE, JAMBE, MAIN, MANGER, OREILLE, PAROISSE, PORTE, RÈGLE, SAUCE, SERRURE, VAINCRE, VÉRITÉ, VOIR.

toux. *See* SAPIN.

trace. *See* BAISER, MARCHER, SUIVRE.

tracer. Tracer le chemin à quelqu'un pour faire quelque chose, To show someone the way to do something.

See also SILLON.

tragique. Prendre les choses au tragique, To take things too seriously, To go [in] off the deep end.

See also RONRON.

trahir. On n'est jamais trahi que par les siens, Save me from my friends. " God keep me from false friends!" —*King Richard III* III, 1.

Se trahir [soi-même], To give oneself away.

train. Aller bon train, To go at a good [round] pace.

Aller son train, To be going on as usual, To be taking its course.

Aller un train d'enfer *ou* un train de chien, To go at a break-neck pace, To go hell for leather.

Être dans le train, To be in the swim, To be abreast of the times, To be up to date (*slang*).

Être en train, To be in the mood ; To be on the road : Quand il est en train, rien ne lui coûte, When he is in the mood, nothing will stop him. Il n'est pas en train de rire, He is in no laughing mood. Il est en train de se ruiner, He is on the road to ruin.

Faire aller quelqu'un bon (*ou* grand) train, To treat someone with a high hand.

Le train ordinaire des jours *ou* Le train-train quotidien de la vie, The daily round.

See also BAL, CHASSE-MARÉE, DIABLE, MAL, MANQUER, MENER, ONZE, POSTE, RÉFORMER.

traînée. Se répandre comme une traînée de poudre, To spread like wildfire.

traîner. Ne pas traîner en affaires, Not to let the grass grow under one's feet.

See also BOUE, BOULET, GÉMONIES.

trait. Avoir du trait, To have a pretty (*or* a dainty) wit.

Ce sont de vos traits, That is just like you, That is you all over.

Partir comme un trait [d'arbalète], To be off like a shot *or* (*slang*) like greased lightning. " I go, I go ; look how I go,—Swifter than arrow from the Tartar's bow."—*A Midsummer Night's Dream* III, 2. " Do you think me a swallow, an arrow, or a bullet ? "—2 *King Henry IV* IV, 3. " We will . . . make them skirr away as swift as stones Enforced from the old Assyrian slings."—*King Henry V* IV, 7. " Bear this sealed brief With winged haste." — 1 *King Henry IV* IV, 4.

Peindre les événements à grands traits, To depict [the] events in bold outline.

See also ADRESSE.

traiter. Il se traite bien, He does himself well *or* proud.

Traiter quelqu'un de fat, de fou, d'impertinent, To call someone a fool, a madman, an impertinent fellow.

See also BRAS, COMPAGNON, GARÇON, HAUT, NÈGRE, PUISSANCE, RUDESSE.

tralala. Être en grand tralala, To be dressed up to the nines, To be got up to kill.

tramer. Il se trame quelque chose, There is something brewing *or* something afoot *or* something in the wind.

tramontane. *See* PERDRE.

tranchant. *See* ARGUMENT, ARME.

trancher. Trancher le mot, To speak out, To put it plainly. Pour [le] trancher net, To cut a long story short. " To end a tale of length."—*Troilus and Cressida* I, 3.

See also BEAU 29, SEIGNEUR, VIF.

tranquilliser. Tranquillisez-vous sur ce point, Set your mind at rest on that point.

transe. Être dans les transes (*ou* dans des transes mortelles) à la pensée de ce qui pourrait arriver, To be on tenterhooks (*or* shivering in one's shoes) at the thought of what might happen.

transiger. Ne pas transiger, To be adamant. " You hard-hearted adamant."—*A Midsummer Night's Dream* II, 2.

transir. *See* PEUR.

transpercer. Être transpercé jusqu'aux os, To be wet (*or* soaked) to the skin, To look like a drowned rat. *Quotations under* MOUILLER.

Transpercer le cœur à quelqu'un *ou* Transpercer quelqu'un de douleur, To pierce someone to the heart, To cut someone to the quick.

travail. *See* AURORE, BÉNÉDICTIN, BŒUF, CHEVAL, CONSACRER, CREVER, HALEINE, PLANCHE, ROMAIN, ROUTINE, TUER.

travailler. Faire travailler son argent, To employ one's money, To turn one's capital to account. Son argent travaille sans cesse, His money (*or* capital) is never idle.

Son esprit, sa tête, travaille, His (Her) mind (*or* head *or* brain) is in a ferment *or* in a whirl. *Quotations under* CHAOS.

Travailler comme un galérien *ou* comme un forçat *ou* comme un nègre *ou* comme un cheval *ou* comme un mercenaire *ou* comme quatre, To work like a galley-slave *or* like a nigger *or* like a horse.

See also POUVOIR, TUER.

travers. Avoir l'esprit de travers, To have a warped disposition.

Il donne dans ce travers, He leans (*or* is inclined) to this bad habit.

Prendre quelque chose de travers, To put a wrong construction on something.

Regarder quelqu'un de travers, To look black at someone.

Se mettre en travers d'un projet, To thwart a project.

See also BONNET, CHAPEAU, ENTENDRE, PARLER.

traverse. Venir (*ou* Se jeter) à la traverse, To intervene (*interfere so as to prevent or modify result*).

See also CHEMIN.

trébuchet. Prendre quelqu'un au trébuchet, To entrap (*or* To beguile) someone (*into doing something against his will or interest*).

tréfonds. *See* FONDS.

treille. Le jus de la treille, The juice of the grape (*wine*).

treize. *See* DOUZAINE.

tremblement. *See* TOUT.

trembler. Trembler dans sa peau, To shake in one's shoes.

Trembler depuis les pieds jusqu'à la tête *ou* Trembler de tous ses membres, To be all of a tremble.

See also FEUILLE.

tremper. Avoir un esprit bien trempé, To have a vigorous mind.

Être trempé jusqu'aux os *ou* Être trempé comme une soupe, To be wet (*or* soaked) to the skin, To look like a drowned rat. *Quotations under* MOUILLER.

trente-six. Tous les trente-six du mois, Once in a blue moon *or* in a while.

See also CHANDELLE, SOT.

tresser. Tresser des couronnes à quelqu'un, To crown someone with glory and honour. " How sweet a thing it is to wear a crown; Within whose circuit is Elysium, And all that poets feign of bliss and joy."—3 *King Henry VI* I, 2.

trêve. *See* PAIX.

tribord. *See* FEU.

tribut. *See* PAYER.

trier. Trié sur le volet, Carefully selected (*things*); Very select (*people*).

triomphe. Le triomphe de la vertu, The triumph of virtue. " Heaven is above all yet; there sits a Judge That no king can corrupt."—*King Henry VIII* III, 1.

Porter quelqu'un en triomphe, To carry someone shoulder high, To chair someone.

triompher. Triompher de tout, To carry all before one.

triste. Avoir une triste figure *ou* une triste mine, Not to look up to the mark, To look white about the gills.

Être triste comme un bonnet de nuit, To have a face as long as a fiddle *or* a long face. " I am as melancholy as a gib-cat or a lugged bear.—Or an old lion, or a lover's lute.—Yea, or the drone of a Lincolnshire bagpipe. "—1 *King Henry IV* I, 2. *Note.*—lugged = worried (*in baiting*).

Faire triste figure *ou* triste mine, To pull a long face. " With tristful visage."—*Hamlet* III, 4.

Faire triste mine à quelqu'un, To give someone a poor, a cold, welcome.

Faire un triste repas, To make a melancholy meal ; To make a poor (*or* a sorry) (*or* a wretched) meal.

Faire une triste figure, To cut a sorry figure, To look sadly out of place, To be very uncomfortable *or* ill at ease.

Il (Elle) est triste comme un lendemain de fête, It is a case of the morning after the night before.

Le temps est triste, The weather is dismal.

See also CHEVALIER, VIN.

trois. *See* BRAVE, ÉTOILE, PELER, QUART, SOT, VIE.

troisième. *See* DESSOUS, ÉLEVER, RAVIR.

trombe. *See* ENTRER.

trompe. Publier quelque chose à son de trompe, To trumpet something abroad, To sound something far and wide, To let all the world know something.

tromper. À s'y tromper *ou* À se tromper, Not to be able to tell one from the other, To be remarkably alike ; To be able to make a mistake : Elle ressemble à sa sœur à s'y (*ou* à se) tromper, One can't tell her from her sister. Il lui ressemble à s'y tromper, He is remarkably like him. Il n'y a pas à s'y tromper, There is no mistake about it.

C'est ce qui vous trompe, That is where you are mistaken *or* wrong.

Se tromper dans son calcul, To be out in one's reckoning.

Tromper le temps, To while away the time.

Tromper les regards, To escape notice.

trompette. Il est bon cheval de trompette, il ne s'étonne pas du bruit, It takes a lot (*or* more than that) to frighten him.

See also DÉLOGER, EMBOUCHER, TAMBOUR.

trompeur. *See* DEMI.

tronquer. Tronquer une citation, To garble a quotation.

trop. Être de trop, To be in the way, To be unwelcome, To intrude.

Trop est trop *ou* Rien de trop, Enough is as good as a feast. " If thou art rich, thou art poor ; For, like an ass whose back with ingots bows, Thou bear'st thy heavy riches but a journey, And death unloads thee."—*Measure for Measure* III, 1.

See also CORDE, CUISINIER, EMBRASSER, FIN, GALON, GRATTER, HÂTER, HAUT, JEU, LONG, OCCUPER, OS, PRÉCAUTION, PROUVER, SOMME, TARD, TONDRE, VIOLENT.

tropique. *See* BAPTÊME.

troquer. *See* AVEUGLE.

trotte. Tout d'une trotte, Without stopping, At a stretch.

trotter. Cette idée lui trotte dans (*ou* par) la tête *ou* la cervelle, This idea keeps running in (*or* through) his head, He can't get that idea out of his head, He can't forget it.

See also ENTENDRE.

trou. Un petit trou mort, A dead-and-alive little hole.

Un petit trou pas cher, A cheap little place in the country [, where one can spend a quiet holiday].

See also AIGUILLE, BOIRE, BOUCHER, BOUTEILLE, LUNE, NORMAND, SOURIS.

trouble. Avoir la vue trouble *ou* Voir

trouble, To be dim-sighted. " My sight was ever thick."—*Julius Caesar V*, 3.

Avoir une vue trouble des choses, To have a confused idea of things.

Le temps est trouble, The weather is murky.

See also PÊCHER.

troubler. *See* FÊTE, MORT.

trouille. Avoir la trouille, To be funky, To have (*or* To get) the wind up (*slang*).

troupe. Aller (*ou* Marcher) en troupe, To go (*or* To walk) in a band (*herded together*).

Aller (*ou* Marcher) par troupes, To go (*or* To walk) in groups (*not herded together*).

La troupe céleste, The heavenly host (*Luke* ii, 13).

See also COMIQUE, TIRER.

troupeau. *See* GALEUX.

trousse. Être aux trousses de quelqu'un, To be after someone, To be at someone's heels (*following him about*).

trousser. Trousser une affaire, To dispatch (*or* To polish off) a piece of business.

See also BAGAGE.

trouver. C'est bien trouvé ! Happy thought !

Cela, c'est trouvé ! (*ironiquement*), What a find !

Où avez-vous trouvé cela ? Where did you get that from ? What put that into your head ?

Trouver à dire à, To take exception to, To find fault with, To carp at ; To have something to say to: Il était si embarrassé qu'il n'a rien trouvé à dire, He was so embarrassed that he could find nothing to say *or* that he lost (*or* couldn't find) his tongue.

Trouver à qui parler, To find (*or* To meet) one's match.

Trouver à redire à quelque chose, To take exception to something, To find fault with (*or* To carp at) (*or* To pick holes in) something.

Trouver le temps long, To find the time hang on one's hands.

Trouver son maître, To find (*or* To meet) one's master.

Vous trouvez ? You think so ?

See also BON 69, 70, BUISSON, CHAUSSURE, CHERCHER, COMPTE, CONNAISSANCE, COUPE, CROIRE, CRUEL, DÉPAYSER, DOUZAINE, EAU, ENCLUME, FILON, FORT, GÂTEAU, JOINT, MAUVAIS, MÉCHANT, NID, PAS, PIERRE, PRENDRE, SELLE, TUF, VERGE, VISAGE.

truchement. *See* ŒIL.

tu. Être à tu et à toi avec tout le monde, To be on familiar terms (*or* To be hail fellow well met) with everybody.

tuer. Avoir une heure à tuer, To have an hour on one's hands *or* an hour to kill.

Je me tue à vous répéter toujours la même chose, I am sick [and tired] of telling you the same thing over and over again.

La lettre tue et l'esprit vivifie *ou* La lettre tue, mais l'esprit donne la vie, The letter killeth, but the spirit giveth life (2 *Corinthians* iii, 6).

On s'y tuait, We were almost squashed to death *or* suffocated (*the crowd was so dense*).

Se tuer à force de boire, To drink oneself to death.

Se tuer à force de travail[ler] *ou* Se tuer de travail, To work oneself to death, To wear oneself out (*or* To kill oneself) with hard work, To wear one's fingers to the bone.

Se tuer à plaisir, To endanger one's health wantonly.

Tuer le temps, To kill (*or* To while away) time.

Tuer quelque chose dans l'œuf, To nip something in the bud. " And therefore think him as a serpent's egg, . . . And kill him in the shell." —*Julius Caesar* II, 1.

See also GRAS, PEAU, PISTOLET, POULE, VER.

tuerie. C'est une vraie tuerie, The crush (*crowd of people*) is dreadful.

tue-tête (à). *See* CRIER.

tuf. Trouver le tuf, To get down to bed-rock.

tuile. Être logé sous les tuiles, To live in an attic.

Il m'est tombé une tuile sur la tête, It was a bolt from the blue (*unexpected misfortune*). " I know his brains are forfeit to the next tile that falls."—*All's Well That Ends Well* IV, 3.

Quelle tuile ! What rotten luck !

Turc. Servir de tête de Turc, To serve as a butt (*of someone's ridicule*).

See also FORT.

tutelle. *See* PRENDRE, TENIR.

tuyau. Avoir des tuyaux, To be in the know.

Dire quelque chose (*ou* Parler) à quelqu'un dans le tuyau de l'oreille, To whisper something in someone's ear, To say something to someone in his private ear. " Your followers I will whisper to the business."—*The Winter's Tale* I, 2. " For I would commune with you of such things That want no ear but yours."—*Measure for Measure* IV, 3.

tympan. Briser (*ou* Rompre) (*ou* Crever) le tympan à quelqu'un (*fig.*), To split someone's ear-drums, To make a deafening noise. *Quotation under* DÉCHIRER.

U

un. C'est tout l'un ou tout l'autre, It is either one thing or the other, There is no middle course.

C'est tout un *ou* Ce n'est qu'un, It's all one, It's all the same, It's as broad as it's long, It makes no difference, It comes to the same thing.

Dire d'un, puis d'un autre, To say first one thing, then another, To contradict oneself.

En savoir plus d'une, To know a thing or two, To know what's what.

Il dit d'une façon et il fait d'une autre, He says one thing and does another. " If for I want that glib and oily art To speak and purpose not."—*King Lear* I, 1. " And be these juggling fiends no more believ'd, That palter with us in a double sense ; That keep the word of promise to our ear, And break it to our hope!"—*Macbeth* V, 8.

Ils ne font qu'un, They are hand in (*or* are hand and) glove with one another.

L'un vaut l'autre, One is as good as the other ; One is as bad as the other ; They are as good, as bad, as each other, It is six of one and half a dozen of the other.

L'un(e) dans l'autre, [Taking] one with the other, Taking it all round, On an average.

Ne faire ni une ni deux, To make no bones about it.

Ne savoir qu'une note *ou* qu'une chanson, To be always harping on the same string, To harp (*or* To keep harping) on one string, To chew the rag (*slang*). *Quotation under* MÊME.

Qui voit l'un voit l'autre, To see one is to see the other, There is no difference between them.

See also AVIS, BOUCHER, CHANSON, DIRE, DONNER, DORMIR, ENTENDRE, EXPLIQUER, FESSE, JOUR, LOUP, MERVEILLE, MOT, MOUTURE, NOTE, NU, NUIRE, ŒIL, OREILLE, OS, PÊCHER, PELER, PERDRE, PIÈCE, PLEURER, PORTER, QUATRE, QUEUE, SAVOIR, SOMME, TIRER, TOUR, VALOIR.

unique. C'est (*ou* Voilà qui est) unique, That's (*or* It's) the limit (*slang*), Who ever heard of such a thing ?

Faire un front unique, To present a united front.

Vous êtes unique, You're the limit (*slang*).

unir. Un homme tout uni, A plain man (*of homely manners*).

See also GESTE.

universel. Cet homme est universel, This man is a walking encyclopaedia.

usage. Faire usage de tous ses moyens, To use every means in one's power.

See also PERDRE.

user. Cet argument est usé jusqu'à la corde, That argument is worn threadbare.

Cette plaisanterie est usée jusqu'à la corde, That joke is a chestnut.

Cette ruse est usée jusqu'à la corde, That trick is played out.

En user familièrement (*ou* librement) avec quelqu'un, To be on familiar terms with someone.

See also BON 27, FOURREAU.

utilité. Cela n'est d'aucune utilité, That is [of] no [earthly] use.

V

vache. Il est de la vache à Colas, He is a protestant.

La vache à Colas, Protestantism.

Une vache à lait (*fig.*), A milch cow.

Une vache n'y retrouverait pas son veau, You never saw such disorder.

See also GARDER, MANGER, MÉTIER, PARLER, PLANCHER.

vague. *See* HUILE, RÊVERIE.

vaillant. N'être pas vaillant, Not to be up to the mark.

See also SOU.

vain. *See* DIEU.

vaincre. Vaincre toutes les résistances, To overcome all resistance, To carry all before one.

See also AVOUER.

vainqueur. Prendre des airs vainqueurs, To put on (*or* To give oneself) the airs and graces of a conquering hero.

vaisseau. *See* BRÛLER.

val. *See* MONT.

valet. *See* MAÎTRE, PROPOS.

vallée. Cette vallée de larmes, This vale of tears (*life here below*).

valoir. Les deux hommes se valent, They are two of a pair, They are both tarred with the same brush.

Se faire valoir, To make the most of oneself; To push oneself forward.

Un tiens vaut mieux que deux tu l'auras *ou* Il vaux mieux (*ou* Mieux vaut) tenir que courir *ou* Mieux vaut un moineau dans la main que la grive qui vole *ou* Un oiseau dans la main vaut mieux que deux dans la haie, A bird in the hand is worth two in the bush.

Vaille que vaille, For what it is worth, For better [or] for worse.

See also AFFAIRE, ARRACHER, AUTANT, AVERTIR, AVIS, BON 21, 73, CHANDELLE, CHIEN, CLOU, CORDE, DIABLE, DIRE, ENCLUME, ENVIE, FAIRE, GRAND-CHOSE, JEU, MÉTIER, OR, PAIN, PARLER, PAROLE, PLIER, POSSESSION, PREMIER, PRÉVENIR, QUATRE, RIEN, SAINT, SAUCE, SOU, TARD, TERRE, UN, VIE.

valser. *See* ARGENT.

vanité. Tirer vanité d'une chose, To take pride (*or* To glory) in a thing, To plume oneself on a thing.

vanter. Il n'y a pas de quoi se vanter, That's nothing to boast (*or, slang*, to shout) about.

vase. *See* EMMIELLER, GOUTTE.

va-tout. Jouer son va-tout, To stake one's all *or* one's last farthing.

vau-l'eau. Aller à vau-l'eau, To go to

rack and ruin (*of an enterprise*), To go to pot (*slang*).

veau. *See* ADORER, GRAS, PLEURER, PLIER, VACHE.

vedette. Avoir (*ou* Occuper) la vedette sur l'affiche, To head (*or* To top) the bill (*of actor*).

Être en vedette (*fig.*), To be in the limelight.

veille. *See* CONSACRER, POISSONNIER.

veiller. *See* GRAIN.

veilleuse. Cette usine est en veilleuse, This works is (*or* These works are) [only] working with a skeleton staff.

Mettre la lumière en veilleuse, To dim the light.

veine. Être en veine, To be in [the] vein (*in the mood to produce something good or great*).

Être en veine de bonheur, To be in luck's way. " Fortune and I are friends."—*Troilus and Cressida* III, 3.

Ne pas avoir de veine, To have no luck, To draw a blank.

See also COUP 70.

velours. Jouer sur le velours, To be on velvet.

See also CHEMIN, GANTER, PATTE.

vénal. C'est une plume vénale, He is a penny-a-liner *or* a hack writer ; He is an inspired writer (*writes what he is told to write*).

venant. À tout venant, To all comers, To all and sundry.

À tout venant beau jeu, I am (He is) ready to take on all comers, Let 'em all come (*slang*).

vendange. *See* ADIEU.

vendre. Ce n'est pas tout que de vendre, il faut livrer (*fig.*), Sellers must deliver the goods.

See also CHAT, CHEMISE, CHER, DÉPENDRE, MÈCHE, OR, PAIN, PEAU.

vendredi. *See* RIRE.

vengeance. *See* CRIER, MORCEAU.

venin. C'est un homme sans venin *ou* qui n'a point de venin, He is a man who bears no malice. " No levell'd malice Infects one comma in the course I hold."—*Timon of Athens* I, 1.

Jeter son venin, To vent one's spite. " Thy reason, dear venom : give thy reason."—*Twelfth Night* III, 2.

See also MORT, QUEUE.

venir. Attendre et voir venir, To wait and see.

Ce qui vient de la flûte s'en retourne au tambour *ou* Ce qui vient de flot s'en retourne de marée, Easy come, easy go, Lightly come, lightly go ; Ill got, ill gone. *Quotation under* AUTRUI.

Elle aura quinze ans, viennent les prunes, She will be fifteen [years old], [come] next summer. " I have known thee these twenty-nine years, come peascod time." — 2 *King Henry IV* II, 4.

En venir à son but *ou* à ses fins, To gain one's end, To achieve one's object, To get what one wants.

En venir aux coups (*ou* aux mains) (*ou* à la violence) sur quelqu'un, To come to blows with someone.

Être mal venu à faire quelque chose, To have no right to do (*or* no reason for doing) something.

Il faut en venir là, It is inevitable ; It comes (*or* amounts) to that.

Il faut voir venir les choses, Wait and see.

Je vous vois venir *ou* Je vois (*ou* Je comprends) où vous voulez en venir, I see what you are driving at. " What you would work me to, I have some aim."—*Julius Caesar* I, 2.

Les choses en sont-elles venues là ? Have things come to such a pass ?

Où (*ou* À quoi) voulez-vous en venir ? What are you [driving] at ? What is your little game ?

Qu'il y vienne, Let him try.

Va-t'en voir s'ils viennent, Tell me another.

Vienne une maladie, un revers, etc., Should illness, a reverse, etc., come.

See also ALLER, APPÉTIT, ATTENDRE, BALLE, BIEN, BOUT, BRÛLER, CHAIR, CHEVEU, CHIEN, COUP 77, DIRE, DORMIR, EAU, ÉCLAT, ENFARINER, FAIT, LOIN, MALHEUR, MARS, MOULIN, NOBLESSE, PAYS, PIED, PREMIER, PRISE, QUEUE, SABOT, SENTIR, TEMPS, TRAVERSE, VENT, VIEILLESSE, VOIE.

vent. Aller contre vent[s] et marée[s] *ou* S'obstiner (*ou* Persévérer) contre vent et marée (*fig.*), To pursue one's course (*or* To persist) in spite of all opposition.

Aller selon le vent (*fig.*), To drift with the current.

Avoir le vent dans ses voiles *ou* le vent en poupe, To be on the high road to success.

Avoir vent et marée, To be favoured by circumstances, To have everything in one's favour. " Sail how thou canst, have wind and tide thy friend."—3 *King Henry VI* V, 1. " My boat sails freely, both with wind and stream."—*Othello* II, 3. " There is a tide in the affairs of men Which, taken at the flood, leads on to fortune ; Omitted, all the voyage of their life Is bound in shallows and in miseries. On such a full sea are we now afloat ; And we must take the current when it serves, Or lose our ventures."—*Julius Caesar* IV, 3.

Il fait un vent à [d]écorner les bœufs, There is a wind enough to blow one's head off, It is blowing great guns, It is blowing a gale. " Blow, winds, and crack your cheeks ! rage! blow !" —*King Lear* III, 2. " The mountain pines . . . When they are fretted with the gusts of heaven."—*The Merchant of Venice* IV, 1.

Qu'en sort-il ? du vent, What does it amount to ? mere words *or* (*slang*) hot air.

Quel bon vent vous amène ? What lucky chance brings you here ? " And tell me now, sweet friend, what happy gale Blows you to Padua here from old Verona ? "—*The Taming of the Shrew* I, 2.

Regarder (*ou* Voir) de quel côté vient le vent, To see which way the wind is blowing, To find out how the wind blows *or* lies *or* how the land lies (*Also in this sense :* Prendre le vent) ; To amuse oneself looking (*idly*) out of the window. " Sits the wind in that corner ? "—*Much Ado About Nothing* II, 3.

Savoir d'où vient le vent, To know on which side one's bread is buttered.

Tout cela n'est que [du] vent *ou* Autant en emporte le vent, That's all moonshine *or* (*slang*) hot air. " This abundance of superfluous breath."—*King John* II, 1.

See also ABATTRE, BATTRE, DESSUS, ENTRER, FLAMBERGE, NEZ, PLUME, ROSEAU, SEMER, TEMPÊTE, TONDRE, TOURNER.

vente. *See* ALLER.

ventre. Avoir le ventre creux *ou* plat, To have an empty feeling *or* an aching void, To be [as] empty as a drum (*very hungry*).

Cet homme n'a rien dans le ventre (*fig.*), This man has nothing in him (*is thoroughly incapable*).

Être (*ou* Se mettre) à plat ventre devant quelqu'un, To grovel before (*or* To cringe to) someone.

Il n'avait que cet ouvrage dans le ventre, This is the only good work he ever wrote.

Je saurai ce qu'il a dans le ventre, I shall find out the stuff he is made of ; I shall discover what is in his mind *or* (*slang*) on his chest.

Passer sur le ventre à quelqu'un (*fig.*), To achieve one's purpose in spite of someone's opposition ; To get the better of someone.

Taper sur le ventre à quelqu'un, To give someone a dig in the ribs (*in offensive familiarity*).

Ventre à terre (*fig.*), At full gallop, Hell for leather.

Ventre affamé n'a point d'oreilles, It's no use preaching to a hungry man. " They said they were an-hungry ; sigh'd forth proverbs,— That hunger broke stone walls, that dogs must eat."—*Coriolanus* I, 1.

See also BOUDER, BROSSER, CŒUR, GRAND, MANGER, PAROLE, RIRE.

venue. Être tout d'une venue, To be straight up and down (*of person's figure, legs*).

ver. C'est un ver de terre, He (She) is a worm. " You froward and unable worms!"—*The Taming of the Shrew* V, 2.

Le ver rongeur, The worm of conscience, Remorse. " If Don Worm, his conscience, find no impediment to the contrary."—*Much Ado About Nothing* V, 2. " The worm of conscience still be-gnaw thy soul!"—*King Richard III* I, 3. " Leave her to heaven, And to those thorns that in her bosom lodge, To prick and sting her."—*Hamlet* I, 5.

Tirer les vers du nez à quelqu'un, To worm secrets out of someone, To pump someone. " I'll have this secret from thy heart, or rip Thy heart to find it."—*Cymbeline* III, 5.

Tuer le ver, To take a glass of spirits first thing in the morning.

Voilà qui n'est pas piqué des vers, That's not so bad *or* (*slang*) so dusty.

See also ÉCRASER, NU.

verbe. *See* HAUT.

verge. Donner des verges pour se [faire] fouetter, To lay up a rod for one's own back, To be asking (*or* looking) for trouble. " You lay out too much pains For purchasing but trouble."—*Cymbeline* II, 3.

Être (*ou* Se trouver) sous la verge de quelqu'un, To be under someone's thumb.

Gouverner quelqu'un avec une verge de fer, To rule someone with a rod of iron.

See also PASSER.

véritable. *See* BESOIN.

vérité. Dire à quelqu'un de grosses vérités *ou* Dire à quelqu'un ses vérités, To tell someone a few plain (*or* home) truths. *See also* Se tenir à quatre, *under* QUATRE.

Il n'y a que la vérité qui offense, Nothing hurts like the truth. " Truth's a dog must to kennel."—*King Lear* I, 4.

Le temps découvre la vérité *ou* Tôt ou tard la vérité se fait jour, Truth will out, Tempus omnia revelat. " Time shall unfold what plighted cunning hides."—*King Lear* I, 1. " Truth will come to light ; murder cannot be hid long : a man's son may ; but, in the end, truth will out."—*The Merchant of Venice* II, 2. " Well, time is the old justice that examines all such offenders."—*As You Like It* IV, 1.

Toutes vérités ne sont pas bonnes à dire, It is not always wise to speak the truth.

See also BRILLER, COUPER, FERMER, PUR.

verjus. *See* AIGRE, JUS.

verre. Cela, Il, est à mettre sous verre, That, He, ought to be kept in a glass case.

Vivre dans une maison de verre, To live an open life (*with nothing to conceal*).

See also CASSER, MÉDECINE, NOYER, TEMPÊTE.

verse. *See* PLEUVOIR.

verser. *See* BON 48, MAIN.

vert. Les raisins (*ou* Ils) sont trop verts, The grapes are sour. " O, will you eat No grapes, my royal fox ? yes, but you will My noble grapes, and if my royal fox Could reach them."—*All's Well That Ends Well* II, 1. " Like a poor beggar, raileth on the rich."—*King John* II, 1.

Se mettre au vert, To take a holiday, a rest, in the country.

See also DIABLE, EMPLOYER, JUS, MANGER, PRENDRE, TAPIS.

vertement. *See* TANCER.

vertu. Vous avez bien de la vertu, It's very good of you to do it (*I not wanting to do it myself*).

See also DRAPER, NÉCESSITÉ, NOBLESSE, TRIOMPHE.

vessie. Il veut faire prendre des vessies pour des lanternes *ou* Il veut faire croire que les vessies sont des lanternes, He would have us believe the moon is made of green cheese.

veste. Remporter une veste, To meet with a check *or* a repulse *or* a rebuff, To get snubbed *or* (*slang*) a smack in the eye.

vêtir. *See* OIGNON, SOMMAIREMENT.

viande. *See* CHARPIE, CREUX, TENDRE.

vice. *See* CLOAQUE, FANFARON, PAUVRETÉ.

victoire. *See* CHANTER.

vide. Tourner dans le vide *ou* Mâcher à vide, To beat the air.

See also GOUSSET.

vider. Vider une querelle, To adjust a difference, To fight (*or* To have) it out.

See also CARQUOIS, SAC.

vie. C'est la vie ! Such is life!

Faire la vie, To live riotously, To go the pace.

La vie à trois, The eternal triangle.

La vie de campagne *ou* La vie des champs, Country life.

Le chien en vie vaut mieux que le lion mort, A live dog is better than a dead lion.

Une vie de cocagne, A life of plenty.

See also ARRACHER, BAIL, BÂTON, CACHER, CÉNOBITE, CHANOINE, CHEMIN, CHER, CHERCHER, CHIEN, COMMUN, COURT, DUR, DURER, JOYEUX, MENER, QUITTER, REGAIN, ROSE, SACRIFIER, TEMPS, TENIR, TRAIN, TUER, VOIE, VOULOIR.

vieillesse. C'est la vieillesse qui vient, A.D. (= *Anno Domini*) is the trouble. " On us both did haggish age steal on, And wore us out of act."—*All's Well That Ends Well* I, 2.

See also BÂTON, CORTÈGE, JEUNESSE.

vieillir. *See* HARNOIS.

vieux. Être vieux comme les rues *ou* comme les chemins *ou* comme le monde, To be [as] old as the hills *or* as Adam.

Il ne fera pas de vieux os, He will not make old bones, He is not long for this world.

Un vieux de la vieille, One of the old guard.

Vieilles rancunes, Bad blood.

See also BARBE, CHASSE, CROÛTON, DÉPOUILLER, DIABLE, HOMME, PIPÉE, POUPÉE, RÉGLER, ROCHE, ROUTIER, SINGE.

vif. Il est vif comme la poudre, He is of an explosive nature. " For I do know Fluellen valiant, And, touch'd with choler, hot as gunpowder, And quickly will return an injury."—*King Henry V* IV, 7. " Zounds, I am afraid of this gunpowder Percy, though he be dead ; how if he should counterfeit too, and rise ? "—1 *King Henry IV* V, 4.

Piquer au vif, To cut to the quick, To touch on the raw, To make a home thrust.

Tailler (*ou* Trancher) (*ou* Couper) dans le vif (*fig.*), To have done with half measures.

See also ÉCUREUIL.

vigilance. *See* ENDORMIR, SURPRENDRE.

vigne. Être dans les vignes [du Seigneur], To be in one's cups.

vilain. Il fait vilain, It is wretched weather.

Un vilain oiseau *ou* Un vilain

merle, A most unpleasant man, A thoroughly nasty man.

See also BOTTE, CHÈRE, COCO, CRAPAUD, DRAP, HURE, JEU, MOUE, NID, OINDRE.

vilenie. *See* MÉDITER.

village. Cet homme est bien de son village, This man moves in a very narrow circle.

See also CHIEN, CLOCHER, COQ, INNOCENT.

ville. Avoir ville gagnée, To score a success.

Être à la ville, To be in town (*not in the country*).

Être en ville, To be in town *or* in the city (*not at home*).

See also COURIR, EMPÊCHER.

vin. Avoir le vin gai, mauvais, tendre, triste, To be merry, quarrelsome, affectionate, melancholy (*or* maudlin), in one's cups.

Être pris de vin, To be intoxicated.

See also BOIRE, CUVER, DANSER, EAU, ENSEIGNE, ENTRE, POINTE, PORTER, SAC.

vinaigre. *See* MOUCHE.

vingt. *See* DONNER, FOIS.

vingt-quatre. *See* SOT.

violence. Faire une douce violence à quelqu'un, To press someone to accept (*something he would like to have but which he refuses from politeness*).

Faire violence à la loi, à un texte, To stretch (*or* To strain) the law, a text.

Se faire violence, To do violence to one's feelings, To make an effort, *e.g.*, pour ne pas éclater de rire, not to burst out laughing.

See also DOUCEUR, VENIR.

violent. Cela est [trop] violent, That (*or* It) is [going] beyond a joke *or* (*slang*) is coming it a bit too strong.

violon. Payer les violons, To pay the piper. Il paie les violons et les autres dansent, He pays the piper while [the] others call the tune.

S'il me fait danser, il paiera les violons, If he calls the tune, he shall pay the piper.

virer. *See* TOURNER.

vis. *See* SERRER.

visage. Sous son vrai visage, In his (her) (its) true colours.

Trouver visage de bois, To find the door shut ; To find no one at home *or* nobody there.

See also ALLONGER, ALLUMER, BON 40, 43, CHANGER, COUPER, DÉCOUVERT, DÉTERRER, MAUVAIS, MONDE, MORT, NEZ, NOM, PAPIER, POUPÉE, RE[N]-FROGNER, RÉPROUVER.

visée. *See* RÉPONDRE.

viser. Viser plus haut, To fly at higher game (*fig.*).

See also SOLIDE.

visière. *See* ROMPRE.

vision. Avoir des visions, To have hallucinations, To see (*non-existent*) things. " Is this a dagger which I see before me, The handle toward my hand ? Come, let me clutch thee :—I have thee not, and yet I see thee still. Art thou not, fatal vision, sensible To feeling as to sight ? or art thou but A dagger of the mind, a false creation, Proceeding from the heat-oppressed brain ? I see thee yet, in form as palpable As this which now I draw." *Macbeth* II, 1.

C'est un homme à visions, He is a man who has crazy ideas.

See also CORNU.

vite. *See* ALLER.

vitesse. *See* GAGNER.

vitre. *See* CASSER.

vivant. *See* BIBLIOTHÈQUE, DICTIONNAIRE, ENCYCLOPÉDIE.

vivifier. *See* TUER.

vivre. Il a vécu (*in the literary style*), He is dead.

Ne pouvoir vivre avec quelqu'un, To be unable to get on with someone.

Qui vivra verra, Live and learn, Time will show, Those that live longest will see the most.

Vivre à discrétion *ou* Vivre comme dans un pays de conquête, To live at free quarters (*be entertained gratuitously*).

Vivre au jour la journée *ou* au jour le jour, To live from hand to mouth, To take no thought for the morrow (*Matthew* vi, 34).

Vivre avec soi-même, To live to oneself, To live in isolation.

Vivre bien ensemble, To get on well together.

Vivre d'industrie *ou* d'expédients, To live by one's wits.

Vivre de régime, To be on a diet.

Vivre ensemble comme Robin et Marion, To hit it off excellently with each other (*of man and woman*).

Vivre et laisser vivre, Live and let live.

See also AIR, AISÉ, APPRENDRE, AUTEL, CÉNOBITE, CHAUME, CHENET, CHIEN, COMMODE, COMMUN, COMPAGNON, COQ, CROCHET, DÉBANDADE, DÉPENS, DIFFICILE, ENNUI, ESPÉRANCE, ESPRIT, ÉTROIT, GOGO, GRASSEMENT, MOURIR, PIED, QUATRE, ROMAN, SEIGNEUR, SOUCI, VERRE.

vogue. *See* ENTRER.

voguer. Voguer à pleines voiles, To forge ahead.

See also GALÈRE.

voici. *See* AUTRE.

voie. En venir (*ou* Se livrer) à des voies de fait sur quelqu'un, To come to blows with someone.

Être sur la voie, To be on the right track.

Être toujours par voie et par chemin, To be always on the move.

La voie étroite (qui mène à la vie), The narrow way (which leadeth unto life) *Matthew* vii, 14. " The steep and thorny way to heaven."—*Hamlet* I, 3. " I am for the house with the narrow gate."—*All's Well That Ends Well* IV, 5.

La voie large (qui mène à la perdition), The broad way (that leadeth to destruction) *Matthew* vii, 13. " The primrose way to the everlasting bonfire."—*Macbeth* II, 1. " They'll be for the flow'ry way that leads to the broad gate and the great fire."—*All's Well That Ends Well* IV, 5.

See also AIGUILLER, BON 32, 35, 55, BOUT, DROIT, FRAYER.

voilà. Et voilà ! So much for that ! And that's that ! " *Clown. Bonos dies,* Sir Toby : for as the old hermit of Prague, that never saw pen and ink, very wittily said to a niece of King Gorboduc, ' That that is, is : ' so I, being master parson, am master parson : for what is that but that ? and is but is ?"—*Twelfth Night* IV, 2.

Ne voilà-t-il pas (que = if + negative), Lo and behold, There now, Well I declare, Well I never, [I'm] blest, *e.g.*, Ne voilà-t-il pas qu'il se fâche, qu'il pleut, Well I declare, if he isn't angry, if it isn't raining.

See also AUTRE, BIEN, CHIENDENT, DIABLE, ÊTRE, FAIRE, HIC, HISTOIRE, NEUF, PARLER, PORTER, UNIQUE, VOULOIR.

voile. Jeter un voile sur quelque chose (*fig.*), To draw a veil over something.

Les voiles de la nuit (*poetic*), The curtain of night. " The day begins to break, and night is fled, Whose pitchy mantle over-veil'd the earth."—1 *King Henry VI* II, 2. " The blanket of the dark."—*Macbeth* I, 5. " Night's black mantle."—3 *King Henry VI* IV, 2. " Night's cloak."—*Romeo and Juliet* II, 2. " The dragon wing of night o'erspreads the earth.—" *Troilus and Cressida* V, 8. " Bescreen'd in night."—*Romeo and Juliet* II, 2.

See also CALER, FORCE, VENT, VOGUER.

voir. À voir la manière dont . . ., To

judge by the way (*someone does something*).

Allez voir là-bas si j'y suis *ou* Va-t'en voir si j'y suis, I'll see you further first.

Allez-y voir ! Get away with you ! (*What you say is nonsense*).

Ceci est à voir *ou* C'est à voir *ou* C'est ce que nous verrons, That remains to be seen, We shall see [what we shall see].

Cela n'a rien à voir à l'affaire, That has nothing to do with it, That is beside the point.

Cela se voit, That is obvious.

En avoir vu de toutes les couleurs, To have had all sorts of experiences, To have been through the mill.

En faire voir à quelqu'un de toutes les couleurs, To behave very badly towards someone, To treat someone abominably.

Je le vois d'ici, I can very well imagine it.

On ne voit que cela, There's no getting away from it.

Vit-on jamais rien de semblable ? Did you ever see such a thing ? Has the like ever been seen ?

Voir, c'est croire, Seeing is believing.

Voir la mort de près (*fig.*), To look (*or* To stare) death in the face (*to narrowly escape death*).

Voir le feu, To be under fire (*of soldier*).

Voir les choses telles qu'elles sont, To look facts in the face.

Voir tout couleur de rose *ou* Voir tout en rose *ou* tout en beau, To see everything through rose-coloured spectacles, To take a rosy view of things.

Voir tout en noir, To take a gloomy view of everything, To look on the dark side of things. " Let's reason with the worst that may befall."—*Julius Caesar* V, 1.

See also AUTRE, BEAU 12, 21, BIEN, BLEU, BOIS, BON 63, 64, BOURSE, BOUTEILLE, BROUILLARD, CHAIR, CHANDELLE, CHEMIN, CIEL, CLAIR, DESSOUS, EMPÊCHER, ÉTOILE, FALLOIR, FERME, FÊTE, FEU, FICELLE, FOND, GOUTTE, GRIS, HAUT, JOUR, LOIN, LOUP, MAL, MAUVAIS, NEZ, ŒIL, OS, PAILLE, PAYS, PEINTURE, PRISME, TAUPE, TROUBLE, UN, VENIR, VENT.

voisin. *See* BON 16.

voisiner. Ne pas voisiner, To keep oneself to oneself.

voix. La voix du peuple est la voix de Dieu, The voice of the people is the voice of God, Vox populi, vox Dei.

See also CHAPITRE, CRÉCELLE, DÉESSE, DEUX, POINTU, RENOMMÉE.

vol. À vol d'oiseau, As the crow flies.

Prendre son (*ou* un) vol trop haut, To fly too high (*be too ambitious*).

Saisir (*ou* Attraper) l'occasion au vol, To seize (*or* To grasp) the opportunity instantly, To leap at (*or* To snatch) (*or* To snap) the opportunity.

Une vue à vol d'oiseau, A bird's-eye view (*of a country, a town, an edifice*). *Cf.* Voir les choses de haut *under* HAUT.

volant. *See* CAMP.

volcan. C'est dormir sur un volcan, It is like sitting on a volcano (*highly dangerous*).

volée. *See* BOND.

voler. Il ne l'a pas volé, He richly deserves it, It serves him right.

Voler de ses propres ailes, To fend (*or* To shift) for oneself, To find one's feet.

Vouloir voler avant d'avoir des ailes, To want to run before one can walk (*fig.*) ; To go to expense before having the wherewithal.

See also ENTENDRE, VALOIR.

volet. *See* TRIER.

voleur. *See* DEMI, FAIRE, PENDRE.

volonté. *See* ACTE.

volume. Faire du volume, To throw one's weight about, To do the heavy, To swank (*all slang*).

vôtre. Vous faites des vôtres, You are up to your tricks.

vouer. *See* OUBLI, SAINT.

vouloir. À qui en voulez-vous ? Whom do you want ? Whom are you looking for ? ; Whom are you aiming at (*attacking*) ? ; What is the (*or* your) trouble now ?

Dieu le veuille, Please God, Please the pigs.

En veux-tu ? en voilà, As much as ever you like, Galore, To be had for the asking.

En vouloir à quelqu'un, To bear someone ill will, To bear (*or* To owe) someone a grudge ; To have designs on someone.

En vouloir à quelque office vacant, à la vie de quelqu'un, To have designs on some vacant post, on someone's life.

Faire de quelqu'un [tout] ce qu'on veut, To twist (*or* To turn) someone round one's [little] finger.

Je m'en veux d'avoir fait cela, I am angry (*or* am vexed) (*or* could have kicked myself) for having done that.

Se vouloir mal de quelque chose, To reproach oneself with something.

Vous l'avez voulu, Georges Dandin (*in speaking to oneself*), It serves you right, It's your own fault, You would have it, You have brought it on yourself, You have only yourself to blame.

Vouloir c'est pouvoir *ou* Celui qui veut, celui-là peut *ou* Qui veut la fin veut les moyens, Where there's a will there's a way.

See also ANTIPODE, BIEN, BOUCHE, CHIEN, COURT, CROIRE, ENTENDRE, FAIRE, FEMME, GARDER, LUNE, MARCHER, MÉNAGER, MINE, PEAU, PIED, PROUVER, REGARDER, RIRE, SAVOIR, SENS, SOUFFLER, TAILLER, VENIR, VESSIE, VOLER.

vous. *See* BALLE, DE, DÉ, ENTRE, FOUR.

voûte. La voûte du ciel *ou* des cieux *ou* La voûte céleste (*poetic*), The vault (*or* The roof) (*or* The floor) of heaven, The welkin. " The azured vault."—*The Tempest* V, 1. " The vaulty heaven so high above our heads."—*Romeo and Juliet* III, 5. " The vaulty top of heaven." —*King John* V, 2. " This majestical roof fretted with golden fire."—*Hamlet* II, 2. " Look how the floor of heaven Is thick inlaid with patines of bright gold."—*The Merchant of Venice* V, 1. " The starry welkin."—*A Midsummer Night's Dream* III, 2. " On the welkne shoon the sterres lyght."—CHAUCER.

See also CLEF.

voyage. Partir pour (*ou* Faire) le grand voyage *ou* Faire le voyage de l'autre monde, To go on one's last journey, To cross the great divide (*die*). " The undiscover'd country, from whose bourn No traveller returns."—*Hamlet* III, 1. " Strange, is it not ? that of the myriads who Before us pass'd the door of Darkness through Not one returns to tell us of the Road, Which to discover we must travel too."—EDWARD FITZGERALD, *Rubaiyat of Omar Khayyam* LXVII.

voyager. *See* MÉNAGER.

vrai. Aussi vrai qu'il fait jour, As sure as eggs is eggs. " As certain as I know the sun is fire."—*Coriolanus* V, 4.

Un vrai des vrais, A true blue.

Vrai de vrai, As true as true [can be], Honest Injun. " As true as truth's simplicity."—*Troilus and Cressida* III, 2.

See also BESOIN, DIRE, FAUX, MONTRER, PORTRAIT, VISAGE.

vu. Au vu et au su de tous *ou* de

tout le monde, To everybody's knowledge, As everyone knows.

vue. À vue d'œil, By eye (*as in* To judge a distance by eye); Visibly. *Cf.* Fondre à vue d'œil *under* FONDRE.

À vue de nez, At a first glance, At a rough estimate.

Avoir des vues sur quelqu'un, sur quelque chose, To have designs on someone, on something.

En vue de l'avenir, With an eye to the future.

Juger à vue de pays, To take a general view (*of a matter*); To judge at a cursory glance.

Marcher (*ou* Se conduire) à vue de pays, To follow the lie of the land (*in walking*).

Parler à vue de pays, To speak off hand *or* out of hand.

See also BAS, CLOCHER, PERTE, PORTER, TROUBLE, VOL.

Y

y. *See* AVOIR, ÊTRE, METTRE.

Z

zéro. C'est un [vrai] zéro *ou* C'est un zéro en chiffre, He is a mere cipher *or* is a nonentity *or* a nobody. " And let us, ciphers to this great acompt, On your imaginary forces work."—*King Henry V Scene at the beginning of the Play.*

zut. Avoir un œil qui dit zut à l'autre, To squint.